ON SOCIOLOGY, SECOND EDITION: VOLUME ONE

ON SOCIOLOGY, SECOND EDITION

VOLUME ONE: CRITIQUE AND PROGRAM

John H. Goldthorpe

STANFORD UNIVERSITY PRESS

STANFORD, CALIFORNIA

2007

Stanford University Press
Stanford, California

Printed and bound by CPI Group (UK) Ltd,
Croydon, CR0 4YY

First edition: Oxford: Oxford University Press. © 2000
by John H. Goldthorpe.

Chapters 2 and 7 were originally published in the
British Journal of Sociology, vol. 42, 1991 and vol. 49,
1998, respectively: chapter 3 in *Comparative Social
Research,* vol. 16, 1997; chapter 5 in *West European
Politics,* vol. 25, 2002; and chapter 6 in the *European
Sociological Review,* vol. 12, 1996.

Library of Congress Cataloging-in-Publication Data

Goldthorpe, John H.
     On sociology / John H. Goldthorpe. — 2nd ed.
        v.   ; cm.
     Originally published: Oxford : Oxford University
Press, 2000.
     Includes bibliographical references and index.
     Contents: v. 1. Critique and program
     ISBN-13: 978-0-8047-4997-8 (cloth : alk. paper)
     ISBN-13: 978-0-8047-4998-5 (pbk. : alk. paper)
   1. Sociology.   2. Sociology—Philosophy.
3. Sociology—Methodology.   4. Sociology—
Research.   5. Social action.   6. Social classes.
I. Title.
HM585.G65   2007
301—dc22
                                        2006020316

Typeset by G&S Book Services in 10/14 Sabon

In grateful memory of my mother,
Lilian Eliza Goldthorpe (1901–2002),
and in hope of a better century for my grandchildren,
Ellie (2002), Bronnie (2004), and Daniel (2005)

CONTENTS

PREFACE

In venturing on this second, revised and now two-volume, edition of *On Sociology*, I have been motivated in two main ways. On the one hand, I have been encouraged by the favourable reception of the first edition, as reflected not just in reviews but also in the generous responses of colleagues who have found the book of value in their own work and in their teaching. On the other hand, though, I have become increasingly aware of further issues that I could relevantly take up, in part as a result of various comments on the lines of 'you said too little about x' or 'what then is your position on y' and in part, too, simply as a result of the progression of arguments and of related research and theory over the years since the first edition appeared.

For their help in making a second edition possible, I am indebted above all to David Grusky for suggesting Stanford University Press as a possible publisher and then to Patricia Katayama of Stanford University Press for her positive and highly constructive response to the idea, even when, at a dark time, I had doubts about it myself. In succession to Patricia, Kate Wahl has been an unfailingly helpful editor during the two-and-a-half years that it took me to complete the work.

In the case of those chapters that appeared in the first edition, I have for the most part engaged in only quite limited editing. I have corrected some errors and more obvious infelicities, made various changes in the interests of terminology consistency, and added references to recent work that seemed to me both relevant and important. The main exception is with chapter 16 in Volume 2, 'Outline of a Theory of Social Mobility', which, in order to take account both of developments in research and in my own thinking, has been entirely rewritten and a good deal extended. Throughout the two volumes I have increased the amount of cross-referencing between chapters—in the hope that, rather than merely irritating readers, this may help persuade them that the essays comprised do in fact have a greater degree of unity than may be immediately apparent.

I noted in the Preface to the first edition that, in contrast to engaging in collaborative research, writing a book such as *On Sociology* is an essentially solitary task in which the need for support and conviviality can be keenly felt. Most of the individuals and institutions that I then thanked for having sustained me in this regard I must thank once again, and with special mention of David Cox, Robert Erikson, and Walter Müller, as friends who can always combine the sharpest of observations with great good humour, and of Liz Martin and her staff in the Nuffield College Library who splendidly maintain its tradition of high-quality service with a smile.

In addition, I am grateful to my colleagues Richard Breen, Tak Wing Chan, Michelle Jackson and Colin Mills for many rewarding discussions, often ranging far beyond the several research projects in which we have of late been engaged; and further to Michelle for her valiant but, alas, often unavailing attempts at improving my IT skills and for dealing womanfully with various disasters that have ensued. Lynn Prince Cooke also greatly lightened my life, through entertaining, bordering on outrageous, lunch-time conversations, not least on the theme of 'when little men cast long shadows, then surely night is coming'.

Finally, I have to thank my wife, Rhiannon, and all other members of my family for their forbearance over the period in which *On Sociology* again preoccupied me, and especially since this was one in which the vicissitudes of family life were especially marked, as the dedication of the new edition reflects.

The Barbican, London
December, 2005

ON SOCIOLOGY, SECOND EDITION: VOLUME ONE

CHAPTER ONE

Introduction to Volume One

This volume brings together a series of essays relating to the present state of sociology that are of a critical and a programmatic character. In the critical essays, I discuss a number of chiefly methodological issues that arise with certain current styles of sociological work—issues that, I believe, have not been given the attention they deserve. In the programmatic essays, I put forward various suggestions about how a new mainstream sociology might be formed that would be characterised, above all, by a closer and intellectually more productive integration of research and theory than is typically apparent today. In this introductory chapter I have two main aims. First, I seek to supply some general background to the essays, and in particular to update the background I provided in the first edition of *On Sociology*. Second, I outline my purposes in writing each essay and, in the case of those that have stimulated commentary and debate, I note criticisms that have been advanced and make some response to what seem to me the more consequential points that have been raised. I take this opportunity of thanking all those who have been ready to read my work and to react to it, even if from positions of radical disagreement.

THE BACKGROUND

In the Introduction to the first edition, I argued that sociology was in a state of general intellectual disarray and one that, were it to continue, must threaten to undermine the substantial institutional progress that sociology has made, within both academia and national research communities and organisations, over the course of the twentieth century. I identified three main sources of this disarray that were, I suggested, of cumulative significance.

    1. A manifest lack of integration of research and theory—the scandal of sociology. Chief responsibility for this situation must lie with those sociological or 'social' theorists who do not accept that the prime purpose of theory is to provide a basis for the systematic *explanation* of social phenomena, as established by empirical investigation, and who would rather treat theory, as van den Berg (1998: 205–206) has aptly put it, 'as a sub-discipline in its own right, and one with its own criteria of utility and relevance that would seem wholly divorced from the needs and concerns of practising sociological researchers'.

    2. A collective failure on the part of sociologists to decide just what kind of discipline sociology is or ought to try to be. The so-called 'reaction against positivism' that developed from the later 1960s led to a return to nineteenth-century preoccupations with the differences between *Geisteswissenschaften* and *Naturwissenschaften* and to a divisive exaggeration of these differences, especially on the part of sociologists not directly engaged in research.

    3. Second-order disagreement over how the disagreement over the nature of sociology should itself be regarded. This is often expressed in—or, rather, covered up by—an appeal to 'pluralism', but to a pluralism that is intended not to promote a vigorous, possibly mortal, competition among differing views but rather an accommodation among their adherents. Such pluralism is justified pragmatically by the need to preserve a semblance of disciplinary cohesion; but often, too, philosophically, by the adoption of some kind of postmodernist stance from which the idea of rational argument as a means of approximating objective truth can be rejected in favour of cognitive, or epistemic, relativism.

Writing now some six years later, I would see little reason for any major revision of this analysis of the condition of sociology.[1] Intellectual disarray persists (cf. Cole, ed., 2001). At the most manifest level, witness the often quite startling differences that can be found in the content even of graduate courses in sociology from one university department to another; or, again, in the character of the papers that could be taken as representative of different sociological journals.[2] Attempts are from time to time made to suggest that this state of affairs is of no great concern or is inevitable or even perhaps in some way desirable (e.g., Abbott, 2001: ch. 1). But such attempts are scarcely convincing—at all events to those viewing sociology from without. Far greater weight has still, in my view, to be given to Huber's argument (1995) that sociology's evident lack of a clear disciplinary core—'what must be retained if the discipline is to continue to exist'—leaves it especially vulnerable to external threats to its intellectual standing and institutional consolidation alike.

However, while I would thus continue to regard the state of sociology as being a precarious if not critical one, I do at the same time believe that, of late, it has become possible to discern a number of developments that provide grounds for a degree of optimism for the future that did not earlier exist or that, at very least, serve to bring greater clarity than before to some central issues. The nature and significance of these developments I can best set out in relation to the three sources of the intellectual disarray of sociology that I listed above, and by taking these in reverse order, that is, from the more general to the more specific.

To start, then, with problems of second-order disagreement over the nature of sociology as a discipline, the possibility of more productive debate has been significantly enhanced by the waning influence of the cognitive relativism that previously provided an apparent legitimation for the avoidance of all foundational questions and in turn for a pluralism of an essentially mindless kind. In particular, postmodernism, the major source of cognitive relativism in the later twentieth century—with its claim that truth is not discovered, through rational procedures, but is rather in various ways 'made'—would now seem to be losing much of its former allure.

In part, this has to be reckoned as the consequence of the internal dynamics of intellectual fashion, to which sociologists appear unduly susceptible, and also of the increasingly damaging criticism to which postmodernist arguments became subject in the course of the 'science wars' of the 1990s (cf. Gross and Levitt, 1994; Gross, Levitt, and Lewis, eds., 1996; Koertge, ed., 1998; Sokal and Bricmont, 1998).[3] However, one should further note, in more positive vein, a number of powerful reassertions by leading philosophers of the continuing validity of what Searle (1993) has called 'the western rationalist tradition' of scientific and scholarly enquiry and of the idea of objective truth as both an intellectual goal and cultural value (see esp. Searle, 1993, 1995, and Nagel, 1997; also Haack, 1998; Williams, 2002). Of particular significance in the present context are Searle's robust defence of the correspondence theory of truth—the theory, anathema to postmodernists, that truth is a matter of correspondence to 'facts in the world'; and Nagel's demonstration of the contradiction inherent in the rejection of the idea of reason as a universal category of thought—since this idea 'is necessarily employed in every purported challenge to itself' (1997: 7).[4]

In this changing intellectual climate, it has then become more difficult than before for sociologists to take an anti-foundational stand and to believe that a relaxed, 'anything goes' attitude in regard to methodology and theory is not only advantageous from the point of view of disciplinary politics but indeed a mark of philosophical sophistication. Rather, greater pressure has been placed on individuals and schools to decide and clearly set out what kind of intellectual enterprise they see themselves as being engaged in and what basic rules of the game they are ready to play by. Clear advantage follows from this.

An illustration is, I believe, provided by the statements of position recently made by the editors of two important collections, the main purpose of which is to uphold comparative historical and other qualitative approaches in macrosociology (and political science) against criticism from more 'positivistically' inclined quantitative researchers and rational action theorists—myself included. In earlier replies to such criticism, and indeed still in some more recent ones (see, e.g., Somers, 1998; and cf. Steinmetz, 2004, 2005), the main defensive resort is to versions of cognitive relativism, such as 'historical epistemology' and radical social constructivism, as a result of which the possibility of any meaningful dialogue about the specifics of research methods and theory formation is removed. However, Mahoney and Rueschemeyer in their introduction to *Comparative Historical Analysis in the Social Sciences* (2003: 22–24) make it clear that they would not wish to appeal to postmodernist or other arguments that 'assume that valid knowledge is inherently illusory'. Rather, they insist that demonstrating empirical regularities and seeking testable theoretical accounts of their causation are integral concerns of comparative historical work. And, in similar vein, Brady, Collier, and Seawright in the first chapter of *Rethinking Social Inquiry* (2004: 18–20) acknowledge, chiefly in response to King, Keohane, and Verba (1994), that although qualitative and quantitative researchers may have different aims, follow different strategies, and use different research tools, both need to follow the same 'logic of inference' and in turn to apply the same principles and standards in the linking of argument and evidence (cf. also Rueschemeyer, 2003: 324–28).

As will later become apparent, I for one am unconvinced by a number of the particular methodological claims that are made in the collections cited, and would wish in these respects to maintain my previous critical stance. But the more important point is that a sufficient degree of consensus does now exist for a potentially productive exchange of views to take place, and thus for a genuine, rather than a merely spurious, pluralism to prevail.[5]

Turning next to issues concerning the kind of discipline that sociology is or should aim to be, I would see the declining influence of cognitive relativism as here again an encouraging development, and likewise the apparent fading out, at long last, of the reaction against positivism—if only as a result of 'positivism' having become used in so many different, and often quite unwarranted, senses as to lose all meaning except, perhaps, as a term of general disapprobation applied to survey-based and other quantitative work.

One indication of this attitudinal shift is the growing number of sociologists, and especially among those with some involvement in or awareness of interdisciplinary work in, say, the medical, educational, or environmental fields, who would now in effect to agree with Popper (1972: 183–86) that 'labouring the difference' between the natural and the social sciences is 'a bore', and often indicates a lack of understanding of the methods of the former as well as of the latter. And, more generally, there would today appear to be a greater readiness once again to make out the case for the social sciences as an enterprise that has a basic methodological commonality with the natural sciences, even if at the same time involving some inevitable differences (see, e.g., Steuer, 2002).[6] In this context, then, the issue does become more sharply posed of whether or not sociology should seek to be part of the social sciences as thus understood.

There is, to be sure, no shortage of authors who, even if not sharing in the postmodernist rejection of the very idea of science, would still adhere to the view that for sociology to aim for scientific status is mistaken and indeed vain (see, e.g., Bryant, 1995; Flyvbjerg, 2001; Jenkins, 2002). The sciences proper—in effect, the natural sciences—are concerned, it is held, with inert physical entities but, in contrast, sociology is concerned with 'self-reflecting humans' (Flyvbjerg, 2001: 32) and it is they who together construct and reconstruct, through their own subjectivity, what counts as social reality. Moreover, sociologists cannot set themselves apart from this process. *Their* concepts are inevitably dependent on, and in interaction with, the concepts that are embedded in the everyday lives of 'lay actors'. Thus, the attainment of cumulative, theoretically grounded sociological knowledge is continually subverted by the very way in which human society is constituted. All general propositions that may be advanced by sociologists are necessarily rendered unstable since such propositions will need to change in response to changes in lay actors' own understandings and interpretations of their social worlds—that is, of social reality—and including those changes that may be prompted by the practice of sociology itself. From this 'impossibilist' position, the ultimate purposes of sociology have then to be seen not as cognitive but rather as moral and political. Sociology, it is argued, should aim to be a mode of public discourse or 'conversation' that offers citizens new perspectives on society, new insights into their own experience within society, and new value positions and vocabularies that can serve as a basis for both social critique and praxis.

However, while arguments on these lines retain wide support, they are now being more often challenged by those who would believe that they amount in effect to selling sociology short; and, further, as setting up an unfortunate division between sociology and other obviously related disciplines, such as economics or psychology, whose practitioners are far less inhibited in their scientific ambitions.

For example, in an important intervention, Boudon (2001) recognises, as a matter of fact, that sociology is 'a house of many mansions' and that what he labels as 'expressive' and 'critical' sociology are prominent within it. Nonetheless, he insists that privilege must be given to 'cognitive' sociology—or sociology as social science—as 'the sociology that really matters'. This is so because while sociology may well serve to express and illuminate individual experience or to inform sociopolitical dissent, it can do so *validly* only on the basis of defensible knowledge claims. Issues of the logical coherence of sociological analyses and of their relation to the findings of systematic investigation cannot be avoided.[7] Moreover, as regards the assertion that a scientific knowledge of society, in the sense of knowledge of a cumulative, theoretically grounded kind, will always remain out of reach, Boudon resorts to a straightforward empirical rejection. In both classical and contemporary sociology, he maintains, there is in fact ample evidence of such knowledge actually being achieved. A tradition of scientific sociology extending from the nineteenth century through to the present can be documented (see Boudon and Cherkaoui, eds., 1999).[8]

At the same time, it is important also to note that in course of the philosophical reaction against cognitive relativism, to which I earlier referred, several elements of the impossibilist position on social science are directly called into question. Thus, Searle (1995: ch. 9) complements his general defence of the correspondence theory of truth with the further argument that while social facts may differ from the more 'brute' facts of nature in depending on human recognition and agreement, this does not prevent a version of the correspondence theory from being viable in their investigation. More specifically, it does not follow, as the impossibilists would appear to suppose, that because the mode of construction of social reality means that it has an *ontologically subjective* character, this must preclude its treatment by social scientists as *epistemologically objective*. Similarly, Hacking (1999: ch. 1 esp.) stresses the error of extending the idea of social construction from the formation of concepts to the 'facts in the world' to which these concepts are applied, including ontologically subjective social facts. Because the concepts of, say, 'market' or 'economy' are socially constructed, it does not follow that the social activities to which these concepts refer have no existence independently of them.[9] And to this it can then be added that although in the case of the social world there may be interaction between the concepts of researchers or theorists and those of lay actors, such interaction does not necessarily occur nor, where it does, must it lead to problems of the fundamental kind that impossibilists would imply.[10]

Finally, then, as regards the lack of integration of research and theory in sociology, the main development that here provides grounds for optimism is the widening interest in a new style of theorising that I would see as holding great potential. This style of theorising is distinctive in that it is explicitly concerned with the explanation of social phenomena—rather than with metatheoretical issues or simply the elaboration of concepts; and, further, in that it seeks such explanation through the identification and analysis of the specific *processes* or *mechanisms* by which such phenomena are generated and sustained or perhaps disrupted and changed (see, e.g., Elster, 1989b; Coleman, 1990; Esser, 1993–2001; Hedström and Swedberg, eds., 1998; Boudon, 2003b; Barbera, 2004; Cherkaowi, 2005; Hedström, 2005).

So far, this new style has been pursued mainly via a commitment to methodological individualism and to primarily micro-to-macro explanations grounded in versions of rational action theory. And this, I should say, is the particular approach for which I subsequently argue both in the programmatic essays in this volume and in the complementary illustrative essays that appear in Volume II. However, such an approach is not integral to theory construction in terms of mechanisms. This could, for example, proceed in a macro-to-micro fashion, with, say, a prime emphasis on the mechanisms that are involved in the structural or cultural conditioning of social behaviour. Opportunity is indeed created for such differing approaches to be set in direct competition with each other as regards the explanatory success that they achieve.

The new style of theorising makes for a closer relationship between research and theory in two main ways. First, it does, at least at its best, start out from regularities already established by systematic empirical investigation and offers explanations of how these come to be as they are—rather than elaborating possible generative processes for social phenomena that may, or may not, be in evidence. In this way, it is then made harder for social researchers to maintain an attitude of general indifference to theory that was not in fact unreasonable for so long as theory remained, to revert to van den Berg's phrase 'wholly divorced from [their] needs and concerns'. Second, mechanism-based explanations of social phenomena are ones that are in turn open, at least in principle, to empirical test. Insofar as the generative processes that are seen as adequate to produce the regularities to be explained are spelled out in some detail, further research can then be undertaken—of, perhaps, a quite different kind to that which established the regularities in the first place—in order to determine whether it is the mechanisms proposed that are indeed at work. Research and theory can thus be brought into a state of continuous interaction.[11]

One other point concerning theory construction in terms of generative processes might be made, especially in relation to the impossibilist position on sociology as social science. Impossibilists lay great stress on the crucial role played in explanation in the natural sciences by general laws that in turn provide the basis for reliable prediction; and sociology, it is observed, has conspicuously failed to arrive at such laws, as indicated by its lack of predictive capacity (see, e.g., Flyvbjerg, 2001: 30–32, 38–40; Jenkins, 2002: 24–27). However, it has for some time been recognised that explanation in the natural sciences, and especially outside of physics, may well not conform to the covering-law model. In the biological sciences mechanism-based explanation would in fact appear quite standard. Explanation consists in determining causal processes or mechanisms that operate at some 'deeper' level than that at which the phenomena of interest are themselves observed (cf. Cox, 1992).[12] It is true that such processes are then typically given a far more unified and cogent theoretical grounding than in sociology. Nonetheless, it remains the case that the explanations produced may still not attain complete generality (as, say, in ecology) and that they may not allow in any strict sense for prediction (as, say, in evolutionary biology).[13]

In other words, the quite radical discontinuity between the natural and the social sciences that the impossibilists would wish to set up is not here apparent. As Lieberson and Lynn (2002) have argued, in regard to models of explanation and more generally, it is in fact the biological sciences, far more than physics, that offer instructive parallels for sociology as social science. Rather ironically, in their preoccupation with the significance of general laws and prediction, impossibilists would seem to fall victim to the kind of misleading preoccupation with physics of which 'positivist' sociologists have been so often accused.

THE CRITICAL ESSAYS

The first four of the essays that follow are of a critical character, and the first three, relating, in turn, to historical sociology, to case-oriented as opposed to variable-oriented approaches in comparative macrosociology, and to sociological ethnography, to some extent go together. My intention, I must stress, is *not* to dismiss these versions of qualitative sociology out of hand but rather to raise methodological issues that I would regard as both serious and unduly neglected. As an indication of the depth of the methodological difficulties that arise with these styles of enquiry, I show how in each case alike their proponents, even while inveighing, often rather imprecisely, against positivism, are, paradoxically, themselves led into positions that are in fact positivistic in quite basic and well-established senses.

The first essay, 'The Uses of History in Sociology: Reflections on Some Recent Tendencies', starts from a rejection of the view advanced by Abrams (1980), following Giddens (1979), that 'history and sociology are and always have been the same thing'. In the essay, I focus on one particular, methodological difference between the two disciplines that, I argue, is of a highly consequential kind: namely, that while historians have to rely solely on evidence in the form of what I call 'relics'—that is, the physical remains of the past of one kind or another—sociologists, insofar as they work in present-day societies, have the further possibility of using various kinds of research procedure in order to generate evidence that did not exist before. I then discuss the implications of this difference for sociologists' research strategies and the more specific problems that it raises for the practice of historical sociology. I conclude with a critique of what I label as 'grand historical sociology': that is, historical sociology that usually aims to deal with large macrosociological issues and that is written on the basis not of relics themselves—or, in other words, of primary sources—but rather on the basis of the preexisting work of historians. I seek to show how, in thus using such secondary (or yet more derivative) sources as their main empirical materials, grand historical sociologists are led, willy-nilly, into accepting what historians themselves have for long recognised and criticised as a positivist conception of historiography, and, in turn, into various formidable methodological problems that they have so far often failed to appreciate, let alone resolve.

The first reaction to this essay came in the form of four critical comments by Bryant, Hart, Mann, and Mouzelis that appeared in the *British Journal of Sociology* (vol. 45, no. 1, 1994). These seemed chiefly motivated by sorrow or anger that I had seen fit to question the methodological foundations of grand historical sociology and thus to show disrespect to such apparently iconic works as Barrington Moore's *The Social Origins of Dictatorship and Democracy* (1966). I have nothing to add here to the reply that I made (1994) at the time.

Subsequent reactions have also centred on my criticism of the use of secondary sources in grand historical sociology. In some cases, the attempt has been made to pass this over as being of relatively minor importance. Thus, Calhoun (1996: 312) argues that what I have to say on this matter could 'largely be rephrased as useful advice' to grand historical sociologists to 'take care' over evidence. But he has then nothing to suggest about the specific methodological procedures that might be followed by way of exercising such 'care': that is, procedures of the kind for which, as I note, Skocpol (1984: 382) called—apparently in vain—over 20 years ago. Mahoney and Rueschemeyer (2003: 18) are in effect yet more cavalier in simply asserting that the use of secondary sources 'need not result in any systematic error' because, typically, the full 'population' of sources is covered, and, in any case, the validity of comparative and related theoretical arguments 'does not hinge on a particular reading of the secondary literature'. I cannot see how this argument stands up. What else *could* the validity of such arguments hinge on, where no primary work has been undertaken? How else is the underlying theory to be tested? Moreover, already in my essay I give the examples of Moore (1966), Anderson (1974b), and Wallerstein (1974–89: vol. 1) all neglecting, where they do not unwarrantedly disparage, studies relating to the English Civil War that do not fit with their preferred interpretation of it as a 'bourgeois revolution'; and I would not, I believe, have much difficulty in presenting further, more recent cases where a similar rather blatant partiality arises.[14]

A far more considered response is that of Lustick (1996). In direct contrast to Mahoney and Rueschemeyer's claim of complete population coverage, Lustick formulates the problem of secondary sources as being the expression, in the context of grand historical sociology, of the more general problem of selection bias in data that occurs in one form or another across virtually the whole range of sociological research. Lustick's main critical—and factually correct—observation on my essay is then that, having identified the key issue of how grand historical sociologists should choose among rival or contradictory sources without undue bias, I do not offer any solution to it; and, he speculates (1996: 610), with reference to the *BJS* comments, that this is why my essay has led to reactions 'that have been so defensive and so nearly, in some cases, hysterical'. For unless some intellectually satisfying solution can be provided, 'the whole field is vulnerable'.

Lustick goes on to suggest (1996: 613–15) that at least the beginnings of a solution might be found if researchers dependent on secondary historical materials were to be more explicitly concerned with 'patterns within historiography', as distinct from 'patterns within History', and ready to treat each possible secondary source as a 'data-point' that is subject to error, whether random or biased. I would regard this as a proposal that should certainly be taken further. To do so would at all events serve to bring discussion of the methodology of grand historical sociology under the general rubric of the logic of inference. I would, however, note that the problem of selection bias does in fact occur at two different levels, as Lustick appears at one point to acknowledge: that is, not only at the level of the researcher's choice of secondary sources but further at the deeper level of the 'natural selection' of primary sources during the passage of time. And the extreme, though not uncommon, case that here arises—I give examples in my essay—is where relics from the past of the kind that would be necessary for making certain inferences have simply not survived to any adequate extent.

In the second critical essay, 'Current Issues in Comparative Macrosociology', I seek primarily to question the idea that certain methodological problems that are well known to arise in quantitative work—what I label as the small N, the Galton, and the black box problems—can in fact be avoided or more readily handled via a qualitative, case-oriented approach. These problems, I argue, are in fact met with in qualitative just as much as in quantitative research, and the distinctive methods supposedly available to the case-oriented approach not only fail to resolve them but also—like the standard procedures of grand historical sociology—often carry wider implications of a rather surprising kind. Most seriously, perhaps, attempts to overcome the small N problem (the problem of 'too many variables and not enough cases') by resorting to 'logical' as opposed to statistical methods of analysis must rest on the—strongly positivist—assumption that the social world is deterministic rather than probabilistic in character and can moreover be studied as such: a probabilistic approach is not required even on account of the problems of uncertainty or error that inevitably arise in all processes of data collection.

The essay was published in its original form in a special number of *Comparative Social Research* (vol. 16, 1997), together with comments by Abbott, Goldstone, Ragin, and Rueschemeyer and Stephens, Teune, and Tilly, to which I replied (1997). More than one of these commentators linked my criticisms of qualitative case studies to those previously made by King, Keohane, and Verba (1994) and also by Lieberson (1992, 1994), and thus construed them as part of a concerted attack on this style of research in sociology and political science (cf. also Adams, Clemens, and Orloff, 2005: 24–25). However, what is by now much better appreciated is that what motivates criticism of the kind in question is not a hostility to qualitative research as such but, rather, a commitment to the view that there is 'one logic of inference' (King, Keohane, and Verba, 1994: ix), to which the particular methodological procedures followed in qualitative and quantitative research must *alike* be subject. As I have earlier remarked, the increasing acceptance of this position among leading proponents of case-oriented research is a notable and welcome development.

Furthermore, from both the initial and later reactions to my essay (see esp. Collier, Brady, and Seawright, 2004: 254–55), it is evident that a large measure of agreement exists on at least one major issue. It is common ground that once empirical regularities have been established, theory is then required as a basis for explaining these regularities: that is, in order to overcome the black box problem of otherwise merely 'mindless' correlations and associations. And to this it may be added that the idea of 'process tracing' as a means of determining possible causal relations, which appears widely favoured among case-oriented researchers, has some obvious similarities to that of mechanism-based explanation to which I previously referred.

Nonetheless, some significant disagreement also remains. Arguments advanced in favour of the qualitative case-oriented approach confirm me in the view I expressed, following various other critics (e.g., Kiser and Hechter, 1991, 1998; Levi, 1997), that this approach is inductivist to a quite excessive degree. Rather than treating the description of the phenomena to be explained, the development of explanatory theory, and then the testing of this theory as methodologically separate phases of the research process, proponents of case studies see it as a virtue that they do in fact disregard any such separation. Thus, Mahoney and Rueschemeyer (2003: 13; cf. also 20–21) stress that, in dealing with small Ns, comparative historical researchers can 'comfortably move back and forth' between their historical data and theory 'in many iterations of analysis as they formulate new concepts, discover novel explanations, and refine preexisting theoretical expectations in light of detailed case evidence'. And likewise Ragin (1997: 30–32 esp.) sees the actual constitution of 'positive' and 'negative' cases—that is, the *explananda* of the analysis—in conjunction with 'the reciprocal clarification of empirical categories and theoretical concepts' as being a central and distinguishing feature of qualitative macrosociology.

The standard objection to proceeding in this extreme inductivist way (cf. King, Keohane, and Verba, 1994: 19–23) is, of course, that if the *explananda*, the theoretical explanation, and the evidence taken as relevant to testing the explanation are all regarded as being open to continuous mutual accommodation, it is then difficult to see how any real progress in evaluating theory can be made. The possibilities for adapting, modifying, or otherwise 'saving' a theory in the face of contrary evidence would appear unlimited.[15]

Ragin (1997: 31) does in fact accept that 'in fairness' to both King and his colleagues and me, it should be recognised that the concerns that lie behind our criticisms are with theory testing rather than with 'concept formation, elaboration and refinement', which, for Ragin, are the prime concerns of case-oriented research. In return, I would have to say that *if* such research has indeed no ambition beyond improving concepts, my grounds for quarrelling with it disappear—although I fail to see why such effort should be put into conceptualisation without then *moving on to* the development of theory per se and its empirical testing. Moreover, it is apparent that Ragin's modesty in this respect would not be shared by Mahoney and Rueschemeyer nor, I would believe, by most other practitioners of this style of research.[16] I would, therefore, wish fully to maintain my critique of its undue inductivism; and I would add that what are represented as instances of the progress that it has achieved (e.g., Mahoney and Rueschemeyer, eds., 2003: part I) are in fact regularly open to question precisely because of the failure to allow the three phases of the research process that I would wish to distinguish an appropriate degree of independence.[17]

The third critical essay, 'Sociological Ethnography Today: Problems and Possibilities', can be seen as closely parallel to the second. I start off from current debates among ethnographers occasioned by the reception of postmodernist ideas. But my main concern is again to question, this time in regard to ethnographic case studies, the effectiveness of methods that can, apparently, transcend any logic of inference and that—as some would see it—offer the possibility of sociological ethnography establishing itself as a radical alternative to positivist (read survey-based and quantitative) forms of research. I argue that, as applied to widely recognised problems of what I call variation within and variation across the locales of ethnography, such methods do not work. The problems in question are again ones ultimately of potential selection bias, and solutions to them are likely to be found only through ethnographers adapting to their own purposes the logic of sampling as this has been developed within the survey tradition. Further, I once more illustrate how efforts to avoid recourse to what is deemed to be positivist methodology can in fact lead to the adoption of *ur*-positivist positions: that is, where attempts to justify generalisations from ethnographies of unknown representativeness turn out to depend on a conception of theory as providing certain knowledge of deterministic, lawlike relations. Finally, though, I suggest that sociological ethnography, in a methodologically enhanced form, could, in some instances, take on an important role in the *testing* of theory, and in particular in testing for the presence of causal mechanisms that are specified at the micro-level of individual action and interaction. In this way, ethnography might be brought into both a complementary and a revealing competitive relationship with survey-based research.

This essay has not, so far as I am aware, attracted any published comments of substance. I have, though, received a number of personal communications from sociological ethnographers expressing support for my general position and confirming the need for what critics would wish to label as a 'positivist' turn. One additional point that has been raised in this connection seems to me quite crucial: that is, the importance of ethnographic, and other qualitative, data being as far as possible archived, in the same way as now routinely occurs with survey data, so that they become open to public scrutiny and available for secondary analysis (cf. Corti and Thompson, 2003). Moves in this direction should be facilitated by the extent to which ethnographers now organise their data in a form suitable for computer-assisted analysis. However, resistance to archiving is already evident, including on the—unfortunately—predictable grounds (see, e.g., Parry and Mauthner, 2004) that archival policies and procedures 'are derived from a positivist quantitative model' that does not apply to qualitative material that should be understood as an individual resource and as personal rather than public property. It is difficult to see how such a position can be compatible with the idea of social science; perhaps it is not intended to be.

The fourth critical essay, the most recent in the sequence, is somewhat different in its motivation from the preceding three, although it too has an ultimate methodological concern. I was prompted to write it by what appears to be a growing tendency for social scientists, but especially sociologists, to hold forth on large issues of the day in an ambitious, but often very loose fashion, under the dubious licence of being (or aspiring to be) 'public intellectuals'. I take up one aspect of one such issue—the impact of globalisation on social class—and seek to show that the claims of 'grand' globalisation theorists are empirically ill informed and often have a quite crude and inadequate theoretical basis. Overall, the changes in class inequalities, class structure, and class politics that these theorists associate with an emerging global society are, to judge by more extensive evidence and more rigorous analyses than they acknowledge, far less 'transformational' than they would suppose, and the connection with processes of globalisation is far more problematic. Notions of 'epochal change' of a kind that requires a quite new avant-garde sociology for its comprehension, are not, I argue, to be taken seriously.

As I have maintained elsewhere (Goldthorpe, 2004a), it is indeed important that sociologists show themselves ready to engage with current sociopolitical issues—but, I would argue, as social scientists rather than as public intellectuals who seek authority for their pronouncements more on the basis of *réclame* than of specialist knowledge. To revert to Boudon's point earlier noted, insofar as sociology moves into its expressive or critical modes, it needs to be securely grounded in sociology as social science. It is of interest that of late other authors, including ones more sympathetic than Boudon or I to the idea of the sociologist as public intellectual, have also sought to highlight the problems of sociology and its different audiences that here arise. Thus, for example, Burawoy has argued (2004a: 1609, my emphasis; cf. also 2004b) that 'An effective public or policy sociology is not hostile to, but *depends upon* the professional sociology that lies at the core of our disciplinary field.'[18] I would hope that these problems will become yet more widely debated as the role of sociologists in public life almost inevitably increases.

THE PROGRAMMATIC ESSAYS

The last four essays in this volume I describe as programmatic. Although they take up a number of different substantive issues, their shared purpose is to give some idea of the main elements of the new mainstream sociology that I would wish to see emerge. The essays thus start out from those aspects of research and theory in sociology over recent decades that I would regard as holding most promise, despite the generally unfavourable context for the advancement of sociology as social science that has prevailed.

On the side of research, the most notable achievements have, I believe, been made in quantitative work. New techniques of analysis have been applied to large-scale data-sets deriving from surveys of increasingly diversified and sophisticated design.[19] This has then resulted in the demonstration, in a wide range of substantive fields, of empirical regularities, over both time and space, that were hitherto unrecognised or only inadequately described. On the side of theory, no comparable progress could be claimed. What can, however, be observed is that with the seemingly final collapse of functionalism in both its liberal and its Marxist forms—*fonctionnalisme rose* and *fonctionnalisme noir*—a revival has occurred of what Boudon (1987) calls the 'individualistic' theoretical tradition in sociology. That is, one in which the explanation of social phenomena is sought not in terms of the functional or teleological exigencies of social systems but rather in terms of the conduct of individuals and of its intended and unintended consequences. This revival has been most marked, and, in my view, pursued to best effect, where the emphasis is placed on individual *action* rather than *behaviour* and, further, where the attempt is made to treat action as being in some sense *rational.*[20]

And such an approach has become closely linked with the growing interest in mechanism-based theorising that I earlier noted as a recent encouraging development.

In the first programmatic essay, 'The Quantitative Analysis of Large-Scale Data-Sets and Rational Action Theory: For a Sociological Alliance', my aim is to argue that proponents of these two more promising concerns of contemporary sociology, labelled as QAD and RAT, could with mutual advantage enter into a closer relationship. QAD, I maintain, needs RAT. It is now clear that, as various critics have insisted, statistical techniques, no matter how powerful in revealing social regularities, cannot at the same time be used to crank out causal explanations of these regularities. A theoretical input is essential and on several counts causal narratives grounded in RAT would in this regard seem an especially attractive proposition. Conversely, RAT needs QAD. As critics have also pointed out, if the capacity of RAT to inform effective mechanism-based explanations is to be more convincingly demonstrated than hitherto, it needs to be seen at work in other than apparently handpicked and often 'data-poor' cases. Probabilistic yet wide-ranging regularities of the kind that QAD can establish would therefore appear as highly appropriate *explananda* in relation to which the full range of application of RAT (and at the same time its eventual limits) could be shown up.

This essay first appeared in the *European Sociological Review* (vol. 12, no. 2, 1996) as the lead item in a special number in which various authors considered the prospects for the kind of alliance that I suggest, and it was then reprinted in a collective volume on the same theme (Blossfeld and Prein, eds., 1998). Much commentary on the essay has been positive. I am evidently not alone in believing that through building on the successes of QAD and the potential of RAT, a substantial component of a new disciplinary core for sociology could indeed be created. At the same time, though, I am left under no illusions about the resistance to be overcome if such a project is to make headway—and not only on the part of those who would seek to reject it out of hand as positivism *redivivus*.

Thus, among proponents of QAD there remain those who have difficulty with the idea of taking theory seriously and who would still wish to believe that QAD is able in itself not only to establish empirical regularities but at the same time to provide adequate explanations of them—even if perhaps with the help of a little 'commonsense' interpretation. Likewise, among theorists, whether proponents of RAT or not, there is often a reluctance to accept that they should be ready to take up the explanatory challenges that are posed by descriptive results deriving from QAD, and especially from what is sometimes dismissed as 'merely administrative' research. Thus, Edling (2000: 5–6), in a further comment on my essay, contends that there is 'no general claim on the part of RAT to explain statistical regularities', and would apparently believe that RAT and QAD 'can be connected in a fruitful way' only 'if the collection of quantitative data is guided by a rational choice theoretical framework' in the first place. Edling fails here to distinguish between two different kinds of research: that which would be appropriate to test a RAT-based explanation of some social phenomenon and that which might be necessary to demonstrate the phenomenon for which an explanation is sought. Research of the former kind will obviously need to be 'guided by' RAT, but it would seem quite unduly restrictive and indeed inappropriate to require the same of research of the latter kind.

The second and third programmatic essays follow on from the first and are closely related. In the second, 'Rational Action Theory for Sociology', I start from the observation that RAT comes in fact in a range of different versions, and I attempt to analyse these by reference to three criteria: the strength of the rationality requirements that are imposed, whether the focus is on situational or procedural rationality, and whether the ambition is to provide a theory of action of a special or a general kind. On this basis, I then try to identify in which form RAT would seem to hold out most promise for sociology, and especially for use in conjunction with QAD. I conclude that sociologists are likely to be best served by RAT that draws on a conception of subjective rather than objective rationality and in turn imposes rationality requirements of 'intermediate' strength; that has a strong emphasis on explaining action in terms of its situational rationality (or, in Popper's phrase, its 'situational logic'); and that seeks to be only a special theory of action although one that is still in various ways privileged.

The general objective that I had in writing this essay was to counter the tendency, widespread among sociologists, to equate RAT with the particular versions of such theory that are most commonly found in economics, and in turn to see RAT as in some way alien and threatening to the very nature of the sociological enterprise. However, from continuing critical responses to RAT, whether or not prompted by my essay, it became evident to me that more needed to be done to try to set right this, and indeed a number of other, mistaken views that persist in relation to RAT: for example, that

RAT has some integral connection with neoliberal political ideology or that it entails an unduly restricted and impoverished view of the human individual or person. Hence, the initial motivation for the third essay, 'Rational Action Theory in Sociology: Misconceptions and Real Problems', which is published here for the first time.

As the title indicates, though, my concern in this essay is not simply with dispelling error. I also set out what I would see as quite fundamental problems that arise with the use of RAT in sociology—but to no less an extent in the pursuit of other theoretical approaches as well. These are, I argue, in the last analysis problems of 'nature and culture' and of 'individual and society' that have been encountered throughout the history of the social sciences or of social thought more generally. But what I further argue is that they are not problems that are open to merely conceptual solutions but rather ones of an ultimately empirical character, our understanding of which will be advanced only by research, and that this will often be research in fields other than that of sociology itself. Moreover, in certain respects, if not in others, advances via research are, I suggest, already being made, and advances from which proponents of RAT in something like the version I would favour can take encouragement.

The fourth and final programmatic essay, 'Causation, Statistics, and Sociology', may appear to be concerned with an issue somewhat removed from those previously considered: that is, that of how the idea of causation is, and might best be, applied in the context of sociological analysis. In fact, this essay can, I hope, help to highlight and integrate certain themes that recur throughout all the preceding essays in this volume.

I distinguish three different understandings of causation deriving chiefly from the work of statisticians. The first, 'causation as robust dependence', is that associated with attempts to make causal inferences through statistical technique alone, without theoretical or other subject-matter input. The second, 'causation as consequential manipulation', is that associated with experimental designs, and especially in applied sciences, where attention centres on assessing the effects of (given) causes—that is, treatments or other interventions—rather than on determining the causes of effects. The first understanding is, I argue, by now outmoded in sociology, and the second, although capable of powerful technical elaboration, is not well suited to a subject in which research must for the most part be nonexperimental and, moreover, in which the concept of action is central. The third understanding of causation that I identify, that of 'causation as generative process', I find far more attractive. In this case, the key idea is that advancing a causal explanation of phenomena that are taken to be evident in a set of data means giving an account of some underlying process that would in fact be capable of bringing the phenomena into being: that is, a process operating at a deeper or more micro-level than that at which the relevant data are themselves observed.

This understanding of causation does then fit well with the mechanism-based, micro-to-macro style of sociological explanation that I would generally favour, and I take it as a basis for proposing an approach to causal analysis that would seem especially appropriate for use in the context of a QAD-RAT alliance. This approach can in fact be represented schematically through the three-stage sequencing of the research process that I already indicated in my critique of excessive inductivism in qualitative macro-sociology. The first stage is that of establishing the phenomena: that is, of demonstrating the social regularities that constitute the *explananda*, with statistical techniques here being used in an essentially descriptive mode. The second stage is that of hypothesising generative processes at the level of action that have explanatory adequacy and that are of a theoretically grounded kind—as, say, in the form of RAT-based narratives. And the third stage is then that of testing the validity—the actual applicability—of the explanations that are thus advanced, using as wide a range of strategies, direct or indirect, and of research methods and analytical techniques, quantitative or qualitative, as can be effectively brought into play.[21]

This essay has in general been well received (see, e.g., the special number of the *European Sociological Review*, vol. 17, no. 1, 2001) and by statisticians as well as sociologists. In addition to recapitulating some key arguments from the critical and programmatic essays of this volume, I would see it as providing a link between these essays and those intended to illustrate the general position that I have taken up which form the larger part of Volume II. Through such illustration, the importance to sociologists of issues of how they should understand—and implement—the idea of causation in their work may, I hope, become more apparent.

CHAPTER TWO

The Uses of History in Sociology
Reflections on Some Recent Tendencies*

To take up again the question of the uses of history in sociology may well appear regressive. For to do so implies, of course, making a distinction *between* history and sociology, which would now be widely regarded as untenable. Thus, for example, Philip Abrams, in his highly influential book, *Historical Sociology* (1980) advanced the argument that since 'history and sociology are and always have been the same thing', any discussion of the relationship of one to the other must be misguided; and Abrams in turn quotes Giddens (1979: 230) to the effect that 'There simply are no logical or even methodological distinctions between the social sciences and history—appropriately conceived'.

As Abrams is indeed aware, the position he adopts is in sharp contrast with that which would have been most common among sociologists in the mid-twentieth century. At this time, sociologists were for the most part anxious to differentiate their concerns from those of historians. For example, much use was made of the distinction between 'idiographic' and 'nomothetic' disciplines. History was idiographic: historians sought to *particularise* through the description of singular, unique phenomena. Sociology was nomothetic: sociologists sought to *generalise* through formulating theories that applied to categories of phenomena.[1] However, all this was in the period before the sociological community lost its nerve over the idea of

*This essay is a revised version of the T. H. Marshall Memorial Lecture for 1989, given at the University of Southampton. For helpful comments on various drafts, I am indebted to Klas Åmark, Robert Erikson, Stephen Mennell, Patrick O'Brien, and, especially, Gordon Marshall and Lucia Zedner.

21

'social science'—before, that is, the so-called reaction against positivism of the late 1960s and 1970s created a new mood in which political radicalism went together with intellectual conservatism.

My first contribution to the debate on 'history and sociology' (1962) dates back to this prelapsarian time, and was in fact a *critique of* the idiographic-nomothetic distinction. My remarks were not especially well received by either historians or sociologists, and this present contribution may, I fear, prove similarly uncongenial. For what I would now think important is that attempts, such as that of Abrams and Giddens, to present history and sociology as being one and indistinguishable should be strongly resisted.[2] To avoid, if possible, being misunderstood, let me stress that I do not seek here to reestablish the idiographic-nomothetic distinction, or at least not as one of principle. I do not believe, for example, that sociologists can ever hope to produce theories that are of an entirely transhistorical kind, nor that historians can ever hope to produce descriptions that are free of general ideas about social action, process, and structure. Nonetheless, good grounds do still remain for refusing to accept the position that *any* distinction drawn between history and sociology must be meaningless.

To begin with, I would argue that the idiographic-nomothetic distinction is still pertinent if taken as one not of principle but of *emphasis*. Historians do—quite rightly—regard it as important that dates and places should be attached to the arguments they advance as precisely as possible. As Thompson (quoted in Stone, 1987) has aptly remarked, 'the discipline of history is above all a discipline of context'. Sociologists—no less rightly—believe that they are achieving something if the time and space coordinates over which their arguments apply can be widened. And, from this, one use of history in sociology is immediately suggested. History may serve as, so to speak, a 'residual category' for sociology, marking the point at which sociologists, in invoking 'history', thereby curb their impulse to generalise or, in other words, to explain sociologically, and accept the role of the specific and of the contingent as framing—that is, as providing both the setting *and* the limits—of their own analyses.[3] However, it is not on such issues that I wish here to concentrate. My aim is rather to focus attention on another major difference between history and sociology that has, I believe, been much neglected but that carries far-reaching implications for sociological practice. This difference concerns the nature of the evidence that the two disciplines use or, more precisely, the way in which this evidence comes into being.[4]

EVIDENCE IN HISTORY AND SOCIOLOGY

As a trainee historian at University College London in the 1950s, I under-
went a standard catechism on method, which began with the question: what
is a historical fact? The answer that had to be given was: a historical fact
is an inference from the relics. This answer struck me then, and still strikes
me, as the best that can be given and as one of considerable significance.
What the answer underlines is the obvious, but still highly consequential,
point that we can only know the past on the basis of what has physically
survived from the past: that is, on the basis of the relics—or of what may
be alternatively described as the residues, deposits, or traces—of the past.[5]
These relics are of very different kinds. They may, for example, be simply
natural remains, such as bones or excrement as are exploited by archaeolo-
gists; or again, artefacts, such as tools, weapons, buildings, or works of art.
But of most general importance are what one might call 'objectified communications': that is, communications in some written form and, especially,
'documents' of all kinds. Whatever their nature, it is these relics, and only
these relics, that are the source of our knowledge about the past. Statements
about the past—historical 'facts'—are inferences from the relics, and can
have no other basis. In short: no relics, no history.

So far as the practice of history is concerned, there are two points about
relics that it seems important to recognise: first, they are *finite* and, second,
they are *incomplete*. The relics that exist are just a limited selection of all
that could have survived, a sample, so to speak, of a total universe of relics,
where, however, neither the properties of the universe nor of the sample are,
or can be, known (cf. Murphey, 1973; Clubb, 1980). The relics of a given period may diminish, by being physically destroyed, but they cannot increase.

It is true of course that not all the relics that exist at any one time are
known about. Historians have always the possibility of discovering 'new'
relics, of adding to the known stock: and it is indeed an important part of
their *métier* to do so. It is also true that from any set of relics, the inferences
that can be made are *in*finite. The 'facts' that the relics yield will tend to
increase with the questions that historians put to them and, in turn, with
the range of the problems they address and with the development of their
techniques of enquiry. However, none of this alters the situation that the
relics themselves, in a physical sense—what is there to be discovered and
interrogated—are finite and are, to repeat, a selection, and probably only a

quite small and unrepresentative selection, of all that could have survived. It must therefore be the case that limitations on the possibilities of historical knowledge exist simply because it is knowledge of the past—because it is knowledge dependent on relics. There are things about the past that never can be known simply because the relics that would have been essential to knowing them did not in fact survive.

Historians, we may then say, are concerned with *finding* their evidence from among a stock of relics. In contrast, and this is the difference I want to stress, sociologists have open to them a possibility that is largely denied to historians. While sociologists can, and often do, draw on relics as evidence in just the same way as historians, they can, in addition, *generate* evidence. This is of course what they are doing when they engage in 'fieldwork'. They are producing, as a basis for inferences, materials *that did not exist before.*[6] And it is, I would argue, such generated evidence, rather than evidence in the form of relics—in other words, evidence that is 'invented' rather than evidence that is discovered—that constitutes the main empirical foundations of modern sociology.

The immediate reason for this difference in the way in which historical and sociological evidence comes into being is obvious: historians work 'in the past', while sociologists *can also* work 'in the present'. However, behind this immediate reason lies the difference of emphasis that I earlier referred to: sociologists do not seek to tie their arguments to specific time and space coordinates so much as to test the extent of their generality. Thus, if a sociologist develops a theory intended to apply, say, to all industrial societies, it will be only sensible at all events to *begin* the examination of this theory through research conducted in contemporary rather than in past industrial societies, and hence through research that permits the generation of evidence rather than imposing a reliance on relics.

If, then, there is here, as I would wish to maintain, a major difference between history and sociology as forms of disciplined enquiry, what follows from it for the uses of history in sociology? The main implication is, I believe, clear enough. Because sociologists have the possibility of producing their own evidence, over and above that of exploiting relics, they *are in a position of advantage that should not be disregarded or lightly thrown away.* In other words, sociologists should not readily and unthinkingly turn to history: they should do so, rather, only with good reasons and in full awareness of the limitations that they will thereby face. Here again I am, I suspect, in some danger of being misunderstood. Let me therefore at once add that I do not in any way seek to suggest that sociology is in some sense a 'superior' discipline to history: rather, I am concerned to bring out just how difficult history is—since, as will later emerge, I believe that some sociologists have clearly failed to appreciate this. Nor do I suppose that generated evidence, in contrast to that in the form of relics, is unproblematic. I am well aware that it too must always be critically viewed as regards its completeness as well as its reliability and validity, and indeed that in these latter respects special problems result precisely from the processes of generation. However, what I do wish to emphasise are the very real advantages that are gained where the nature and extent of available evidence is not restricted by the mere accidents of physical survival; where, moreover, the collection of evidence can be 'designed' so as to meet the specific requirements of the enquiry in hand, and where questions of the quality of evidence can always be addressed, as they arise, by generating yet further evidence through which to check and test the original.[7]

SOME ILLUSTRATIONS OF THE ARGUMENT

To develop these arguments, I now turn to particular cases. To begin with, it may be helpful if I give an example of what I would regard as a mistaken— one might say, perverse—recourse to history on the part of a sociologist. I take here Kai Erikson's book, *Wayward Puritans* (1966), which is a study of social deviance within the seventeenth-century Puritan community of Massachussetts Bay.

In his Preface, Erikson states his aims clearly. He begins with certain hypotheses about social deviance drawn from a Durkheimian position, and he aims to examine two hypotheses in particular: first, that some amount of deviance is functional for a community in helping it to define its moral and social boundaries, and thus in preserving its stability; and second, that, because of this functionality, deviance within any community will tend to be at a fairly constant level over time. Erikson then proposes to take Massachussetts Bay as a case study. 'The purpose of the following study', he writes (1966: vii–viii), 'is to use the Puritan community as a setting in which to examine several ideas about deviant behavior. In this sense the subject matter of the book is primarily sociological, even though the data found in most of its pages are historical'. And, he goes on, 'The data presented here have *not* been gathered in order to throw new light on the Puritan community in New England but to add something to our understanding of deviant behavior in general, and thus the Puritan experience in America has been treated in these pages as an example of human life everywhere'. Judged in the light of this statement, *Wayward Puritans* is, I would argue, a failure—and indeed a necessary failure—because of its reliance on historical materials. The hypotheses that Erikson starts from are not seriously examined, and could not be, simply because Erikson does not have the evidence needed for this among the relics at his disposal.

Thus, as regards the first hypothesis, on the functionality of deviance, Erikson draws largely on court records, indicating the response of the authorities to antinomianism, Quakerism, and alleged witchcraft. But he has little evidence of how *the community at large*, as distinct from the authorities, reacted to such deviance or, for that matter, to its treatment by the authorities. In other words, he has no adequate basis on which to determine whether, in consequence of the deviance he refers to, there was, or was not, a stronger definition of the moral and social boundaries of the community. So far as popular perceptions and evaluations are concerned, he is without means of access. Likewise, in treating the second hypothesis, on the constant level of deviance, Erikson has to rely on official crime statistics, which, for well-known reasons, give only a very uncertain indication of the actual level of social deviance, and are influenced in their trend by a variety of other factors. However, unlike the sociologist of deviance working in contemporary society, Erikson cannot investigate in any detail the processes through which the official statistics were constituted, nor can he collect data of his own that could provide alternative estimates—as, say, through some form of 'victim survey'.

To be sure, the hypotheses that Erikson addresses are not ones that would be easily tested under any circumstances. But, given that they derive from a theory that pretends to a very high level of generality, there is all the more reason to ask why Erikson should impose on himself the limitations that must follow from choosing a historical case. Why should he deny himself the possibility of being able to generate his own evidence, to his own design, and under conditions in which problems of reliability and validity could best be grappled with? Any sociologist, I would maintain, who is concerned with a theory that *can* be tested in the present should so test it, in the first place; for it is, in all probability, in this way that it can be tested most rigorously.[8]

I would now like to move on to consider cases where the recourse of sociologists to history *would* appear to have the good reasons that, I earlier maintained, should always be present. Here my aim is to illustrate what such reasons might be, but also—when they are acted on—the difficulties that may be expected.

Sociologists, one might think, will most obviously need to turn to history when their interests lie in social change. However, it should be kept in mind that a recourse to the past—or, that is, to the relics thereof—is not the only means through which such interests may be pursued: repeated surveys and life-course and panel studies, for example, are all ways of studying social change on the basis of evidence that is, or has been, collected in the present. Sociologists, I would argue, are compelled into historical research only when their concern is with social change that is in fact historically defined: that is, with change not over some analytically specified length of time—such as, say, 'the life cycle' or 'two generations'—but with change over a period of past time that has dates (even if not very precise ones) and that is related to a particular place. Sociologists have a legitimate, and necessary, concern with such historically defined social change because, as I have earlier suggested, they wish to know how widely over time and space their theories and hypotheses might apply.[9]

One illustration of what I have in mind here is provided by Michael Anderson's book, *Family Structure in Nineteenth Century Lancashire* (1971). Anderson is concerned with the hypothesis that in the process of industrialisation, preexisting forms of extended family and kinship relations are disrupted. Specifically, he is interested in whether or not this hypothesis holds good in the British case, that of the 'first industrial nation'. Thus, to pursue this issue, Anderson aims to examine just what was happening to kinship relations in Britain at the time when, and in the place where, the 'take-off' into industrialism is classically located. In contrast, then, with Erikson, Anderson has a quite clear rationale for turning to historical research. A second illustration is provided by Gordon Marshall's book, *Presbyteries and Profits* (1980). Marshall is concerned with the 'Weber thesis' that a connection exists between the secular ethic of ascetic Protestantism and 'the spirit of capitalism'. In the long-standing debate on this thesis, the case of Scotland has several times been suggested as a critical one, in that, in the early modern period, Scotland had a great deal of ascetic Protestantism—that is, Calvinism—yet showed little in the way of capitalist development. Marshall's aim is then to reexamine the Scottish case for the period from around 1560 to the Act of Union of 1707. Marshall points out that Weber himself always emphasised that his argument on the role of the Protestant ethic in the emergence of modern capitalism was intended to apply *only to the early stages* of this process: once a predominantly capitalist economy was established, its own exigencies, in the workplace and market, would themselves compel conduct generally consistent with the 'spirit of capitalism' without need of help from religion. Again, then, Marshall, like Anderson, has obviously good grounds for his recourse to history.

Now before proceeding further, I should make it clear that I have the highest regard for the two studies to which I have just referred. Both make signal contributions to the questions they address; and, for me, they stand as leading examples of how in fact historical sociology should be conceived and conducted. I say this because I want now to go on to emphasise the severe limitations to which the analyses of both authors are subject: *not* because of their deficiencies as sociologists, but simply because of the fact that they were forced into using historical evidence—forced into a reliance on relics—rather than being able to generate their own evidence within a contemporary society.

The relics on which Anderson chiefly relies are the original enumerators' books for the censuses of 1841, 1851, and 1861. On this basis, he can reconstruct household composition according to age, sex, and kinship relations, and he can also to some extent examine the residential propinquity of kin. But this still leaves him a long way short of adequate evidence on the part actually played by kinship in the lives of the people he is studying and on the meanings of kinship for them. He attempts to fill out the essentially demographic data that he has from the enumerators' books with material from contemporary accounts. But these would, I fear, have at best to be categorised as 'casual empiricism' and at worst as local gossip or travellers' tales. Titles such as *Walks in South Lancashire and on its Borders, A Visit to Lancashire in December 1862*, and *Lancashire Sketches* give the flavour. Anderson is in fact entirely frank about the problem he faces. 'It must of course be stressed', he writes (1971: 62), 'that just because interaction with kin occurred it is no necessary indication that kinship was important. The real test, which is quite impossible in any precise way in historical work, would be to examine the extent to which kinship was given preference over other relational contacts (and the reasons for this preference), and the extent to which contacts with kin fulfilled functions which were not adequately met if kin did not provide them'.

The point I want to make here would perhaps best be brought out if one were to compare Anderson's study of kinship with one carried out in contemporary society—let us say, for example, Fischer's study (1982) of kinship and of other 'primary' relations in present-day San Francisco. The only conclusion could be that the latter is greatly superior in the range and quality of data on which it draws, and in turn in the rigour and refinement of the analyses it can offer. And the point is, of course, not that Fischer is a better sociologist than Anderson but that he has an enormous advantage over Anderson in being able to generate his own data rather than having to rely on whatever relics might happen to be extant.

Turning to Marshall, one finds that he has problems essentially the same as those of Anderson. One of Marshall's main concerns is that Weber's position should be correctly understood, following the vulgarisations of Robertson, Tawney, Samuelson, and other critics; in this respect Marshall makes two main points. First, Weber was not so much concerned with official Calvinist doctrine on economic activity as with the consequences of *being* a believing Calvinist for the individual's conduct of everyday life—consequences that the individual might not even fully realise. In other words, Weber's thesis was ultimately not about theology but subculture and psychology. Second, Weber's argument was that the Protestant ethic was a necessary, but not a sufficient, cause of the emergence of modern capitalism; there were necessary 'material' factors also, such as access to physical resources and to markets, the availability of capital and credit, and so on. Thus, Marshall argues, in evaluating the Weber thesis, it is not enough to look simply for some overt association between theology, on the one hand, and the development of capitalist enterprise on the other. What is required is more subtle. It is evidence that believing Calvinists, on account of their acceptance of a Calvinist worldview, were distinctively oriented to work in a regular, disciplined way, to pursue economic gain rationally, and to accumulate rather than to consume extravagantly—so that, *if* other conditions were *also* met, capitalist enterprise would then flourish.

Marshall's position here is, I believe, entirely sound. But it leads him to problems of evidence that he can in fact never satisfactorily overcome, despite his diligence in searching out new sources and his ingenuity in using known ones. And the basic difficulty is that relics from which inferences can systematically be made about the orientations to work and to money of early modern Scots are very few and far between. In other words, what is crucially lacking—just as it was lacking for Anderson and indeed for Erikson—is material from which inferences might be made, with some assurance of representativeness, about the *patterns of social action* that are of interest within particular collectivities. As Clubb (1980: 20) has observed, the data from which historians work only rarely allow access to the subjective orientations of actors *en masse*, and inferences made in this respect from actual behaviour tend always to be question-begging. And Marshall, it should be said, like Anderson, sees the difficulty clearly enough. He acknowledges (1980: 35) that it may well be that 'the kind of data required in order to establish the ethos in which seventeenth-century Scottish business enterprises were run simply does not exist'—or, at least, not in sufficient quantity to allow one to test empirically whether Calvinism did indeed have the effect on mundane conduct that Weber ascribed to it.

THE PROBLEM OF 'GRAND HISTORICAL SOCIOLOGY'

Let me at this point recapitulate. I have argued that history and sociology differ perhaps most consequentially in the nature of the evidence on which they rely, and that this difference has major implications for the use of history in sociology. I have presented a case of what, from this standpoint, must be seen as a perverse recourse to history on the part of a sociologist; and I have now discussed two further cases where, in contrast, such a recourse was justifiable, indeed necessary, given the issues addressed, but where, nonetheless, serious difficulties arise because of the inadequacy of the relics as a basis for treating these issues. In the remainder of the essay, I would like to move on from these instances of sociologists resorting to history in the pursuit of quite specific problems to consider, with my initial argument still in mind, a whole genre of sociology that is in fact *dependant on history in its very conception*. I refer here to a kind of historical sociology clearly different from that represented by the work of Anderson or Marshall, and that has two main distinguishing features. First, it resorts to history because it addresses very large themes, which typically involve the tracing out of long-term 'developmental' processes or patterns or the making of comparisons across a wide range of historical societies or even civilisations. And second, it is based largely or entirely not on inferences from relics but rather on 'history' in the sense of what historians have written—or, in other words, not on primary but on secondary, or yet more derivative, sources.

The idea that sociologists might proceed by taking the results of historical research as their main empirical resource in developing wide-ranging generalisations and theories is not of course a new one. It was in fact a nineteenth-century commonplace. Its plainest expression was perhaps provided by Herbert Spencer when he wrote (1904, vol. 2: 185; cf. also 1861/1911: 29) that, for him, sociology stood to works of history 'much as a vast building stands related to the heaps of stones and bricks around it', and further that 'the highest office which the historian can discharge is that of so narrating the lives of nations, as to furnish materials for a Comparative Sociology'. From the end of the nineteenth century, this understanding of the relationship between history and sociology met with severe criticism and rather rapidly lost support. Historians had indeed never taken kindly to the idea that they should serve as some kind of intellectual under-labourers, and sociologists became increasingly interested in developing their own methods of data collection.[10] However, in more recent times, a notable revival of what might be called 'grand historical sociology' has occurred. This revival was led by the appearance of Barrington Moore's *The Social Origins of Dictatorship and Democracy* (1966) and was then consolidated in the United States by the subsequent work of Wallerstein (1974–89) and Skocpol (1979) and in Britain by that of Perry Anderson (1974a, 1974b), with other authors such as Hall (1985) and Mann (1986) following in the wake.[11] What I would now wish to argue is that the practice of these authors does in fact raise again all the difficulties inherent in Spencer's programme, and that the use of history in sociology as exemplified in their work is problematic in a far more fundamental way than in any of the studies earlier considered.

The authors in question would certainly not wish to represent their position in terms similar to those of Spencer. They would rather incline to the idea that history and sociology are one and indivisible; and, instead of viewing historians *de haut en bas*, they would surely wish to include them in the joint enterprise as equal partners.[12] Nonetheless, the fact remains that grand historical sociology in its twentieth-century form, just as in its nineteenth, takes secondary historical sources as its evidential basis, and must therefore encounter the methodological difficulties that are entailed, even though its exponents have thus far shown little readiness to address, or even acknowledge, them. The root of their predicament is richly ironical. The revival of grand historical sociology can be seen as one expression of the 'reaction against positivism' within the sociological community to which I referred at the start, and yet its practitioners' own *modus operandi*—the use they seek to make of secondary sources—must depend on what is an essentially positivistic conception of *historiography*, to which they would, I suspect, be reluctant to give any explicit support.

The catechism that I was put through as an undergraduate had a clear objective. It was to prompt a rejection of the view that the past—or at least certain well-documented aspects of the past, such as 'high' politics—could in principle be reconstructed, fact by fact, so that the distinction between history in the sense of what actually happened in the past and history in the sense of what is written about the past might be elided. Against this 'positivist' conception of historiography—as it was indeed labelled (see, e.g., Collingwood, 1946/1993: 126–33)[13]—it was urged on us that historical facts could not be cognitively established as a collection of well-defined items or entities, each independent of the rest, which, when taken together, would then dictate a specific and definitive version of the past. Rather, historical facts should be recognised as no more than 'inferences from the relics'; and inferences that had always to be weighted, so to speak, according to the security of their grounding, which were often interdependent—that is, stood or fell together—and which were of course at all times open to restatement, whether radically or through the most subtle changes of nuance.

Now, to repeat, I very much doubt if grand historical sociologists would wish to take up the defence of positivist historiography as against this latter view. But it is difficult to see how, *in practice*, they can avoid *assuming* an essentially positivist position. For even if the procedures they follow in producing their sociology do not actually require the elision of the two senses of history, they still cannot afford to recognise a too indeterminate relation between them. Grand historical sociologists have to treat the facts, or indeed concatenations of facts or entire 'accounts', that they find in secondary sources *as if they were* relatively discrete and stable entities that can be 'excerpted' and then brought together in order that some larger design may be realised. In anti-positivist vein, Becker (1955) expressly warned that historical facts should *not* be thought of as possessing 'solidity', 'definite shape', or 'clear persistent outline', and that it is therefore especially inapt to liken them to building materials of any kind. But the very procedures of grand historical sociologists push them back, willy-nilly, to Spencer's idea of using the stones and bricks of history to construct the great sociological edifice, and constructional metaphors do indeed reappear. Thus, for example, one finds Skocpol (1979: xiv) remarking that 'primary research'—which the comparativist 'has neither the time nor (all of) the appropriate skills to do'—'necessarily constitutes, in large amounts, the foundation upon which comparative studies are built'. However, I would then wish to respond that the constructions that result are likely to be dangerously unsound. In particular, I would argue that in grand historical sociology the links that are claimed, or supposed, between evidence and argument tend to be both *tenuous* and *arbitrary* to a quite unacceptable degree.

As regards the first charge, it is, I would suggest, instructive to consider some fairly specific arguments advanced by a grand historical sociologist, and to note the 'authorities' that are invoked as providing its factual basis; then, to work back from these citations—through perhaps other intermediate sources that are involved—until one comes to direct references to relics of some kind. What, I believe, one will typically find is that the trail is longer and harder to follow than one might have expected, and that, not infrequently, it reaches no very satisfactory end. For example, in *Social Origins of Dictatorship and Democracy*, Moore spends several pages reviewing aspects of English economic history over the late medieval and early modern periods, and then concludes as follows (1966: 14):

> In the light of this general background there would seem to be little reason
> to question the thesis that commercially minded elements among the landed
> upper classes, and to a lesser extent among the yeomen, were among the main
> forces opposing the King and royal attempts to preserve the old order, and
> therefore an important cause, though not the only one, that produced the
> Civil War.

However, if one actually examines the sources that Moore cites, both before and after this passage, the grounding of his argument is very far from apparent. Indeed, it is quite unclear just what is the evidence, at the level of relics, in the light of which there would be 'little reason to question' the thesis that Moore advances. In the authorities referred to—the main ones are Tawney

(1912, 1941/1954) and Campbell (1942)—there is in fact remarkably little 'evidence' bearing in any direct way on the crucial link that Moore seeks to establish between economic position and political action. And such as there is cannot be regarded as evidence in the sense that relics themselves are evidence or, for that matter, the data of a social survey are evidence. Rather, what one has are series of inferences, often complex and indeed often quite speculative, which are drawn from relics that are manifestly incomplete, almost certainly unrepresentative, and in various other ways problematic— as the authors to whom Moore refers are themselves well aware. In other words, such 'facts' as are here available cannot be understood as separate, well-defined modules, easily carried off for sociological construction purposes, but would be better regarded simply as strands in heavily tangled, yet still often rather weak skeins of interpretation.

In effect, then, what grand historical sociologists seem to me to be generally doing is not developing an argument on the basis of evidence, in the manner of 'primary' historians or again of sociologists working on their own research data, but rather, engaging in interpretation that is of, at least, a second-order kind: that is, in interpretation of interpretations of, perhaps, interpretations. And in consequence, I would maintain, the connection between the claims they make about the past and relics that could conceivably serve as warrant for these claims is often, as in the passage from Moore that I have quoted, quite impossibly loose. Following the practices that are here illustrated, history must indeed become, in Froude's words (1884, vol. l: 21) 'a child's box of letters with which we can spell any word we please'.

As regards my second charge, that of arbitrariness, the idea of historiography as a matter of inferences from relics that are finite and incomplete is again directly relevant. It follows from this that historians working on the same topic, and indeed on the same relics, may quite reasonably come to quite different conclusions, as of course they may for other reasons too. But it further follows that there may be little or no possibility of their differences ever being resolved because the relics that would be necessary to settle the disputed issues simply do not exist. For grand historical sociologists, this then raises a major problem: where historians disagree, and may have perhaps to remain in disagreement, *which* secondary account should be accepted? By what criteria should the grand historical sociologist opt for one of two, or more, conflicting interpretations? Thus, to return to Moore and his treatment of the economic and social origins of the English Civil War, the question one may ask is: why, on this notoriously controversial matter, and one plagued by a lack of relevant evidence, does Moore choose largely to follow what has come to be thought of (not altogether fairly) as the 'Tawney' interpretation rather than any of its rivals? By the time Moore was writing, it should be said, the idea that the 'rising', commercially oriented gentry were key actors in the parliamentary opposition to the King and his defeat in the Civil War was in fact fast losing ground among English historians, both to interpretations that gave the leading role to other socioeconomic groupings and, more important, to ones that questioned whether political allegiance in the Civil War period had any close association at all with economic position and interest.[14]

The answer to the question I have posed is, I believe, as obvious as it is unsatisfactory. Moore favours the interpretation that fits best with his overall thesis of the 'three routes to modernity'; in other words, that which allows the English Civil War to be seen as an instance of a successful 'bourgeois revolution'. However, he still fails to present any serious case for this choice. Supportive sources simply receive accolades, such as 'excellent analysis' or 'unsurpassed account', while less congenial ones are disparaged as 'conservative historiography' (see, e.g., 1966: 6, 14, and the Appendix).[15] This clearly will not do. But if mere tendentiousness is not the solution, what is? In the end, of course, any rational way of evaluating a secondary source must involve some judgment on the inferences made from the primary sources—that is, from the relics. But once this is recognised, the methodological bind in which grand historical sociologists find themselves becomes only more apparent. Their large designs mean, they tell us, that they cannot themselves be expected to work directly from the relics but must rely on the studies of specialist authorities. However, they are then either forced into positivistic assumptions concerning the 'hardness' and 'solidity'—and also the 'transportability'—of the evidence that these works can yield; or, if they accept that what these sources provide is no more than rival complexes of inference and interpretation, then they must explain how they propose to choose among them *without knowledge of* the primary sources. Where historians themselves draw on secondary sources, it may be added, as, say, in situating their own primary research or in writing surveys of a field, issues of the availability, and quality of sources are typically discussed. Moreover, in the case of survey articles, and likewise in the writing of textbooks, authors are not under pressure to defend a particular interpretation but can present a

review of different positions. Grand historical sociologists, in contrast, usually cannot afford such evenhandedness; they need to use—that is, to choose
among—secondary sources as evidence for or against a particular thesis.[16]

Since, then, I have been so critical of the methodological basis of grand
historical sociology, I should, before finishing, consider what its exponents
have themselves had to say on the matter. In fact, as I have already implied,
they have said remarkably little. Methodological issues tend to be raised, if
at all, in the early pages of their books, but then only to be dealt with in a
quite perfunctory and unconvincing manner (see, e.g., Moore, 1966: x–xi;
Skocpol, 1979: xiv–xv; Anderson, 1974a: 8; Mann, 1986: vii–viii, 3–4,
31–32). However, there is one statement by Skocpol, from the concluding
chapter of a collection that she edited on the subject of method in historical
sociology that is of interest in several respects. Skocpol writes as follows
(1984: 382):

> Because wide-ranging comparisons are so often crucial for analytic historical
> sociologists, they are more likely to use secondary sources of evidence than
> those who apply models to, or develop interpretations of, single cases . . .
> From the point of view of historical sociology, . . . a dogmatic insistence on
> redoing primary research for every investigation would be disastrous; it would
> rule out most comparative-historical research. If a topic is too big for purely
> primary research—and if excellent studies by specialists are already available
> in some profusion—secondary sources are appropriate as the basic source of
> evidence for a given study. Using them is not different from survey analysts re-
> working the results of previous surveys rather than asking all questions anew.

I would note, first of all, about this passage how clearly it shows the
pressure that bears on grand historical sociologists to move towards the positivistic, Spencerian programme—'excellent' historical studies by specialists
can be 'the basic source of evidence' for the wide-ranging sociologist. And
also revealing is the reference to 'redoing the primary research', as if it were
apparent that the same result as before would necessarily emerge. Second, I
would point out that Skocpol is quite mistaken in the analogy she seeks to
draw with survey-based research. The 'secondary analysis' of survey data to
which she refers differs from the grand historical sociologist's use of secondary sources, precisely because it *does* entail going back to the 'relics': that is,
at least to the original datatapes and perhaps also to the original questionnaires or interview schedules. And it is then these materials that serve the
secondary analyst as evidence, not the interpretations of the original ana-

lyst, which may be, and indeed often are, disputed. Thus, a closer parallel would be between the secondary analyst of surveys and the historian who again works through and reinterprets a body of source materials discovered and initially analysed by a predecessor. Third, I would remark that by way of providing a rationale for the methodology of grand historical sociology, Skocpol has little at all to offer. Apart from her mistaken *tu quoque* argument directed at survey researchers, all she in fact says is that it would be 'disastrous' for grand historical sociologists if they were to be forced back to primary sources—which is scarcely a way of convincing sceptics.

What is actually of greatest interest is what Skocpol goes on to acknowledge in the paragraph that immediately follows the one from which I quoted: namely, that 'it remains true that comparative historical sociologists have not so far worked out clear, consensual rules and procedures for the valid use of secondary sources as evidence' and further that in this respect 'varying historiographical interpretations' is one obvious problem to be addressed. 'Certain principles', Skocpol believes, 'are likely to emerge as such rules are developed'. But, one must observe, so far at least, grand historical sociology is *not* significantly rule governed; its practitioners enjoy a delightful freedom to play 'pick-and-mix' in history's sweetshop.[17]

To sum up, then, I have argued that the view that history and sociology 'are and always have been the same thing' is mistaken and—dangerously—misleading. Sociology must, it is true, always be a historical discipline; sociologists can never 'escape' from history. It is therefore highly desirable that they should be historically aware—by which I mean, aware of the historical settings and limits that their analyses will necessarily possess, even if these settings and limits may never be precisely determined. But history and sociology can, and should, still be regarded as significantly different intellectual enterprises. A crucial source of the difference, I have sought to show, lies in the nature of the evidence that the two disciplines use: in the fact that historians have for the most part to rely on evidence that they can discover in the relics of the past, while sociologists have the considerable privilege of being able to generate evidence in the present.

As regards, then, the use of history in sociology, what I have sought to stress is that sociologists should not underestimate, or readily give up, the advantages that they can gain from having evidence that is 'tailor made', whereas historians have usually to 'cut their coats according to their cloth'.

Where sociologists are compelled into historical research, by the very logic of their enquiries, then, I have suggested, they must be ready for a harder life—for research typically conducted, as one historian has put it, 'below the data poverty line' (Clubb, 1980: 20). They must not only learn new techniques but also to accept new frustrations; in particular, those that come from realising that issues of crucial interest are, and will probably remain, beyond their cognitive reach. Historical sociologists such as Anderson and Marshall have learnt well, and much of what they can in turn teach us stems from their sensitivity to just what manner of inferences the relics available to them can, and cannot, sustain. In contrast, grand historical sociologists seem to me to have, so far at least, shied away from the major intellectual challenges that historiography poses, and to have traded implicitly on a conception of it that I doubt they would wish openly to defend. Until, then, they do meet the challenges before them, and provide a coherent methodology for their work, the question must remain of how far this does possess a real basis in the relics of the past or merely an illusory one in a scattering of footnotes.

CHAPTER THREE

Current Issues in Comparative Macrosociology*

I seek in this essay to intervene in what is in fact a rather long-standing debate within comparative macrosociology, but one which appears of late to have acquired new vigour. The contending parties in this debate are now usually characterised as exponents of quantitative, variable-oriented methodologies, on the one hand, and of qualitative, case-oriented methodologies, on the other (see, e.g., Ragin, 1987; Rueschemeyer, 1991; Janoski and Hicks, eds., 1994; King, Keohane, and Verba, 1994; Mahoney and Rueschemeyer, eds., 2003; Brady and Collier, eds., 2004). I shall, however, argue that while the issues caught up in the protracted and complex exchanges that have occurred do include ones of major importance, the form that the debate has taken has not been especially helpful in highlighting just what these issues are, nor yet in pointing to ways in which they might be more effectively addressed.

I develop my position as follows. To begin with, I give a brief account of the contrast, or opposition, that has been set up between variable- and case-oriented approaches. I then pursue my central argument by considering three rather well-known methodological problems that are encountered in the practice of comparative macrosociology. These problems are ones that have in fact been chiefly discussed in connection with variable-oriented research. But, I aim to show, they are present to no less a degree in case-

*This essay is a revised and extended version of the Vilhelm Aubert Memorial Lecture for 1993, given at the University of Oslo. For information, advice, and critical observations on previous drafts, I am indebted to David Collier, Anne Gauthier, Andrew Hurrell, Olli Kangas, Philip Kreager, John Stephens, Laurence Whitehead, and Timothy Wickham-Crowley.

oriented studies and, contrary to what several prominent authors have maintained or implied, the latter can claim no special advantages in dealing with them. Largely on account of misconceptions in this regard, I conclude, much recent discussion has tended to obscure, and divert attention away from, questions of method that comparative macrosociology does now need to engage with more actively—in whatever style it may be carried out.[1]

VARIABLE- VERSUS CASE-ORIENTED APPROACHES

The variable-oriented approach to comparative macrosociology stems from a now famous proposal made by Przeworski and Teune (1970: ch. 1; cf. Zelditch, 1971: 269–73): that is, that the ultimate aim of work in this field should be to replace the proper names of nations (or of states, cultures, etc.) with the names of variables. Przeworski and Teune first illustrate the logic they would recommend by examples such as the following. Rates of heart attack are lower in Japan than in the United States. But, in seeking an explanation for this, we do not get far by treating the differing rates as simply 'Japanese' or 'American' phenomena. Rather, we have to drop proper names—or adjectives—and introduce generally applicable variables: that is, variables on which each nation can be given a comparable value. Thus, in the case in point, one such variable might be 'per capita consumption of polysaturated fat'.

Przeworski and Teune then of course go on to provide further illustrations of their position drawn from the social sciences; and, by the present day, one could in fact add to these entire research programmes in sociology—and political science—that essentially follow the approach that they advocate. As a paradigm case here, one might take research that is aimed at explaining cross-national differences in the size and institutional form of welfare states (for reviews, see Quadagno, 1987; O'Connor and Brym, 1988; Huber, Ragin, and Stephens, 1993). In such research, the names of nations are typically replaced by such variables as 'GNP per capita', 'proportion of population over age 65', 'degree of trade-union centralisation', 'share of left-wing parties in government', and so on. That is to say, these are the independent variables, by reference to which the dependent variables—cross-nationally differing aspects of welfare provision—are to be accounted for. The relationships that actually prevail between independent and dependent variables are then investigated statistically, through various techniques of multivariate analysis.

It is, for present purposes, important to recognise what Przeworski and Teune were defining their position *against*. Most importantly, they sought to challenge the historicist claim that any attempt to make macrosociological comparisons must fail in principle because different national societies are *sui generis*: that is, are entities uniquely formed by their history and culture, which can be studied only, so to speak, in their own right and on their own terms.[2] In opposition to this, Przeworski and Teune point out that being 'comparable' or 'non-comparable' are not inherent properties of things: whether meaningful comparison is possible is entirely a matter of the analytic concepts that we have at our disposal. Thus, apples and oranges may appear to be non-comparable—but only until we have the concept of 'fruit' (cf. Sartori, 1994). At the same time, though, Przeworski and Teune do insist that *if* the historicist position is accepted, then it must indeed follow that a comparative macrosociology is ruled out. If nations can only be studied as entities in themselves that will not allow of any kind of analytic decomposition— if, in other words, nations can only be studied holistically—then comparisons *cannot* be undertaken. Considered as wholes, nations *are* unique, and 'holistic comparison' is thus an impossibility. As Zelditch (1971: 278) later put the point: 'There is nothing else on earth quite like the United States (or the Navaho, or the Eskimo . . .) taken as a whole. Therefore the rule of holism [in comparative work] yields a clear and straightforward contradiction: only incomparables are comparable'.

However, if the variable-oriented approach thus developed out of a critique of holism, the case-oriented approach is usually taken to represent a revival of holism, and indeed one directed against the kind of analytic reductionism that Przeworski and Teune would favour. Thus, for example, Ragin (1991: 1–2) would regard it as being the very raison d'être of case studies that they allow a return to holism in comparative research: that is, they allow nations, or other macrosocial units, to be considered as 'meaningful wholes' rather than serving simply as the basis on which 'to place boundaries around the measurement of variables'.

It must, though, be noted that the holism that Ragin and others thus set against multivariate analysis is not as radical as might at first appear. Case studies are indeed regarded as the only way in which macrosocial entities can be treated in their distinctive historical contexts, in their proper detail, and as each constituting, as Skocpol and Somers (1980: 178) put it, 'a complex and unique sociohistorical configuration'. But this, it turns out, does not imply a historicism of a quite thoroughgoing kind, which would deny the validity of any concepts that are formed in order to transcend particular cases (cf. Skocpol, 1994: 328–29). It is still seen as permissible to abstract from different cases certain of their features or attributes, which can then be compared for theoretical purposes. In other words, variables *are* identified, even if sometimes behind a verbal smokescreen. Where holism enters in is with the insistence that, in any comparison, the unity of the particular cases involved should always be preserved. What is required is that, in the process of comparison, cases should always remain identifiable as such, rather than being decomposed into variables that are then interpreted only in the course of the simultaneous analysis of the entire sample of cases under investigation.

In actually pursuing holistic comparisons in this sense, exponents of the case-oriented approach appear to have found their chief methodological inspiration in the logic of John Stuart Mill (1843/1973–74): specifically, in Mill's 'canons', or rules, of experimental induction—the 'Method of Agreement', the 'Method of Difference', and so on (see, e.g., Skocpol, 1979: 36–37, 1984: 378–81; Skocpol and Somers, 1980: 183–84; Ragin, 1987: 36–42). Following Mill, it is believed, each case included in a comparative enquiry can be taken as representing the presence or absence of a given phenomenon of interest—each case, that is, can be taken as a 'naturally occurring' experiment relating to this phenomenon. Inferences regarding the causation of the phenomenon can then be drawn by considering which *other* features are *concomitantly* present or absent, and by in turn applying Mill's logical rules to the resulting set of comparisons. Thus, Skocpol, in her well-known study of social revolutions (1979) seeks to explain their outcomes by comparing national cases, on the one hand, in terms of whether or not revolutionary attempts succeeded and, on the other hand, in terms of the presence or absence of what she takes as likely determining factors: for example, various features of the agrarian economy and class structure, international pressures, and internal political crises.[3]

It might seem that in both multivariate and logical comparisons alike the aim is in effect to control variation in the making of causal inferences—so that the two approaches are not, after all, so very far apart. And, indeed, the application of Mill's methods in the comparison of cases has not infrequently been represented as itself a form of multivariate analysis (e.g., Smelser, 1976: ch. 7; Skocpol and Somers, 1980: 182–83; Dogan, 1994: 35). However, as other commentators have pointed out (e.g., Lieberson, 1992, 1994), there is one quite fundamental difference. The various forms of multivariate analysis used in quantitative work are statistical techniques, and the propositions to which they give rise are therefore *probabilistic*: they are based on associations or correlations that need not be perfect. In contrast, the methods proposed by Mill, being logical in character, entail propositions of a *deterministic* kind: they entail relationships that are entirely invariant. As will later be seen, this is a difference that matters, and indeed to overlook it is to neglect a major development in the history of sociological analysis: that which, in the course of the nineteenth and early twentieth centuries, saw sociology become part of 'the probabilistic revolution' (cf. Krüger, Daston, and Heidelberger, eds., 1987; Krüger, Gigerenzer, and Morgan, eds., 1987; and also vol. II, chs. 8 and 9).

The distinction between variable- and case-oriented approaches is not then a meaningless one. It captures an important divergence in preferred styles of comparative macrosociological research and further, one may suspect, in basic assumptions about the character of social phenomena. But, I would argue, focusing on this distinction will not in itself provide the key to an understanding of the more taxing methodological problems that arise in the conduct of such research; nor are attempts at combining or synthesising the two approaches likely to make the main contribution to overcoming these problems, since they are in fact ones that confront both approaches alike. This argument I now seek to sustain with reference to what may be labelled as (1) the small N problem, (2) the Galton problem, and (3) the black box problem.

THE SMALL N PROBLEM

The small N problem arises in that, if nations or other macrosocial entities are taken as units of analysis, the number available for study is likely to be quite limited. Where individuals are the units, populations can be sampled so as to give Ns of several hundreds or thousands, but where nations are the units, N cannot rise much above one hundred even if all available cases are taken, and is often far less. In applying techniques of multivariate analysis, serious difficulties tend therefore to be encountered in that N is not much greater than the total number of variables involved. Statistically, this means that there are too few degrees of freedom, that models become over-determined, that intercorrelations among independent variables cannot be adequately dealt with, and that results may not be robust. Substantively, it means that *competing* explanations of the dependent variable may not be open to any decisive evaluation. Thus, it has been claimed (Huber, Ragin, and Stephens, 1993) that, for just these reasons, the research programme on the determinants of state welfare provision—in which analyses based on a maximum of around 20 nations have been typical—has by now reached a virtual 'impasse'. Theories privileging different sets of determinants can claim similar degrees of statistical support.[4]

The small N problem is then a real and troubling one. However, what I would wish to question are suggestions to the effect that it is a problem *specific to* the variable-oriented approach to comparative macrosociology, and that the case-oriented approach in some way or other allows it to be solved or circumvented. Most explicitly, Skocpol (1979: 36; cf. Rueschemeyer, 1991: 27–28, 32–34) has maintained that application of the methods 'laid out' by Mill 'is distinctively appropriate for developing explanations of macro-historical phenomena' when the small N problem arises; that is, 'when there are too many variables and not enough cases'.[5]

This claim calls for comment in several respects. To begin with, it is unclear whether Skocpol realises that Mill himself (1843/1974: Book VII, ch.7 esp.) went to some lengths to explain that his rules of induction, being developed for use in the experimental sciences, were *not* appropriate to the study of social phenomena and that, if used, would be likely to prove inconclusive if not actually misleading. At all events, Skocpol fails to take sufficient account of certain assumptions on which Mill's methods depend but that, as various critics have followed Mill in observing (e.g., Nichols, 1986; Lieberson, 1992), are assumptions rarely, if at all, defensible in social research. For example, Mill's logic presupposes that, in any analysis, *all* of the relevant causal factors can be identified and included—that is, that there are no unmeasured variables; and further that there is no multiple (or 'plural') causation, nor again any interaction among causal factors.[6]

At the same time, though, Skocpol *is* well enough aware that Mill's canons are designed to lead to causal propositions of a deterministic kind—and does not appear much disturbed by this fact (cf. also 1984: 378). What, therefore, her argument would appear to come down to is this: that, in circumstances where there are too few cases for the satisfactory evaluation of probabilistic theories, deterministic ones may nonetheless be established. However, to accept this position, it should be noted, one must be ready to believe not just that the social world is indeed subject to deterministic theory rather than being inherently probabilistic. One must *further* believe that sociohistorical *data* can be obtained that are of such a quality and completeness and that are so error-free, that a probabilistic approach is not even required for the purposes of relating these data to (deterministic) theory (cf. Lieberson, 1992: 106–107; King, Keohane, and Verba, 1994: 59–60). This latter implication at least is one that, I suspect, would be found by most sociologists, on due reflection, to be far more daunting than the small N problem itself.[7]

Various attempts have been made to develop the logical analysis of relatively small numbers of cases so as to overcome some of the more obvious limitations of Mill's methods in the context of social research. Most notable in this connection is perhaps the technique of 'qualitative comparative analysis' (QCA) proposed by Ragin (1987, 2000), which is based on Boolean algebra. This technique aims to alleviate the small N problem by allowing inferences to be drawn from the maximum number of comparisons that can be made, in terms of the presence or absence of attributes of interest, across the cases under analysis. And, at the same time, it does permit—indeed is primarily directed towards—the analysis of multiple causation and interaction effects. Thus, Ragin (1994b: 328) maintains that while a regression exercise with, say, seven explanatory variables and only 18 cases would be generally regarded as untrustworthy, QCA would make possible the examination of all 128 (i.e., 2^7) different combinations, as present or absent, of the causal conditions involved: that is, it would enable the analyst to address a degree of causal complexity far beyond the reach of regression.

Given the nature of QCA, Ragin would then further argue, it allows the macrosociologist to combine analysis with holism in that the distinctive features of particular cases need never be lost sight of. However, although this may be so, it is still somewhat misleading for Ragin to represent QCA as being a *synthesis* of the case- and variable-oriented approaches, for, as he indeed recognises (1994b: 305–306), QCA remains, no less than Mill's methods, entirely logical and nonstatistical in character. And it does therefore still share with the latter the major disadvantages of being unable to make any allowance either for missing variables or for error in the data used.

Moreover, with QCA these disadvantages combine with two other evident weaknesses of the technique: its requirement that all variables should be treated as ultimately two-valued; and its high degree of sensitivity to the way in which each case is coded on each variable. Thus, where essentially continuous variables are involved, such as 'GNP per capita', 'proportion of population over 65', and so on, these must be reduced (with, of course, much loss of information) to more or less arbitrary dichotomies; and all subsequent results will then be strongly dependent on the way in which particular cases are allocated. If, on account of error in the original data, or in its treatment, even a single case happens to be placed on the 'wrong' side of a dichotomy, the analysis could well have a radically different outcome to that which would have been reached in the absence of such error. In an application of QCA, it should be noted, the independent variables are simply shown to be causally relevant—or not; no assessment of the *relative strengths* of different effects or combinations of effects is, or can be, made.[8]

In sum, the fact that QCA remains a logical technique means that its results are far more exposed to major distortion, both by difficulties in the selection of independent variables (cf. Amenta and Poulsen, 1994) and by the occurrence of error in data, than are results derived from statistical techniques. And whether, then, QCA does actually mark any significant advance in the treatment of the small N problem, as, for example, Skocpol has claimed (1994: 309), must remain open to very serious doubt.[9]

What, I would argue, it is above all else necessary to recognise here is that *au fond* the small N problem is not one of method at all but rather of data: more specifically, it is a problem of *insufficient information* relative to the complexity of the macrosociological questions that we seek to address. Thus, insofar as exponents of the case-oriented approach in effect choose to restrict themselves to small Ns, they are unlikely ever to avoid the difficulties of 'too many variables and not enough cases' or, as King, Keohane, and Verba (1994: 119) put it, 'more inferences than implications observed'—no matter what resorts to Millian logic, Boolean algebra, or other technical devices they may attempt. Conversely, what is vital to overcoming the small N problem is in principle easy to state, albeit in practice toilsome, even where possible, to achieve: that is, simply to increase the information that we have available for analysis.

One way in which this can sometimes be achieved is by exploiting more fully the experience of those nations (or other macrosocial units) for which we do have good data sources. Thus, in comparative welfare state research various investigators (e.g., O'Connor and Brym, 1988; Korpi, 1989; Pampel and Williamson, 1989; Huber, Ragin, and Stephens, 1993; O'Connell, 1994) have by now taken up the lead given by econometricians and demographers and have pooled data for the same set of nations for several different time-points. Observations—and degrees of freedom—are in this way increased, and appropriate checks and corrections can be introduced into analyses in order to allow for the fact that the successive waves of information thus acquired are not, of course, entirely new and independent (see, e.g., Stimson, 1985; Hicks, 1994). Such a pooling strategy can then, despite technical problems that may still arise with it, be reckoned as a valuable resource for macrosociologists following a variable-oriented approach; and King, Keohane, and Verba (1994: 221–23) have recently suggested various analogous procedures that might profitably be taken up in qualitative studies.[10]

More important, though, for the variable- and case-oriented approaches alike, is to increase the number of units to which comparisons extend; and further (cf. Przeworski, 1987) to widen their geographical and sociocultural range, so that the greater variation thus obtained in supposed causal factors can improve the chances of deciding between competing theories. This will often mean bringing Third World nations into the analysis, and problems of data quality, which must always be of central concern in comparative work, may on this account be accentuated (cf. Dogan, 1994: 40–41). However, the challenge thus posed should not be shirked. Bradshaw and Wallace (1991: 166) have argued for the particular appropriateness of case studies in the Third World, since, they maintain, calls for rigorous quantitative research must be biased against poor nations that lack adequate data or even computers. Although this view is clearly well intentioned, I would still regard it as quite wrongheaded. Either the assumption is being made that case studies are, in some mysterious way, immune to problems of the reliability and validity of data with which quantitative researchers have to struggle or else case studies are being recommended for Third World use as some kind of 'inferior good'. It would surely be, from all points of view, a better strategy for First World social scientists to seek to help their Third World colleagues to collect *whatever* kinds of data, and to undertake *whatever* kinds of analysis, are in fact demanded by the nature of the substantive problems that they wish to pursue.[11]

THE GALTON PROBLEM

The Galton problem is named after the nineteenth-century British polymath, Francis Galton. In 1889 Galton famously criticised a pioneering comparative analysis by the anthropologist, Edward Tylor. Tylor (1889) claimed to show complex associations (or what he called 'adhesions') among economic and familial institutions across a wide range of societies, past and present. These associations he then sought to explain from what we would now think of as a functionalist standpoint. Galton (1889), however, questioned the extent to which Tylor's observations were *independent* ones, and pointed out that 'institutional' associations might arise not only under the pressure of functional exigencies or through other processes operating *within* societies but might also be the result of processes of cultural diffusion *among* societies.

The problem of distinguishing between processes of these two kinds has subsequently plagued cross-cultural anthropology (Naroll, 1970; Hammel, 1980), and it obviously arises in comparative macrosociology to no less a degree. Thus, to revert to the investigation of welfare state development, it would be rather implausible to suppose that this development has proceeded quite autonomously in each national case, and free of such external influence as might have been exerted by the examples of, say, Bismarckian social policy in the nineteenth century, or the Beveridge Plan for postwar Britain, or, more recently, the 'Scandinavian Model' (cf. Therborn, 1993).

Moreover, the Galton problem could be regarded as potentially more damaging at the present time than ever before. Claims that the treatment of nations as independent units of analysis has been untenable ever since the emergence of a 'world system' in the seventeenth century (Hopkins, 1987; Hopkins and Wallerstein, 1981) or that there now exists 'a highly institutionalised world polity' (Meyer, 1987: 42) might well be thought exaggerated. But it could hardly be denied that, by the twenty-first century, the independence of 'national' observations is likely to be compromised, and not merely by the acceleration and intensification of cultural diffusion but further through the quite purposive actions of a whole range of international or multinational political and economic organisations. In this way, as Przeworski (1987) has recognised, the threat is created that the small N and Galton problems run together, as we enter into a 'globalised' world in which N = 1.

Lack of independence in observations, as well as limits on their number, does then undoubtedly create serious difficulties for cross-national research. However, just as with the small N problem, what I would wish first of all to stress is that while the difficulties in question may be most *apparent* with the variable-oriented approach, they are by no means restricted to it; the case-oriented approach enjoys no special immunity.

Thus, the assumption that nations can be treated as units of analysis, unrelated to each other in time and space, is one required by the logical methods of comparison that are favoured in case-oriented research no less than by statistical methods. And indeed where historical cases are involved, the Galton problem is then likely to be encountered in a particularly trouble-some form. The scarcely disputable fact that situations and events occurring at one time tend to have been influenced by situations and events occurring earlier clearly breaches the assumption of the independence of cases—as built into Mill's or any other logical method—and in a way that is not easily remedied. Thus, for example, one finds that Skocpol, in her study of revolu-tions (1979: 23–24, 39), has obviously to recognise that the course of the Chinese revolution up to 1949 was in various ways influenced by events in Russia in 1917 and subsequently. But this recognition has then to be kept quite apart from her logical analyses of the factors that determine revo-lutionary success, which in fact it threatens to compromise (cf. Burawoy, 1989). In other words, the use of Mill's canons and of narrative accounts that crucially rely on temporality cannot be integrated, but have to be left to play separate, and ultimately incompatible, explanatory roles (see further Kiser and Hechter, 1991: 12–13; Griffin, 1992: 412–13; cf. also Skocpol, 1994: 338).

Despite this, the Galton problem has in fact met with only a rather limited appreciation—and response—among exponents of case-oriented research. McMichael (1990) has proposed a solution through what he calls 'incorporated comparisons', which is apparently intended to take over the insights, while avoiding the 'rigidity', of a world-system perspective. But because he presents his approach as an 'interpretative' one that can proceed 'without recourse to formal methodological procedures or a formal theory'

(1990: 388), it is not easy to evaluate (nor, I would have to say, to understand). Another reaction is that of Sztompka (1988) that, however, is less an attempt to grapple with the Galton problem than a capitulation to it, and one that might be seen as somewhat opportunistic. The severity of the problem in the modern world, Sztompka maintains, is such that the whole agenda of comparative macrosociology needs to be changed—towards in fact a concentration on case studies! 'Globalisation' has, in Sztompka's view, already made societal homogeneity and uniformity the norm. Thus, the central aim should no longer be to establish cross-national similarities or regularities of variation, using 'hard', quantitative techniques; rather, comparative work should now focus on the description and interpretation of 'enclaves of uniqueness'—that is, those deviant cases that stand out against globalisation—and, for this purpose, should follow a 'soft', qualitative approach. Sztompka does not tell us just how such enclaves of uniqueness are to be identified in the absence of systematic comparison. But, in any event, in arguing as he does, as if an extreme version of the convergence thesis had in fact been realised, he takes up a position that is well beyond the empirical evidence (see further ch. 5).

In addressing the Galton problem more pertinently, there are, I would suggest, two main points that need to be recognised. First, it is not so pervasive a problem as Sztompka and others (e.g., Scheuch, 1989; Allardt, 1990) would have us suppose. It is perhaps most regularly encountered in the comparative study of *public policy*, and especially of economic and social policy. For the pressures directly exerted by both international organisations and internationalised economies may alone bring about some degree of uniformity of policy among nation-states, quite apart from any diffusion of values and beliefs (Schmitter, 1991). At the same time, though, it is not difficult to point to other areas of comparative research in which the Galton problem is far less apparent.

Consider, for example, research into the class inequalities that occur in attainment and in transition rates at successive branching points in young people's educational careers. This research has revealed that in many modern societies such inequalities display a surprising degree of persistence over time (Shavit and Blossfeld, eds., 1993; and see further vol. II, chs. 1–4); but further that variation in the detailed pattern of inequality from society to society stems largely from differences in national educational institutions, which would seem endowed with substantial autonomy. Thus, even though governments—prompted, say, by international economic competition or 'world-system ideology' (cf. Ramirez and Boli, 1987)—may have engaged in essentially similar programmes of educational expansion and reform, the processes of social selection that are distinctive to their indigenous institutions have proved hard to eradicate (see esp. Müller and Karle, 1993; Ishida, Müller, and Ridge, 1995; Shavit and Müller, eds., 1998; Shavit, Arum, and Gamoran, forthcoming). Here, then, evidence of convergence through globalisation is, to say the least, not conspicuous.[12]

Second, it should be understood that, even where clearly present, the Galton problem does not necessarily preclude comparative analysis of a systematic kind. If, in a comparative study, national observations are known not to be independent, for whatever reason, it may still be possible to proceed by incorporating the processes that create this situation as an element in the analysis. That is, in the language of the variable-oriented approach, one can seek to model interdependence itself, as in fact demographers and statistically minded geographers have been doing for some time (see, e.g., Berry, 1970; cf. Przeworski, 1987; Breen and Rottman, 1998). In the context of welfare state research, a notable pioneering contribution in this regard is that of Usui (1994). In a study of state-sponsored social insurance policies in a sample of 60 nations, Usui applies techniques of event history analysis in order to investigate how the development of these policies was influenced not only by domestic factors but further by the establishment of the International Labor Office in 1919 and by its subsequent worldwide activities.

The further large potential of attempts at thus modelling interdependence may be brought out by reference to the work of Castles and others (Castles, ed., 1993), who have introduced into comparative policy research the idea of 'families of nations'. Instead of attention centring on nations as 'unattached singles', they argue, more account should be taken of the affinities that exist among groupings of nations, as a result of shared histories and cultural traditions. Castles has in fact suggested (1993: xv–xvi) that recognition of such affinities may indicate the 'outer limits' of the Przeworski-Teune programme of replacing the proper names of nations with the names of variables. For policy similarities and differences among nations 'may be attributable as much to history and culture and their transmission and diffusion amongst nations as to the immediate impact of the economic, political and social variables that figure almost exclusively in the contemporary public policy literature'. And, Castles believes, the former kinds of effects are difficult to accommodate within the 'prevailing intellectual paradigm', as represented by the variable-oriented approach.

Now, as regards his substantive point on the importance of historically formed cultural patterns that transcend national boundaries, Castles may well be right. And, as will be apparent later, I share his concern with determining just where the theoretical limits of macrosociology, in whatever style it may be conducted, must in the end be drawn. But I do not see why the variables that replace the names of nations in quantitative analyses of comparative public policy need be *only* variables thought likely to have an 'immediate impact', nor why one cannot, in principle at least, also include variables that do indeed seek to capture nations' historical affinities and the longer-term influences that derive from them. Indeed, I would argue that to attempt to do precisely this is the obvious way to explore further the idea of families of nations. In other words, there seems no reason why the insights provided by Castles and his associates should not serve as the starting point for appropriate quantitative analyses that would enable us to form more reliable judgments on what is, after all, crucially at issue: that is, the *relative importance*, in regard to policy developments and repertoires, of inter- as opposed to intra-societal, and of 'historical' as opposed to 'contemporary' effects.[13]

In sum, we should not be led into believing that claims regarding globalisation or the existence of a world system or of families of nations necessitate some quite radical transformation of cross-national comparative macrosociology, and least of all one that would entail its restriction to case studies. In dealing with the Galton problem—where there are good grounds for supposing that it does indeed exist—the variable-oriented approach has resources that are in fact only beginning to be exploited.

THE BLACK BOX PROBLEM

The black box problem, even more than the small N or Galton problems, has been linked with the variable-oriented approach (see, e.g., Rueschemeyer, 1991: 26; Abbott, 1992a: 54–62). A quantitative analysis may be undertaken that is successful in accounting for, in a statistical sense, a significant part of the variation in the phenomenon of interest—let us say, the sizes of welfare states. But such an analysis, it can be objected, still tells us rather little about just what is going on at the level of the social processes and action that underlie, as it were, the interplay of the variables that have been distinguished. We know the inputs to the analysis and we know the outputs from it, but we do not know much about why it should be that, within the black box of the statistical model that is applied, the one is transformed into the other. The problem is of course mitigated if 'intervening' variables are also included in the analysis, so as to give it a more finely grained character; and further if both explanatory and intervening variables are chosen on theoretical grounds, so that certain causal processes may at least be implied. Nonetheless, it can still be maintained that the black box problem is seriously addressed only to the extent that such processes are spelt out quite explicitly, so as to provide a causally adequate account of the actual *generation* of the regularities that are empirically demonstrated (see further chs. 6 and 9 this volume).

The black box problem, thus understood, has been seized on by exponents of case studies in order to make the claim that the results of quantitative analyses must in effect *depend on* case studies for their interpretation. Thus, Huber, Ragin, and Stephens (1993) have argued that the problem of conflicting explanations of the growth of welfare states can only be solved through a 'dialogue' between variable- and case-oriented research, and that it is case studies that must play the crucial part in identifying 'actual historical causal forces'. Likewise, Rueschemeyer (1991: 28; cf. also Rueschemeyer, Stephens, and Stephens, 1992: ch. 2) has maintained, with reference to comparative research into capitalist development and democracy, that in this area the tradition of historical case studies is 'far richer in theoretical argument and analysis' than is that of quantitative work. Rueschemeyer accepts that quantitative studies have established a clear positive association between capitalist development and democracy; but, he is convinced, the 'key to the black box' that mediates this association will only be found in theory inspired by case studies and, especially, in 'explanatory ideas grappling with historical sequences'.

Again, however, I would wish to call into question the privileged status that is thus accorded to the case-oriented approach. To begin with, it should be recognised that while, just as with the small N and Galton problems, the black box problem may be most apparent in quantitative work, it does in fact arise equally with the case-oriented approach where logical methods of comparison are applied. Contrary to what Rueschemeyer suggests (1991: 32–33), logical methods too can only establish empirical regularities that may, at most, point to causal relations: they do not, in themselves, provide an account of the actual *processes* involved (cf. Burawoy, 1989). And if, to this end, 'analytical induction' is accompanied by some narrative of historical sequences, then this, for reasons earlier noted, cannot be part of the logical method itself but only in fact a rather awkward, if not inconsistent, appendage to it.

I would, furthermore, argue that the *theoretical* achievement of case studies is, in any event, a good deal less impressive than the authors cited above attempt to make out. Where the unity of cases is preserved—where cases are studied holistically, rather than being decomposed into variables— it is indeed possible, at least in principle, to provide detailed descriptions of 'what happened' in each case, and with due regard for the specific contextual features involved. But to have a narrative account of a sequence of historical events is *not* the same thing as having a theoretical account, even if one accepts—as I would be ready to do—that a historical narrative can itself constitute a form of explanation.[14] Most crucially, perhaps, such a narrative need not extend beyond the particular instance to which it is applied, or comparative narratives beyond the set of cases compared (cf. Skocpol and Somers, 1980: 195). In contrast, a theoretical account must have *some* claim to generality. The explanation it provides of what is going on within the black box of a statistical or of a logical analysis cannot be merely one that is inductively extracted from the actual events involved in the instances covered by the analysis; it has rather, to be derived from a theory that could, indeed should, apply to *other* instances falling within its intended scope or domain.

It might of course be suggested, and I would find it unexceptionable, that specific narratives may serve as a valuable resource for theory development: that is, by prompting attempts to conceive of some more general ideas that would allow the accounts given in different cases to be fitted into a deductive structure of argument. In other words, detailed case studies could play a *heuristic* role in the 'context of discovery', prior to the testing of any resulting theory against further, independent cases in the 'context of validation'. However, the distinction here involved is one that proponents of the case-oriented approach appear to find uncongenial, and that Rueschemeyer, for example (1991:32–33; cf. Rueschemeyer, Stephens, and Stephens, 1992: 36; Skocpol, 1994: 330), flatly rejects. The view that seems rather to be favoured is that the process of theory development should be advanced by successive inductions from particular cases—so that it becomes in effect essentially *merged with* the process of theory testing. The matching of developing theory against new inductions and its modification where it is found not to hold go on as one, seamless activity.

It is, however, in just this regard that the case for case studies becomes least convincing. The crucial point is that if a theory is formed in such an essentially inductive way—without, so to speak, any deductive backbone—then it is hard to see how it can be genuinely tested at all. As it stands, such a theory does no more than recapitulate observations; and it is, moreover, difficult to know exactly how it would be properly extended beyond the particular circumstances from which it has been obtained so that an independent test might be attempted. Or, to put the matter the other way around, if a theory amounts to no more than an assemblage of inductions, the possibilities for 'saving' or 'patching' it in the face of contrary evidence are virtually unlimited. Generality can be claimed for so long as such a theory appears to fit the cases to which it is applied. But when it fails to fit, it can then be maintained that 'causal homogeneity' no longer holds, and that a somewhat different theory is required; and, in all of this, analysts can congratulate themselves on their 'sensitivity to context'![15]

However, the arbitrary delimitation of the scope of a theory—that is, a delimitation that the theory does not itself provide for—is an evident weakness. Thus, in the context of welfare state research, Korpi (1989: 324; cf. Korpi and Palme, 2003: 442) has critically remarked that theories of state autonomy, as advanced by Skocpol and others (e.g., Orloff and Skocpol, 1984; Weir and Skocpol, 1985) on the basis of qualitative case studies 'leave ample room for flexible *ad hoc* explanation', and has urged the need for such theories to be formulated in a way that would expose them to more stringent empirical critique. And yet more prominently, the charge of arbitrariness has been levelled against Skocpol's treatment of the Iranian revolution (1982), when taken in relation to her previous analyses (1979) of the French, Russian, and Chinese revolutions (Nichols, 1986; Burawoy, 1989; Kiser and Hechter, 1991). In the Iranian case a significant, yet seemingly quite ad hoc, theoretical shift is introduced in that popular urban demonstrations become a 'functional substitute' for peasant revolts and guerrilla activity (cf. Skocpol: 1994: 313–14).

Finally in this connection, I would also question whether the account offered by Rueschemeyer, Stephens, and Stephens of the association between capitalist development and democracy does in fact bear out their contention that case studies afford a privileged ground for the development of theory capable of overcoming the black box problem. Their account fails in this respect, I would suggest, precisely because of the degree to which the analysis of their cases leads them to hedge about their central argument on power struggles among social classes with exceptions and qualifications—relating to cross-national differences in the social construction of class interests, in the possibilities for class alliances, in the form of civil society, in the role of the state, in the impact of transnational relations, and so on (1992: 269–81 esp.). Not only does the ratio of explaining to 'explaining away' thus seem rather low but, further, it is notable that when these authors come to address the key issue of the 'generalisability' of their theory beyond the cases they have examined (1992: 285)—to, say, east Asian or east-central European nations of the present day—what they have to offer is not a series of derived hypotheses that would be testable against such new cases but yet more discussion of additional factors to be considered.[16] Now it may be that the awareness that Rueschemeyer and his colleagues here display of complexity and causal heterogeneity is empirically warranted. But, if so, what they have provided is a demonstration of the inherent difficulty of forming a theory of the relationship between capitalist development and democracy, and not that theory itself.

For macrosociologists seeking to treat black box problems more effectively, I would then argue, case studies, whether historical or otherwise, have no distinctive value, and an absorption in their specificities may indeed divert attention away from what is in fact crucially required: that is, theory that is as general as it is possible to make it. As Kiser and Hechter (1991) have maintained, in a strong critique of the quality of theory in comparative historical sociology, to illuminate the black boxes represented by mere empirical regularities, we need more than just a redescription of the latter within a 'theoretical (*sc.* conceptual) framework', which appears indefinitely modifiable as our database expands. Rather, theory must be sought that is general in that it permits the specification of causal processes, which, if operative, would be capable of producing the regularities in question *and* would have a range of *further* implications of at least a potentially observable kind (see further ch. 9). To the extent that theory is general in this sense, it can then claim both greater explanatory power, which theory must always seek, and greater openness to empirical test, which it must never evade.[17]

I would, moreover, add that such a concern with generality in theory might help macrosociologists to see the relevance of history to their enterprise in a different, and, I believe, more appropriate, way to that which appears currently in mode among exponents of the case-oriented approach. Instead of a recourse to history being regarded as essential to the development of theory, it might be better understood as marking the *limits of theory*: that is, the point at which what is causally important in regard to certain empirical findings is recognised not in recurrent social situations and processes that might be the subject of theory but rather in contingencies, distinctive conjunctures of events, or other singularities that theory cannot comprehend.

Because the foregoing argument is put somewhat abstractly, I may try to illustrate it with reference to the primarily quantitative work that I have undertaken with Robert Erikson on comparative social mobility (Erikson and Goldthorpe, 1992a). Perhaps the most notable finding of this work was that when intergenerational class mobility was considered net of all structural influences—or, that is, as 'social fluidity'—rates and patterns showed a surprising amount of stability over time within nations and, further, a significant commonality across nations. Such a degree of *in*variance does then strongly underline the need for general theory. Hypotheses on the causal processes capable of producing temporal constancy and cross-national similarity of the kind that our quantitative analyses revealed will need to be derived from a theory of considerable scope: that is, from a theory that is precisely *not* 'sensitive to context' (unlike the theories of national 'exceptionalism' in regard to mobility, which our results called into doubt) but that is applicable to societal contexts widely separated over both time and space. And in this respect, I should say, Erikson and I were able to make only a very modest beginning—on which, however, I have later tried to build (see vol. II, ch. 7).[18]

We also found, though, that insofar as variation in social fluidity *did* occur cross-nationally, we could not account for it, to any large extent, in terms of other generalisable attributes of societies, in the way that the Przeworski-Teune programme would require (cf. also Breen and Luijkx, 2004b). Our analyses pointed here to the far greater importance of historically formed cultural or institutional features or political circumstances that could not be expressed as variable values except in a quite artificial way. For example, while *levels* of social fluidity were not highly responsive to the overall degree of educational inequality within nations, *patterns* of fluidity did often reflect the distinctive, institutionally shaped character of such in-equality in particular nations, such as Germany or Japan. Or again, fluidity was affected less by the presence of a state socialist regime per se than by the significantly differing policies actually pursued by the Polish, Hungarian, or Czechoslovak regimes on such matters as the collectivisation of agriculture or the recruitment of the intelligentsia. In such instances, then, it seemed to us that the retention of proper names and adjectives in our explanatory accounts was as unavoidable as it was desirable, and that little was to be gained in seeking to bring such historically specific effects within the scope of theory of any kind.

In sum, black box problems—essentially problems of making sense of empirical findings—are unlikely to be alleviated by comparative macroso-ciologists striving in effect to transcend the distinction between theory and history. For such attempts tend to lead merely to a weakening of our under-standing of theory and of historicity alike, and in turn to a blurring of crucial differences in the nature of theoretical and historical explanations. A strat-egy of greater long-term promise would be to continue to pursue sociological theory that amounts to more than just the elaboration of concepts and that aspires to generality in the sense indicated above, but at the same time to show due modesty in accepting that, for any kind of macrosociology, and no matter how theoretically accomplished it may eventually become, 'history' will always remain as a necessary residual category.[19] It may, furthermore, be a consequence of such a strategy that certain phenomena that macro-sociologists have sought to study—and including, perhaps, revolutions or other kinds of 'regime transition'—turn out to be ones on which theory can give relatively little cognitive grasp at all. That is to say, while it may be of interest to write the comparative history of these phenomena—their history as viewed within a common conceptual framework—they appear just too few, too interdependent, and too causally heterogeneous for anything of much use to be said in theoretical terms. In instances where the indications accumulate that this is indeed the case, then the course of wisdom must surely be to accept the situation with good grace. Macrosociologists will still be left with a very great deal to do, and there have not, after all, ever been any guarantees that a sociology of everything should be possible.

I have argued that, while a divergence can certainly be observed between variable- and case-oriented approaches to comparative macrosociology, to concentrate attention on this divergence, or even on ways of overcoming it, does not provide the best focus for understanding and addressing major methodological issues that are encountered in this field. As King, Keohane, and Verba have emphasised (1994: ch.1), we may distinguish between quantitative and qualitative *styles* of research in the social sciences, but each must still strive to meet the exigencies of the same underlying logic of inference and contend with the problems to which this common requirement gives rise. Through an examination of three such problems, recurrent within comparative macrosociology, I have tried to show how each can, and does, occur in the context of variable- and case-oriented work alike. These problems are not in fact ones on which alternatives in research styles have much bearing, but are of a more elementary, which is not to say easier, kind. Thus, the small N problem is essentially a problem of insufficient information on which to base analyses—or, that is, on which to draw in making inferences; and it can be resolved, or mitigated, only by more extensive data collection, aided by techniques for exploiting to the full the information that is at any time available. The Galton problem, where it arises, is one of observations lacking a property—independence—that we would like to assume in our analyses; and, to the extent that interdependence among our units of observation is simply a feature of the way the world is, we must deal with this situation by seeking to represent the interdependence (or, better, the processes creating it) within our analyses, so that we do not just recognise its presence but also assess its importance. And finally the black box problem is one of how we move from descriptive to causal inferences or, that is, go beyond our empirical findings and the regularities they allow us to establish to an understanding of how these regularities are generated. Here what is crucial is to construct theory in a way that maximises both its explanatory power and its openness to test against further empirical research—and that also allows us to see as clearly as possible where the limits to theoretical explanation are reached.

In this essay, criticism has been more often directed against case-oriented than against variable-oriented research. This is not an expression of hostility on my part to qualitative research as such, whether in macrosociology or more generally, and especially not to such research of a historical character. Rather, it reflects my view that it is proponents of the variable-oriented approach who have, at all events, better appreciated and responded to the problems I have considered, while proponents of the case-oriented approach have sometimes failed to recognise that they too need to address these problems or, as I suggested at the start, have made claims to the effect that they dispose of special and privileged means of bypassing or overcoming them. My critical comments have then been chiefly directed against such claims. I have sought to show that they do not, at least as so far presented, have any very secure basis, and that, if they are to be maintained, they will need to be demonstrated far more cogently than hitherto. I would doubt if this will prove possible, because I see no reason at all to believe in such special and privileged means. The small N, Galton, and black box problems pertain to quite basic issues that are likely to arise in any instance of comparative macrosociological research, whatever the style in which it is conducted. Whether investigators choose to work quantitatively or qualitatively, with variables or with cases, the inherent logic of these issues remains the same, and so too therefore will that of any solutions that may be achieved.

CHAPTER FOUR

Sociological Ethnography Today
Problems and Possibilities*

I start in this essay from the rather curious state that has by now been reached in the debate within sociology between proponents of ethnographic and of survey-based research—a debate that represents one expression of larger and yet more complex oppositions between qualitative and quantitative or case- and variable-oriented styles of data collection and analysis.[1]

Sociologists favouring ethnographic research, whether as actual practitioners or on more general grounds, were prominent in the so-called 'reaction against positivism' of the late 1960s and 1970s, when survey methodology and its supposed philosophical foundations became a prime focus of criticism. In the face of this attack, the response of sociologists engaging in survey research, or reliant on the secondary analysis of its results, could only be described as muted. Few, it seems, were able to raise sufficient motivation to offer any systematic reply. The effort made in this respect by Marsh (1982) is distinguished not just by its quality but also its rarity. However, what is today striking is the degree to which, despite the rather one-sided nature of the debate, the continuing contributions from supporters of ethnography have changed in their tone. Although 'positivist' still tends to serve as an all-purpose pejorative qualifier, calls for the outright rejection of the survey method are far less frequently heard and more common are pleas—albeit made on differing grounds—for ethnography to be accepted

*For advice, information, and comments on an earlier draft of this essay, I am indebted to Richard Breen, Robert Erikson, Roger Goodman, Peter Hedström, Martín Sánchez Jankowski, Janne Jonsson, Jennifer Platt, Federico Varese, and, especially, Martyn Hammersley, and Wout Ultee.

as an essential complement to survey research (see, e.g., Orum, Feagin, and Sjoberg, 1991; Hammersley, 1992; Katz, 1997; Burawoy, 1998). Such arguments indeed often appear to be of an essentially defensive kind, being linked to complaints that in contemporary sociology ethnographic work is unduly neglected or undervalued on account of the dominance that survey research has come to exert. But in some instances too they go together with a recognition that it is the scientific credentials of ethnography that are now increasingly in question—even to the extent that a 'crisis' of ethnography exists (e.g., Hammersley, 1991: 15; Snow and Morrill, 1993; Vidich and Lyman, 1994: 38–43; Brewer, 2000: 38–48, 172–74).

How, then, has this situation come about? Why is it that even though proponents of survey-based research did not for the most part bother to respond to radical criticism of their methodology, the survey tradition remains strong, both within sociology and social research more generally, while it is now among the ethnographers that methodological concerns and uncertainties are most apparent?

One explanation for the continuing importance of survey research that has been offered, and that has been underwritten by at least some supporters of ethnography, is of an entirely external kind. Survey research, it is argued, owes its success to the fact that it is an instrument of power or must at all events collude with power: 'power is its precondition' (Burawoy, 1998: 16). This is so not only because such research requires substantial resources of a kind likely to be available only to government, big business, or major foundations. In addition, knowledge deriving from survey methodology is knowledge that is formed—in the name of objectivity—from outside and above the 'life-world' of those studied, and that is in turn aimed essentially at *control*. Moreover, it is held, from the hegemonic position that they thus enjoy, the proponents of survey research can seek to impose their standards on other sociologists, ethnographers in particular, and to subject the work of the latter to 'inappropriate criticism' (Burawoy, 1998: 15; cf. Stoecker, 1991). Ethnography is thus disfavoured and threatened; nonetheless, it still serves as the basis of an alternative, but equally valid, paradigm of social enquiry to that represented by survey research. Because ethnographers usually operate individually, in a 'craft' rather than a 'bureaucratic' mode, they need only modest resources and can thus avoid becoming compromised by power. Moreover, by entering directly into the life-world of their subjects, they seek to produce knowledge for the purposes not of control but rather of empathetic understanding, and especially so in the case of marginal, stigmatised, dispossessed, or otherwise subordinate and powerless groups.[2]

Such an account may have an appealing rhetoric but it does not stand up to serious examination. It is of course true that governments and other powerful agencies do routinely use survey research in order to collect information in the course of forming, implementing, and monitoring their policies. This could indeed be taken as good evidence that survey research *works*—that it is a cost-effective way of producing information of a sufficiently reliable and valid kind to allow useful analyses of social phenomena to be made. However, it is also the case that many sociologists, and of widely differing political commitments, from neoconservatives through to Marxists, undertake survey research on a quite independent basis; and, further, that many more reanalyse the data-sets of official surveys for their own purposes, often very different from those for which the surveys were initially designed, and then present new results and interpretations that may be highly uncongenial to official positions. A less simplistic explanation both of the success of survey research and of the current difficulties of ethnography would therefore appear to be needed, and one that is able to give due attention to internal as well as to external factors.

The argument that I wish to advance begins with the claim that the methods of enquiry that are used across the natural and the social sciences alike are informed by what might be referred to as a common logic of inference—a logic of relating evidence and argument. The application of this logic presupposes that a world exists independently of our ideas about it, and that, in engaging in scientific enquiry, we aim to obtain information, or data, about this world, which we can then take as a basis for inferences that extend *beyond* the data at hand, whether in a descriptive or an explanatory mode. This logic of inference can never be definitively codified: it has, rather, to be adapted and elaborated via the particular methodologies that are appropriate to different subject-matter areas and their problems. This work has been achieved with greatest coherence and refinement in the case of experimental methods, especially in the natural sciences. But, since the end of the nineteenth century, significant advances have also been made, of importance to both the natural and the social sciences, in the methodology of the statistical analysis of observational data (see further vol. II, chs. 8 and 9). And the possibility of further developments is of course entirely open.[3]

The logic of inference, it must be stressed, does not guarantee that the knowledge that we acquire with its aid is certain. All processes of inference are in fact inherently *un*certain, on account both of inadequacies in data and of human tendencies towards error and bias. Recognition of the logic of inference serves rather to ensure that, in the application of any particular method, as explicit an understanding as possible exists of the *grounds* on which inferences are made and conclusions reached and in turn, therefore, of the grounds on which these inferences and conclusions *may be subject to rational criticism*. It is, in other words, by reference to this logic that questions can be raised and debated of just how scientific claims follow from the evidence that is presented in their support and of what further evidence, were it to be adduced, would result in these claims coming to be seen as mistaken. In sum, one could say, it is the logic of inference that provides the basic rules according to which the 'friendly-hostile co-operation' that Popper (cf. 1966: ch. 23; 1994: ch. 3 esp.) regards as essential to scientific activity is carried on, and that enables this activity to assume a social and public rather than merely a personal and private character.

In outline, my argument will then be that while both survey research and ethnography began with at least an implicit commitment to the logic in question, this commitment has not been similarly sustained. Where problems in survey research have been encountered by its practitioners, or have been pointed out by critics, an effort has been made to overcome these problems essentially by methodological refinements or innovations consistent with this logic; and this effort I would see as being a key factor in the achievements of survey research. In contrast, the history of ethnography, and especially its recent history, must from this point of view appear as far more chequered. Sociological ethnographers have responded on widely divergent lines to the problems of method with which they have been confronted. Some—though so far relatively few—have indeed been ready to accept that the logic of inference in ethnography can be no different to that which applies in survey research or in the case of any other kind of scientific method, and have sought to advance ethnographic procedures accordingly. Others, under the influence of intellectual upheavals in social anthropology (see esp. Clifford and Marcus, eds., 1986; Clifford, 1988) and of related postmodernist and other irrationalist fashions, have taken up a radically different position that in fact entails relinquishing all social scientific claims in favour of an understanding of ethnography as simply 'writing'. The ethnographer aims not to *represent* some independently existing life-world or culture but rather to give a fictive account of a self-exploratory 'experience of the other', and one to which the critical standards of art rather than of science must apply (cf. Gellner, 1992). Further, though, many sociological ethnographers—perhaps a majority—have sought a 'third way', by pursuing which they would be able to avoid what they would see as the equally unacceptable extremes of either a capitulation to 'positivism' or the abandonment of their scientific credentials. The appealing idea is that some kind of alternative, non-positivist, version of social science might be formulated—characterised as 'critical', 'humanistic', 'reflexive', or whatever—which would be able to claim parity of esteem with its positivist counterpart, and which the practice of ethnography would then exemplify.[4]

What, however, I seek ultimately to show is that no such third way will prove viable or, at all events, *not insofar as* the rejection of or departure from 'positivism' also implies an abandonment of the idea of a single logic of inference and leads to efforts to devise special methods of enquiry and analysis that are believed to be in some way exempt from this logic. It is obviously open to ethnographers to secede from social science altogether—although they must then be ready to accept the various consequences of so doing.[5] But if they wish to retain a place within social science, this cannot be entirely on terms of their own choosing. Rules of the game do exist, and while failure to comply fully with them may be regarded as endemic, it is nonetheless important that the obligation always to try in principle to do so should be accepted.

In substantiating the argument that I have sketched out, I begin, in the second section of the chapter, by recalling an early confrontation between ethnographic and survey research, in which the methodological problems that have most seriously troubled ethnography, at least as conducted in the context of modern industrial societies, were first made apparent: that is, what I label generically as *problems of variation*. In the third and fourth sections, I elaborate on these problems, and question attempts to deal with them, which would seem to suppose that ethnography can in some way or other claim a special and privileged status. I suggest, rather, that solutions must be sought following the same basic logic as is applied in survey research. In the fifth section, I start by noting criticisms made of survey research from the side of ethnography, and, in particular, in regard to what I label as *problems of context*. By in fact following through the logic of inference, survey researchers, I seek to show, have produced a more effective response to these problems than seems often to be appreciated and have thus set an example that ethnographers might follow.

However, there is, I recognise, one respect in which the criticism still carries real force, and especially in its degree of convergence with that from other sources. This concerns the neglect in much survey-based sociology of the social processes, or 'mechanisms', through which regularities demonstrated at the level of relations among variables are actually generated and sustained, and the failure to see that causal explanations of these regularities cannot themselves be given through the analysis of variables but have rather to refer to the action and interaction of individuals (see further chs. 6 and 9). In developing, but above all in *testing* such explanatory accounts, I then conclude, an opportunity arises for an—methodologically enhanced— ethnography to make good its claim to be a vital part of the modern sociological enterprise and to engage in potentially highly revealing competition with survey-based research.

SURVEYS VERSUS ETHNOGRAPHIES: THE HISTORICAL ORIGINS

From the early nineteenth century onwards, as other European nations followed Britain into rapid industrialisation, questions of poverty, labour relations, and, more generally, 'the condition of the working classes' seized the attention of humanitarians and moralists, social reformers, and politicians of all persuasions. At the same time, such questions also became a leading concern of social investigators, often private individuals but, increasingly, representatives of the state or other public bodies or of various voluntary associations. In Britain, from the 1830s, Royal Commissions and other forms of official enquiry became important agencies of research, alongside local 'philosophical' and 'statistical' societies. In continental Europe, the traditions of German *Universitätsstatistik* and of the French *enquête*, which dated back to the eighteenth century, were adapted to new circumstances and requirements. The character of the research thus undertaken was diverse but, from the standpoint of the present, much could in fact be regarded as prototypical survey work. Information on a set of issues or topics was collected, on some more or less standard pattern, for relatively large numbers of individuals, and was then subjected to analysis, possibly though not necessarily numerical, before presentation. However, from the mid-nineteenth century a new method of research was developed, in part as an extension of, but in part also as a reaction against, the survey approach. This was the 'monographic' method of Frédéric Le Play and his followers, which, in retrospect, may be seen as sociological ethnography in one of its earliest manifestations (cf. Zonabend, 1992).

Le Play was trained and had worked as a metallurgist and mining engineer before becoming preoccupied with social problems and acquiring a detailed knowledge of the statistics of his day. He had little regard for 'philosophical' sociology, such as that of Comte, and believed that all science was founded on the close and sustained observation of the phenomena of interest. From this position, he was led to question various practices that were common in enquiries into working-class occupations or family life. For example, Le Play objected to the extent to which such enquiries tended to rely on information obtained from persons regarded as local authorities, such as civil servants, clergy, or doctors, rather than on information that was collected firsthand by appropriately trained investigators, either through the observation of workers or from interviews with them. Further, he maintained, only through such direct—and prolonged—contact with workers and their families could an adequate range and quality of information be acquired. It was important to know not only about workers' physical conditions of life, economic resources, family budgets, and so on, but also about their life histories and aspirations and their moral beliefs and values; and in order to gain this more intimate knowledge in a reliable way, it was essential, Le Play held, for investigators to secure the confidence of workers, to speak to them in their own language and idiom, and to 'enter into their minds' (Silver, ed., 1982: 41–75, 171–83).

In the first edition of his major work, *Les Ouvriers européens* (1855), Le Play presented 36 monographs on particular families, expanded in the second edition (1877–79) to 57, in relation to a two-way typology: type of worker by type of society. On this basis, he believed that he could generalise from the individual case studied to the category that it was taken to represent—and, in turn, elaborate an empirically grounded theory of the institutional differentiation of social systems as well as a normative theory of social order. This generalising confidence shown by Le Play, and by others who supported him in the use of the monographic method, would appear to have owed much to the statistical sociology of Quetelet (see further vol. II, ch. 8). According to Quetelet (1835/1842), *l'homme type*, who could in fact be equated with *l'homme moyen*—the average individual within any social category—was the proper focus of social scientific attention. For in the characteristics of this individual could be seen displayed in their pure form the effects of all constant or systematically varying causes that were at work; whereas with other individuals the tendency of their characteristics to deviate from the average in accordance with the 'error law'—that is, the normal distribution—served to show that they resulted from various unconnected 'accidental' causes of no particular scientific interest. Even a single case, if truly typical in this statistical sense, could therefore be taken as carrying general significance (cf. Desrosières, 1991, 1993: ch. 7 esp.). However, when towards the end of the nineteenth century the monographic method became subject to increasingly frequent counterattacks from proponents of survey research, it was on the issue of what might be called typological generalisation that criticism focused.

By the time in question, Quetelet's 'statistics of the average' were in fact being superseded by the 'statistics of variation' pioneered by Galton—for whom averages were merely fictitious and variation the scientifically important reality. And it was in turn problems of variation that increasingly concerned survey researchers. This concern arose primarily out of their efforts to devise ways of constructing 'representative samples' of populations, or, in effect, to develop a logic of descriptive inference from part to whole, and thus to be able to show that surveys, even if only 'partial investigations', could still effectively substitute for complete censuses. At the same time, though, they were led directly to challenge the adequacy in this respect of the typological approach. Kiaer, the leading advocate of representative sampling, objected to a reliance on typologies as a basis for social investigation essentially on the grounds that they could not satisfactorily accommodate the variation in individual cases that was present in real life. Even if the rationale of the typologies that were formed was itself sound, Kiaer argued (1901), a reliable basis for generalisation still did not exist. This was because a concentration on types neglected not only extreme cases that might fall altogether outside the typologies used but further, and more seriously, all of the variation that occurred *around* the types that were distinguished. Other, more detailed criticism of the work of Le Play and the Le Playistes then served to bring out that problems of variation in fact arose *at two different levels*: that is, first, in regard to the choice of the individual cases that were taken to represent a type and, second, in regard to the generalisations that were made from a series of instantiated types to the 'whole': that is, the national population or other collectivity of interest.

In choosing the actual subjects of their monographs, Le Play and his followers would appear to have had no very specific procedures. Le Play himself, although objecting to the practice of using local authorities as sources of information, still largely depended on them for advice on which families could be seen as average and thus typical within one of his predefined categories. Le Play regarded such authorities as embodying the accumulated knowledge and wisdom of their communities, but there was little reason for sceptics to accept this view. It was in fact argued against Le Play that his authorities could well be biased, in particular in a conservative direction, and inclined to pick out families accordingly: for example, ones whose members could be relied on to express general acceptance of the status quo and emphasise solidarity rather than conflict. Such criticisms gained support from the results of several re-studies that were made in localities and among groups of workers who had been represented by one of Le Play's monographs. The re-studies tended to find less harmony in community and workplace relations and less satisfaction among workers than Le Play's accounts had indicated (cf. Lazarsfeld, 1961; Goldfrank, 1972; Silver, ed., 1982: 54–75). Finally, aside from the question of the typicality or otherwise of the subjects of particular monographs, the issue could also be raised, as it was for example by Halbwachs (1933), of whether Le Play did not seriously underestimate the diversity in standards and styles of living of workers associated with any one of his types, and to the point at which their analytical value had to be called into doubt.

When seeking to generalise on the basis of their monographs, the Le Playistes then found that problems of variation were compounded. To begin with, even supposing that their typological categories were well represented by their monographs—that the latter did refer to 'average' cases—there was the problem of estimating the numerical importance to be attached to each category. Le Play himself showed little interest in this matter. Some of his followers, however, believed that a solution could be found in the use of official statistics, arguing that these could provide the essential information for forming such categories—'*les moyennes qui conduisent le monographe à son type*'[6]—while at the same time indicating their relative size. But the further problem of the extent of variation around each type remained, so that it was still unclear just how the monographic method could lead to what

Kiaer referred to as '*une vraie miniature de l'ensemble qu'on observe*': that is, one that would accurately reflect both types *and* the nature and extent of deviations from them. Moreover, if typological categories were in effect to be determined on the basis of the categories of official statistics, then the question could be raised of why cases for study should not be chosen simply by sampling within these categories or some combination of them.

This was in effect the strategy followed by the survey researchers in their quest for representativeness. Thus, Kiaer's pioneering study carried out in Norway in 1894 (in connection with retirement pension and sickness insurance reforms) had a two-stage design. A number of districts were chosen by reference to census statistics so as to be representative of the country as a whole and then households in which detailed interviews were to be conducted were selected within each district with the specific aim of capturing the full range of variation that existed in economic and social conditions: that is, through what was known as 'purposive sampling' (Kiaer, 1895).[7]

Subsequently, however, in the light of work by Bowley (1906, 1926; cf. also Bowley and Burnett-Hurst, 1915) and various others, sampling methods became increasingly informed by probability theory, as this was developed by the successors of Galton. And then with the decisive intervention of Neyman (1934), all forms of purposive sampling were in fact called into question as lacking a clear theoretical basis and as leaving open a serious possibility of bias, and appear to have been rather rapidly abandoned. A new approach developed in which the purposive element in survey design was clearly separated from sampling procedures. This approach comprised, first, the a priori 'stratification' of the population under study or, in other words, its proportionate division in the light of already well-established knowledge of certain aspects of its heterogeneity and of the purposes of the survey; and then, second, the 'probability', or, that is, the *random*, sampling of units *within* strata (cf. Seng, 1951; Kruskal and Mosteller, 1980; Hansen, 1987).

With such stratified random sampling, survey researchers in fact arrived at a broadly satisfactory solution to problems of variation, as they perceived them: that is, as problems of inferring characteristics of populations via estimates from samples with a relatively small and known degree of error. Ethnographers did not, however, make any comparable progress. As I seek in the next two sections to show, what might be called, on the one hand, *problems of variation within the locales of ethnography* and, on the other hand, *problems of variation across locales* have persisted; and, although they have been recurrently addressed, no agreement even on the general approach to be taken to them would seem so far to have emerged, let alone procedures that might become codified as standard practice.

PROBLEMS OF VARIATION WITHIN LOCALES

There would seem to be broad agreement on at least three characteristics of sociological ethnography that set it in contrast with survey work (cf. Brewer, 2000: 10–11). First, it is research undertaken in 'natural' situations, as opposed to ones specifically set up for research purposes, such as that of the formal interview (or laboratory experiment). Second, it is research conducted via the ethnographer's own observation, in some degree participant, within the situation or situations studied, supplemented by interviews with actors of an informal, unstructured kind—'interviews as conversations'. And third, it is research aimed at the elucidation of actors' own definitions of their situation and of the meanings that they give to their actions within it, rather than, or at least prior to, the imposition of the investigator's concepts, as must in some degree occur where formal interview schedules or questionnaires are used.[8] But, given these characteristics, the following issue then inevitably arises. When the ethnographer is in the field—in the locale of the ethnography—what principles of selection should guide the observation and conversations in which he or she actually engages? Since anything approaching total coverage will rarely be feasible, just *who* should be observed and questioned and, in turn, have *their* patterns of meaningful action and *their* understandings of the life-world of the locale recorded and, ultimately, analysed?

In ethnographic work in classical social anthropology, much reliance was in fact placed on local authorities—otherwise known as 'key informants'. It would seem to have been accepted that such individuals could be identified in a fairly unproblematic way and that, with some prompting and checking, they could provide the basis for adequate accounts of at least the major institutional and cultural features of the (mostly tribal) societies that were studied. As Cohen (1984: 223) has put it: 'The chief could tell us about politics and war and hunting; the priest or shaman or witchdoctor about religious, magical or mystical affairs' and so on. Moreover, as Cohen also notes, it tended to be assumed that the cultures in question were 'monolithic' and that actors were highly socialised into them. Thus, it was scarcely envisaged that a widening of the range of informants might lead to a significantly different picture of the society being formed.[9]

Whether such a degree of confidence in key informants' accounts was justified may well be doubted.[10] But, for present purposes, the more relevant point is that in the case of ethnography undertaken in modern societies, the idea of such informants pronouncing authoritatively on monolithic cultures is not one that could be given any very serious consideration. Nor indeed is it. In textbooks on ethnographic methods for sociologists problems of variation within locales are generally recognised and so in turn are ones of selection—or, that is, of sampling—in the course of data collection (see, e.g., Burgess, 1984: 53–59, 61–75; Miles and Huberman, 1984: 41–42; Johnson, 1990; Hammersley and Atkinson, 1995: 45–53; Fetterman, 1998: 32–33; Brewer, 2000: 76–82). Correspondingly, a disregard for such problems is taken to constitute grounds for legitimate criticism. Thus, to take one notable example, Hammersley and Atkinson (1995: 111–12) point out that Willis (1977) bases an ethnography of working-class boys in a secondary school largely on conversations with one grouping, 'the lads', who represent a well-defined counter-school subculture, while more or less ignoring another grouping that he identifies, the 'ear-'oles', who accept school norms and values. Willis, they object, provides no good reasons for endorsing 'the lads' as being the genuine 'spokesmen for the working class', nor any explanation for why, having found evidence of significant subcultural variation, he then denies the 'ear-'oles', and possibly other groupings too, the right to a voice. Moreover, various other, less obvious possibilities of unaccommodated variation leading to bias in ethnographies have been commented on: as, say, where certain very helpful, but not necessarily representative, individuals or groups threaten to dominate the data collection process or where influential 'gatekeepers' or 'sponsors', through whom access to a locale has been achieved, then seek to slant the direction of the research and the choice of interviewees in a particular way (cf. Hammersley and Atkinson, 1995: 59–67, 133–34).[11]

However, recognising problems is one thing, devising generally accepted solutions to them, another. And in this latter regard, a reading of both textbooks and sociological ethnographies themselves would suggest that still almost everything remains to be done. The main difficulty, I would argue, is that, on account perhaps of the fraught intellectual climate within which they now operate, even those ethnographers who most clearly see the need for methodological development and codification around the idea of a logic of inference are wary of complying too readily with what might be labelled as 'positivist' requirements and at the same time are too indulgent towards supposed alternative approaches. Thus, so far as problems of variation within locales are concerned, a number of such alternatives are in fact entertained, each of which, though, can be shown to have rather basic shortcomings.

To begin with, the suggestion has been made (see, e.g., Orum, Feagin, and Sjoberg, 1991: 19–21; Fetterman, 1998: 11–12) that resorting to the kind of inference that is typically involved in survey work, that is, from sample to population, is not the only way in which the representativeness of an ethnography can be underpinned. The 'verisimilitude' of any such qualitative account, or its 'authenticity', 'plausibility', or 'undeniability', can also be communicated to its readers by its literary style—a means that is less readily available in the case of quantitative analyses. However, the trouble here is, rather obviously, that the appreciation of style as creating an effect of verisimilitude and so on is not at all the same thing as having evidence of representativeness, and is moreover a highly subjective matter. What strikes *me* as an ethnography that 'rings true' may strike *you* as quite unconvincing; and we could then only pursue the matter in a rational way by moving from style to substance: that is, to the strength of the grounds, of the linkage between evidence and argument, on which the claim of representativeness is made—or, in other words, by moving back to the logic of inference.[12]

Again, it has been maintained that while sampling of some kind may be necessary in data collection within the locale of an ethnography, this need not be—perhaps should not be—the probabilistic sampling characteristic of survey work (cf. Johnson, 1990: ch. 2; Stewart, 1998: 35, 47). Thus, one alternative that has been proposed is what is called 'judgmental' or 'opportunistic' sampling. Ethnographers should be alert to whatever possibilities for observation or conversation may happen to come their way and should then decide on which to concentrate in the light of their judgment of which are most 'appropriate' (Fetterman, 1998: 32–33) or most likely to prove rewarding (Burgess, 1984: 54–55). However, just as where appeal is made to the stylistic effects of an ethnography, the difficulty arises of disputed cases. *You* may think that an ethnographer has shown sound judgment in his or her selection but *I* may suspect, say, that data collection has been recurrently biased in favour of a particular theoretical or ideological position.[13] And again the only way to proceed would be to get down to an examination of the actual grounds on which judgment was exercised.

A yet further variety of nonprobabilistic sampling that has been seen as well suited to ethnography is then 'theoretical sampling', as advocated by Glaser and Strauss (1967: ch. 3 esp; cf. Strauss and Corbin, 1990: ch. 11). This is evidently sampling that, rather than trading on happenstance, is of a highly purposive kind. The central idea would appear to be that the process of data collection should be controlled by emerging theory, with the aim of allowing the investigator to try out and elaborate new concepts and categories until 'saturation' is reached: that is, until no further elaboration is empirically warranted. As Bryman has pointedly observed (1988: 117), theoretical sampling seems to be far more often referred to than actually used; and it is, moreover, unclear whether Glaser and Strauss intended it as a solution to problems of within-locale variation. But, even if they did, it is still hard to see how it could in fact answer. The ethnographer could let emerging theory dictate the selection of observations and conversations up to whatever point without thereby gaining any assurance that the data resulting from such sampling would adequately reflect the range of variation to be contended with. Indeed, insofar as the theory being developed was mistaken from the outset, the path then followed in data collection might be systematically biased towards *un*representative instances.[14]

In sum, two main points may be made. First, reliance on inadequate or in effect pseudo-solutions to problems of variation within the locales of ethnography can serve only to undermine what is claimed as one of ethnography's greatest strengths, especially in relation to survey-based research: that is, its capacity not only to 'tell what it's all about' but further to 'tell how it is' from the actors' point of view. For all too often, as things stand, it is left quite unclear just how critical readers of an ethnography might assess whether they are indeed being told about all, or only a part, of what is going on and are being given insight into the subjectivity of all, or only of some, of the actors involved.[15]

Second, in search of more effective solutions, ethnographers have in fact no alternative but to go down the same road as did survey researchers: that is, to adopt procedures that are in some way or other based on the demonstrated advantages of probabilistic sampling. Some such procedures have indeed been proposed for ethnographic work and occasionally implemented, most often, perhaps, in the case of the observation of patterns of action over time (e.g., McClintock, Brannon, and Maynard-Moody, 1983; cf. Burgess, 1984: 64–71). But it would seem important that they should become quite standard both in this regard and in the selection of interviewees also. Apart from misplaced fears of an apparent surrender to the hegemony of 'positivist' methodology, the main obstacle to a movement in this direction would appear to be similarly misplaced doubts about practicalities.

It has, for example, been held (Burgess, 1984: 75; Fetterman, 1998: 8–9) that random sampling will often be inappropriate or at least insufficient in an ethnography because certain individuals or groups *have* to be covered—that is, their selection could not be left to chance—on account of the particular positions, roles, or statuses that they occupy or of their crucial theoretical relevance. But if such firm a priori knowledge or clear theoretical direction is indeed available, then some form of stratification could be adopted with, if need be, differential sampling ratios (including, perhaps, some of 100 percent) within strata.[16] Again, it has been argued that because the locale of an ethnography is usually not all that well defined, sampling frames would be difficult to construct (Hammersley and Atkinson, 1995: 136–37). But what is overlooked here is that quite similar situations arise in survey research, so that some amount of slippage has regularly to be acknowledged between the theoretical population of a study and that which is actually sampled. Moreover, ethnographers could well have some compensating advantages in regard to sampling. In survey work a major problem now emerging is that of increasing, and most likely increasingly biased, nonresponse. In the small-scale setting of an ethnography not only might relatively high response rates be expected but, in addition, a better knowledge of nonrespondents, and in turn a better estimation of any resulting bias, should be possible.

In all of this, it is essential that the point earlier made should be kept in mind: that pursuing methods responsive to the logic of inference is desirable *not* because reliable and valid results are thus guaranteed (though the chances of such results may be enhanced) but rather because the processes through which results, of whatever quality, are produced are thus made *transparent* and shortcomings from ideal requirements, which are in some degree inevitable, are fully exposed. The adequacy of surveys in capturing variation in phenomena of interest within populations can be, and routinely is, evaluated by critical reference to such matters as sampling frames, sample design, response rates, and response bias. The adequacy of ethnographies in capturing within-locale variation should be open to evaluation on a comparable basis.

PROBLEMS OF VARIATION ACROSS LOCALES

Ethnographies are a form of case study in which the unit of study is usually not the individual but rather a social entity of some kind—a group or network, a community, or an organisation—that is treated in a holistic way. In consequence of this and of the emphasis on intensive and prolonged fieldwork, it is common for an ethnography to be confined to the study of a single unit or to no more than two or three. Only rarely, one could say, does the number covered amount to double figures. How the units that will constitute the locale or locales of an ethnography are to be chosen is then a question of evident importance. In the context of classical social anthropology the argument could be made that it was in fact of value to carry out ethnographic work among *any* people or in *any* region not hitherto studied, before truly indigenous cultural and institutional forms disappeared for ever. But such an argument is of obviously less help to the sociological ethnographer. For the latter, the fundamental difficulty is that any kind of unit in which he or she has an interest may be expected to show some common features from one locale to another within the larger society but also some non-negligible degree of variation, and that it is then unlikely to be apparent from the study of only a small number of units which findings provide a reliable basis for sociological generalisation and which do not. If research is undertaken within, say, industrial work groups, or isolated villages or inner-city schools, how is the ethnographer to know how much and what part of what he or she observes is indeed recurrent across work groups, villages, or schools of the kind in question or is limited only to the particular locales that happen to have been picked out, each of which will of course have its own distinctive articulation with the larger society?

It has sometimes been suggested that ethnographers can simply side-step the issue of how far their findings can be generalised by viewing ethnographies as being entirely idiographic in intent: that is, as being concerned purely with the description of the cases studied in all their detailed uniqueness and for their own intrinsic interest. But while this is in itself a defensible position, it is a difficult one to hold to, at all events for those who would wish to argue for the continuing importance of ethnography in sociological research, and in fact most ethnographers do seek to draw conclusions from their work of some degree of generality. Cases are, after all, usually understood as being cases *of* something.[17] Moreover, problems that are in this regard created by variation across locales are no less regularly and openly acknowledged in textbooks on ethnographic research than are those arising from variation within locales (see, e.g., Burgess, 1984: 59–61; Miles and Huberman, 1984: 36–41; Bryman, 1988: 87–91; Hammersley, 1991: 24–27, 102–103; Silverman, 1993: 160–62; Hammersley and Atkinson, 1995: 42–45; Stewart, 1998: ch. 5; Brewer, 2000: 76–82). However, what has here once more to be said is that, although acknowledged, these problems have not so far been treated in ways that have been able to command general acceptance— nor indeed in ways that would deserve to do so; and, again, it would seem, largely on account of a misguided concern to find alternative approaches to ones that might be thought too tainted by positivistic methodology and, in particular, as this is taken to be applied in survey work.

Thus, just as it has been supposed that a solution to problems of within-locale variation can be achieved without any consideration of inference from sample to population—by appeal to 'verisimilitude' and so on—so too it is believed that in regard to problems of variation across locales the idea of statistical generalisation can be discarded in favour of that of 'naturalistic generalisation'. The latter, one understands, is successfully achieved when the findings of an ethnographic case study prove to be 'epistemologically in harmony with the reader's experience and thus to that person a natural basis for generalisation' (Stake, 1978: 5; cf. Denzin, 1989) or when the data 'resonate experientially and phenomenologically' with the reader (Snow and Anderson, 1991: 165). In this case, there is in fact a more or less explicit acceptance that what to one reader is a valid generalisation need not be so to another; and not on account of any issue that would be open to rational examination and debate but simply in consequence of their having led different lives. What 'resonates' with me may well not resonate with you, and there, unfortunately, the matter has to rest.

Likewise, the proposal of judgmental or opportunistic sampling as an alternative to probabilistic sampling for within-locale observation is paralleled by the argument that ethnographers can equally well proceed on the basis of opportunism tempered by judgment in their selection of locales. Considerations of representativeness, it is suggested, are of less importance in this respect, at least initially, than are those of ease of access, prior knowledge of the locale, the availability of insider contacts, or mere physical convenience (Burgess, 1984: 59–61; cf. Spradley, 1980). If there is reason to believe that the choice of locales thus made may limit the extent to which generalisation will be possible, this can then be taken into account—that is to say, the ethnographer can use his or her judgment as regards representativeness— when eventually drawing conclusions from the study. However, as with such an approach to sampling within locales, the difficulty that arises is that of knowing on just what grounds this crucial judgment is being exercised or, in turn, could be challenged by critics. It would seem to be supposed that, after the fact, the ethnographer somehow has information to hand on the nature and extent of the variation that exists across locales that was not available before sampling or was not deemed relevant to this task.

Finally, though, one further argument regarding the problem of variation across locales should be noted that does in fact recognise that *some* logic of inference is needed in order to underpin the process of generalisation but maintains that this is not the *same* logic as that which is appropriate in survey work. The origins of this argument lie in the distinction made by Znaniecki (1934) between 'enumerative' and 'analytic' induction. Its most explicit exposition is, however, to be found in a much-cited paper by Mitchell (1983). For Mitchell, Znaniecki's distinction is in fact best interpreted as one between two kinds of inference rather than induction: that is, 'statistical' inference and 'causal' inference. Generalisation in survey-based sociology depends on a form of statistical inference and in turn on a sample being representative of the population from which it is drawn. However, with an ethnography, or indeed any kind of case study, generalisation must rely on causal inference—on the analysis establishing certain 'essential' causal linkages among social phenomena, which, if found in the locale under study, will then necessarily be found in all comparable locales: 'We infer that the features present in the case study will be related in a wider population not because the case is representative but because our analysis is unassailable.' There is thus no point in the ethnographer trying to find typical locales; a concern with this issue simply reflects confusion over the two kinds of inference. In fact, the causal linkages that can be extrapolated from a single ethnography may well be most clearly revealed within idiosyncratic locales (Mitchell, 1983: 200, 204).

The question that at once arises here is of course that of how the ethnographer is in fact able to identify essential causal linkages within the body of empirical data that a particular locale provides. The answer Mitchell gives—and it is the only one conceivable—is: on the basis of theory. Preexisting theory enables 'significant elements' to be identified in the data, and the extent to which generalisation is possible depends on the 'adequacy' of the further theoretical developments that are achieved (1983: 202, 203). But what has then to be observed is the nature of the demands that are thus made on theory. To be viable, Mitchell's approach requires theory that, as well as allowing generalisable causal processes to be conceptually separated out from 'the unique circumstances' of the ethnography, is furthermore *both* deterministic in character, so that the analysis of just one case is enough, *and* entirely correct in substance, so that the analysis becomes 'unassailable'.

The understanding of theory implicit in Mitchell's position is then one that, ironically, might well be described as positivist in something close to the original, nineteenth-century sense: theory is seen as giving certain knowledge of necessary, lawlike relations.[18] Today, such an understanding would not find great philosophical support, within the social sciences at least; nor, more to the point, can sociology in fact claim to have produced theory of the kind in question. Consequently, compelling instances of its use in the way that Mitchell would envisage are difficult to cite. Individual ethnographies may of course serve as the basis for the development of theory; but this is theory which, far from being unassailable, must then be exposed to test, and not least in order to determine the range of applicability, from one context to another, of the causal processes that it postulates.[19]

In sum, whether the aim is simply description *or* theoretical advance, the problem of variation across the locales of ethnographies cannot be avoided; and neither, I would then argue, can the conclusion that, just as with problems of within-locale variation, solutions must be sought on the basis of the same sampling procedures that have become standard in survey work. Moreover, here too, it would seem, many ethnographers have moved some way towards accepting this conclusion, even if only implicitly, and more would be likely to do so, and more openly, were it not for the influence of poorly examined inhibitions about supposedly positivist methodology.

Thus, for example, ethnographies are quite often taken as a basis for descriptive generalisation on the grounds that the case or cases studied *can* be regarded as typical or representative of some population within which

they fall. Or again, ethnographies are held to have theoretical significance
on the grounds that they relate to cases that offer strategic advantages for
research because of their 'deviant', 'leading edge', or 'critical' character or
because they minimise or maximise certain crucial contrasts (cf. Platt, 1988;
Stewart, 1998: 58–59). But to argue thus can of course only mean that
the importance of variation across locales, and likewise of the positioning
of particular locales within this variation, *is* recognised; and, further, that
some knowledge in these respects is claimed or supposed. Indeed, one can
readily find recommendations made (e.g., Orum, Feagin, and Sjoberg, 1991:
15; Hammersley, 1992: 189–90), much on Le Playiste lines, that official
or other statistics produced via survey research should be utilised in order
to establish the degree of typicality, or the nature of the atypicality, of ethnographic locales—and even while, perhaps, the general inappropriateness
of the sampling approach of survey work to the selection of such locales is
maintained.

However, of yet greater significance in this regard is the fact that a number of ethnographies can by now be cited in which just this approach is explicitly pursued. For example, one could cite here Jankowski's study (1991;
cf. also 2002) of American urban gangs or Halle's study (1993) of artwork
in individuals' homes and its personal and social significance in communities of differing class composition. Thus, to take the former case in more
detail, Jankowski's research is based on 37 randomly selected gangs from an
ethnically stratified list of all gangs known to be active in three major cities
with widely contrasting ecological features. From the standpoint of a survey
research handbook, the sampling is by no means perfect—as Jankowski
realises—and, in view of the practical difficulties attendant on his choice
of research topic, it is difficult to see how it could have been. Nonetheless,
problems of variation across locales are clearly confronted, and what must be
stressed is that shortcomings in the procedures followed do not detract from
the ultimate virtue that derives from them: that, once more, of transparency.
We know the rationale according to which Jankowski came to work in certain locales rather than in others; we have the essential information that we
need in order to evaluate his sampling, to point to ways in which bias might
have been introduced, and to form judgments for ourselves of how far his
findings are likely to be applicable to urban gangs in America at large. Work
such as this does then constitute a challenge to which other sociological
ethnographers should show themselves ready to respond. If such a sampling

approach to the problems of across-locale variation can be implemented, with the advantages indicated, in the study of urban gangs, then why not in what would in general be the more favourable circumstances of studies of workplaces, local communities, and schools? Or, if there *are* better approaches to such problems, then their superiority should be demonstrated, with studies such as Jankowski's serving as benchmark.[20]

PROBLEMS OF CONTEXT IN SURVEY RESEARCH AND POSSIBILITIES FOR ETHNOGRAPHY

In the foregoing, I have maintained that problems of variation, both within and across locales, that were raised in criticism of the earliest efforts at sociological ethnography still persist today, and that little agreement has emerged about how a solution to these problems might be achieved. I turn now to what can be seen as a corresponding range of problems that are associated with survey-based sociological research, and that have in fact been frequently pointed to by proponents of ethnography: that is, what may be called problems of context. I aim to show *en passant* that survey researchers have in certain respects responded to these problems in a manner that ethnographers could find instructive, but my main concern is with one problem that remains and that, moreover, provides new possibilities for ethnography to demonstrate its continuing importance to the sociological enterprise.

As earlier suggested, it is characteristic of ethnography that it is carried out in natural situations and relies on participant observation and 'interviews as conversations' in order to reach, at least as a primary goal, some understanding of the meanings that individuals give to these situations and to the patterns of social action in which they are involved. In contrast, it has then been claimed, survey-based research must, through its essential techniques, *abstract* individuals from their natural situations—that is, from their social contexts—and thus introduce into the research process a significant degree of artificiality. A sample of individuals is selected from within a population, usually a quite large one, and data are collected from the members of this sample via questionnaires or formal interviews following a prepared schedule. But, it is held, to ground sociological enquiry in the study of such 'atomised' individuals is likely to prove in various ways misleading. For example, the attitudes and beliefs that individuals express in interviews, in response to more or less standardised questions, may be largely products of the circumstances of the interview itself rather than attitudes and beliefs that would actually guide the actions of the respondents in the course of their everyday lives. In other words, one set of problems of context in survey research are in effect those of the reliability and validity of the data obtained. In addition, it has been contended that survey data, whatever their quality, must be subject to serious restriction in their scope. In relating to the attributes of individuals, or to individuals' perceptions and reports, such data cannot provide any direct information pertaining to the supra-individual level of structured social relationships, which, as well as being of interest in itself, will also of course condition and influence the experience and action of individuals. A further problem of context in survey research is then that of how such 'contextual effects' are to be detected and their importance assessed.

Problems of the kind thus far indicated are, however, ones that survey researchers have for long recognised. They are, moreover, ones that in recent years they have addressed with greater success than hitherto, and essentially, it could be said, *by following through the basic logic of their established methods of data collection and analysis.* Thus, in regard to problems of the reliability and validity of data, and of subjective data in particular, a variety of statistical techniques have been developed directed towards, on the one hand, determining the extent to which such problems exist and, on the other, enabling due allowance to be made for the error present in data in the course of their analysis. At its most sophisticated, what this approach entails is the elaboration of probability models for survey response in which such response is taken to be a function *both* of the attributes of individual respondents *and* of the questions they are asked, the context in which they are answered, and so on (for a particularly instructive series of papers on the issue of 'non-attitudes', see Converse, 1964, 1970; Duncan, 1982; Brooks, 1994a, 1994b).

Likewise, the problem of contextual effects has been addressed by extending the data collection process in survey research so as to include information not only on individuals but further on the social entities in which they are involved—groups, networks, communities, organisations, and so on—which can of course also be sampled, and by then applying to such hierarchically structured data-sets various techniques of multilevel modelling. It thus becomes possible for estimates to be made of the actual degree to which variation at the individual level shows association with contextual factors—for example, variation in academic performance with features of schools or variation in voting with features of constituencies—independently of variation in the attributes of individuals themselves (here a relevant series of papers would be Lazarsfeld, 1959; Blalock, 1984; DiPrete and Forristal, 1994).

Indeed, in consequence of such advances, survey researchers might well consider themselves now to be in a position to mount a strong counter-critique of ethnography. It could, for example, be pointed out that conducting interviews as conversations rather than more formally does not in some magical way simply make problems of the reliability and validity of data disappear; these problems demand serious attention from ethnographers also. Or again it could be remarked that while in ethnographies contextual effects are often claimed or supposed, this is not to say that they are actually demonstrated through some method that is open to critical inspection.[21] However, I do not seek here to pursue such issues but rather to take up a further problem of context in survey-based research, underlined by ethnographers, which I would see as being of a different order to those considered above and with which sociologists reliant on such research have yet to come to terms.

Ethnographers have often maintained that the ultimate concern of their research is with social processes: that is, with patterns of situated social action and interaction, continuing through time, that are integral to the life-worlds that they explore. Their methods of enquiry, based on a long-term involvement in natural situations, are those most apt to the understanding of such processes, whereas in this regard survey research, with its focus on the atomised and in turn 'decontextualised' individual, is at a serious disadvantage. Such a position is, moreover, readily developed into the further argument that, because of the privileged access that it gives to social processes, ethnography must play a key role in the study of social causation (see, e.g., Miles, 1983: 117). Survey research is well suited to establishing associations among social phenomena, at all events at the level of statistical relations among variables; but ethnographic research comes into its own when it is a matter of explaining in terms of social processes why these relations are found. Thus, for instance, Fetterman (1998: 3) maintains that while a survey approach would be more appropriate than ethnography in determining the distribution of different ethnic groups across a national occupational structure, ethnographies would be required in order to show how unequal ethnic representation in specific occupations is actually brought about—to show how this outcome is actually produced 'on the ground'.

For present purposes, this argument gains in significance in the degree to which it can be allied with forceful criticism from other quarters of the idea that social causation can be established directly via the statistical analysis of survey data (see further chs. 6 and 9). On the one hand, it has been objected by theorists of social action that 'variable sociology' cannot itself provide causal explanations of the regularities it describes, since such explanations must ultimately refer to the action and interaction of individuals through which the demonstrated relations among variables are actually created. On the other hand, it has been pointed out by statisticians that inferences that are thought to be derived from the causal modelling of survey data cannot in fact come from such modelling alone, since this must itself rest on theoretical assumptions (whether recognised or not) about social processes, which are then quite crucial to the validity of the results obtained.

There would therefore appear to be an emerging consensus that in attempts at explaining established social regularities, the elaboration of what might be called their underlying generative processes—or, alternatively, 'causal mechanisms' (cf. Hedström and Swedberg, eds., 1998; also Blossfeld and Prein, eds., 1998)—is indeed essential. And in this way, I would then argue, an opportunity is opened up for sociological ethnography to establish its role as an essential complement to survey research on rather more specific and more secure grounds than those hitherto advanced. This opportunity would consist *not* in ethnography pursuing any special advantage as regards the actual construction of accounts of generative social processes, as, say in the inductive style envisaged by Mitchell or again in that favoured by proponents of grounded theory, but rather in ethnography providing a distinctive medium through which such accounts, whatever their provenance, *could be exposed to empirical test.*[22]

If it is accepted that explanations of observed social regularities have in the end to be given micro-to-macro rather than macro-to-micro—that is, in terms of situated social action and of its intended and unintended consequences rather than by reference to the functional and structural exigencies of social systems—it would then seem to follow that such explanations, in the form of narratives of action, will be open to most direct test through precisely the kind of intensive, context-embedded study in which ethnographers engage. That is to say, it is through this kind of enquiry that it should be possible to see hypothesised generative processes, or what has been called 'local causality' (Miles and Huberman, 1984: 15), actually at work. Thus, to return to Fetterman's example of disparities among ethnic groups in their representation in different occupations, one could question his implied view that ethnographers are in some way in a privileged position to suggest generative processes. But one could at the same time recognise that, once such explanations for the established regularities have been proposed—as, say, in terms of adverse 'labelling' and discrimination by employers or of migration chains and ethnic social networks—then ethnographic research would appear an apt way of investigating whether processes of the kind invoked do in fact operate. It would certainly be difficult to retain belief in their efficacy if, in well-designed and sustained fieldwork in a series of appropriately selected locales, no indication of their presence could be found.

Insofar, then, as sociological ethnography does have advantages over survey-based research in its capacity to study social action and interaction in context, it is, I would maintain, primarily through the testing of accounts of generative social processes that this advantage can, and should, be exploited. However, further in this regard, two qualifications need to be made.

The first is that if ethnography is to contribute effectively to sociological analysis in the way in question, it is essential that the problems of variation both within and across locales that were earlier reviewed should indeed be dealt with through ethnographers taking more seriously than hitherto the logic of sampling as this has been developed in survey research. On the one hand, it has to be recognised that, because the social regularities that are to be explained will themselves be probabilistic, the accounts of generative processes that are suggested will need to be ones that are directed towards capturing central tendencies in social action and its consequences. There is no requirement, nor any warrant (see further ch. 6), for deterministic explanations, such as those to which analytic induction supposedly leads, and in which *every* 'seemingly anomalous' case (cf. Becker, 1992: 210–12) is covered. In testing hypothesised accounts, it will therefore be vital that fieldwork procedures should enable within-locale variation to be appropriately handled and, in turn, make it possible for a fairly reliable understanding to be reached of what patterns of action (if any) can be regarded as representing central tendencies in a given locale and of the nature and extent of the variation that occurs around them. For example, in the case of the under- or over-representation of ethnic groups in different occupations, individual instances illustrative of almost *any* conceivable causal process *might* be encountered in the course of fieldwork. But the sociologically important issue is that of deciding just which of the processes that have been proposed are sufficiently dominant in the locale studied to be capable of generating, as an aggregate effect, the regularities in the pattern of association between ethnicity and occupation that are generally observed.[23]

On the other hand, it would seem no less vital that ethnographic research should be so designed that problems of across-locale variation are also adequately treated: that is to say, so that some rationally defensible basis exists for generalisation from the findings that particular ethnographies yield. Even if social processes that have been suggested as generating a given outcome are clearly in evidence within a given locale, or set of locales, the question will still remain of whether these processes could be expected to operate similarly in other locales. There is of course no reason why a particular outcome should not be produced in several different ways and, perhaps, ones of widely differing prevalence from one context to another. Thus, ethnic disparities in occupational attainment could be found, say, in one locale to be brought about primarily through direct discrimination by employers but, in another, more through the timing of waves of immigration and their social organisation. The empirical testing of hypothesised generative processes, whether via ethnography or otherwise, should then be such that this issue of causal heterogeneity can be seriously addressed, rather than being invoked, as it often tends to be in 'grounded' theorising, merely as an excuse for adhocery. Moreover, a more secure handling of problems of across-locale variation in this regard would also be important in helping theory construction that does have a stronger deductive component to go beyond simply the accumulation of what Coleman (1964: 516) aptly calls 'sometimes-true' theories and Elster (1990: 247–48) merely 'causal models' as distinct from theories. Testing whether *possible* causal processes are actually realised in locales that can be reliably positioned within a range of variation is of obvious relevance to what must be the further ambition of explicitly spelling out domains of application: that is, of developing theories that comprise coherent accounts of which of the causal processes that they specify will in fact be most likely to operate in which kinds of context.[24]

The second qualification that should be made to the idea of ethnography playing a distinctive role in the testing of explanations given in terms of causal social processes can be simply stated. It is that while ethnography's role may here be distinctive, this is not to say that it will be unchallenged. A quite different, and in fact largely contrasting, approach can be identified, and one, moreover, that could be implemented essentially within the survey research tradition.

This approach starts from the position that while micro-to-macro accounts of generative processes of action are indeed crucial to sociological explanation, the study of these processes in themselves is highly problematic. This position may be given a philosophical justification on broadly Humean lines: causation itself cannot be directly observed but must always be in some way or other a matter of inference from observations. But more relevantly, perhaps, for present purposes, the pragmatic argument is also advanced that a convincing research methodology for determining patterns of social action and interaction has yet to be developed and, in particular, as regards the understanding of actors' subjectivity. The capacity of social scientists to gain access to actors' values, beliefs, attitudes, goals, or preferences, let alone to their more complex mental constructions, such as 'definitions of the situation', is viewed with a radical scepticism—and regardless of whether this access is sought via observation or interviews, participant rather than nonparticipant observation or informal rather than formal interviewing techniques.[25]

From this position, then, it is maintained that in seeking to test explanations of established social regularities in terms of causal processes of action, the most viable strategy will be to focus not on immediate but rather on more indirect implications. That is to say, instead of attempting to observe the hypothesised processes actually in operation 'on the ground', within particular locales, it will be better to proceed by asking: if these processes are indeed generating the regularities in question, then what *other* regularities, similarly open to reasonably secure empirical demonstration, are implied and ought to be discovered? Thus, in seeking to test the claim that it is the discriminatory practices of employers that create a skewed occupational distribution of certain ethnic groups, it will be less effective to try to observe such discrimination as it actually takes place within firms or communities— what exactly would this entail?—than to spell out what other consequences should be expected if discrimination is indeed in operation and then to see whether evidence of these can be found, as, say, from extensive survey research. The case of discrimination in employment (whether by ethnicity, gender or otherwise) is in fact a particularly apt one to take here since, pre-cisely on account of the difficulty of proving its occurrence directly, much attention has been given, for policy and legal as well as academic reasons, to specifying what could be regarded as indirect indicators of discrimination at work: for example, differing patterns across groups in the relation between qualifications and experience, on the one hand, and levels of pay or rates of promotion, on the other.

It is not my purpose here to come to any final judgment on the merits of hypothesis testing via what might be called the direct or indirect approaches. Although I would regard the issue as being one of the most important and difficult that arises in contemporary sociology, and indeed in social science more widely,[26] it will, I believe, be decided only in the light of long-term ex-perience of relative performance. Moreover, while the two approaches might appear to diverge sharply on basic principles, there would in practice seem to be no difficulty and some evident advantage in, for the time being at least, pursuing them together. In the present context, the main conclusion to be drawn from the foregoing discussion is then that if in this regard sociologi-cal ethnography is to compete effectively, the need is yet further underlined for renewed attention to be given to its methodological basis: that is, both in relation to problems of within- and across-locale variation, which, as I have sought to show, are a specific historical legacy, and at the same time in relation to problems of the reliability and validity of data, and of subjective data in particular, which are problems that ethnography does not escape but shares with the survey tradition.[27]

In this essay, I have examined the idea that ethnography might represent a radical alternative to 'positivist' sociology of the kind that finds its main empirical resource in survey-based research. I have maintained that while sociologists can of course apply a variety of different research methods, all must in some way or other be conformable to the same underlying logic of inference through which a basis is provided for the rational construction and criticism of scientific arguments. If, then, an ethnography that rejects positiv-ism is an ethnography that rejects this logic, such an ethnography must place itself outside social science—which is indeed, according to some currently influential irrationalist authors, its only conceivable location. I would regard these authors as totally misguided, but their position is, in this respect at least, a consistent one. Correspondingly, I have argued, those ethnographers who wish to retain their social scientific credentials must in principle accept a commitment to research methods that do acknowledge the logic of inference, and must therefore in practice aim either to show just how the methods characteristic of ethnography are in fact informed by this logic or to modify and develop them appropriately. What I have chiefly aimed to criticise are claims to the effect that there is some 'third way' available: one that will allow ethnographers to continue to work honourably within the social scientific community but under, as it were, a different aegis to its other members and with the benefit of some special and privileged methodological licence.

I have pursued detailed criticism on these lines with reference to a set of problems that appear quite crucial in sociological ethnography and that were apparent from its very origins: that is, problems of variation both within and across the locales of ethnography. While these problems have been readily recognised by ethnographers, they still remain without any generally accepted solution. Basically the same problems—in effect those of making inferences from part to whole—were encountered by survey researchers and, for their purposes, were rendered tractable through the development of sampling methods. However, on account, it would seem, of inhibitions over the apparent acceptance of a positivist approach, ethnographers have made no concerted effort to adapt the logic of sampling to the circumstances of their own style of research, and have instead shown a predilection for various alternative, 'third way' solutions. On examination, these prove rather obviously inadequate, and most commonly, one could say, because they are not of a kind that involve objective, transparent procedures nor therefore that are able to allow for any critical assessment of their application in particular cases.

In regard, then, to problems of context, which have been endemic in survey-based sociology on account of its focus on the decontextualised individual and which have afforded ethnographers evident possibilities for critique, I have noted that survey researchers have in certain respects responded in promising fashion, essentially by extending the logic of their standard techniques. Nonetheless, any sociology that remains entirely at the level of relationships among variables is still vulnerable to the charge, which others have of late joined ethnographers in pressing, that it cannot adequately address issues of social causation; or, more specifically, that it cannot itself penetrate to the processes of situated social action and interaction that alone can be the source of the empirical regularities that it describes. Ethnography, with its focus precisely on such processes, would thus seem here to have a clear advantage. But this advantage, I have then argued, should be understood as lying not in the distinctive capacity of ethnography to produce causal accounts of established social regularities, as, say, through inductive procedures, but rather in ethnography constituting a style of research with an evident appropriateness to the empirical testing of such accounts, however they may be derived. Any form of 'local causality' that is hypothesised in the form of generative social processes should, it may be held, be open to demonstration through appropriately sited and conducted ethnographic research, if it does indeed operate.

It is then on this basis that sociological ethnography may most convincingly be represented as, at all events, an essential complement to survey-based research. However, what I have further maintained is that an ethnography capable of sustaining such a claim, in what for the foreseeable future will be a difficult and contested area, will not be one that appeals to some ill-conceived and unconvincing 'third-way' methodology. To the contrary, in order to rise to the competitive challenges that it will surely face, ethnography must cease, as one author (Katz, 1997: 410–11) has put it, to 'beg off' the kinds of methodological issue with which survey research has for long grappled, and instead aim to make its own contribution in this regard.

Finally, I should no doubt acknowledge that for a sociologist who is not an ethnographer to write an essay in this vein could well be regarded as something of an impertinence, if not worse. There are, however, two points that I would put forward in mitigation. First, as I noted at the outset, sociological ethnography would now seem to be widely regarded, among its practitioners as well as outsiders, to be in a state of disarray, if not crisis. There is little agreement about the way ahead and methodology appears to be the main source of contention. Second, as I would read the situation, those who wish to see ethnography as accepting the same underlying 'rules of the game' as survey-based, and indeed other, methods of sociological research are not at the present time in the ascendancy. Intellectual fashion is against them and would appear, rather, to encourage increasingly avant-garde ethnographies such as, say, would culminate in 'the sixth moment' envisaged and celebrated by Denzin (1997).[28] If this judgment is anywhere close to the mark, then no apology at all for intervention from without is required: ethnography is obviously far too important to be left to ethnographers.

CHAPTER FIVE

Globalisation and Social Class*

An effort to achieve greater clarity is by now an essential preliminary to any essay on globalisation. To this end, it would seem important, first of all, to distinguish between concepts and theories of globalisation: that is, between nominal propositions about how globalisation might most usefully be understood and real propositions about the causes or consequences of globalisation, as understood in one way or another. A review of the current literature would suggest that, in the case of concepts and theories alike, sharply contrasting positions can be identified according, chiefly, to the degree of ambition that they display. By way of introduction, I shall therefore outline these positions and note those concepts and theories of globalisation that will be of greatest concern to me in this essay.

Concepts of globalisation can be divided into those that would represent globalisation narrowly, as indeed a primarily economic phenomenon, and those that would represent it more largely as an economic but at the same time as a political, social, and cultural phenomenon.

For economists, globalisation is a process whereby economic activity of all kinds is increasingly organised and conducted in ways that cut across politically defined national or regional boundaries. Thus, the advance of globalisation is revealed by various indicators of the degree of cross-national and cross-regional integration of markets for capital, labour, goods, and

*For information and advice, I am indebted to Tony Atkinson, Richard Breen, Geoffrey Evans, Duncan Gallie, Pablo Beramendi, Andrew Hurrell, Sanford Jacoby, Anand Menon, Colin Mills, Walter Müller, Yossi Shavit, Mike Smith, Stefan Svallfors, and Chris Whelan.

services. However, for most political scientists, globalisation would also signify a process through which—in part as a response to the globalisation of economic activity—new agencies of governance of an international or a transnational kind are created, so that greater substance is given to the idea of a world political as well as a world economic order. And finally, at least some sociologists would wish to see globalisation as further entailing social structural and cultural changes that reflect the growing interdependence and more frequent and rapid interaction of individuals and organisations across space and time and that are now leading if not to a world society, then at all events to the emergence of a new 'cosmopolitan' social order.

Theories of globalisation can likewise be divided into two main types. On the one hand, there are those that offer accounts of present-day processes of globalisation that recognise or imply an essential continuity with earlier experience, at least within the modern period of history. On the other hand, there are those that give accounts that stress the historically unprecedented nature of contemporary developments and indeed their radical *dis*continuity with the past.

Theories of the first kind tend to be associated with a relatively narrow, economic understanding of globalisation. The economists and economic historians who chiefly advance or support such theories would not seek to deny that a new wave of globalisation is now in train, nor that this shows a number of distinctive features. But they would at the same time point to basic similarities between the current and previous waves—those, say, of the 1950s and 1960s or of the decades before World War I—and, most importantly, in the micro-level mechanisms through which globalisation is generated and through which it in turn exerts its economic, and perhaps also its political and social, effects (see, e.g., Bairoch, 1996; Oman, 1999; O'Rourke and Williamson, 1999).

Theories of the second kind may also be associated with a primarily economic view of globalisation but more often go together with wider-ranging conceptions. What is in any event maintained is that globalisation in its contemporary phase has a different dynamic to the globalisation of earlier periods and is, moreover, of a 'transformational' character: we are today witnessing a historical disjunction and the beginning of a new epoch. This epochal change may be represented in terms chiefly of economics or of political economy—as, say, expressing the emerging triumph of free-market capitalism within a liberal-democratic world political order (e.g.,

Reich, 1991; Ohmae, 1995; Strange, 1996). But it is more often represented within a larger perspective as one that brings about a new stage of modernity—'second', 'reflexive', or 'post' modernity—and thus a whole new context not just for economic and political action but for 'human being and human doing' in general.

The concern of the present essay is with the impact of globalisation on social class—in the more advanced societies of the present day. While I shall therefore be much concerned with globalisation in its economic aspects, it is on 'grand' theories of globalisation that I focus. Such theories have of late been chiefly advanced by sociologists, but by sociologists who seek to go beyond their professional role and to write as—often self-styled—'public intellectuals' (see esp. Giddens, 1990, 1994, 2000; Albrow, 1996; Castells, 1997, 2000a, 2000b; Gray, 1998; Beck, 2000a, 2000b, 2000c). What these authors hold in common is that not only a new world economy and world polity are now in the making but, at the same time, a radically new sociocultural order. And it proves to be central to this claim that fundamental changes are occurring in the nature of class inequalities and of the class structures in which they are grounded, and that *these* changes then play a key role in other macro-level transformations, especially via their effects on political action, organisations, and institutions.

In what follows, I treat in turn three sets of arguments on the lines indicated that relate to the effects of globalisation on

1. economic inequalities among members of different classes,
2. class structures in themselves, and
3. the relationship between class and politics.

In each case, I begin with an exposition of the arguments and I then proceed to a critical examination of their theoretical coherence and their conformity with the available empirical evidence.[1] What emerges is that the underlying theory is often naïve and underdeveloped and that the linkage to the findings of relevant social science research is weak and, sometimes, nonexistent. Overall, the upshot of my critique is that, in some instances, processes of globalisation have not occurred in the way or to the extent that the authors in question would suppose; and that, in others, such processes, even where present, have not had the effects attributed to them. While I recognise that such a critique is limited to only one aspect of those theories of globalisation that claim epochal change, I conclude by suggesting that certain issues are raised that must call into question the more general validity of these theories and in turn the *modus operandi* of their authors; and further that, at least in the case considered, the sociologist as public intellectual does not, intellectually, cut a very impressive figure.

GLOBALISATION AND CLASS INEQUALITIES

During the years of the long boom that followed on World War II, it was widely believed that, as living standards generally improved within western nations, class inequalities, of both condition and opportunity, were tending to decline. However, since the ending of the long boom—say, from the mid-1970s onwards—such an optimistic view has become a good deal more difficult to sustain. Perhaps most disturbing has been evidence of a widening inequality in earnings and also in household incomes with, seemingly, a rather clear class basis. Specifically, the main losers would appear to be unskilled wage workers in manual or routine nonmanual occupations, whether through the stagnation or decline of their real earnings, even under conditions of continuing economic growth, or the increasing risk of long-term or recurrent unemployment.

It is, then, widely held by globalisation theorists that this 'new inequality' must be understood primarily as a consequence of the progressive integration of world markets, and in particular of increasing world trade, rather than of economic or sociopolitical processes operating within the boundaries of nation states and thus, potentially at least, subject to their control. The central argument here is the following. In the global economy more developed nations are increasingly open to trade with less developed nations in which unskilled labour is cheap. In these latter nations, therefore, goods of a labour-intensive kind can be produced at a far lower price than in the former, with the result that unskilled workers in more advanced societies are inevitably disadvantaged in one way or another. Either they must accept a fall in their wage level—as has occurred most notably in the United States; or, if their wages are maintained by union power or by protective legislation, then they must face an increase in their level of unemployment—as has occurred in continental European countries.

No protection against this economic logic, it is held, can be provided by the institutional forms or policy repertoires of particular nations. Competition on an ever more global scale acts as a kind of universal acid, eroding the distinctive features of the national capitalisms of the mid-twentieth century. Supposedly sovereign states have, willy-nilly, to accept the global free market and indeed are compelled, as Gray (1998: 78) puts it, to engage in the 'competitive deregulation' of their economies. A mechanism of 'downwards harmonisation' is thus in operation: 'Every type of currently existing capitalism is thrown into the melting pot'.

Moreover, as well as creating greater inequality in primary incomes in the form of earnings, globalisation is also seen as having major implications for secondary incomes: that is, those incomes that result when, in addition to earnings, taxes, on the one hand, and state benefits, on the other, are taken into account. The 'downwards harmonisation' enforced by the global economy extends, it is argued, beyond the labour market policies of nation-states to their tax and expenditure policies also. Capital will flow, and especially through the agency of multinational corporations, to those countries that are most 'investment friendly' in imposing the lowest tax burdens on firms (and their senior executives) and in giving priority to expenditure not on social benefits but rather on developing transport, communications, and other facilities in ways that will enhance productivity. Thus, in Beck's words (2000a: 4), multinational corporations are now in a position 'to play off countries or individual locations against one another, in a process of "global horse-trading" to find the cheapest fiscal conditions and the most favourable infrastructure'.

As a result, the capacity of nation-states to pursue policies that might offset greater inequality in primary incomes and in turn redress class inequalities becomes ever more constrained. Intensified global competition and the centrality thus given to productivity impose strict limits on the resources that can be raised through taxation in order to fund social welfare services (cf. Castells, 2000b: 354–55) and in effect, according to Giddens (1994: 74–75), rule out 'attempts to use the welfare state as a redistributive mechanism'. Rather than succeeding, such attempts are more likely to be counterproductive through deterring investment, reducing levels of wealth creation, and thus damaging those individuals and families they were intended to help. In short, as part of the larger process in which national political autonomy is undermined, globalisation throws social-democratic welfare states into crisis. For Beck (2000a: 96) they are 'caught in a downward spiral'; for Giddens (1994: 74–75, 140; cf. Gray, 1998: 64, 88–89), they are part of 'a now lapsed historical endeavour'.

Such arguments are advanced with great confidence and have attracted wide public attention. One may, however, still ask just how secure is their theoretical and empirical basis and, in particular, when they are viewed in the context of a larger body of social science literature than that to which their proponents usually refer. The issues in question are in fact ones that have been of interest not only to grand globalisation theorists but also to those who have concentrated more narrowly on globalisation as an economic phenomenon and to a range of other social scientists, less concerned with privileging globalisation as a theme than with understanding class inequalities or welfare state development in their own right.

To begin with, it may be noted that in their accounts of the impact of globalisation on inequalities in earnings, the authors cited above appear in fact to be essentially reliant, though they may not in all cases realise it, on certain basic propositions in neoclassical economics: that is, ones deriving from what is usually known as Heckscher-Ohlin trade theory. This theory provides an explanation of why in general, as trade becomes more open, 'locally scarce' factors of production, which are overpaid in a closed economy, will fall in price in response to shifts in demand, at the same time as 'locally abundant' factors, formerly underpaid, will rise in price. Thus, in an increasingly global economy (abundant) unskilled labour in less developed societies will benefit, but (less abundant) unskilled labour in more developed societies will be disadvantaged, with declining demand leading either to falling wages or, insofar as wages do not fall, to greater unemployment. However, what globalisation theorists do not appear to appreciate is, first, that the Heckscher-Ohlin theory is, though rigorous, a highly abstract one that holds good only under a range of assumptions; and second, that its applicability to present economic realities has become increasingly called into question.

For example, Atkinson (1999b) has pointed out that a simple two-bloc, less developed/more developed nation, model is, from the point of view of realism, scarcely defensible, and that, at very least, a distinction *within* the more developed, OECD nations between the United States and the Eurozone (EZ) would seem required. But, once such a distinction is made, what then follows from the neoclassical theory is that, insofar as the EZ takes the strain of the fall in demand for unskilled labour via increased unemployment, wage levels should be unaffected in either the EZ *or* the United States. And, further, any way of modifying the analysis so as to accommodate the fact that in the U.S. wage differentials between skilled and unskilled labour *have* widened, is then likely to carry the implication that these differentials will widen in the EZ also and that unemployment will fall. In short, the Heckscher-Ohlin theory does not provide a very satisfactory basis for claims that intensifying world trade is the key factor in explaining *at one and the same time* the declining wages of unskilled workers in the United States and their rising risks of unemployment in Europe.

Furthermore, Atkinson, among others (see, e.g., Smith, 1999, 2001) has also observed that, on close examination, the detailed facts of increased earnings inequality turn out to be more complex than is usually supposed. Thus, as well as there being wide cross-national differences in the extent to which such an increase has occurred, the increase seems rarely to have been of a sustained kind, and it would therefore seem more appropriate to think of episodes of rising—or falling—inequality than of general and secular trends (cf. also Atkinson, 1997). Again, and yet more significantly, at least in those nations where growing inequality has been most evident, such as the United States and the UK, this no longer reflects only, or even primarily, a worsening of the position of unskilled wage workers. Over recent years much of the increased dispersion has occurred in the *upper* reaches of the earnings distribution—that is, one may suppose, as a result of relative gains made by higher-level salaried employees (for the UK, see further Goodman and Oldfield, 2004; Goldthorpe and McKnight, 2006).[2]

Once these features of widening earnings inequality are recognised, an explanation in terms of the progressive development of world trade must then appear a priori far less plausible, and various alternative explanations, emphasising, for example, technological, organisational, or demographic changes or, perhaps, quite short-term and nation-specific factors, such as changes in processes of wage and salary determination, correspondingly gain in credibility.

In these circumstances, an empirical approach aimed at assessing quantitatively the relative importance of various possible causal factors would appear appropriate, and a series of studies of the kind in question has in recent years been carried out. So far as trade is concerned, the findings from such studies have in fact shown a large degree of consistency, despite sharp differences in, and debates over, methodology. In a comprehensive review paper, Slaughter and Swagel (1997) sum up the emergent consensus as follows: while the effect of increased world trade on the growth in inequalities in earnings in advanced societies over the last decades of the twentieth century has not been zero, it has still been 'only modest'. Thus, typical results would be ones showing trade effects to explain somewhere between 5 and 20 percent of this growth (cf. also Rodrik, 1997). Moreover, the position is not greatly altered if, in addition to the direct effects of trade on inequality, those possibly arising from the 'exporting' or 'outsourcing' of jobs by multinationals or from the inward migration of labour are also taken into account.

Thus, Slaughter and Swagel observe, the impact of globalisation on widening earnings inequality must be judged, so far at least, to be a good deal less than what might be expected from 'purely anecdotal evidence' or again from sweeping assertions about the irresistible consequences ever-intensifying international competition. And in turn, insofar as the relevance of trade theory is still maintained, one conclusion that might be drawn from the results reviewed is (1997: 16) 'that on balance the advanced economies have *not* in fact become substantially more open to trade' [emphasis in original]—because, say, as tariff barriers have fallen, they have been replaced by other barriers such as voluntary export restraints and bilateral protectionist agreements.

It has, however, to be said that detailed and technically sophisticated research of the kind that Slaughter and Swagel consider would appear to have had little influence on grand globalisation theorists. Such research is rarely, if at all, cited in their work and, one must then suppose, they either are unaware of it or choose to ignore it.[3]

A situation essentially similar to the foregoing is, moreover, to be found when one moves on to the further issue of the implications of globalisation for secondary incomes, and, more specifically, for the capacity of national governments to use fiscal and social policy to offset rising earnings inequality. On the one hand, globalisation theorists again seem to have a less than certain grasp of the theory on which they—implicitly more than explicitly—rely; on the other hand, there is a substantial body of directly relevant research that, for whatever reasons, but to their cost, they largely ignore.

Claims that national welfare states can no longer achieve redistributive goals because of the constraints imposed on fiscal policy by trade and capital market integration and by the increased mobility of firms and individuals relate to the 'efficiency effects' of globalisation, and to what might be regarded as the *supply* side of the political market. If these effects alone are taken into account—as is largely the case among the globalisation theorists earlier cited—then the argument that welfare states aiming at income redistribution among social classes will face fiscal crisis can be made with some apparent force. But, theoretically, it is important to recognise that globalisation may have not only 'efficiency effects' but 'compensation effects' also. That is to say, on the *demand* side of the political market, globalisation may lead to mounting pressure on national governments to raise public spending in order to provide various forms of protection against market dislocations and the increased likelihood of different social groups experiencing sudden reversals in their economic fortunes. The crucial question then becomes that of whether it is efficiency effects or compensation effects that are to be reckoned as having greater relative importance; and at this juncture theory has again to give way to empirical enquiry.

In fact, a good deal of quantitative research on this question has of late been undertaken, which can be seen as parallel with that previously referred to on the impact of globalisation on earnings inequality; while the findings are somewhat less consistent than in the latter case (see, e.g., Quinn, 1997; Rodrik, 1998; Garrett, 2000), a significant amount of agreement, at least as regards more advanced, OECD countries, can once more be discerned. Here, a valuable review paper is that by Schulze and Ursprung (1999). The main conclusion that these authors extract from the work they survey is that the extent to which the efficiency effects or the compensation effects of globalisation predominate on welfare state development is cross-nationally variable, but that a key factor in determining the outcome can be identified: that is, the form of political institutions. In societies endowed with political institutions that facilitate the *collective* representation of interests, most notably the institutions of 'neo-corporatism' or of 'consociational democracy', (demand-side) compensation effects tend to be the stronger, while in other societies (supply-side) efficiency effects are more likely to prevail.

In other words, the evidence from 'encompassing and sophisticated' empirical investigations does not bear out 'the extreme opinion, often heard in the media and from armchair social scientists that globalisation is bound to destroy the fabric of social welfare states' (Schulze and Ursprung, 1999: 344–45). The tax and social policies of national governments are not inevitably caught up in a 'race to the bottom' (see also the detailed study of fiscal regimes by Olewiler, 1999). An extended welfare state remains entirely possible and redistributive policies can still be successfully pursued, *provided* that there is adequate electoral support *and* that collective—

including, of course—class interests have an effective means of expression (cf. also Swank, 1998; Hirst and Thompson, 1999: ch. 6; Korpi and Palme, 2003).[4]

It is also relevant to add that Schulze and Ursprung, in a rather similar way to Slaughter and Swagel, are led to comment that research that finds globalisation to have less dramatic effects than has often been asserted tends in turn to suggest that claims about the extent of globalisation itself may be exaggerated. And they indeed emphasise (1999: 345) that while the economies of advanced societies are currently more integrated than they used to be, the reality at the turn of the century 'does, in no way, resemble the notion of a single and uniform global economy'.[5]

GLOBALISATION AND CLASS STRUCTURE

Globalisation theorists would see the progressive integration of world markets as a key factor in increasing economic inequality between individuals and families occupying what could, descriptively, be treated as different class positions. However, these theorists would at the same time regard the idea of class structure as being of rapidly declining value in attempts at understanding either the causes or the consequences of the new inequality. The idea of class structure, it is held, is tied to that of the nation-state, but, today, inequality, even if still viewed in class terms, must be linked to processes operating within the world economy rather than, as Albrow puts it (1996: 159–60), associated with 'the social structure of a national entity'. And, further, globalisation itself serves in various ways to loosen the connection that exists, both in fact and in popular consciousness, between economic—and wider social—inequalities and the class positions that individuals or families hold. For Beck (1992: 88), social inequality becomes in its nature increasingly 'classless'; modern world capitalism is 'a capitalism without classes'. For Giddens (1994: 143), 'Class for the most part is no longer experienced as class', but rather as a variety of constraints and opportunities—in the formation of which globalisation plays a crucial role. The more detailed arguments that are then advanced in support of these claims relate to two main themes: insecurity and mobility.

As regards insecurity, what is most frequently maintained is that, in the context of the global economy, the threat, if not the reality, of job loss and unemployment is no longer largely confined to individuals in less advantaged class positions but becomes quite pervasive. Previously, it was for the most part the working class—that is, manual wage workers and their families—who bore the stresses and costs of economic fluctuation. But, in the global epoch, salaried professional and managerial employees become similarly exposed to insecurity. Job loss, unemployment, and resulting poverty, Beck asserts (2000a: 153; cf. Giddens, 1994: 142–44), 'correspond less and less to class stereotypes'. Indeed, world capitalism is a capitalism without classes essentially because the quantity of paid labour of all kinds is 'rapidly shrinking' and we are now approaching 'a capitalism without work' (2000a: 58–59).

In this last respect, it should be said, other globalisation theorists might not go to Beck's extreme, and would see 'classless inequality' as resulting more from the radical transformation of work than from its disappearance. Thus, Castells (2000a: 290) argues that 'the traditional form of work', based on full-time employment in a specific occupation and also entailing a 'career pattern over the life-cycle' is being 'slowly but surely eroded away'. Gray (1998: 29, 71–72, 111) likewise believes that global capitalism has revolutionised the nature of work and emphasises the decline of 'the bourgeois institution of the career or vocation' and its replacement by the idea of the 'portfolio person' without permanent attachment to any particular occupation or organisation. Today, Gray holds, much of the workforce 'lacks even the economic security that went with wage-labour', so that, rather than the main tendency in class structural change being the *embourgeoisement* of the working class, as was confidently predicted in the 1960s, it is in fact 'the de-bourgeoisification of what remains of the former middle class'. All work, whatever might once have been the class structural location of those performing it, is now brought down to the same level of 'commodification'.[6]

As well as creating generalised economic insecurity, the rapid rate of change within the world economy is also regarded by globalisation theorists as a source of increasing rates and new forms of social mobility that further serve to reduce the significance of class. The continuity of occupational and class membership, both across generations and over the course of individuals' own working lives, is undermined and so too then is class as the basis of social identity. For example, Giddens contends (1994: 92, 144) that, especially as a result of the decline of the industrial working class and the breakup of 'traditional' working-class communities, fewer people now 'automatically follow' in their parents' footsteps, while greater opportunities for upward mobility from blue- to white-collar jobs mean that 'class is less of a "lifetime experience" than it was before'. Of obvious influence here (cf. Giddens, 1994: 143) is Beck's notion (1992: ch. 3) of the 'individualisation' of social inequality as in effect the counterpart to its 'classlessness'. Beck argues that although individualisation must still 'compete' with the experience of class as collective fate, it is nonetheless the case that what were formerly 'class biographies' and 'somehow ascribed' are now being transformed into 'reflexive biographies' that 'depend upon the decisions of the actor' (1992: 88).

Finally, though, it should be noted that even while emphasising the classless or individualised nature of the new inequality, globalisation theorists are much attracted to a further idea that would appear to imply inequality of—in some sense—a structured kind: that is, the idea of 'social exclusion', which, in the global age, is to be preferred to that of poverty. While the risk of poverty was experienced primarily by members of the working class, social exclusion, it is held, comes about through a variety of processes that can pose a threat to individuals and families across a wide range of class positions. Moreover, social exclusion, according to Giddens, is 'not about gradations of inequality but about mechanisms that act to detach groups of people from the social mainstream' (1998: 104), and further that it is 'not a matter of differing from others in degree—having fewer resources—but of not sharing in opportunities that the majority have' (2000: 105). The idea of social exclusion is likewise taken up by Gray (1998: 29–31), Castells (2000b: 71–73,128–52), and Beck (2000a: 50–51, 152–54) and, in the case of these authors, is linked to that of an 'underclass' or 'new *lumpenproletariat*' that is seen as a quite distinctive product of global capitalism. The underclass indeed gives direct and dramatic expression to globalisation by bringing elements of the Third World into the First.[7]

Arguments on the lines indicated are, again, ones that have achieved public resonance. But, again too, the question of their theoretical and empirical grounding is one that can, very pertinently, be raised.

To start with perhaps a rather obvious target, claims of the kind made by Beck to the effect that the inequalities of global capitalism are becoming classless if only because we are fast approaching a workless capitalism are scarcely to be taken seriously, and indeed well merit Krugman's label (1999) of 'globaloney'. Theoretically, they provide a prime example of the 'lump of labour' fallacy—the fallacy that there is only a limited amount of work to be done in the world and that, as productivity rises, the number of jobs available must therefore fall. Empirically, they are without foundation. Further, though, even the seemingly less extreme positions reviewed tend to derive from unwarranted interpretations or extensions of the results of such research and analysis as are, rather sporadically, cited in their support.

Thus, as regards economic insecurity, it is true that after the ending of the long boom of the postwar years rates of unemployment in general increased in advanced societies, though with much temporal and cross-national variation; and, further, that falls in the average length of job tenure have been recorded across most kinds of occupation, though usually very modest ones. However, this does not in itself constitute evidence that the link between class position and insecurity of employment has been broken. And indeed the findings of the more systematic research that has actually focused on this link would suggest that, while it has possibly weakened somewhat in the United States (Farber, 1997; but see also Diebold, Neumark, and Polsky, 1997), elsewhere its strength has been little affected. For example, Gallie and others (1998: ch. 5 esp.) analyse complete employment histories of a representative sample of the British workforce over a series of birth cohorts and show that for men, though not for women, some increase in worklife instability has occurred. But they also show, in the case of men, that structural factors are far more closely associated with the risks of instability than are individual attributes and, further, that it is class position that remains 'critical' so far as vulnerability to unemployment is concerned. In the 1990s, just as in the 1970s, men in skilled working-class jobs were two-and-half times more likely to become unemployed than were those in professional and managerial positions, and men in unskilled working-class jobs were three times more likely. More recent analyses (Elias and McKnight, 2003; Goldthorpe and McKnight, 2006) provide general confirmation of these findings (see further vol. II, ch. 6) and they have been replicated for various other contemporary societies.[8] In the light of such research, the idea that employment insecurity is now losing its class structural basis or that what were formerly 'class biographies' become 'reflexive biographies', expressing individual choice, must then appear as merely fanciful.

Again, there is evidence from many economically advanced societies, though most notably from the United States, that a growth in nonstandard forms of work has extended to some degree into the higher levels of white-collar employment—as, say, in the form of short-term contracts for professional staff. And there are also indications that firms are less ready than previously to offer assurances of lifetime continuity of employment even to their managerial personnel, who are now more exposed to losing their jobs as a result of downsizing, delayering, and other organisational changes that may occur in economic good times as well as bad. But none of this can be thought sufficient to give serious backing to claims that the 'bourgeois institution of the career' is now at an end or that a universal commodification of labour is in train.

One important point that such claims leave out of account is that non-standard forms of work carry very different implications at different levels of employment (see again Gallie et al., 1998: ch. 6). Thus, professionals on short-term contracts are in a far less disadvantageous situation than are routine wage workers employed on a temporary basis in, say, retail or hotels and catering. While for the latter temporary work may well become a 'trap', for the former it more often serves as a 'bridge' into better, more permanent positions.

More generally, very little evidence has been mustered, and even for the United States, specifically to show that professional and managerial careers are in decline—provided only that careers are seen as being made *between* as well as within organisations, which is, after all, scarcely a novel idea. Indeed, Jacoby (2000), starting from a rejection of Sennett's view (1998) that there is now 'no long term' in American life, reviews a large body of research that indicates that the *stock* of 'career-type' positions in the American economy is little diminished. And similarly in Britain a major programme of research into 'The Future of Work' has produced powerful evidence of the persistence of professional and managerial career structures (cf. Taylor, 2002 and vol. II, ch. 6). The extent to which understandings on continuity of employment have been dropped from the 'implicit contracts' between firms and their higher-level employees is easily exaggerated; and even where this is the case, understandings on continuity of *employability*—as furthered via appropriate training, 'planned experience', and so on—are typically substituted. Generalisations from Silicon Valley à la Castells are simply invalid.[9]

In short, while individuals in essentially routine types of work, even if white collar, may increasingly be employed on the basis of various approximations to spot contracts, this is *not* the case with the vast majority of those in professional and managerial positions. Rather than 'the transformation of work' in the global economy removing the class character of inequality, the differentiation of employment contracts persists—and, it could be said, for good organisational and thus economic reasons—and can itself be regarded as the abiding foundation of the class structures and associated inequalities that are generic to modern 'employee' societies (see further vol. II, ch. 5).[10]

The grounds on which globalisation theorists argue that the pervasiveness of economic insecurity now undermines the significance of class must then be reckoned as tenuous. But the basis of their contention that a similar effect results from new levels and patterns of social mobility is difficult to discern at all. For example, in maintaining that in the advanced societies of today fewer people than previously are found in the same class positions as their parents, Giddens (1994) cites no supporting evidence—which is scarcely surprising since little indeed could be found. Research into class mobility in these societies (for a brief review, see vol. II, ch. 7 and also Goldthorpe, 2005) has amply demonstrated that the net association between class origins and destinations continues to be characterised by a high degree of temporal stability—thus again undermining the idea of the transformation of 'class' into 'reflexive biographies';[11] and the further implication then is that any changes in total mobility rates must be overwhelmingly determined by structural effects. Such effects did in fact lead to modern societies experiencing particularly high rates of intergenerational mobility at a relatively *early* stage in their industrialisation, as men and women flooded out of agricultural into nonagricultural employment (Erikson and Goldthorpe, 1992a: ch. 3). But, so far at least, the class structural changes of the 'global age' have been a good deal less dramatic and, correspondingly, there is now a tendency for total mobility rates to level out (Breen, ed., 2004) or even, as in Britain, to decline somewhat (Goldthorpe and Mills, 2004). While intergenerational stability within the contracting working class—on which Giddens focuses—is indeed falling, this is offset by *increasing* intergenerational stability within the much expanded professional and managerial salariat.

Moreover, this development is also inconsistent with Giddens' argument, again unsupported, that class is now less of 'lifetime experience' than it was previously. The salariat is in fact characterised by distinctively high levels of worklife retention, which appear to have been little if at all affected by its growth. And at the same time, and quite contrary to what Giddens would suppose, opportunities for individuals to achieve upward mobility from manual into nonmanual employment in the course of their working lives are tending to *decline*. This is the result of recruitment to professional, and increasingly also to managerial, positions now being made directly from among those completing their educational careers and, in part at least, on the basis of their formal qualifications (see, e.g., for Britain, Gershuny, 1993, and for Sweden, Tåhlin, 1993). In sum, while worklife mobility between different occupations or different industries or economic sectors is quite probably on the increase—whether in consequence of globalisation or not—all the empirical indications are that worklife mobility between different *class* positions is actually falling. In this sense at least, class is, if anything, becoming *more* of a 'lifetime experience'.[12]

Finally, when globalisation theorists maintain that in understanding the new inequality the concept of social exclusion (complemented perhaps by that of the underclass) must become central, it has to be said that this is, once again, far more a matter of assertion than of demonstration. The idea of social exclusion arose in European political discourse (Paugam, 1996), in which context, as several authors have observed (e.g., Atkinson, 1998; Kleinman, 1998), its very vagueness has obvious advantages; and attempts to give it the degree of clarity required for its useful application in sociological research and analysis must be reckoned as having, so far at least, achieved little.

One immediate indicator of this failure is the lack of even a broad consensus on how the socially excluded are to be enumerated. For example, in the case of present-day Britain, Giddens (2000: 53) represents them as only a small minority—'5 percent or so of the population'. Gray, however (1998: 30), puts the proportion much higher at around 20 percent, though regarding this as 'a magnitude of social exclusion unknown in any other European country'. But Castells (2000b: 375–77) and Beck (2000a: 50–51, 153; 2000c: 2) would clearly regard the socially excluded as already forming a quite substantial minority in most societies—according to Beck, at least 30 percent in Germany—and one that, in consequence of globalisation, is steadily growing. For Castells, the socially excluded can, apparently, be equated with 'the mass of generic labour'; for Beck, they are those 'without purchasing power' or who are in precarious, nonstandard, and 'nomadic' work and who, through a process of the 'Brazilianisation' of the world, may well come to represent 'the future majority of mankind'.

The main problem of definition at the source of these wildly divergent estimates is, evidently, that of specifying just what social exclusion is exclusion *from* (cf. Kronauer, 1998). In this regard, reference is usually made in some way or other to a social 'mainstream', but this merely serves to expose the inadequacy of the concept itself. Thus, Giddens (1998: 103) characterises the excluded as being 'cut off from the mainstream of opportunities that a society has to offer'. However, one has then to ask what meaning can possibly attach to such a phrase, given that all of the most important opportunities—in education, employment, housing, and so on—are well known to be structured in a highly unequal way and very clearly, even if not only, on the basis of class. Just what *is* the mainstream?[13]

In this regard, it is of interest to note the findings of one of the most detailed studies to date of the nature and generation of extreme and (possibly) multiple and cumulative social disadvantage in a society highly exposed to the global economy—the Republic of Ireland. Nolan and Whelan (1999: ch. 8) emphasise, on the one hand, the 'strikingly strong relationship' that exists between being in poverty (defined in terms of both low income and lifestyle deprivation) and holding a working class position—with the high risk of frequent or lengthy unemployment being the major mediating factor; and, on the other hand, the difficulty of identifying any distinctively excluded subgroup *within* the working class that is created through the effects of early life experience, subculture, or neighbourhood. Those suffering severe social disadvantage, Nolan and Whelan conclude, are the unlucky victims of economic changes that increase the risks of such misfortune for 'the manual class as a whole', and not members of an underclass whose formative experiences or current situation set them apart, in some qualitative way, from the mainstream, even of the working class itself.[14]

In sum, rather than social exclusion being now a key concept in the analysis of inequality, its significance must be reckoned as far more political than social scientific. In understanding the new inequality, just as the old, the concept of a class structure, grounded in the differentiation of employment relations, would appear still to retain its central importance.

GLOBALISATION AND CLASS POLITICS

For grand globalisation theorists, as I earlier remarked, changes in the pattern of class inequalities and in the nature of class structures themselves play a key role in mediating between the economic and the other macro-level transformations of the global age. This point is perhaps best illustrated by the importance that these theorists attach to the argument of 'the decline of class politics'. In brief, this argument claims that while in the epoch of 'first' modernity it was social class that provided the main structural basis of politics, in the epoch of 'second', 'reflexive', or 'post' modernity that is created by globalisation class politics give way to new kinds of politics reflecting the radically different structural, and also cultural, conditions under which political action is pursued. In turn, the new forms of political mobilisation and organisation that develop, promote, or indeed compel similarly fundamental changes across the major institutions of governance, both national and international. The particular processes through which theorists represent these transformations as being actually brought about are quite diverse and some differences, at least of emphasis, are apparent. The following, however, are recurrent themes.

First, the dissolution of class structures, associated with globalisation, is taken as in various ways weakening specific linkages between class and party that were previously well established. For example, Gray (1998: 32), referring to Britain 'where electoral allegiance and class culture have always been closely and deeply connected', sees the impact of global capitalism, accentuated by Thatcherite free-market policies, as encouraging voters to abandon their class-based loyalties. Initially, the destruction of old industries and of traditional working-class communities favoured the Tories, but the fact that Thatcherism was perceived as contributing significantly to the generalisation of economic insecurity then had a converse effect—the corrosion of Tory support within the middle classes. Again, Giddens (1998: 20) argues that the reduction in size of the working classes of all western societies must lead to dramatic shifts in the class relations 'that used to underlie voting and political affiliation', if only because left-wing parties can now no longer afford to restrict their electoral appeal essentially to the working class.

Moreover, as well as former class-party alliances being thus undermined, yet wider-reaching political implications are also believed to follow from the generally waning influence of class position on experience and action. In this way, it is held, class divisions become a less important basis for the formation of social identities, and are superseded in this regard by other divisions that in the global age take on major political significance—in particular, by those reflecting what Beck (1992: 101) calls the more 'ascribed' characteristics of race and ethnicity, gender, and sexuality. It is issues associated with these divisions that increasingly shape political conflicts and policy agendas in advanced societies, and in turn it is the social identities that derive from them that become crucial to political commitment. Thus, Castells (1997) sees the construction or reconstruction of such identities as the key to new social movements, both reactive in regard to globalisation (populist, fundamentalist) or proactive (environmentalist, feminist), that, in his view, are now transforming politics in the First World as much as in the Third. Similarly, Albrow (1996: 150–51; cf. Beck, 2000a: 107) directly counterposes to 'old-style class politics' the 'new identity politics' that centre on 'the relative positions of groups whose very existence is problematized by processes of global social change'—but that at the same time offer the possibility of political action that can transcend national boundaries.

Finally, though, not only is it believed that class politics are thus giving way to forms of politics grounded in other social divisions but, further, that 'social cleavage' politics in general are now increasingly rivalled by politics in a quite different and novel mode—what Giddens (1994: 14–15, 90–92) refers to as 'life politics'. In contrast to politics based on considerations of material interests and life chances, life politics express value choices and lifestyles. The issues and conflicts that arise do not map onto old, class-based left-right oppositions (cf. Beck, 2000a: 1–2) but have a wider significance. They concern 'how we should live in a world where everything that used to be natural (or traditional) now has in some sense to be chosen, or decided about.' It is 'thinking in life-political terms' that in fact lies behind the environmentalist and feminist movements, although life politics has various other manifestations. Somewhat more specifically, Giddens (1998: 20–23, 35–37; cf. Albrow, 1996: 194–95) underwrites Inglehart's thesis (1977, 1990, 1997) of the rise of 'post-materialism' in the politics of the advanced democracies. With rising prosperity, and as the influence and guidance of tradition and custom weaken, individuals' engagement in politics has less and less to do with their economic well-being but increasingly reflects their personal search for autonomy, self-fulfillment, and meaning in their lives. In this regard, 'a sea-change in people's attitudes and aspirations' has occurred through which the contours of electoral, and of democratic politics more generally, have been radically reshaped.

I have previously sought to show that the claims made by globalisation theorists concerning changes in class inequalities and in class structures themselves have, at best, only a very uncertain grounding in the relevant social science literature. As regards class politics, the situation is somewhat different. The idea that class divisions, and perhaps other forms of social cleavage, are of waning influence on political partisanship has in fact, in one version or another, been advanced and supported by a number of political scientists and sociologists and, for some, might even count as the emerging orthodoxy in the field. However, it has still to be noted that globalisation theorists do in fact make only very limited reference to the relevant research (Inglehart being most often cited) and, further, that they go clearly beyond the authors of this research in representing globalisation as a key causal factor. Further still, they entirely ignore the forceful attacks that have of late been made on the thesis of the decline of class, or of social cleavage politics more generally: attacks that, so far at least, have received no very adequate response (cp. Inglehart, 1997, and Evans, 2000).

For example, claims of class dealignment in electoral politics were challenged in the British case by Heath and his colleagues at a relatively early stage (Heath, Jowell, and Curtice, 1985) on the basis of new quantitative techniques of a clearly superior kind to those used in previous work. It was made possible for analysts to go beyond the use of crude class (manual/ nonmanual) and party (left/right) dichotomies, and also to assess the underlying strength of class-party linkages while controlling for changes in the relative size of classes and of the overall popularity of parties (see further Goldthorpe, 2001; and for the United States, Manza and Brooks, 1999: ch. 2). A further work (Evans, ed., 1999) then brings together a series of national and cross-national comparative studies that have exploited and developed these techniques and that report findings that allow the editor to conclude as follows (Evans, 1999: 4): 'the thesis of a generalized decline in the class basis of voting in advanced industrial societies is, quite simply, wrong' (see also Brooks, Nieuwbeerta, and Manza, 2006; Andersen, Yang, and Heath, 2006).

In elaboration of this bald statement, two additional points may be made of particular relevance to the arguments of globalisation theorists that were previously reviewed. First, it does not of course follow from the conclusion reached that class dealignment in voting is *never* in evidence: what is rejected is the idea of such dealignment occurring as part of an encompassing epochal transition, whether driven by globalisation or some other force. Levels of class voting must, rather, be understood as showing both wide cross-national variation and over-time fluctuation. And indeed the longer the historical period that can be covered, the more apparent it becomes that class voting could be at a distinctively *low* level in the supposed heyday of traditional industries and working-class communities (see, e.g., Weakliem and Heath, 1999, on Britain in the 1930s).[15] Second, class dealignment—a reduction in the *level* of class voting—has to be distinguished from class *re*alignment—a change in the *pattern* of class voting. Thus, even if some long-established class-party alliances are now in evident decay, as authors such as Gray and Giddens emphasise, this need not imply that, overall, the level of class voting is being reduced. New linkages between class and political partisanship may be replacing the old (for a good illustration in the case of the United States, see Hout, Manza, and Brooks, 1999).

Also of relevance here is a significant theoretical shift that current empirical work has prompted. Because both class dealignment and realignment in voting appear to be more place- and time-specific than universal and secular, there are good reasons for seeking their explanation as much in political, as in the macrosociological terms that globalisation theorists favour: that is to say, in terms of parties' electoral programmes and strategies and of their policies when in office. The basic insight here is that class voting is likely to be low insofar as parties do not actually give voters the opportunity to vote on the basis of their class positions and associated interests (Weakliem and Heath, 1999; Evans, Heath, and Payne, 1999). Thus, even if globalisation plays a part in the general reduction in the size of working classes in advanced societies, this does not in itself entail a decline in class voting, as Giddens would seem to suppose. Whether such a decline occurs will depend essentially on the responses made by left-wing parties and, specifically, on whether, rather than seeking to *extend the range* of their *class* appeal (cf. Korpi, 1983 on the Swedish Social Democratic Party), they ostentatiously abandon class politics and aim in fact to become centrist, catchall parties. Moreover, even if it is the latter strategy that is favoured, it still does not follow that the influence of class on electoral politics will simply disappear. Even if, in consequence of such a strategy, the association between class and voting does weaken, it may well be that the association between class and *non*voting strengthens. Witness the concern of New Labour in Britain that its 'Third Way' politics could be threatened by its former 'heartlands' (*sc.* working-class) supporters increasingly taking what Swedish Social Democrats know as the 'sofa option'.[16]

Finally, as well as making it increasingly difficult to link globalisation to a general process of class dealignment in voting, recent research also throws serious doubt on further claims either to the effect that other forms of social

cleavage are superseding class as a basis of social identity and thus of political commitment or that social cleavage politics are in general giving way to
a new kind of politics expressing individuals' autonomous value choices.

Of particular interest here are recent studies carried out in the United
States and in (West) Germany, as two national cases in regard to which both
of these latter claims have been strongly pressed. Manza and Brooks (1999)
analyse data from studies of American presidential elections from the 1950s
to the 1990s and examine changes over this period in the extent to which
voting was patterned according to race, religion, gender, and class. Some
shifts occurred, but scarcely ones that would support the idea of a transformation of the political scene. Race increased in its influence on vote but
was from the first always the most important cleavage; religion, the second
most important, declined slightly in its effects; gender increased in influence
but remained clearly the least important cleavage; while class was unaltered
in its effects up to the last election covered, that of 1996, when it weakened
somewhat, chiefly as a result of the defection of unskilled workers from the
Democrat cause. Moreover, Manza and Brooks find that the *total* effect of
all four cleavages on voting, rather than declining, actually showed some
tendency to increase over time. In other words, political partisanship in the
United States was, if anything, *more* socially structured in the mid-1990s
than it was 40 years before. If, then, social identities or postmaterialist or
other value-orientations characteristic of the 'new politics' *have* become of
greater significance in the American case, this, it would seem, has occurred
without the old politics being in any fundamental way disturbed.

For Germany, Müller (1999) draws on surveys containing information
on party preferences carried out between 1976 and 1994 and, as regards
social cleavages, produces results that are yet more clear-cut than those of
Manza and Brooks. The influence of class, religion, and gender on partisanship show few changes over time—rather, a remarkable stability—even
though clear differences in patterns of party choice are apparent across birth
cohorts. Further analysis of these differences reveals *inter alia* significantly
greater support for the Greens among men and women who were born and
grew up after World War II. However, what Müller then goes on to demonstrate is that, in accounting for preferences for the Greens (or indeed for
other parties) across different classes, individuals' scores on Inglehart's own
scale of postmaterialist value orientations are in fact of little importance.
In contrast, Green support turns out to have a rather clear *social* basis—

that is, within a segment of the salariat made up of professionals and semi-professionals working in the social welfare and cultural fields, who may, Müller suggests, be less attracted to the environmentalist movement by their distinctive values than by their distinctive interests.

In short, it is again the case that the more systematic, detailed, and technically adequate the research one considers, the greater the gap that is apparent between what this research reveals and the visions of the new world order that globalisation theorists conjure up. New political issues, new political alliances, new sociopolitical movements can all be seen emerging—as indeed they have regularly done throughout the modern period. But the idea that a new identity politics or life politics is now exerting a transformatory effect and radically undermining the basis of politics in class and other long-established social cleavages finds no serious support.[17]

In the foregoing I have considered arguments advanced by grand globalisation theorists regarding the effects of globalisation on class inequalities, class structure, and class politics. I have found these arguments to be generally ill-founded. The changes that are seen as following from globalisation, insofar as they are in evidence at all, turn out to be far less dramatic, far more limited, and also far more cross-nationally variable than the authors in question would suppose; and in turn, the extent to which they are in fact the outcome of processes of globalisation becomes increasingly open to question. The critique that I have advanced does of course refer to only one aspect of theories that would regard the current phase of globalisation as being transformational in character. Nonetheless, it must, I believe, carry negative implications that are of some wider significance. For one thing, it may be asked why, if these theories lead to arguments of such obvious inadequacy concerning social class, one should expect them to be of any greater value in understanding the significance, or lack of significance, of globalisation for other aspects of contemporary social change. Further, though, my critique suggests that in the very way in which grand globalisation theories are conceived and then developed and upheld, there are at least two underlying problems that must seriously detract from their general credibility.

First, proponents of these theories would seem simply to *assume* that the idea of epochal change is a valid one to pursue. There is, however, little reason to accept this assumption. While proclaiming that such change is in train may well be a good strategy for gaining attention (and for hyping books), its intellectual merits are dubious. Historians have become increasingly aware of what has been termed 'the fallacy of discontinuity'—the conceit that 'the present is fundamentally different from the periods that preceded it' (Jacoby, 2000: 1224). It would, for example, be now widely recognised that what was once subsumed in school textbooks under such headings as 'The Renaissance' or 'The Industrial Revolution' was not in fact well understood until the idea of epochal change was in effect abandoned and attention was focused on persistence as well as change, and on change of a long-term and gradual as well as of a more sudden and abrupt kind. And for social scientists this should in no way be surprising. For the systematic study of social change from, say, the time of Ogburn (1922) onwards has served chiefly to show that change in different institutional and cultural domains typically proceeds at differing rather than at similar rates, so that societal transformation is always a far less likely outcome than more complex situations that are characterised by marked and quite possibly long-lasting leads and lags.

From this standpoint, then, the opposition that has been set up within the debate on globalisation—as, for example, by Held et al. (1999: 9)—between the 'transformationalists' and the 'sceptics' who believe that 'nothing much has changed' is seriously misleading. What can be, and indeed chiefly is, postulated as against the transformationalist position is *not* virtual stasis but rather what might be called 'normal' change: that is, change of the kind that has been characteristic of what we now think of as modern societies for several centuries—change that may occur in some respects with startling rapidity while in others only so slowly that it is in fact the degree of continuity that is most in need of explanation.[18] I cannot find that transformationalists have anywhere systematically set out the grounds on which they would wish to claim that either current globalisation processes themselves or their supposed consequences are such that the idea of epochal rather than normal change is necessary to their comprehension.

Second, grand globalisation theorists would appear to have no very adequate view of how their arguments—which they would, presumably, want to represent as having some social scientific status—should be sustained. Thus, as I have sought to show, in their treatment of a range of issues relating to social class, their use of the relevant body of social science research is at best patchy and selective and at worst simply nonexistent. A general inspection of the references and bibliographies that are to be found in their publications would indeed suggest that for most of these authors such research is not a very important point of intellectual reference—far less so than, say, the writings of other theorists, past and present, the output of think tanks, or the columns of social and political commentators.[19]

Part of the problem here may lie in the view taken by some globalisation theorists that so deep and far-reaching are the changes with which they are grappling that, if they are to be adequately comprehended, corresponding changes, amounting to a paradigm shift, are called for in the social science that is to be applied to this task. But, unfortunately, what is then said about the nature of the new social science that the global age requires is vague in the extreme. Beck, for example (2000a: 48–52, emphasis in original), urges a reversion to some form of 'dialectical thinking' that, we are assured, *'alone makes possible the sociological investigation of globality'* but that in fact remains entirely unexplicated; Albrow (1996: chs. 1 and 9 esp.) calls for a return to 'epochal theory'—likewise left as little more than a phrase; while Urry (2000) sees the need for a collection of new categories and meta-phors capable of capturing 'global networks and flows'. Rather than such self-styled *'avant garde* social science' (Beck, 2000c: 22) being taken as the key to the understanding of globalisation—or indeed of anything else—no grounds have yet been provided, I would suggest, for regarding it as any-thing other than intellectual bluff and bluster.

A more general difficulty, though, would seem to be that globalisation theorists have persuaded themselves that *cross-national comparative* sociol-ogy and political economy, of the kind that I have in fact chiefly drawn on in the foregoing, is no longer a viable proposition. Since globalisation has created a new world social order within which not only former economic and political barriers are transcended but also those of space and time them-selves, the nation-state, it is argued (e.g., Beck, 2000a, 2000b; Urry, 2000) can no longer serve as an appropriate unit of social analysis and the basic strategy of cross-national comparative work is therefore undermined. How-ever, leaving aside the manifestly question-begging nature of this position, the assumption that cross-national research and analysis must suppose what Beck (2000a: 23–24) calls 'the container theory of society' and thus en-tail the neglect of cross-national interdependencies, is totally mistaken—as is best indicated by comparativists' long-standing concern with what they know as the Galton problem and with ways of overcoming it (see ch. 3, pp. 48–52).[20]

I would then conclude, first, that the social science that we already possess does in fact offer a far better possibility than avant-garde alternatives of gaining a serious understanding of globalisation and its consequences; and, second, that cross-national comparative work is of particular relevance— indeed, is indispensable—in addressing the crucial issues of just how far processes of globalisation have diminished the political autonomy of nation-states and have narrowed down the range of variation in national institutional forms, social structures, and cultures. Grand globalisation theorists would do well to abandon the pose of 'public intellectuals' and get down to some serious reading in the journals.

CHAPTER SIX

The Quantitative Analysis of Large-Scale Data-Sets and Rational Action Theory

For a Sociological Alliance*

In sociology today, the quantitative analysis of large-scale data-sets (QAD) and the deployment of rational action theory (RAT) are not closely related activities. In this essay, however, it is my aim to show that they could with advantage become highly complementary features of the sociological enterprise, and, further, that the desirability of creating stronger ties between QAD and RAT is in fact well brought out by an examination of the main lines of criticism that each presently encounters.

For the purposes of my argument, I define both QAD and RAT in rather broad terms. QAD is taken to cover any analysis of extensive social data— though typically data collected via survey research—that involves the statistical investigation of relationships existing among variables. RAT refers to any theoretical approach that seeks to explain social phenomena as the outcome of individual action that is construed as rational, given individuals' goals and conditions of action, and that is thus made intelligible (*verständlich*).[1] Throughout the chapter, I illustrate methodological points that arise by reference to substantive work. For the most part, such illustrations are drawn from research in social stratification, not just because this is my own field of special interest but also because it is that from which examples have in fact been most often taken in previous discussion of several issues that are of central concern.

To account for the lack thus far of any special relationship between

*Earlier drafts of this essay benefited greatly from comments made by Peter Abell, Hans-Peter Blossfeld, David Cox, Nan Dirk De Graaf, Dudley Duncan, Ray Fitzpatrick, Martin Hollis, Colin Mills, Garry Runciman, Ian Shapiro, and Wout Ultee.

QAD and RAT would require an excursus into the history of sociology (cf. vol. II, chs. 8 and 9). Here, it must suffice to say that insofar as sociologists engaging in QAD have sought to relate their work to theoretical issues, they have shown no particular interest in RAT—as opposed, say, to structural-functionalism or Marxism—while advocates of RAT have been concerned to emphasise its generality and in turn its applicability in *all* styles of empirical enquiry. Thus, Friedman and Hechter (1988: 212) represent the 'agnosticism' of RAT in regard to different types of data and techniques of analysis as being one of its main attractions; and Boudon (1987) has gone further in maintaining that the 'individualistic paradigm' in sociology, by which he intends a version of RAT, differs from the 'nomological paradigm', in which the quest is for evolutionary or functional laws, in being just as apt to the explanation of historical *singularities* as of macrosocial regularities of the kind that QAD is able to display.

In some contrast with these prevailing attitudes and arguments, the position I here maintain is that exponents of QAD and of RAT could now derive particular advantage through paying more attention to each others' work, recognising the potential complementarities that exist, and in effect entering into a collaborative alliance. Although I would not wish to suggest that such an alliance should be of an exclusive kind, I do believe, and will seek to show, that there are at the present time rather specific reasons why QAD needs RAT and RAT needs QAD; and further, that the particular emphases and modifications that an alliance would encourage, if not necessitate, on either side would be ones likely to be beneficial to the future development of QAD and RAT alike.

THE NEED OF QAD FOR RAT

In recent years it has become a standard criticism of QAD that, although typically based on 'individual data', such as that collected from respondents to surveys, it tends to be conducted without systematic reference to the idea—let alone to a theory—of *individual action*. For instance, Abbott (1992a) has undertaken a detailed textual examination of what he takes to be a representative case of QAD (Halaby and Weakliem, 1989, a study of the influence of worker control on the employment relationship), and has argued that, in general, the analyses offered are couched in terms of variables and their effects rather than of individuals and the courses of action that they follow. It is, in other words, variables rather than individuals that 'do the acting'. Individuals are not seen as acting themselves but merely as being 'the locale for the variables doing their thing' (Abbott 1992a: 55–56). It may be possible, Abbott recognises, to trace a 'narrative' of the action underlying the analysis—that is, a narrative that entails the relationships empirically established among variables—which is of an *implicit* kind, but it tends to be only where unexpected and problematic results are thrown up that such 'interpretation' is attempted in any more explicit way. These exceptional instances are, however, highly revealing. They bring out the fact that practitioners of QAD do in the end accept, even if only covertly, that causality in social processes cannot be established from quantitative analyses in themselves but is rather 'logically dependent' on action narratives (1992a: 57).

Abbott's critique forms part of a more general consideration of the practices of 'standard positivist' sociology, which he evidently sees as being in need of more or less radical reconstruction. However, it has to be noted that his animadversions on QAD are scarcely novel, and what is in the present context of particular interest is that among those who have previously advanced essentially similar arguments are indeed well-known exponents of RAT who would not normally be counted within the anti-positivist camp.

For example, Coleman (1986a: 1314–315) was one of the first to observe the seeming paradox that sociologists engaged in 'empirical, statistical survey research' are largely reliant on individual data but analyse such data with little apparent concern for questions of individuals' purposes or intentions. Supposedly causal explanations of individuals' *behaviour* are given in terms either of their social characteristics or features of their environment, and without reference to any 'intervening action orientation'. The success of this approach tends then to be gauged simply by the amount of variation in behaviour that is 'accounted for', and no need for explanations to be systematically related to a theory of action is recognised. Likewise, Boudon (1987: 61–62), taking the particular example of quantitative studies of social mobility and status attainment, has maintained that in these studies 'the units of analysis are not individuals but variables'. The influence of one variable on another—for example, of education on occupational status—is presented in some quantified form and then, typically, findings of this kind 'will be considered final results'. In other words, no effort is made to show how the statistical relations between variables derive from their 'real causes', that is, the actions of individuals.[2]

Practitioners of QAD might well reply that critical comment on these lines is somewhat disingenuous. They are not, they would say, *quite* so naïve as simply to identify association among variables with patterns of social action and interaction, nor thus to suppose, for example, that a man's education 'causes' his occupation in the same way that, say, a sprained ankle would cause him to limp. And, they might go on, the reason why action narratives are often only implicit in their analyses is that they are typically concerned with testing substantive hypotheses, the theoretical derivation of which is already provided elsewhere. For example, they are concerned with investigating whether or not the association between education and occupational status is strengthening over time because such a tendency is a direct implication of a well-known theory of changing social selection under advanced industrialism: that is, a theory that holds that such selection becomes increasingly meritocratic as criteria of 'achievement' replace those of 'ascription' (see further vol. II, chs. 2 and 7). In turn, this emphasis on hypothesis testing also explains why fuller interpretations tend to be given of problematic results. Where empirical findings do not conform with the theory under examination, the provision of some alternative understanding of their generation at the level of social action is obviously called for.

However, even if such a response is justified, it is of course still one that accepts rather than disputes the central claim of the authors previously cited: namely, that QAD in itself is incomplete and that its contribution to sociology will be seriously limited unless it is allied in some way or other to accounts of social action. And once this claim is accepted, it is then difficult to deny the desirability of such accounts being in all instances as explicit and detailed as it is possible to make them. For, apart from anything else, how far QAD can serve as an effective means of testing theories of macrosocial processes will heavily depend on the degree of their elaboration at the micro-level. Thus, simply to show a strengthening association over time between education and occupational status is in itself of rather little help in evaluating the theory of an increasing meritocratic emphasis in social selection. As several commentators have observed, such a finding is equally consistent with a rival theory that sees the dominant tendency as being not so much towards meritocracy as credentialism: that is, an increasing use of formal qualifications in selection, promoted by interested occupational associations and educational bodies, and in which managements connive more for reasons of convenience than demonstrated efficiency. In other words, the two theories differ crucially in the action narratives, or 'story-lines', by which they account for the *same* empirically observed tendency. And a requirement for any useful adjudication between them must therefore be that this difference is fully spelled out so that the alternative narratives can themselves be exposed to further empirical test.

The need for QAD to become more theoretically informed has, moreover, of late been forcefully underlined as a result of criticism emanating from a quite different quarter to that so far considered: that is, criticism not from theorists who might feel unduly neglected, but rather from statisticians who have become increasingly sceptical of some of the more ambitious versions of QAD that have been attempted within sociology and other non-experimental social sciences.

In this regard, several papers by Freedman (1985, 1991, 1992a, 1992b, 1997, 1999; cf. also Holland, 1988; Clogg and Haritou, 1997) on the uses— or abuses—of structural equation, and in particular causal path, models have perhaps been of greatest impact. Although these interventions have provoked some lively debates, the main outcome would appear to be a widening acceptance, and even on the part of those using such models, of their limitations and dangers. In the late 1960s practitioners of QAD were offered the attractive possibility that structural equation modelling might serve in sociology as a substitute for experimental methods, and, by the 1980s, this approach had in fact become firmly established in many areas of empirical work. As Berk has observed, 'few . . . questioned the fundamentals; causal inferences followed automatically from structural equation models' (1988: 155). Today, however, a clearly different situation prevails.

At a technical level, the criticisms advanced by Freedman and others of causal path modelling in sociology focus on the dubious validity of the stochastic assumptions that need to be made about the distributions, individual and joint, of the variables involved.[3] In turn, much of the debate that has ensued has been concerned with just how far such assumptions are in fact breached, how much this matters, and how far any shortcomings that do occur can be made good by various technical 'fixes'. For present purposes, though, what is of greater interest is the degree of consensus that appears to have emerged on a number of more fundamental matters concerning the relationship of modelling to theory.

First, it would by now seem to be widely accepted that it is *not* in fact possible to derive causal inferences automatically from the results of statistical modelling, whether deemed structural or otherwise, nor indeed, some would wish to add, from *any* kind of investigative methodology, even an experimental one. As Hope has put it (1992: 32), in a response to Freedman, few present-day epistemologists would expect to find, in either the social *or* the natural sciences, 'a Baconian organum for grinding theories out of observations'. And from this position, causality is then more readily understood as a theoretical claim than as a directly accessible feature of the world itself.[4]

Second, it is in turn generally agreed that, far from theory being output from causal path and such-like analyses, it is, rather, necessary input to them. Thus, in a causal path diagram, the ordering of variables, at the very least, must be given by theory, and what the analysis then provides is quantitative estimates of the various effects that are taken to be operating on the dependent variable. It follows that if the theory is wrong, that is, *inconsistent with the social processes actually generating the data*, the statistical calculations will be vitiated. Freedman argues (1992a) that a model seriously intended as a structural one should be sufficiently well grounded theoretically to enable predictions to be made of the results of *interventions* in the system of variables it represents—but that there is little reason to believe that the quality of theory informing causal path models in sociology is sufficient to give them this capacity. And Hope (1992: 34) concurs: for the most part, he accepts, such modelling, 'does *not* license counterfactual claims'.[5]

Third, there appears also to be consensus, albeit with differences of emphasis, that in sociology causal path and other models that have been represented as 'structural' would for the most part be better regarded as having simply *descriptive* functions: that is, as serving to show only patterns of association, not causation. Thus, Hope suggests (1992: 34–36) that causal path analysis should be understood as attempting not to model microsocial processes per se but rather to provide a summary of their overall, macrosocial *outcomes*. In status attainment research, for example, causal path models do not tell us about the ways in which individuals actually get qualifications, are offered jobs, take up jobs, and so on, but about the patterns that ultimately emerge 'from a manifold of decisions: personal, institutional and political' and 'when all social forces have exerted their effects'. Correspondingly, Freedman would himself acknowledge (e.g., 1992a, 1992b) that, at this descriptive level, some intriguing and consequential facts about social stratification have been produced by causal path analyses, even though he might wish also to argue that simpler statistical techniques could have served just as well and with less risk of their results being misinterpreted.

The common ground that would seem to have been established within the debate on statistical modelling might therefore be summed up as follows. Even in its most advanced forms, QAD cannot serve as a source of explanations in itself. It would, rather, be better regarded as, in the first instance at least, a source of *explananda*—a means of establishing evidence of regularities that *call for* theoretical understanding. Moreover, the contribution that QAD may in turn make towards reaching such understanding will not be through the demonstration of causal processes directly. It may, perhaps, be so devised as to help investigators form ideas about such processes (see, e.g., Cox and Wermuth, 1993) but, even so, its primary importance must again lie in the provision of evidence: in this case, evidence that, as Freedman puts it (1992b: 111), can 'serve as a link in a chain of reasoning about causes' where, however, 'the causal inference rides on the argument, not on the magic of least squares'. In other words, the argument itself must be not statistical but substantive: it must be concerned not with relations among variables but with the ways in which the data constituting the *explanandum* are actually brought into being.

The distinction here taken up between descriptive and structural models is one that is in fact echoed and developed in a wider context in recent contributions by several other commentators: for example, by Cox (1990) in separating 'empirical' from 'substantive' models or by Rogosa (1992) in contrasting 'statistical models' per se with 'scientific models' as expressed in statistical form. What is, evidently, the shared concern is to bring out the difference (though without supposing it to be absolute) between applying statistical techniques, on the one hand, in what might be called a pretheoretical mode in order, as Merton (1987) has put it, to 'establish the phenomena' and, on the other hand, in order to model the processes through which—from some theoretical standpoint—the phenomena are seen as being produced.[6]

Once, then, such a discrimination in the uses of QAD is made—instead of QAD being taken as providing, as it were, *explanandum* and explanation simultaneously—the need for an independent theoretical input becomes apparent. And, I would add, the development of QAD itself may at the same time be expected to benefit. That is, through further encouragement being given to tendencies already apparent for its practitioners to break free from a preoccupation with statistical methods constructed around the idea of normal and continuous distributions and to attempt to treat their data with greater *descriptive* fidelity. The growing attraction of sociologists in recent years to alternative techniques such as loglinear modelling or event history analysis can, I believe, be largely understood from this point of view.[7] It is not difficult to show—and status attainment research using path analysis would serve well to illustrate the point—that problems are likely to arise if the descriptive work necessary to establish the specific explanatory tasksthat theory must address is not adequately accomplished *before* the modelling of causal processes is attempted.[8]

If, then, it is accepted that in sociology the uses of QAD, far from being a substitute for theory, can be properly understood *only in their relation to theory*, the question which in the present context remains is, of course, that of why such theory should be RAT. Proponents of RAT might wish simply to say that, following on the intellectual collapse of structural-functionalism in both its liberal and Marxist versions, RAT represents the only theoretical approach now on offer that has serious explanatory potential, at least at a macrosocial level (cf. Kiser and Hechter, 1991) or, perhaps, to make out a general case for RAT's 'paradigmatic privilege' (cf. Abell, 1992). However, two further arguments may be advanced to suggest the *special* suitability of RAT as theory to be utilised in conjunction with QAD.

First, as earlier noted, QAD is usually undertaken with data-sets that result from survey work or other extensive data-collection exercises. In such investigations, the amount of information that can be obtained about the characteristics of particular individuals, or about events or decisions in which they have been involved, is subject to obvious constraints, and has moreover to be elicited in a fairly standardised form via questionnaires or interview schedules. It is therefore scarcely feasible to build up information of the highly differentiated kind that might result from more intensive research, carried out, say, within a limited social milieu by means of repeated interviewing, or observational methods. However, it is a feature of RAT that it does not require accounts of individual actors or action that are based on 'thick' description. Neither the psychology nor the phenomenology of human action is a focus of analytic attention: no attempt is made to capture the full diversity of the cognitive or motivational aspects of action nor of the nuances of its subjective meanings. The primary analytic concern of RAT, at least as typically deployed in sociology, is with elucidating the micro-to-macro link: that is, with showing the ways in which a number, and often a very large number, of individual actions come together so as to generate macrosocial phenomena of interest. And no more descriptive detail or theoretical understanding is sought at the individual level than is called for by efforts to this end (cf. Coleman and Fararo, 1992; Abell, 1992).[9] Thus, what are often seen as the characteristic limitations of survey-type data are not in fact ones likely to create major difficulties in the use of RAT, of the kind that clearly could arise where attempts are made to treat individual action through either psychological or phenomenological approaches that, as Lindenberg (1992: 7) has put it, 'are greedy with regard to information about each individual'.[10]

Second, though, it is not just that the type of data usually subjected to quantitative analysis may be unable to support elaborated accounts of individual action: it is also the case that the action narratives that are typically required in order to complement QAD *should not be* ones that aim either at descriptive or explanatory completeness. Consider the kind of narratives advocated, for example, by Becker (1992), following Znaniecki (1934), with illustrations drawn from case study research in the tradition of Lindesmith (1948) or Cressey (1953). The aim here is, Becker tells us, to give, step by step, 'the story of how something *inevitably* got to be the way it is'. Narrative analysts in this tradition 'are not happy unless they have a *completely deterministic* result'—and, indeed, to the extent that 'Every negative case becomes an opportunity to refine the result, to rework the explanation so that it includes the seemingly anomalous case' (1992: 210, 212, emphases added).[11] Now one might wish to question whether deterministic accounts of action can in fact be a serious goal for sociologists (or adhocery a serious methodological principle). There are good grounds for viewing the social world, or at all events the basis of its study, as being necessarily probabilistic in character (cf. Duncan, 1984: ch.8; Lieberson, 1992; King, Keohane, and Verba, 1994: ch.2). But, for present purposes, the important point is that storytelling in the manner favoured by Becker *is simply not consistent with the kinds of result that QAD produces*. As Becker himself points out, the regularities that are established by QAD *are* of a probabilistic kind, and it must then follow that 'completely deterministic' accounts of the underlying action would lead to such regularities being *over*-explained. Or, to put the matter another way, if deterministic theory were indeed appropriate for understanding the ways in which macrosocial regularities are generated at the level of individual action, one would expect the probabilities shown up by QAD to be much closer to 1—and 'variation explained' to be much closer to 100 percent—than is in fact the case.[12]

So far as the analysts to whom Becker refers do come anywhere near to demonstrating 'inevitable' outcomes, it is, one may suggest, only because their accounts rely less on theory that has any claim to generality than on the invocation of conditions highly specific to the milieux within which their case studies are conducted. However, the regularities that emerge from QAD tend to be of greatest interest, considered, that is, as *explananda*, where, though only probabilistic, they nonetheless hold *across* different milieux, set apart in time and space and in turn, perhaps, in their institutional and cultural contexts. Thus, in stratification research, examples of such regularities would be the persistence over decades of class inequalities in educational attainment and mobility chances, or the extent of similarities in patterns of social fluidity, both across subpopulations within national societies and among such societies themselves (see further vol. II, chs. 2, 7 esp.). If, therefore, a better understanding of regularities of this kind is to be obtained, theoretical accounts with priorities just the reverse of those implied by Becker are what is required. It is generality, not determinacy, that must be sought.

In this respect, then, RAT has obvious attractions. The action narratives to which it gives rise do not, or at least need not, relate to specific actors or to specific courses or conditions of action at given times or places, but can rather be treated as narratives of a highly generalised character. Their aim is not to 'tell the whole story' in any particular case, even supposing this were possible, but to capture *common* elements or, in other words, patterns of action that recur in many cases. This they seek to do through having a structure that is implicative rather than conjunctive: that is to say, the steps that RAT narratives comprise are linked together in the form of 'practical syllogisms' (cf. von Wright, 1971) rather than just temporally. The purpose of these narratives is not to demonstrate how something inevitably got to be the way it is as, so to speak, a piece of natural history, but rather to bring out what in the Popperian version of RAT would be called the 'logic' of a certain *type* of situation (Popper, 1966: ch. 14, 1957: ch. 29, 1985; and see further ch. 7). Given that certain goals are pursued under certain conditions, the idea is to show which courses of action the various actors involved would then be expected to follow according to some criterion of rationality and, of course, with what consequences. These actions and consequences will not necessarily be observed. What is common to a certain set of situations—the underlying logic that the RAT narrative seeks to capture—need not be what actually generates action in any *particular* instance: the whole story is *not* being told. But, on the other hand, RAT would appear adequate to the task of capturing central tendencies in action and thus of providing explanations of the probabilistic, yet often wide-ranging, regularities in social action and its outcomes that QAD has the ability to reveal.

THE NEED OF RAT FOR QAD

If it is by now a standard criticism of QAD that it neglects the actors and the processes of action that generate the regularities it displays, it is a yet more routine criticism of RAT that it derives from a conception of the actor and of the nature of action that is of a quite unrealistic kind (see, e.g., Etzioni, 1988; Frank, 1990; Smelser, 1992; Archer and Tritter, 2000). Put at its most simple, the objection to RAT is that human beings frequently do not, and perhaps *cannot*, act in a rational manner, and therefore that a theory of rational action, however rigorously it may be developed from its initial assumptions, will in its actual application to most areas of social life have at best only a limited explanatory power.[13]

In more detail, it may be argued that any coherent idea of rational action must imply a certain relationship between actors' ends or goals, their beliefs, the evidence they have for these beliefs, and the actions that then follow. Actors act rationally when, in the light of well-grounded beliefs, they choose those courses of action that are best calculated to realise their goals (cf. Elster, 1989b: ch. 4). Such a schema, however, makes apparent just how rationality could at several different points be threatened and, perhaps, defeated. Individuals may not know just what their goals really are: they may be uncertain, confused, ambivalent, or inconsistent. Again, the beliefs that guide their actions may not be well grounded but, rather, ill informed, uncritically held, muddled, or just plain wrong. Further, in moving from beliefs to action, individuals may not succeed in finding that course of action that, given their goals, would be optimal for them: they may fail to consider all the possibilities, miscalculate probabilities, or indeed not calculate at all but simply act in unthinkingly habitual or impulsive ways. And, finally, even where individuals do have well-defined goals, well-grounded beliefs, and are capable of determining the best way to proceed to their goals, they may still lack the *will* to act as they know that they should.[14]

Moreover, it is not just that such deviations from the requirements of rational action can plausibly be suggested: their quite regular and widespread *occurrence* would seem beyond serious doubt. Apart from the experience of everyday life, there is by now an impressive array of research findings in the psychological literature (for a review, see Sutherland, 1992), to show that individuals do display strong propensities to fall into irrational, or at all events nonrational, thought and action in a great variety of ways.

It is, then, perhaps not surprising that advocates of RAT, in responding to the charge that their approach lacks realism, have sought in the main to argue on heuristic and methodological rather than on empirical grounds. Thus, what they have most usually contended (see, e.g., Elster, 1979: part iii; Abell, 1992) is that it is necessary at least to *begin* with an idea of rational action, since it seems only by reference to this that other kinds of action can be usefully identified; and, further, that it is when action is treated as being in some sense rational that it becomes most readily intelligible or, in other words, can most obviously be treated as something other than mere behaviour.

Such replies have force (as I shall argue further in the following chapter). Nonetheless, they might be thought in themselves a not entirely adequate basis for a major programme of theory development, and the importance is thus highlighted of a first way in which RAT could benefit from an alliance with QAD. What I would suggest is that insofar as RAT is used together with QAD—that is, in order to account for regularities in action and in the outcomes of action as demonstrated by QAD—it is possible to provide a stronger and more positive reply to those who would question the foundations of RAT in the way that has been indicated.

The gist of the argument to be made is captured by Hernes's observation (1992: 427; cf. Surowiecki, 2005) that aggregates may be regarded as more rational than their individual members, and its underlying mathematics have been well set out by Stinchcombe (1968: 67–68, n. 8)—albeit in a somewhat different context to the present.[15] The crucial analytical point may be put as follows. Suppose that in their actions in some respect the members of an aggregate or collectivity are subject, on the one hand, to an influence that bears on all alike and, on the other hand, to a variety of influences not deviating *systematically* from the common influence and bearing only on particular individuals or small groups. It can then be shown that even if the common influence is clearly weaker than the 'idiosyncratic' influences taken together, knowledge of the former is still likely to allow a large part of the variation in the behaviour of the aggregate to be accounted for. This result comes about—and will, other things being equal, emerge the more strongly the larger the aggregate—essentially because the effects of the idiosyncratic influences tend to cancel out and thus leave the effects of the common influence, even if relatively weak, as still the decisive ones at the aggregate level. When, therefore, RAT is used to provide an explanation for probabilistic regularities revealed by QAD, it is no longer necessary to suppose that all actors concerned at all times act in an entirely rational manner: *only* that the tendency to act rationally, in the circumstances that prevail, is the common factor at work, while deviations from rationality are brought about in a variety of ways and with a variety of consequences.

Consider, for example, the following finding reported on the basis of quantitative studies (e.g., Handl, n.d.; Portocarero, 1987; Erikson and Goldthorpe, 1992a: ch. 7) carried out in several different modern societies. In these societies a marked degree of class homogamy prevails and, further, the level and pattern of the association that exists between the class origins of women and the class positions of their husbands is with only small—though cross-nationally recurrent—exceptions (see vol. II, ch. 7, n. 22) essentially the same as that existing between men's class origins and the class positions they eventually obtain through their employment. In other words, if it is known how men of a given class origin have become distributed within the class structure in the course of their employment, it can be predicted, with no great inaccuracy, how their 'sisters' will have been distributed by marriage.

Now, the decision to marry and the choice of a marriage partner have in fact been singled out by critics of RAT (see, e.g., Scheff, 1992: 102) as instances of action where the nonrational may be expected to loom large; and, for the purposes of the argument at least, let this be acknowledged. However, it does *not* then follow that the possibility is precluded of giving an explanation of the above finding in terms of RAT: an explanation, that is, which would seek to show how the regularity revealed, and also the recurrent exceptions to it, are generated by men and women pursuing similar goals in marriage and labour markets alike, and thus exploiting class-linked resources and responding to class-linked constraints to the best of their abilities. All that needs to be supposed to make a RAT explanation viable in principle is that some, even if quite small, element of rationality is the *shared* feature among the actors involved. As March puts it (1978: 588), 'Even a small signal stands out in a noisy message'; or as Hernes concludes (1992: 428) 'a gleam of rationality in minds that are otherwise obscure and cloudy goes a long way in explaining what happens in aggregate. We do not always need strong assumptions of rationality in order to benefit from rational actor models.'[16]

In order to bring out more clearly the force of the argument here being advanced, it may be helpful also to refer to a contrasting case: that is, one in which a RAT approach is taken to the explanation not of a probabilistic regularity in social action but rather of a unique event—Boudon's (1987) 'historical singularity'. What has in this regard become almost a paradigm case, in discussion among philosophers at least, is the great British naval disaster that occurred off the coast of Tripoli in 1893 when in the course of a complicated manoeuvre attempted by the British Mediterranean Fleet two battleships collided and over 350 men, including the Commander-in-Chief, Vice-Admiral Tryon, lost their lives.

This event was first taken up by Watkins (1963, 1970; see also Jarvie, 1972: ch. 1; Runciman, 1983: 203–207) in order to illustrate an argument that explanation in terms of 'the rationality principle' or 'the logic of the situation' has a general validity: that is, it need not be restricted to instances where actors succeed in attaining their goals as intended but is just as applicable to those particular cases where they fail to do so and indeed where their actions 'seem more or less irrational or even downright crazy' (1970: 167). Watkins seeks to show that one can go beyond what he calls 'non-rational pseudo-explanations' for Admiral Tryon attempting the 'impossible' manoeuvre that led to the collision—that is, explanations suggesting that he was drunk, suffering from fever, or otherwise deprived of his senses. One can instead provide a rational reconstruction of the incident in which Tryon and all others involved are seen as acting in ways that, given their objectives and the prevailing circumstances, are quite intelligible. The disaster is explicable as the outcome of misunderstandings of an entirely understandable kind.

However, the difficulty here is that Watkins's reconstruction relates essentially to what happened *after* Tryon had thought up the fateful manoeuvre. It does not explain just why Tryon wished to undertake such a manoeuvre nor, more seriously, why he gave orders for it in such an elliptical and indeed perplexing form that, as Watkins's own account recognises, Tryon's subordinates were themselves required to engage in 'rational reconstruction' in order to make any sense of his intentions—a task in which, understandably, they failed. Moreover, what also remains exogenous is the fact that Tryon quite frequently gave orders that appeared designed to challenge his officers to query or defy them. One may, therefore, accept Watkins's account as plausible and in fact illuminating so far as it goes but still maintain that in explaining the disaster major weight must rest with idiosyncratic aspects of Tryon's conduct, on which a clinical psychologist might best be qualified to throw light. Considered as a rational actor, Tryon would seem to fall at the very first hurdle: that is, to have been uncertain or ambivalent as to what his objective was—to have the manoeuvre efficiently carried out, to give his subordinates a combined intelligence and initiative test, or to assert his right to their unquestioning obedience.[17]

For present purposes, the point to be emphasised is then that, *pace* Boudon (1987), using RAT in order to understand regularities in action established in respect of situations recurring within a relatively large aggregate or collectivity *is* a quite different proposition from using RAT to 'make sense' of a historical singularity (cf. Popper, 1994: ch. 8)—and a more readily defensible one. In the former case, a strong argument exists to show how, in principle, rationality in action, even if no more than a 'gleam', could nonetheless be the decisive influence in generating what is empirically observed; in the latter case no such argument can be made. Indeed, in any particular situation and sequence of action it is entirely possible—as Watkins's account of the Tryon disaster could be taken to show—that even though most of the actors involved do act rationally for most of the time, what chiefly determines the outcome is still just one expression of unreason.

The charge of an undue lack of realism in its basic assumptions is that which has been most often levelled against RAT. However, over recent years, as publications expounding and elaborating RAT in one form or another have become more numerous, a further, though related, line of criticism has emerged: namely, that while much effort has indeed gone into theory development, too little has gone into theory *application*, so that the explanatory payoff of RAT in regard, at all events, to the classic problems of sociological analysis has remained disappointingly small. Thus, for instance, Ultee (1991: 47), in evaluating the work of Dutch exponents of RAT (e.g.,

Lindenberg and Wippler, 1978; Lindenberg, 1982, 1983), has concluded that although their 'meta-analytical schemes' illustrate how central issues of macrosociology, such as those of solidarity and inequality, *might* be addressed on the basis of RAT, 'since their approach has not been linked to specific substantive questions, high yields are not to be expected in the near future'. And it is of further interest to note that Green and Shapiro (1994) have taken up an essentially similar position in launching a forceful critique of the 'pathologies' of RAT—in the form of rational choice theory—within American political science. Devotees of rational choice theory, Green and Shapiro argue, are more concerned with its elaboration than with its empirical testing; they can claim rather few instances in which the theory has demonstrated real explanatory power in regard to major political science questions; and it is suspicious that their efforts at application tend to show to best advantage in fields that are 'evidence poor'.

While such judgments might be thought unduly negative—at all events if the achievements and potential of RAT are evaluated in relation to those of other theoretical approaches—it could scarcely be denied that the style in which RAT has thus far been typically presented is such as to attract critical comment of the kind illustrated. The crucial distinction that here arises is well expressed by Hechter when he writes (1987: 55–56) that there are two possible grounds for advancing new theory: first, in order to explain, or to explain better than before, a particular set of findings and, second, in order to resolve a theoretical problem per se. In his study of group solidarity, Hechter makes it clear that his grounds are the latter; and it would be true to say that in the work of most other leading proponents of RAT a similar emphasis is to be found. Furthermore, a tendency is now apparent to go significantly further than Hechter down the road of, so to speak, 'autonomous' theory development—and in just the way that Ultee and Green and Shapiro would regret.

Thus, while Hechter does focus his attention on a specific social phenomenon, group solidarity, and aims to develop a general theory of it (1987: 168), Elster, for example, appears to have come to the view that the quest for theory in this sense should be abandoned, and that social scientists should concentrate simply on formulating causal models or what he prefers to call 'mechanisms': that is, 'small and medium sized descriptions of ways in which things happen' or 'a little causal story, recognizable from one context to another' (1990: 247–48; cf. Hedström and Swedberg, 1998a). As identified and collected, such mechanisms could come to serve as a toolbox, or depository, of explanatory devices to which social analysts could resort as and when might seem appropriate (Elster, 1989b: ch. 1). Likewise, Hernes suggests (1992: 425–26; cf. also 1989) that what RAT permits is the accumulation of models that are of a 'sometimes-true' character (cf. Coleman, 1964: 516–19): that is to say, they are capable of providing the 'inside story' or 'sociologic' of real-life action *insofar as they happen to 'match' it*. However, if a particular model does not give a good match, then another must be taken from the depository of such models or a new one devised.

Although I would regard mechanism-based theory as in fact representing a development of major potential in contemporary sociology, arguments such as the foregoing can scarcely allay fears of theory development becoming increasingly detached from central substantive concerns.[18] For as Hernes (1992: 427) well recognises, abstract models can be constructed to which 'there never has corresponded any real phenomena and never will—they are, so to speak "never-true" theories. But to make them up and play with them may nevertheless provide deep pleasure—as any journal in theoretical economics evinces'. Indeed, the reference here to economics may perhaps be yet more apposite than Hernes intended. For it is in economics that it has become most apparent that the position that he and Elster adopt creates a serious difficulty regarding the relationship between theory and research. As several recent writers on the methodology of economics have observed (see esp. Blaug, 1991, 1992: chs. 3, 4, 16; Hutchison, 1988), if theory is formulated in such a way that its 'domain of application' remains unspecified, it becomes immune to falsification through empirical findings: every apparent refutation can be countered by the argument that the theory was being applied to the 'wrong' kind of case, and the theory may then be returned, unscathed, to the depository. But the question in turn arises: if research cannot be designed in order to test theory and if the validity or otherwise of a particular line of theoretical development cannot be judged by reference to research, how are either theorists or researchers to gain any indication of what the most profitable direction and focus of their efforts might be? The crucial activities of setting research against theory, or theory against research, lose all creative tension; it is, in Blaug's apt phrase, 'like playing tennis with the net down'.[19]

If, therefore, as indeed seems the case, a real danger exists of the connection between RAT and the research process becoming increasingly tenuous and problematic, a second way may be identified in which RAT could benefit from closer ties with QAD. That is—to revert to Hechter's distinction—by its proponents concentrating more on the application of RAT to specific explanatory tasks, rather than on theory development for its own sake, *and taking QAD as their preferred source of explananda*. Authors of expository works may be justified in presenting merely illustrative applications of RAT and, perhaps, ones chosen to demonstrate its power in a particularly striking way. But if, at all events, the case for paradigmatic privilege is to be furthered, then sceptics will need to be persuaded of the explanatory value of RAT across a range of issues that are less evidently handpicked and of widely acknowledged substantive importance (see further Goldthorpe, 2004a). And they will also need to be shown how, in the light of research, RAT can in fact be evaluated against rival approaches—as well as one RAT-based explanation against another. From this standpoint, then, the empirical regularities revealed by QAD would appear to provide an especially appropriate opportunity for RAT to establish its claims: *hic Rhodus, hic salta!* These are regularities of a macrosocial character, emergent from the actions of large numbers of individuals, often over lengthy periods of time, and thus ones in regard to which RAT, with its primary analytic focus on the micro-to-macro link, should be able to show off its potential to good effect. And, as already argued, they are *explananda* in regard to which RAT can operate without the necessity for any very strong—that is, obviously unrealistic—assumptions of individuals acting always and entirely in a rational manner. In addition, though, two other grounds can be set out in favour of RAT combining with QAD in the way I would propose.

First, the empirical regularities that are demonstrated by QAD, while more extensive in space and time than those likely to emerge from ethnographies or other kinds of case study, tend also to be both more reliable and more refined than those that may be built up on the basis of, say, historical sources or official statistics or by applying cut-and-paste methods to existing monographic literature. In other words, resorting to QAD should generally facilitate the process of 'establishing the phenomena': that is, of ascertaining, before one proceeds to explanation, that there is, in Merton's words (1987: 2–6), 'enough of a regularity to require and allow explanation'. This should be a matter of particular importance for proponents of RAT, since seriousness in establishing the phenomena would seem the best way of countering suspicions that they are inclined to elaborate theory for its own sake rather than to serve specific explanatory purposes, or to set up problems in just such a way that favoured theories can be shown to be apposite—for example, by postulating certain 'stylised facts' that, on examination, may turn out not to be facts at all (cf. Green and Shapiro, 1994: 35).[20]

Second, and yet more important, where regularities revealed by QAD are taken as *explananda*, greater possibilities would appear to exist than with regularities based on other forms of data and analysis for the testing of rival hypotheses. Within the context of QAD, these hypotheses can be set against the same or similar data-sets and their performance directly compared. Proponents of RAT, I would then suggest, may in this way gain advantage from the standpoint of, so to speak, both offensive and defensive strategy.

On the one hand, opportunity is thus provided of meeting the charge that the strength of RAT explanations is often not compared with that of explanations of differing theoretical provenance (cf. Green and Shapiro, 1994: 36–38) and, further, of demonstrating the superiority of the former in a compelling fashion. As an apt illustration here one may take studies of the *consequences* of social mobility—for reproductive behaviour, patterns of sociability, political partisanship, and so on. That mobility does indeed have consequences in these respects is indicated by a substantial body of research findings: the phenomena are established well enough. However, quite different explanations have been suggested of how the observed regularities are produced. A broad contrast might in fact be made between explanations in terms of changing economic interests, resources, and constraints, which are implicitly if not explicitly RAT based, and explanations in terms of status striving, frustration, or anxiety that are of a more 'psychologistic' nature. It is usually not possible to judge between such rival explanations just by inspecting the data as presented in the form of percentage distributions or through other relatively simple descriptive statistics. But advances in modelling technique, culminating in 'diagonal reference' models, a form of nonlinear logistic regression (Sobel 1981, 1985; De Graaf and Heath, 1992; Clifford and Heath, 1993), have steadily improved the chances of making effective evaluations. And such evaluations have then proved mainly to go in favour of hypotheses more consonant with a RAT approach.[21]

On the other hand, hypothesis testing in the context of QAD would appear to offer a rewarding approach to a crucial problem of RAT itself that has preoccupied its more thoughtful supporters no less than critics: namely, that of just where the boundaries of its explanatory range should be taken to lie. As Elster (1989b: 36) has remarked, 'The first task of a theory of rational choice is to be clear about its own limits'. So far, the tendency has been to treat this task in a rather introverted way as essentially a theoretical or indeed philosophical one, and empirical materials have been drawn on, if at all, for only illustrative purposes. However, several instances can by now be cited of a more systematic empirical approach being taken—that is, an approach through QAD; and the stage may well have been reached at which, from a sociological standpoint at least, such endeavours will prove more fruitful than further resort to data-free *lucubrations de chambre*.

For example, to return again to the study of class inequalities in educational attainment, Gambetta (1987) has specifically investigated the extent to which a RAT approach would appear capable of accounting for the differing careers that are typically followed by working- and middle-class children within the Italian educational system. Applying logit modelling to survey data, he produces results that are in large part consistent with the hypothesis that these children, and their parents, are in fact engaged in the rational pursuit of life plans, although ones differentially 'filtered' both by class-linked constraints and by expectations of success in more ambitious educational options. Such a hypothesis would, at all events, appear better supported than alternatives that would see educational choices as in effect spurious, because essentially predetermined by either class structural or class cultural forces. However, Gambetta does recognise *some* evidence of 'sub-intentional' influences being also present. Both working- and middle-class children display, he suggests, 'inertial' tendencies that would seem to reflect a degree of *over*adaptation to their objective situations: that is, the former tend to be too pessimistic about their chances of educational success, while the latter are too optimistic. To this extent, then, it could be supposed that not just random, but socially structured, restrictions on rationality operate in a 'behind-the-back' way, which must in its nature lie beyond the reach of RAT. (In vol. II, chs. 2–4, various related issues arising from the RAT explanation of educational differentials are further considered.)

Similarly, Weakliem and Heath (1994) have examined—also using logit modelling techniques, though of a more advanced kind than those deployed by Gambetta—how far RAT-based hypotheses can account for the persisting association in British electoral politics between vote and class. The result is that RAT again emerges with a good deal of credit: the class-vote association *can* to a substantial extent be explained in terms either of individuals' policy preferences or of their retrospective assessments of parties' records that are consistent with their perceived class interests. But, again too, a qualification appears to be required. Some part of the class-vote association still remains that is *not* explicable in these terms and that Weakliem and Heath cannot show to be mediated by any set of attitudes or beliefs, but that *is* related to measures of individuals' exposure to class-linked 'social influence'. In other words, the suggestion is once more that a behind-the-back process, and one, therefore, that RAT cannot accommodate, is at work.

In sum, through recourse to QAD as the basis of hypothesis testing, the explanatory value of RAT, relative to that of other theoretical approaches, can be brought out and at the same time knowledge, which one may hope will be cumulative, can be gained of the circumstances and of the ways in which the limits of RAT in sociological explanation are most likely to be encountered. And it might in this latter respect be added that the recognition of such limits does then lay down a fair challenge to theorists of different orientation to spell out just how they would wish to understand the nature of the influences that have to be invoked when the explanatory resources of RAT are exhausted, rather than these being left as merely 'residual' effects.[22]

The starting point of this essay was a recognition of the fact that in present-day sociology rational action theory and the quantitative analysis of large-scale data-sets are concerns pursued largely in isolation from each other. Certainly, no special relationship between them is recognised or actively sought. Insofar as QAD has been directed towards theoretical issues, no tendency is apparent for these to be ones particularly associated with RAT rather than with other theoretical approaches; and while proponents of RAT have been among the sharpest critics of QAD for its failure to spell out the theory of action that it typically presupposes, they have at the same time wished to emphasise the equal appropriateness of RAT as a basis for all styles of sociological enquiry, regardless of the differing kinds of problem, data, or analytical method involved.

My main purpose in the chapter has, however, been to show that, especially when the nature of current criticism of both QAD and RAT is examined, it is apparent that a closer *rapport* between them would in fact be to their mutual benefit. QAD clearly does need to be informed by some explicit theory of action, at all events where it is used with more than purely descriptive ambitions; and RAT, in view especially of its claims to generality rather than determinacy, would appear distinctively suited to providing accounts of the generation of the probabilistic regularities, often extensive in time and space, that QAD has the capacity to reveal. Conversely, proponents of RAT should find in the results of QAD empirical materials that offer particularly attractive opportunities for demonstrations of RAT's capacity to elucidate the micro-to-macro link: that is, ones that relate to issues of major substantive interest and that at the same time allow extreme assumptions of rationality in social life to be relaxed in the direction of greater realism. Furthermore, insofar as QAD is thus taken as a preferred source of *explananda*, significant advantages would also seem likely to follow, both in making out the case for the superior explanatory power of RAT relative to that of other theoretical approaches and in addressing the question of the boundaries to its explanatory range that RAT must still ultimately accept.

CHAPTER SEVEN

Rational Action Theory for Sociology*

In publications that have appeared over the last two decades, a number of sociologists have sought to persuade their colleagues to become more familiar with rational choice theory, or what might more broadly be called rational action theory (RAT), and to make greater use of it in their substantive work (see, e.g., Coleman, 1986a, 1990; Friedman and Hechter, 1988; Lindenberg, 1990; Abell, 1992; Esser, 1993–2001; Hedström, 1996; Boudon, 2003a, 2003b). I am in general sympathetic to the arguments that these authors have advanced; and it may be useful here to say that I also share in

1. their commitment to methodological (as distinct from ontological) individualism or, that is, to the *explanatory* primacy of individual action in relation to social phenomena;[1]
2. their belief that a theory of action must therefore be central to the sociological enterprise; and
3. their further belief that while in the choice of such a theory, its aptness to problems of the macro-to-micro link is an obvious consideration, yet more important is the fact that *analytic* primacy in sociology lies with the consequences (intended or unintended) of individual action or, that is, with the converse, micro-to-macro link (see esp. Coleman, 1990: ch. 1).

However, the present essay does not aim to make out once again the general case for RAT. My concerns differ from those of the authors previously referred to in the following way. I start from a more explicit recogni-

*I am particularly indebted to Adam Swift for a lengthy critique of an earlier draft of this essay, and also, for helpful comments and advice, to Raymond Boudon, Richard Breen, Cecilia Garcia-Peñalosa, Michael Hechter, Rolf Höijer, Martin Hollis, David Lockwood, and Federico Varese.

tion than has perhaps so far been made that RAT is not a highly unified intellectual entity. Rather, there is a whole family of RATs and, as well as 'family resemblances', significant differences have also to be observed. In Chapter 6, I sought to show that distinctive advantages might follow from a collaborative alliance between sociologists favouring RAT and those engaged in the quantitative analysis of large-scale data-sets; and, for this purpose, I believed it sufficient to understand RAT in a largely undifferentiated fashion. Here, in contrast, my main purpose is to analyse the varieties of RAT according to several criteria that I shall set out, and then to address the question of where, within the variation displayed, sociologists might best look for the particular kind of RAT that would hold out greatest promise for them. In other words, instead of comparing RAT in rather general terms with other major theoretical approaches pursued by sociologists and in setting out its strengths and defending its alleged weaknesses, I will be primarily concerned with comparisons made *within* the RAT family and with the advantages and disadvantages for sociologists of RAT in its differing versions.

It might therefore be supposed that this essay will be chiefly of interest to sociologists who are already in some degree convinced of the merits of a RAT approach. I would, however, hope that, at least among more open-minded sceptics and critics, it could lead to a better appreciation of RAT—if only in countering the view, still prevalent among sociologists (see further Chapter 8), that RAT is no more than a dubious import from economics, and in showing that, when considered in its full diversity, RAT can be seen to have deep roots within the classic sociological tradition.

One other preliminary remark should be made. Consistently with the position indicated in points (1) to (3) above, I take it that the phenomena with which sociologists are concerned are social regularities of some kind that can be established, on a probabilistic basis, within collectivities ranging from national populations, through variously defined subpopulations, down to the level of local communities, associations, households, and so on.[2] The typical explanatory task is then to show how these regularities are created and sustained or, perhaps, modified or disrupted, through the action and interaction of individuals. As argued in Chapter 6, the model of the actor to be used in this task does not have to be one that is capable of capturing all the particular features—all the idiosyncrasies—of the actions of the flesh-and-blood individuals involved, but only the central tendencies in their actions that are seen as relevant to the explanation that is being sought. Thus, if a RAT approach is adopted, it need not be claimed that all actors at all times act in an entirely rational way: only that the tendency to act rationally (however this may be construed) is the most important common—that is, nonidiosyncratic—factor at work. The 'law of large numbers' will then ensure that it is the rational tendency that dominates. An analogous point could of course be made with respect to rival theoretical approaches, such as, say, those that would see patterns of action as being primarily shaped by individuals' responsiveness to shared cultural values or social norms. It is, therefore, on the basis of such an understanding that any empirical evaluation of different approaches must in the end be made. As Sen has argued (1986: 11; and cf. 1987), while there is little doubt 'that getting at actuality via rationality' will entail distortion, the important questions are those of how much distortion and of what kind (e.g., systematic or nonsystematic), and of whether differing assumptions about the motivation of individual action would do better or worse: 'Ultimately, the relative advantages of . . . alternative approaches have to be judged in terms of their results'.

THE VARIETIES OF RAT

How the varieties of RAT are understood will of course depend on the criteria of differentiation that are applied. Here, I will adopt three such criteria that seem to me those most relevant to the task in hand. I will aim to distinguish different kinds of RAT according to whether they

1. have strong rather than weak rationality requirements,
2. focus on situational rather than procedural rationality, and
3. claim to provide a general rather than a special theory of action.[3]

How far, and in what ways, these criteria are interconnected will, I hope, emerge as the discussion proceeds.

Strong Versus Weak Rationality Requirements

Rational action may be understood as action of an 'outcome-oriented' kind in which certain requirements are met regarding the nature of, and the relations among: actors' ends or goals, their beliefs relevant to the pursuit of these ends, and the course of action which, in given circumstances, they then follow.[4] However, from one version of RAT to another, these requirements appear as stronger or weaker.

Rationality requirements may be seen as at their strongest where they extend to actors' ends in themselves, as well as to their beliefs and the action they take towards their ends on the basis of their beliefs. It has, however, to be said that no version of RAT has gained wide acceptance in which the requirement of rationality of ends—or of associated values or preferences—has been understood in a *substantive* sense. This reflects the difficulties that have been encountered in attempts to specify criteria for such substantive rationality. All those that have at various times been formulated—and including those embodied in 'critical sociology' in the sense of the Frankfurt School—have proved highly contestable (cf. Elster, 1983b: 35–42, 1989c: 5–7). Rather ironically, what might be called the Humean view of reason as applying *wholly to means*, and not to ends, has in this way been reinforced.

Most commonly in RAT the nature of actors' ends is then regarded as being exogenous to the theory and thus unrestricted. Actors' ends are to be determined empirically, and may be 'ideal' as well as 'material', altruistic as well as egoistic, and so on.[5] Insofar as rationality requirements do here arise, they are ones of only a *formal* kind relating to consistency or lack of contradiction. Thus, in the version of RAT expressed in mainstream economics consistency in preferences is required in the sense of transitivity: if an actor prefers a to b and b to c, then a must also be preferred to c. It should, though, be noted that the further requirements that are in this case imposed—that preferences should display what are technically known as 'completeness' and 'continuity'—are *not* ones of rationality, but simply of the mathematical techniques through which economists seek to represent preferences by a utility function (Farmer, 1982: 185–87). In other words, 'economic man' here takes on peculiarities that need not be attributed to 'rational man' per se (see further Elster, 1983b: 8–10, 1989c: 9–10; Hausman, 1992: ch. 1).

It is when one turns to the treatment of beliefs within RAT, and of the relation of beliefs to action, that variation in rationality requirements of a more significant kind becomes apparent. Economics undoubtedly provides the instances in which requirements in these respects are strongest. Thus, in RAT as applied in much neoclassical economics questions of the rationality of beliefs and of the grounding of action in beliefs are simply dealt with by the *assumption* that actors have perfect knowledge and use this in the best way possible to achieve their ends—that is, to maximise their utility (or, in the case of entrepreneurs, their profit). Moreover, even where limits on actors' information are recognised, in situations of risk or uncertainty, it is still supposed that they have as much information and can calculate as accurately as such situations will allow in order to maximise their 'expected', or 'subjectively expected', utility. What is involved here remains formidable. As Simon has put it (1983: 13–14), it is assumed that the actor

> contemplates, in one comprehensive view, everything that lies before him. He understands the range of alternative choices open to him, not only at the moment but over the whole panorama of the future. He understands the consequences of each of the available choice strategies, at least up to the point of being able to assign a joint probability distribution to future states of the world. He has reconciled all his conflicting partial values and synthesized them into a single utility function that orders, by his preference for them, all these future states of the world.

Thus, whether the complications of risk and uncertainty are acknowledged or not, the issue of realism would seem bound to arise: that is, the issue of whether actors do in fact make choices according to the rationality requirements that utility theory entails. And since it has been possible to show empirically that, very commonly, they do not (see, e.g., Schoemaker, 1982; Hogarth and Reder, eds., 1986; Appleby and Starmer, 1987), those theorists who would set a relatively high premium on realism in basic assumptions have sought to develop other versions of RAT in which such requirements are clearly weaker. The key idea that has been exploited in this connection is that of *subjective*, as opposed to *objective*, rationality: that is, the idea that actors may hold beliefs, and in turn pursue courses of action, for which they have 'good reasons' in the circumstances in which they find themselves, even though they may fall short of the standard of rationality that utility theory would presuppose.

Within economics, and administrative science, the best-known example of RAT modified in this way is the theory of 'bounded rationality' that has been elaborated by Simon and his associates and followers (see esp. Simon, 1982: vol. II, 1983, 1986; Gigerenzer and Selten, eds., 2001; Augier and March, eds., 2004). Proponents of this theory argue that even where actors have complete information, the sheer complexity of situations may be such—as, say, in chess—that to maximise is simply not feasible, and it becomes rational, from the actor's point of view, to 'satisfice' instead: that is, to act so as to meet certain criteria that, in the actor's judgment, indicate that a course of action is 'good enough'. And it is then further held that where, as is usually the case, actors have *in*complete information, satisficing is unavoidable. For the question arises of how far it would be rational to try to obtain *more* information, and it is doubtful if any optimality criteria can in this respect be specified (cf. Elster, 1983b: ch. 1, 1989c: 15–17). At some point, a decision must be taken, on subjective grounds, to act on the information that is already to hand.

A further version of RAT based on the idea of subjective rationality but oriented towards more sociological concerns is that developed by Boudon (1989, 1994) and, in his most recent work, labelled as the 'cognitivist model' (1996, 1998, 2003b, 2003c). One of Boudon's main interests is in how individuals may, with good reason, hold, and in turn act on, beliefs that are objectively mistaken. A key source of inspiration for his work in this respect is the neo-Kantianism of Max Weber and Simmel and, in particular, the latter's argument (1900/1978, 1905/1977) that reasoning that is perfectly valid in itself may lead to false beliefs because it is carried out in the context of certain implicit, unexamined propositions (a priori) that are inappropriate—though perhaps far from evidently so. What Boudon then maintains is that where individuals appear to act in a way that falls short of rationality because of their mistaken beliefs, it should not be automatically supposed that these beliefs are in some way externally caused: for example, that they are, in the jargon of cognitive psychology, beliefs formed 'hot' under affective influences, such as desires, fears, or frustrations. They may well be beliefs formed 'cold' through inferential processes that, while they happen to be misleading in the particular context of their use, are in themselves sound enough. And Boudon would indeed argue that sociologists should seek to go as far as they can in explaining mistaken beliefs on just these lines. For in so doing they can treat true and false beliefs as being reached by essentially similar processes, rather than as calling for quite different kinds of explanation; and at the same time they can make adherence to mistaken beliefs intelligible in a way that it could not be if externally caused.

Finally here one other example of RAT should be noted in which the requirements of—subjective—rationality are at their weakest: that is, that embodied in the 'analysis of situational logic' as proposed by Popper (see esp. 1957, 1972: ch. 4, 1994) and developed by various of his followers (e.g., Jarvie, 1964, 1972; Watkins, 1970; Agassi, 1975; cf. also Hedström, Swedberg, and Udéhn, 1998). In this case, the aim is to understand action as rational simply in the sense of being 'appropriate' or 'adequate', given actors' goals and given their situation of action, *which is taken to include their beliefs*. In effect, then, not only actors' goals but their beliefs also are exempted from rationality requirements. What is important is not the differentiation of beliefs in terms of the degree of rationality with which they are held—Popper would deny that it is possible to justify beliefs rationally (cf. Caldwell, 1991: 22–23)—but rather the fact *that* they are held and their specific content. Indeed, proponents of this approach would argue that it can, and should, be applied to instances where actors hold, and act on, seemingly quite irrational, even crazy, beliefs—as, for example, in Jarvie's (1964) study of Melanesian cargo cults. If a view is taken of the actors' situation that is larger than, and indeed encompasses, their own, then, it is supposed, some underlying 'logic' to their action will be discovered. In other words, just as in neoclassical economics, rationality is assumed *ab initio*, even if in a much more attenuated sense. It has, though, further to be recognised that no claim is made that the assumption that individuals do act appropriately or adequately to the situations in which they find themselves—'the rationality principle', as Popper calls it—is *true*. Indeed, Popper acknowledges (1994) that, taken as a universal principle, it is certainly false. Nonetheless, its retention is warranted on methodological grounds in that it is essential to the formulation of specific explanations of action of a kind that do stand or fall by empirical tests. This last point has given rise to a good deal of puzzlement and discussion (see, e.g., Hands, 1985; Caldwell, 1991; Blaug, 1992: 231–33). It is, however, one that should become clearer when Popper's position is again considered in the following section.

Situational Versus Procedural Rationality

Within the family of RAT, variation in the strength of rationality requirements relates in a rather complex way to the further variation that occurs in the emphasis that is given to rationality in action as situationally rather than as procedurally—or, one might say, psychologically—determined.

To revert to mainstream economics, it is clear that in this case rationality in action is understood essentially as a response or *re*action to the situation—that is, a market situation of some kind—that actors face. Given their preferences, the way for them to act rationally, as it is assumed that they will act, is situationally constrained to an extreme degree (cf. Latsis, 1976). Thus, as several authors have noted, the paradox arises that the theory of rational choice *par excellence* turns out to imply that little real choice in fact exists: for, typically, the actor's situation is characterised as a 'single-exit' one. Economic man becomes, in Hollis's words (1994: 185–86), 'a mere throughput' between his preferences, which he need only arrange in order, and the 'automatically computed' choice that ensures that his utility is maximised. Indeed, for some economists (e.g., Friedman, 1953; Becker, 1976), such a pattern of choice is *so* automatic that it need not even be supposed that actors are conscious of following it or could therefore explain just what they had done.[6]

In most obvious contrast to this position is that taken by Simon and his followers. Their project of constructing a weaker but more realistic version of RAT around the idea of subjective rationality goes together with a concern to shift the analytic focus of RAT away from the situation of action to the acting individual. If one begins with the idea of objective rationality, Simon argues (1982: part viii esp.), then all conditions of interest are located 'outside the skin' of the actor; but with the idea of subjective rationality, which implies satisficing rather than maximising behaviour, attention has to centre on conditions existing 'inside the skin' of the actor and in particular on human computational—that is, information-processing—capacities and the constraints that *they* impose. Thus, exponents of the behavioural economics and administrative science that have been inspired by Simon's work start from the evidence, already referred to, that the requirements of objective rationality are rarely attained in real-world decision making, and aim to model the processes of thinking and choosing involved in such action in ways more consistent with the findings of modern experimental psychology. Insofar as rational action is invoked, they would maintain, its nature and its limits have in this way to be given a defensible empirical grounding.

Other social scientists, with somewhat wider substantive interests, have accepted this basic position, but have then sought to develop further versions of RAT sensitive to *both* procedural and situational influences and to their interaction. For example, in several contributions Lindenberg and Frey (e.g., Lindenberg, 1989, 1990; Frey, 1992; Lindenberg and Frey, 1993) have tried to provide more secure psychological foundations for the idea of subjective rationality stemming from the actor's own 'definition of the situation' by drawing on 'prospect' or 'framing' theory (cf. Kahneman and Tversky, 1979). And a complementary perspective is represented by Boudon, who, as earlier noted, is likewise concerned with the formation of subjectively rational, even if objectively mistaken, beliefs, but for whom it is also important that the psychological processes here involved should be better understood as regards their *social* determination. Boudon would thus wish to see the cognitive psychology that informs RAT being grounded in a new 'cognitive sociology' or what he alternatively describes as 'a new sociology of knowledge'. It would be the task of the latter 'to try to identify and clarify typical situations where the mental processes characteristic of subjective rationality lead to false beliefs' (1994: 247).

Finally, though, it is important to note that acceptance of the idea of subjective rather than objective rationality can still go together with a quite undiluted, and principled, commitment to situational determinism. This is demonstrated by the position taken up by Popper and the analysts of situational logic.

For Popper it is vital to establish that a commitment to methodological individualism in no sense entails a commitment to 'psychologism': that is, to the view that any social science must ultimately be based on, and reducible to, the operation of 'psychological laws of "human nature"' (see esp. 1966: ch. 14, 'The Autonomy of Sociology', also 1976a: 101–104, 1994; cf. Agassi, 1975). To the contrary, the model of the individual actor employed in the social sciences should, so far as 'internal' characteristics are concerned, be a minimal one, and the rationality that is taken to characterise this actor calls for little, if any, psychological elaboration. From this standpoint, then, no great interest need attach to the computational issues on which Simon focuses, nor indeed to any other aspects of the psychological functioning of individuals. What is important is not actors' mental states or processes but the nature of the beliefs or, as Popper would rather have it, of the (objective) *knowledge* that is situationally available to them and in which their (subjective) understanding is anchored (see esp. 1972, 1976a). The rationality principle, the principle that actors do act appropriately or adequately in the situations in which they find themselves, then simply serves—and is indeed sufficient—to 'animate' the analysis (Popper, 1994: 169): that is, to enable it to be seen why the action taken does indeed follow from what the analysis has revealed about actors' goals and about the constraints and possibilities of their situation, relevant knowledge *y compris* (cf. Langlois, 1986: 229–31). Or, to adopt the idiom favoured by von Wright (1971, 1972), one could say that the rationality principle ensures that a 'practical syllogism' is in fact carried through.[7]

It should therefore be now more apparent why Popper does not seek to defend the rationality principle empirically but rather on methodological grounds (cf. Farr, 1985). Its methodological significance is that, in being substantively 'almost empty', it requires that it is the situation of action that becomes the focus of attention: 'that we should pack or cram our whole theoretical effort, our whole explanatory theory, into an analysis of the situation' (Popper 1994: 169–71). And it is, then, to what follows from this effort, rather than to the rationality principle that directs it, that empirical tests are applicable and that should 'take the strain' if these tests are unfavourable (cf. also Farmer, 1992).

A General Versus a Special Theory

The two criteria so far considered thus generate wide differentiation within the family of RAT, and they would, moreover, appear to be directly crosscut by the third criterion still to be introduced: that is, that of the extent to which versions of RAT aim to provide a general rather than a special theory of action.

Limits to the explanatory scope of RAT are reached, by definition, wherever the concept of action itself appears as inappropriate and gives way to that of behaviour that must be externally explained: that is, in psychological or biological terms that do not entail any reference to actors' intentions. But the further issue of relevance here is that of how far different forms of RAT recognise yet narrower limits resulting from the existence of types or domains *of action* in regard to which, however, the concept of rationality offers little explanatory purchase. It is again convenient to begin with RAT as found within economics: not, though, in this respect as representing an extreme case but rather as illustrating in itself more or less the full range of possibilities.

Numerous examples could be cited from the history of economics of attempts to define the scope of RAT, as expressed in economic analysis, by reference to certain domains of action characterised in terms of motivation or of institutional context. Thus, economic analysis is said to apply to action that is directed towards the pursuit of wealth or to the satisfaction of material needs and wants, or again to action that occurs within systems of exchange based on money and markets. In all these instances, then, economics is treated as, in Hausman's (1992) phrase, 'a separate science', and RAT in turn as a special theory.

However, the development of more ambitious claims can be traced back

at least to Robbins (1949: ch. 1 esp.), who explicitly rejects any 'classificatory' approach to the delimitation of economic analysis. Such analysis, he
argues, should be seen as applying not to particular domains of action but
rather to particular *aspects* of action *in general*. It applies, in his view, wherever questions arise of the relation of means to ends or, more exactly, of 'the
disposal of scarce means' which have 'alternative uses'—that is, which could
be used in order to satisfy competing ends. In other words, RAT, as deployed
by the economist, is the appropriate theory of action in all circumstances in
which such 'economising' is entailed; it has no restriction to action occurring
within economic relations or institutions as conventionally understood.

The tendency here apparent towards 'economics imperialism' can then
be seen as reaching its culmination in the work of Becker (see esp. 1976).
For Becker, RAT, and indeed RAT in the form of utility theory, is capable
of serving as a quite general theory of social action, which is just as applicable to the explanation of, say, crime, church attendance, or suicide as
of consumption patterns or share dealings. *All* social action can be viewed
from the standpoint of individuals maximising their utility from a stable set
of preferences and accumulating optimal amounts of information and other
inputs to the multiple markets, monetised or not, in which they are involved.
Where action appears to deviate from the expectations of utility theory,
little is gained, Becker would argue, from resorting to explanations in terms
of irrationality, cultural tradition, value commitment, value shifts, and so
on—just as might seem convenient. For such explanations are essentially
ad hoc and indeed often contradictory. In contrast to those that derive from
a theory of rational action, they lack a coherent basis, and the question is
left unanswered of just why human action should be sometimes rational but
sometimes not. Where seemingly anomalous findings arise, therefore, the
better strategy is simply to reanalyse the situation on the assumption that
some feature of it was initially misunderstood.

Other versions of RAT may be identified that also seek to provide a
generalisation of economics but that appear somewhat less imperialistic in
that they are to a greater degree influenced by behavioural economics of the
kind pioneered by Simon. For example, Frey (1992) has sought to show that
such economics, as informed by cognitive psychology and also by social-
psychological theories of perception and learning, can be developed into a
'science of human behaviour' of a quite comprehensive kind (cf. also Hirshleifer, 1985; Lindenberg, 1990). However, perhaps the position that can in

this respect be most interestingly set alongside Becker's is that of Popper and the Popperians.

For Popper, the analysis of situational logic is certainly an approach to be followed in all the social sciences—and in the humanities, too, insofar as the explanation of action is involved. At one point Popper does in fact state that his aim is that of generalising utility theory (1976a: 117–18). None-theless, it is clear that he would at the same time wish to trace back the origins of his approach to the hermeneutic tradition of textual scholarship and historiography (1972: ch. 4; cf. Farr, 1983, 1985), and such origins are strongly indicated in the way in which generality is sought, in particular, the accommodation of action that is not, at first blush, readily understood as ra-tional. The weakening, or 'emptying', of the concept of rationality in the way that was earlier noted can be seen as a direct application of the 'principle of charity' in interpretation that characterises the hermeneutic tradition. That is to say, observed action is as far as ever possible to be 'reconstructed' *as* rational, in the situation in which it occurs, so that it may in turn be rendered intelligible—*verständlich*—rather than being left to explanation of a merely external kind.

Finally, though, while all efforts made to apply RAT across the social sciences, and beyond, reflect the evident appeal of moving towards a more unified theory of action, it has also to be noted that, of late, a greater aware-ness would seem to have emerged among its proponents of the need to recog-nise its explanatory limits: that is, not only in regard to (subintentional) behaviour but, further, in regard to (intentional) action that still cannot usefully be brought under the rubric of rationality. Thus, Boudon, who rep-resents his 'cognitivist model' as an extended form of RAT (1996, 1998, 2003b), would still acknowledge that 'hot'—that is, emotionally charged—processes as well as 'cold' ones can and do lead to mistaken beliefs and ac-tion based thereon. And again Coleman, who grounds his major theoretical work (1990) in RAT and, implicitly, draws on its varieties in a quite eclectic fashion, does nonetheless at various points give an important place to modes of action that lie beyond its explanatory range, in particular in the formation of trust relations and of 'social capital' more generally.

In other words, although these authors are much concerned to show that RAT *can* provide compelling accounts of many social phenomena not usually thought of as exhibiting rationality in action—for example, magic and ideologies, panics, mob violence, and revolutions, or indeed the forma-

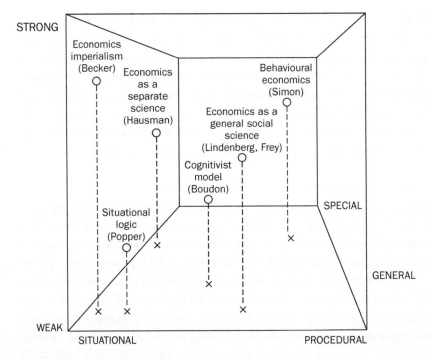

Figure 7.1. Varieties of RAT

tion of the normative structures to which other theories of action appeal—they would still in the end accept that RAT can be no more than a special theory. Thus, rather than striving in the manner of the followers of Becker or Popper, *always* to find *some* way of 'saving' action as rational, they would in effect take up a position that has been somewhat more openly expressed by Elster (1989b, 1993; cf. also Fararo, 1996): that is, that RAT should be viewed not as itself constituting a general theory of action but rather as being that currently available special theory around which the effort to achieve greater generality could best be organised.

WHICH RAT FOR SOCIOLOGY?

The outcome of the foregoing analysis of the varieties of RAT can be graphically, if somewhat crudely, represented as in Figure 7.1. I turn now to the question of where, within the 'space' of the variation thus displayed, the interest of sociologists could best focus, and in this regard I assume two desiderata. Sociologists should be looking for the kind of RAT that (1) can offer greatest explanatory power in regard to action generating social regularities via the micro-to-macro link but that (2) will be most likely, where its explanatory power fails, to promote further research through 'progressive problem shifts' rather than merely defensive 'immunisation stratagems' (cf. Lakatos, 1970). I will proceed by reference to the same three criteria of differentiation as previously used, although, as will become apparent, evaluations made from one to another are not always independent.

Strong Versus Weak Rationality Requirements

Versions of RAT that impose the strong requirements of objective rationality are attractive in that they allow clear predictions to be made about how actors will—or indeed *should*—act in given situations. Economists appear irrevocably committed to such strong forms of RAT in which the positive and the normative are in effect combined. As Hausman has remarked (1992: 278), the methodological distinctiveness of their discipline would appear to be dependent on such theory. However, from a sociological standpoint, two major disadvantages arise. First, and as previously noted, the assumptions involved appear unrealistic and indeed in various respects empirically untenable. Second, where these versions of RAT fail, problem shifts are not typically recognised of a kind that would seem likely to guide sociological research onto more promising lines.

For example, in the face of action that evidently does not conform to the criteria of rationality that are imposed, one response is simply that of postulating hitherto unrecognised features of the situation—unobservable 'psychic' income or costs seem a favourite option (e.g., Becker, 1976: 7, 11)—which, once taken into account, render the action rational after all. Thus, rather than the theory stimulating further research of any kind, it is in effect closed, and would appear to degenerate into little more than a set of tautologies.[8]

Alternatively, if action is accepted as truly anomalous, it has then to be accounted for in terms of 'residual categories', the inadequacies of which, at least for purposes of sociological analysis, were classically exposed by Parsons (1937: ch. 2 esp.). Only two possibilities appear to exist. One is for the action in question to be treated as *irrational*—that is, as action that has *failed to be* rational as a result of 'ignorance or error' (themselves left unexplained). In effect, the emphasis is here shifted from the positive to the normative character of the theory, and it is the actor, not the theory, that is deemed to be 'wrong'. The other possibility is for the action to be reconstrued simply as behaviour that is then to be explained externally by reference to nonsocial aspects of the situation, notably 'heredity and environment'. But in this way the scope for a *verstehende* sociology is severely, though arbitrarily, reduced. Not only is no conceptual space allowed for action of a nonrational kind, but neither for action that, while not rational by the criteria imposed, could still be open to interpretation—that is, could be made intelligible—as rational in the circumstances in which it occurred.

There would therefore seem little doubt that sociologists will be best served by some version of RAT that is weaker than that of mainstream economics in requiring only subjective rationality: that is, a version that treats as rational both holding beliefs and acting on these beliefs where actors have 'good reasons' for so doing. However, the crucial question that then of course arises is that of how, once the standard of objective rationality is dropped, 'good reasons' are to be understood. RAT in its stronger forms may unduly limit the possibilities for *verstehen*; but problems can also be created if, in the attempt to make action intelligible as subjectively rational, the principle of charity in interpretation is stretched too far. Thus, with Popperian analyses of situational logic and the abandonment of any concern with the rationality of beliefs, the threat of a lapse into tautology again all too clearly looms (Gibson, 1976). And even where empirical tests of such analyses can be specified, it may still often be difficult to know (cf. Hollis: 1987: 187–88) just how far the rationality in action that is reconstructed does indeed reflect reasons that were actually operative—or merely the ingenuity of the analyst.

One may, then, agree with Boudon (1994: 254–55) that the most appropriate basis for RAT in sociology will be a conception of the—subjective—rationality of actions and of related beliefs that has requirements of an intermediate strength. But what must of course in this case be further provided is some means of defining the bounds of this conception: that is, not merely via a formal typology of action but via criteria that can be applied so as to determine just which of empirically ascertained modes of action are and are not comprised.

This is a crucial but far from easy task, and one that I do not claim here to accomplish in any definitive way; much will in any event depend on how well proposed solutions fare in actual research practice. However, as a starting point, I would suggest that one should hold on to the idea of rational action as being outcome oriented or 'consequentialist' (cf. Elster, 1991), in the sense that it derives from some kind of cost-benefit evaluation made by actors of the different courses of action that are available to them relative to their goals (whatever the nature of these might be). Such evaluation need not be conducted entirely explicitly or continuously, let alone correctly from an objective point of view; but it should at all events be sufficient to ensure that actors have a capacity to respond appropriately, as they would see it, to their situation of action and to changes therein, and to the trade-offs that arise between one possible course of action and another. In turn, then, non-rational action may be identified in that its evaluation in these terms either does not occur or is overridden by other kinds of motivation.

For example, with the purely typological distinction between rational and 'traditional' action (cf. Weber, 1922/1968: 24–26), a problem arises if patterns of action that are grounded in cultural tradition appear at the same time to possess a clear underlying rationality. For example, in studies of peasant societies traditional agricultural practices have often been represented as providing effective solutions to various problems of socioeconomic organization. However, what could in such cases be taken as the key consideration is whether these patterns of action are adaptable to situational change. If in the face of change that erodes their former effectiveness they are nonetheless maintained simply because this is what tradition itself demands—because 'this is what has always been done'—and regardless of the fact that the achievement of recognised goals is thus frustrated, then attempts at rational reconstruction would appear misguided. The degree of charity required becomes self-defeating.[9]

Likewise, the distinction between rational action and action that expresses adherence to a social norm may prove difficult to implement in that action of the latter kind could itself be rational: that is, where it follows from an assessment of costs and benefits in terms of the sanctions, negative and positive, that are associated with a norm. And here too then the decisive issue could be seen as that of how far the action in question is open to modification in the light of its probable consequences and of those of other courses of action that are available, or that become available as the situation of action changes. If the degree of actors' commitment to a norm, or underlying value, unconditionally dominates what would otherwise have been their choice of action on the basis of comparative cost-benefit evaluations, so that they comply with the norm to their recognised (net) cost, then it would again seem best to acknowledge that the limits of the applicability of RAT are reached. Attempts at saving such action as rational, that is, at making it appear outcome oriented, could no doubt be envisaged: for example, by interpreting it as having the ultimate goal of maintaining actors' integrity, identity, or self-image. But to resort thus to an understanding of rationality in terms of what Coleman (1990: ch. 19) has called the individual's 'internal action system', or of 'multiple selves', while of evident fascination for philosophers, would seem likely to create far more problems than it solves so far as RAT in sociology is concerned, and especially if it is kept in mind that the *explananda* here are typically regularities evident in or deriving from action on the part of large numbers of individuals.[10]

What the instances considered above have in common is that they relate to modes of action that are not usefully treated as rational in that actors in effect accept ideational constraints on their ability to respond to their situation in ways that they could appreciate as being to their advantage. While intentionality has clearly to be recognised, the determination of such action comes into conflict with the idea of rationality insofar as, to adapt an argument from Sen (1977, cf. also 1986), a wedge is driven between actors' personal *choices* and their personal *welfare* (and even if the latter is allowed to entail more than simple self-interest).[11]

An approach on the lines indicated is clearly open to both refinement and extension. But, by pursuing it, sociologists have the possibility of developing a version of RAT, based on 'intermediate' rationality requirements, that can claim ample explanatory scope while at the same time being protected against the damaging consequences of either tautological closure or a resort to residual categories of a too capacious kind.[12]

Situational Versus Procedural Rationality

In regard to the strength of rationality requirements, a strategy of the *via media* can then be advocated. However, when one turns next to the issue of whether, in the sociological application of RAT, attention should focus on situational or on procedural rationality, such a strategy appears a good deal less appropriate. Here in contrast, the strong case, I would believe, is that in favour of sociologists taking up a rather extreme position: that is, one well towards the 'situational' end of the range of variation that was earlier described.

The more negative side of this case has in fact already been made by various authors, drawing on the basic insight of Popper—or indeed of Weber—that sociological explanation, even when grounded, as it should be, in individual action, does not have to depend on any elaborated psychology of the acting individual.[13] As earlier remarked (ch. 6, n. 10), Lindenberg (1985, 1990) has usefully distinguished between the concepts of $individual_1$, appropriate to psychology where both analytic and explanatory primacies lie at the individual level, and $individual_2$, appropriate to sociology (or economics) where explanatory primacy is again at the individual level—via the principle of methodological individualism—but analytic primacy shifts to the aggregate, or macro-, level. And others have then gone perhaps further than would Lindenberg himself in maintaining, on essentially Popperian lines, that in the context of RAT $individual_2$ should remain 'psychologically anonymous'. That is to say, the model of the rational actor should be endowed with no more than the minimum 'inside-the-skin' attributes necessary for the explanatory purposes in hand—most obviously, of course, some capacity for rational action (see further Chapter 8). Little explanatory advantage is to be gained if lower-level processes invoked in order to account for higher-level regularities are themselves of a yet more complex character (cf. Coleman and Fararo, 1992; Stinchcombe, 1993).

More positively, however, it could also be argued that a version of RAT with a situational rather than a procedural emphasis is particularly appropriate for sociology—at all events once the requirement of objective rationality is abandoned. The question that then arises is that of just how action may fall short of the objective standard, but in such a way that it is still open to understanding as subjectively rational. For Simon, given his 'inside-the-skin' preoccupations, it is above all the limitations of human information-processing capacities that preclude objective rationality, and actors are thus subjectively rational when they do the best they can in the face of these limitations: that is, by aiming to satisfice rather than to maximise. For Popper, in contrast, objective rationality is primarily constrained by deficiencies in information—or knowledge—per se, and actors are subjectively rational when they do the best they can in the light of beliefs derived from the knowledge that is situationally available to them.

Thus, while Simon's procedural concerns direct research attention to aspects of individual psychology, Popper's situational concerns lead to clearly more sociological questions. The former approach may well be apt to the study of relatively formal decision making as, say, by business or administrative leaders—to which Simon and those influenced by him have indeed chiefly devoted their efforts. But the latter approach would appear that better suited to understanding central tendencies in the kinds of decision that are made, usually of course in a far less formal and explicit way, by individuals in the course of their everyday lives, and that sociologists pursuing RAT are in turn likely to invoke as the basis of their explanations of emergent macrosocial regularities: for example, such decisions as whether to leave school or to stay on (see further vol. II, chs. 2–4), to get married and to whom, to have children and how many, to vote for this party rather than that, to participate in a voluntary association or social movement, to engage in a criminal activity, and so on.

Boudon, as earlier noted, urges the need for an understanding of subjective rationality that is supported by both cognitive psychology and a new cognitive sociology. It may, however, be further remarked that of the many illustrations that Boudon (1994, 1996) gives of his argument, it is those where objective rationality can be seen to be restricted by situational limits on knowledge, rather than by failures purely in information processing, that appear to carry the larger sociological significance. This is so, I would suggest, because inferential errors of the latter kind, at least as they arise in everyday life, will tend to be more readily corrected, simply by processes of social learning, than will those of the former kind that have a structural basis (cf. Elster, 1983b: 144–48).[14]

In short, I would believe that Abell (1992: 198; cf. Friedman and Hechter, 1988) is right in maintaining that, for sociologists wishing to comprehend subjective rationality, the modelling of actors' 'information environments' must be of primary concern: that is, unlike (most) economists, sociologists should aim to treat the information available to actors as a product of the social relations in which they are involved. Abell's position, it may be added, is thoroughly Popperian, not just in his effective underwriting of Popper's methodological injunction to 'pack or cram' as much explanatory effort as possible into the analysis of the situation of action but again in his recognition that the social structuring of knowledge is a no less important aspect of that situation than the structuring of other resources of, say, a material kind.[15] And where such comprehensive situational analysis is achieved, it could well be that the Popperian conclusion will in turn be found to hold good: that the need for sociologists to address questions of procedural rationality at the level of individual psychology is rather slight.

Finally, the point should here be made that while explanations of action in terms of situational rationality take the form of reconstructions *ex post actu*, rather than entailing predictions, this in no way precludes their testing or indeed their refutation. To the contrary, it may be seen as a further advantage of a focus on situational rather than procedural rationality that it leads to explanations that are preeminently open to criticism on grounds of fact and of logic alike. On the one hand, the analysis of situations of action depends, as Koertge (1975: 445) has put it, on 'independent evidence for each component', with special importance attaching to the empirical grounds for any 'unorthodox utilities' that may be attributed to actors; and claims thus made would seem more readily challenged than 'psychological hypotheses' about actors (cf. also Latsis, 1976: 22; Tsebelis, 1990: 40), especially where large numbers are involved. On the other hand, the attribution of rationality to actors that 'animates' situational analyses can, as earlier noted, be regarded as the completion of a practical syllogism which may in turn be questioned, and again without reference to mental states. A critic could accept the description provided of the situation of action but still seek to show that the actors involved could, just as rationally, have acted in some other way to that observed—that is, that the situation was not a 'single-exit' one and that the explanation offered is at all events incomplete; or, more radically, that the syllogism advanced is in some respect flawed, so that no adequate basis is in fact provided on which the observed action can be comprehended as rational—that is, that a new analysis must be essayed.[16]

A General Versus a Special Theory

The foregoing does then in some large part predetermine the view that I take on the question of whether RAT should be considered as a general or a special theory of action. If one argues, as I have done, that sociologists should opt for a version of RAT that refers to action that can be treated as subjectively rational, but with full recognition then being made of the need to delimit what shall count as such action and to focus enquiry on its situational understanding, it obviously follows that RAT in such a version will be a special theory. Certain modes of action, as well as externally caused behaviour, must be seen as lying outside its scope. There is, however, one important challenge that can be raised against this position that I should address, and one important qualification to it that I would myself wish to make.

As earlier noted, accepting RAT as a special theory of action avoids the difficulties encountered by versions that claim generality when forced by anomalous findings into either tautology or a reliance on dubious residual categories. But, as was also noted, if RAT is viewed as only a special theory, then the question can be seriously pressed, as, for example, it is by Becker (1976: 14), of just why action should be 'compartmentalised' so that it is sometimes viewed as rational but sometimes not.

The most promising approach to a solution is, I believe, for exponents of RAT to seek to avoid merely ad hoc appeals to varieties of nonrational action by developing the capacity of their theory actually to explain under what conditions such action is likely to occur in sociologically significant ways. A valuable lead in this regard is given by Hechter (1994). Action that follows from an unconditional commitment to 'immanent' as opposed to 'instrumental' values is, Hechter argues, most likely to cut across patterns of rational action where immanent values are neither universal (e.g., biologically determined) nor merely idiosyncratic but, rather, distributed non-randomly among populations—as, say, in relation to class, ethnicity, or gender. Research should then focus on the processes of action—which may themselves be open to interpretation as rational—through which heterogeneous values come to be thus distributed and in turn, perhaps, institutionalised into normative structures.

It is of particular interest that the way in which Hechter would thus treat what he refers to as the 'interference' of value commitments in rational action runs essentially parallel to that in which Boudon would treat the deviation of subjectively rational action from objective standards. That is, instead of seemingly anomalous action being accommodated ad hoc, the aim is to 'endogenise' it through a genuine theoretical development. And, as Hechter implies (1994: 320), insofar as this can be achieved, the challenge can then be thrown back to critics such as Becker to likewise endogenise the manipulation of utility functions to which they *in extremis* are inclined to resort.

Hechter's paper can also serve to introduce the qualification that I would make to the idea of RAT as a special theory of action. Although RAT should be thus regarded, it can at the same time, I would argue, claim to be a *privileged* theory: that is, not just one theory of action among others but rather *the* theory with which attempts at explaining social action should start and with which they should remain for as long as possible (cf. Abell, 1992; Boudon, 1994, 2003b). Thus, it is from this standpoint entirely appropriate that Hechter should pose his problem as being that of the 'interference' that in certain social contexts value-committed action creates.

In fact, most proponents of RAT, in whatever version, would implicitly or explicitly share in this view, even if not always on the same grounds. And it is then in this respect that they are brought together in sharpest conflict with proponents of other theories of action who are led to maintain a more or less contrary position: that is, that it is nonrational action, for example, action guided by values and social norms or prompted by emotions, on which explanatory effort should in the first instance focus, with rational action then being treated as itself a derivative of certain normative and affective conditions (see esp. Etzioni, 1988: 90–92, 152; also Denzin, 1990; Scheff, 1992). As stated at the outset, it is not my intention in this essay to become involved in the general debate over RAT. So although I regard this latter line of argument as quite uncompelling, I shall here respond to it only indirectly in seeking to restate the case for the privilege of RAT in the version that I would see as having greatest attraction for sociologists. This case comprises three different though connected points.

First, it may be held that the very idea of rational action is *prior to* that not only of irrational but also of nonrational action. Rational action is action of a kind in which certain requirements are met regarding the nature of, and the relations among, actors' ends, their beliefs, and the courses of action that they in fact follow. Just as, then, stronger and weaker conceptions of rationality are defined as these requirements are made more or less demanding, so are departures from particular conceptions of rationality to be defined in terms of certain associated requirements not being met. In other words, we need some idea of rationality in action as setting a pattern that may or may not be followed before we can talk about irrational or nonrational action: the latter only 'make sense', as Elster has put it (1979: 154; cf. 1989c: 28–30), 'against a background of rationality' (cf. also Davidson, 1976, 1980). How we might proceed the other way around is difficult to envisage, and it can thus be claimed that other theories of action in effect derive their conceptual basis from RAT.

Second, this conceptual privilege is linked to what might be called hermeneutic privilege. Here the argument is that, whether as social scientists or

indeed as social actors ourselves, we can best say that we understand the action of others—that it becomes intelligible to us—when we can construe this
action as rational. Thus, as Hollis has expressed it (1987: 6–9), it is through
the category of rationality, rather than through the vaguer one of 'meaning',
that the problem of 'other minds' and, in turn, that of 'other cultures' can be
most effectively approached. It is rationality 'which lets us make most objective yet interpretive sense of social life'. Any *verstehende* sociology must
then crucially rely on RAT, and especially on a version that invokes subjective rather than objective, and situational rather than procedural rationality.
Where observed social regularities can be ultimately accounted for in terms
of actors pursuing their goals as best they know how in the situations in
which they find themselves, we can claim that the action and interaction
involved is intelligible to us in a fuller sense than if, say, we are forced in the
end (as we may be) to appeal to actors' unreflective conformity to tradition
or to their unyielding value commitments. For in these latter cases—at all
events if we are not ourselves under the sway of the traditions or values in
question—problems of interpretative understanding still obviously remain
(cf. Weber, 1922/1968: 6–7; cf. Tsebelis, 1990: 44–45).

Third, the hermeneutic privilege of RAT can be connected with a further
claim of explanatory privilege: that is, a claim as regards *erklären* as well as
verstehen. If it is the case that a satisfactory explanation is one that serves
to resolve intellectual tension, then it would seem an especially appropriate *terminus ad quem* for sociological analysis that it can show as rational
the action generating the social regularities that it addresses. In Coleman's
words (1986b: 1), the rational action of individuals has 'a unique attractive-
ness' as the basis of sociological theory since 'the very concept of rational
action' is one of ' "understandable" action that we need ask no more questions about'; or as Hollis (1977: 21) succinctly puts it, 'rational action is its
own explanation'. Conversely, it is when RAT fails, when there is no way of
denying the prevalence of systematic irrational or nonrational action, that
'black boxes' remain and there is clearly more explanatory work to be done
(cf. Boudon, 1998, 2003b).

In this essay, I have sought to distinguish versions of RAT according to
whether they have strong or weak rationality requirements, focus on situational or procedural rationality, and purport to be general or only special
theories of action. Sociologists, I have then maintained, will tend to be best

served by a form of RAT that has rationality requirements of intermediate strength, that has a primarily situational emphasis and that aims to be a theory of a special, although at the same time a privileged, kind. To revert to the space delineated in Figure 7.1, the area I would recommend for sociological colonisation thus lies at a middling height, far to the left and closer to the back than the front, with, say, the position allocated to Boudon marking its lower-right-front corner. The arguments I have advanced do, I would like to think, have a degree of coherence which a summary on the following lines may serve to bring out.

If a subjective conception of rationality such as that I have advocated is adopted, serious efforts must be made to complement this conception in two different respects. First, it is important to analyse the conditions under which actors come to act—systematically rather than just idiosyncratically—in a way that is rational from their point of view, even if deviating from the course of action that would be objectively rational. Second, criteria must be developed by reference to which action that is open to understanding as subjectively rational can be demarcated from action that is not, and analyses in turn undertaken of the conditions under which such nonrational action—again when of a systematic kind—is most likely to occur. Progress in both these directions then requires that sociologists should concentrate their explanatory efforts on the situation of action rather than on the psychology of the acting individual. While still adhering to a RAT approach, they may aim to show how social structural and procedural features of this situation may subvert objective, though not subjective, rationality (as in Boudon's new sociology of knowledge); or, further, lead to subjectively rational action being crosscut by action with clearly different motives and meanings (as in Hechter's proposed sociology of immanent values).

Even in such an extended version, RAT would claim to be only a special theory of action. Its exponents might, indeed should, be expected to push the theory to its furthest limits—to seek in effect to reduce accounts of social regularities in terms of cultural traditions, values, and norms as far as possible to ones given in terms of rational action—because of the distinctive hermeneutic and explanatory advantages that could thus be gained. But such reductionism would always require empirical justification, while appeals that might still be made to nonrationality, rather than being ad hoc, would be provided with their own sociological grounding.[17]

CHAPTER EIGHT

Rational Action in Sociology*
Misconceptions and Real Problems

In the two preceding chapters, I have advanced arguments from several different, but, I hope, consistent, points of view in favour of rational action theory (RAT) being given a central role in sociological explanation and understanding. To repeat, I opt for 'rational action theory' as a term that has a broader reference than that usually intended by the more common 'rational choice theory'. I take it to cover an entire family of theoretical approaches in the social sciences that have in common the aim of explaining social phenomena as the outcome of individual action that can—in some way—be construed as rational.[1] Within this family resemblance, however, significant differences arise, and in Chapter 7 I sought to analyse these differences and, further, to specify the features of the version or versions of RAT that sociologists would, in my view, be likely to find most apt to their purposes: that is, a version or versions with rationality requirements of intermediate strength, with a situational rather than a procedural emphasis, and that aim to provide a special rather than a general theory of action, although a special theory of a privileged kind.

In the present essay I have two further concerns. First, I attempt to identify and to dispel several misconceptions in regard to RAT that still appear widespread among sociologists. Second, though, I recognise that to succeed in this does not then mean that RAT is problem-free. Rather, it allows attention to focus on certain quite fundamental and still largely unresolved

*For advice, information, and helpful comments on earlier drafts of this essay I am indebted to Bob Allen, Richard Breen, Hartmut Esser, Oliver Grant, Douglas Heckathorn, Peter Hedström, and Michael Macy.

problems that confront proponents of RAT—but problems, I aim also to show, that equally confront proponents of other theoretical approaches, or at least of any that has the explanation of social phenomena, rather then merely conceptual elaboration, as its goal.

MISCONCEPTIONS

The misconceptions about RAT that are most common among sociologists would seem to be of three main kinds, each of which, I would suggest, is linked with the perception of RAT as posing a particular kind of *threat*: specifically, a disciplinary threat, an ideological threat, and what, for want of a better word, I will call an existential threat. This may help explain why the misconceptions persist and also, perhaps, why they cannot always be regarded as being entirely unwilled.

The first kind of misconception, which is associated with the sense of a disciplinary threat, could, in its essentials, be expressed as follows.

The idea, central to RAT, of explaining social phenomena in terms of individual action understood as far as possible as rational is 'unsociological'. It is an alien idea taken over from economics or, worse, represents a form of 'economics imperialism' against which sociologists have to defend themselves.

In this case, the immediate source of the misconception is fairly obvious: that is, a failure to recognise the varieties of RAT, which then leads to an equation of, or confusion between, RAT as deployed in mainstream economics and RAT more generally. Such a lack of discrimination, and the disciplinary defensiveness that accompanies it, is particularly well illustrated in a work produced by members of the Department of Sociology at the University of Warwick (Archer and Tritter, eds., 2000)—heroically entitled, *Rational Choice Theory: Resisting Colonisation*—to which I can therefore usefully refer.

Neither individually nor collectively do the contributors to this volume indicate the extension that they would wish to give to the term 'rational choice theory'. To be sure, it is evident enough what they see as the main target of their resistance movement. This is what I would describe as RAT in versions that are found chiefly in economics: that is, versions with strong rationality requirements that assume that actors have the level of information and of calculating capacity necessary to 'maximise' or 'optimise' and, further, that actors are always egoistic. Now to construe rational choice theory in this way is not in itself unreasonable. However, both individual contributors to the volume and the editors do at various points clearly imply the existence of *other* versions of RAT, in use in sociology, and even, in some cases, openly acknowledge them—yet without these other versions being given any very serious consideration.[2] Consequently, it is left quite uncertain whether, or how far, the arguments that are advanced against the RAT of economics are intended to have a wider relevance and, if so, what force they would then carry. Moreover, the suspicion cannot be entirely suppressed that this rather unsatisfactory outcome arises because the Warwick authors are indeed opposed to the use of RAT in sociology in *any* form—and primarily because of its grounding in methodological individualism (on which more later)—but choose strategically to focus their attack on the RAT of economics so that 'economics imperialism' can then be invoked as a means of rallying disciplinary support for their position.[3]

Other examples of this same kind of misconception concerning RAT, which in effect consists in taking the part for the whole, could readily be cited (e.g., Hirsch et al., 1987; Denzin, 1990; Smelser, 1992; Baert, 1998). By way of correction, the following point has then to be stressed. To suppose that any attempt at deploying RAT in relation to social phenomena must imply a capitulation to economics and thus, to quote Denzin (1990: 172), 'a turning away from the subject matter of sociology itself', is to show a rather gross disregard for the history of the social sciences. For RAT, in the broad sense that I have indicated, is far from being an accomplishment of economics alone and has in fact deep roots also in the sociological tradition.

This aspect of the intellectual origins of RAT is in fact well brought out in a series of studies by Boudon (1987, 1998–2000), who shows that within classical sociology there was always to be found, alongside the holistic or nomological paradigm, most notably exemplified in the work of Durkheim, a rival, individualistic paradigm. Within the latter, explanations were sought of macro- as well as of microsocial phenomena in terms of individual action *and*, so far as possible, in terms of action that could be understood as rational. To this end (and in contrast with the situation in classical economics) rationality was treated subjectively as well as objectively: that is, from the point of view of the actor as well as from that of the analyst. And it thus became an essential part of the analyst's task to establish empirically the situation in which action occurs and the actor's knowledge of and objectives within this situation, so that the subjective 'logic' of the course of action actually followed, even if not at first apparent, could be effectively reconstructed.

Boudon identifies Tocqueville as a prototypical exponent of the individualistic paradigm. But, unsurprisingly, it is in the work of Max Weber that Boudon sees the paradigm as having its most important expression. For Weber, rationality was the key to transcending the division between 'understanding' and 'explanation' that lay at the heart of the *Methodenstreite* of his day. And it is Weber who first suggests the idea, now central to RAT in sociology, that the concept of rationality is, on the one hand, that through which the understanding of action can be most reliably achieved and, on the other, that in which the explanation of action can be 'most finally' grounded (see, e.g., Weber, 1903–06/1975; cf. Norkus, 2000 and also vol. II, ch. 8)

Boudon further documents the significant contributions that were made in the context of the individualistic paradigm, even if from differing standpoints, by Simmel, Tarde, and Pareto. And other contemporary exponents of RAT in sociology have in effect supplemented Boudon's project in recognising clear continuities between their own work and that of earlier authors as, for example, Esser (1993) writing on Schütz and Hedström, Swedberg, and Udéhn (1998) on Popper.[4] In the light of this body of scholarship, it could then be said that those who are concerned to safeguard sociology against what they represent as the alien influence of RAT are led to take an unduly partial view of what constitutes the sociological tradition; and, in seeking to associate the individualistic paradigm exclusively with economics, end up, ironically, selling sociology short.

Finally, it is relevant here to note two further points, both of which relate back to the diversity of RAT. First, although falling within a distinctive and long-established paradigm within the discipline, the RAT of present-day sociology is itself still far from unitary. As shown in Chapter 7, important differences of view occur over such questions as how far the concept of rationality can be broadened and how far, in reconstructing action as subjectively rational, the 'principle of charity' can be applied without analytical sharpness being thereby lost and the threat of tautology arising. Second, the RAT of economics is *also* not as monolithic as is often supposed and, of late, would seem to have become significantly less so. In particular, it may be noted that Simon's arguments (see esp. 1982, ii; 1983) to the effect that economic analysis could be more realistically based on a conception of bounded rather than of infinite rationality, which for some time remained decidedly heterodox, are now being increasingly accepted, developed, and applied (for a major review, see Conlisk, 1996; cf. also Augier and March, eds., 2004).

What is thus indicated is the error of supposing that the crucial issues regarding RAT are ones being fought out—and that can only be fought out—between the true defenders of the sociological faith and the barbarian economists at their gates. These issues today concern sociologists and economists alike, and there is in turn evident opportunity for cross-disciplinary engagement and exchanges of a productive kind. It is of course true that quite explicit programmes of economics imperialism have in the past been launched, most notoriously, perhaps, by Becker (1976), but in fact no very serious threat to sociology has ever in this way been created (cf. Baron and Hannan, 1994). And further, even if such programmes are of a kind that few sociologists could find congenial, it should still be recognised that they had a worthy objective: that of overcoming incompatibilities and achieving greater integration among theories of action across the social sciences. Favourable prospects now exist of moving towards this objective, not through imperialism but rather, one might say, through confederation.

The second kind of misconception that sociologists commonly hold about RAT is one that is, rather obviously, linked with the sense of an ideological threat. This misconception is on the following lines. *The attempt to explain social phenomena in terms of individual action understood as rational is motivated by more than purely social scientific concerns. It is also the expression of an extreme individualistic worldview and provides the intellectual basis for neoliberal ideologies, programmes, and policies that disregard social solidarity and treat the unrestricted pursuit of self-interest as natural and beneficent.*

To illustrate, Archer and Tritter (2000: 1–3) in introducing the collection of papers by the Warwick sociologists, earlier referred to, claim that rational choice theory has 'underpinned the neoliberal reforms of the public sector in much of the Western industrial world' and in turn 'the rollback of the traditional welfare state and withdrawal of its services'. And they go on to underwrite the view 'that there is rather more than an "elective affinity" between philosophical individualism and the methodological individualism which forms the explanatory charter of rational choice theory'. Similarly, if somewhat more obliquely, Sciulli (1992: 164) argues that it is a 'background assumption' of rational choice theory that 'actors' relatively unfettered pursuit of their own preferences is more likely to yield and sustain a benign direction of social change—a stable, liberal-democratic society—than any effect to restrain this pursuit with institutionalized norms'. And Rule (1997: 82) maintains that rational choice theory has at least 'expressive associations' with liberalism in projecting 'a view of the social world as composed of calculating, utility-maximising actors pursuing ends that are essentially *divisible*—that is, capable of being attained without regard to the utilities of other actors'.

Once again it may be noted that rational choice theory is apparently being interpreted in the sense of—to use my own terminology—RAT as deployed in economics, even though the authors cited are all specifically concerned with sociological applications. However, this is not the only source of the multistranded misconception that here arises, in disentangling which it is in fact essentially problems over 'individualism' that have to be addressed.

To begin with, Archer and Tritter are of course quite correct in saying that methodological individualism provides the 'explanatory charter' of RAT. However, there is no reason for then supposing that any necessary connection exists between *methodological* individualism and individualism as an economic or political creed: that is, there is no reason for supposing that the former entails the latter. If such entailment is what Archer and Tritter wish to suggest through the somewhat coy phrase 'rather more than an elective affinity', one can only echo Max Weber (1922/1968: 18): 'It is a tremendous misunderstanding to think that an "individualistic" method should involve what is in any conceivable sense an individualistic system of values'.[5]

If empirical confirmation of this point is needed, it should be enough to note the development in the 1980s of rational choice Marxism (e.g., Roemer, 1982; Elster, 1985; Roemer, ed., 1986) into which methodological individualism was naturally incorporated. And rational choice Marxism must of course further count as evidence against the weaker claim that a connection between the different forms of individualism exists simply at the level of elective affinity or of Rule's 'expressive associations'—as indeed must evidence, even if only from everyday observation, of proponents of RAT being, say, committed social democrats. In short, the linkage between the positions that individuals take up in the philosophy of the social sciences, on the one hand, and in economic and political affairs, on the other, must be reckoned a good deal more complex, and looser, than the authors earlier cited would try to make out—and sometimes, it would seem, with primarily rhetorical intent.[6]

However, even if not always innocent, this first level of misconception that I have identified does often appear to stem from a second: that is, from the further mistaken supposition that methodological individualism implies *ontological* individualism—or, worse, from a failure to see the need to make a clear distinction between the two (e.g., Archer and Tritter, 2000: 7). Methodological individualism claims that all social phenomena are to be explained, ultimately, as the consequences, intended or unintended, of individual action; only individuals act and, in the last analysis, only individual action has causal efficacy in the social world. But methodological individualism does *not* claim that only individuals *exist*. That is ontological individualism—and might in fact be somewhat more plausibly associated with an individualistic worldview. For example, when Margaret Thatcher famously stated that 'society does not exist—only individuals and [somewhat inconsistently] families', she was being an ontological, and not, or not just, a methodological individualist.

For methodological individualists, proponents of RAT included, no difficulty at all arises in accepting the independent reality, beyond that of individuals, of cultures, and of social institutions and other social structural features (see esp. Popper, 1972: 158–68). These are recognised as being emergent from individual action, and it is further recognised that, as they exist at any one time, such emergent entities will then condition the actions of individuals: that is, will create opportunities for, and impose constraints on, such action. Indeed it may well be that in practice—that is, for the purposes of particular enquiries—cultural and social structural features are simply taken as givens; but, even so, the argument that they must ultimately be understood as themselves the outcome of individual action is still in principle maintained (cf. Hedström and Swedberg, 1998a: 11–13).[7]

These points require emphasis because they are relevant to yet another aspect of misconceptions over individualism in RAT: that which associates RAT with an undue *voluntarism* or, in other words, with a tendency to exaggerate, with ideological motivation, the extent to which in a liberal form of society individuals are free not only to choose their own ends or goals but also to pursue them just as they will.

Under RAT, it is indeed assumed that in pursuing as well as choosing their goals, actors do have 'degrees of freedom'. However, it is *not* assumed that this freedom is unlimited—quite the contrary. In any attempt at developing an explanation based on RAT, the first steps are to establish the feasible set of actions, or the opportunity structures, for the different actors involved, given their goals; and then to consider, from the actors' points of view, the costs, as well as the benefits, of choosing one possible course of action rather than another. In Volume II illustrations of exactly this approach are provided in regard to the explanation of class differentials in educational attainment and of patterns of intergenerational class mobility. What in fact typically emerges from such applications of RAT in the field of social stratification is that individuals in more advantaged class positions have systematically 'better' choices to make than individuals in less advantaged positions. And it may even be the case that, for the latter, the courses of action that appear best suited to the achievement of their goals, under the constraints that they face, are also ones that will, in aggregate, help perpetuate the overall structure of inequality in which they are implicated. Findings of this kind can then scarcely be regarded as ones that consort well with neoliberal ideology. RAT is just as likely to bring out what has been aptly called 'the back of the invisible hand' as its more benign and equitable consequences.

On the issue of voluntarism, what proponents of RAT, as methodological individualists, would primarily oppose are claims that individuals have in effect *no* choices to make or that their sense of choosing is merely illusory. They would, for example, reject Marxist claims that individuals are no more than the 'bearers' of inexorable historical forces, or functionalist claims that in effect they act out the exigencies of social systems, or culturalist claims that they simply realise the prescriptions of the culture or subculture into which they were socialised. And what would then in turn be rejected is the idea that it is in historical forces or functional exigencies or cultures that social causation ultimately inheres.

There is one last misconception that has to be noted among the series relating to the 'individualism' of RAT—that in which it is taken to imply *egoism*. RAT, it is claimed, presupposes that individuals invariably seek their own interests and with an asocial disregard for the interests of others. Leaving aside the rhetorical advantage that may again be sought from such a claim, the main source of the misconception itself is probably to be found in the somewhat ambiguous idea of 'self-interest'. Under RAT the assumption is indeed made that actors choose their own goals, and their choices might then, in this sense, be described as self-interested. However, the goals chosen need not be ones that are self-interested in the further and stronger sense of relating to actors' own welfare rather than the welfare of others: or, to follow Sen's nice distinction (1986: 7–8), 'self-goal choice' need not entail an exclusive concern with 'self-welfare goals'.

It is true that certain analytical advantages can be gained from taking the stronger view of self-interest, and in some versions of RAT these are exploited (cf. Hechter, 1994). But there is still no difficulty in principle in regarding altruistic as well as egoistic goals as ones that can be rationally pursued. Under RAT, as critics indeed often remark (see further below), rationality refers entirely to means and not to ends. Where altruistic goals are postulated, what is in fact chiefly important in applications of RAT is that strong empirical evidence of such goals should be provided so as to ensure that altruism is not just being invoked ad hoc as a means of 'saving' a RAT-based explanation, and through in effect a recourse to tautology (Koertge, 1975).[8]

The third kind of misconception concerning RAT that I want to take up is that associated with what I call an existential threat. It might be expressed in the following way. *Whatever conception of rationality is adopted, the attempt to privilege rational action in sociological explanation remains restrictive and unrealistic. Individuals constantly act in ways that diverge from rationality in any sense, and not only because of ignorance and error but also because of their values and their emotions. Human beings are far more than just cold calculators.*

Again, Archer and Tritter's critique of RAT serves as a useful source. These authors (2000: 5–6) rightly see it as major claim of RAT that it allows for the understanding and explanation of action, for 'hermeneutics and causality', to be pursued together. But, they contend, this claim rests on the assumption that human actors are beings who 'all of the time' act 'solely' on the basis of instrumental rationality—an assumption that is empirically untenable. In particular, Archer and Tritter stress the importance in determining action of value commitments or 'ultimate concerns' that 'are simply expressive of who we are' and that do not depend on any kind of cost-benefit analysis. RAT is, in other words, founded on a quite impoverished view of the human individual or person (cf. Douglas and Ney, 1998; Dupré, 2001: 153, 183). A somewhat similar position is taken up by Scheff (1992: 102) who, however, focuses more narrowly on RAT's neglect of emotions. 'Important decisions', he argues, 'often are made impulsively' with actors 'taking into consideration few if any of the possible options, and considering few or none of the consequences'. The discounting of emotions in RAT, Scheff believes, mirrors the general tendency in modern societies for emotions to be suppressed.

The misconception in this case concerns the ultimate objective of RAT. This is *not* to provide a comprehensive and detailed account of human decision making but rather to explain social phenomena: that is, to show how regularities of one kind or another that have been empirically established in social life are created, sustained, and, under certain conditions, disrupted and changed. To this end, RAT does not in fact require the assumption that all actors act all of the time in an entirely rational way: proponents of RAT can readily acknowledge that this is far from being the case. The assumption that is crucial for RAT is a different one. It is that in the explanation of social phenomena in terms of individual action, rationality can claim a privileged role in that it expresses the most frequent *common* influence on action. And here the important consideration is (cf. Gellner, 1990: 18) that, given rationality, the same aim will in similar circumstances tend to call for the same action. In contrast, nonrational action will express a wide range of more idiosyncratic influences that can therefore in aggregate be expected in some large degree to cancel out. In the generation of social regularities it is thus rational action that is likely to represent the decisive central tendency, and even if many—or indeed most—of the individuals involved do act in a nonrational fashion (see further and for an example ch. 6, pp. 128–30).[9]

Once this is understood, then a line of counterargument can be pursued that *is* of an entirely pertinent kind. As Rule remarks (1997: 91), it could be that rational action is *not* privileged in the way that is being supposed: nonrational action may also in some cases 'lend regularity to social process'. Rule himself does not make any specific suggestions in this regard but it is not difficult to think of at least one kind of action that is quite pervasive and that could be expected to be systematic in its outcomes: namely, action guided by social norms that are grounded in culturally shared beliefs and values and, perhaps, enforced via close interpersonal relations (cf. Edling, 2000; Hedström, 2005).

In response to such an objection, it might, first of all, be observed that, contrary to what some critics of RAT would suppose (e.g., Archer, 2000: 51), norm-oriented action may not be nonrational: that is, where it is itself of an instrumental character—where the actor chooses to follow a norm, rather than to break it, on the basis of some assessment of the costs and benefits of so doing (cf. Coleman, 1990: ch. 10). Nonetheless, insofar as norm-oriented action is not instrumental but reflects, rather, the actor's acceptance of a norm arising out of moral commitment or, to use Archer and Tritter's phrase, 'ultimate concerns', then a challenge to RAT has surely to be recognised.

This challenge might be met by attempts to extend RAT so that it would still be capable of accommodating action of the kind in question: for example, by postulating an 'internal action system' (Coleman, 1990: ch. 19) within which individuals can perform analyses of purely psychic costs and benefits. But, on grounds previously set out (ch. 7, p. 155), I would regard this as a dubious strategy that could easily lead to RAT becoming tautologous. It would seem preferable, at least for sociologists, to take RAT in a version that aims to provide only a special rather than a general theory of action and so acknowledges space for alternative theories. From this position, it can then be regarded as an empirical matter how well RAT and rival theories, including theories that privilege norm-oriented action, actually perform in particular instances: that is, in explaining particular social phenomena of interest. This is in fact an issue that will arise at various points in Volume II, in particular in regard to the explanation of class differentials in educational attainment (chs. 2–4); and I there hope to show that, in this case at least, RAT-based explanations do in fact fare better than the alternatives that have been proposed.

In sum, RAT does not need to operate with the idea of the human actor as being no more than a cold calculator. Its key assumption is more subtle: namely, that it is the rational element in individual action that is the prime source of regularity in social life. It is possible that this assumption will in certain instances prove mistaken and thus misleading. In Sen's words (1986: 11), it may be the case that 'getting at actuality via rationality does distort our approach to actuality'. However, as Sen then goes on to argue, from a social scientific point of view the crucial questions that follow are those of how much distortion is created and of what kind—systematic or nonsystematic—and, further, of whether, in the light of empirical assessment, *other* approaches do better or worse.[10]

In the foregoing, I have tried to show that the misconceptions about RAT that are most widespread among sociologists are not only fairly radical but tend also to go together with an affective response to RAT. I have suggested that RAT is perceived as being in various ways threatening, whether to sociology itself or to sociopolitical and human values to which many sociologists adhere. I have then sought further to show the nature of these misconceptions—that is, why they *are* misconceptions—and, in turn, why the threats they appear to pose are, for the most part, illusory. RAT is not an unsociological importation from economics; the methodological individualism on which RAT is founded has no logical, and probably no very strong empirical connection with any kind of individualistic ideology; and RAT does not imply a view of the human actor as devoid of moral sense or emotion.

I hope that I have thus made it easier for RAT to be considered on its merits rather than in a way coloured by concerns that are in any event scarcely relevant to its value as theory; or that, at very least, I have made it harder for misconceptions about RAT to be perpetuated as a means of avoiding such consideration. However, none of this should be taken to imply that I regard RAT as being unproblematic. To the contrary, I believe that in efforts to develop RAT, and especially RAT for sociology, fundamental problems do indeed arise. These are, however, problems that critics of RAT as well as its proponents need more seriously to address, because they are ones that are crucial for sociological theory *in general*. It is to these problems that I now turn.

REAL PROBLEMS

The two basic problems that I wish to discuss are, as I will show, connected and, stated rather baldly, are the following.

1. The problem of rationality itself. Where does rationality in action 'come from'? Is the capacity for rational thought and action a universal human capacity, a generic property of *homo sapiens*? Or, rather, is the capacity, or at all events the propensity, for rationality in action a distinctive sociocultural product, specifically of the modern West?

2. The problem of the ends,[11] to which action, rational or otherwise, is oriented. Where do they 'come from'? How far can they be treated as universal or, alternatively, as simply random—as expressions, say, of the freedom of human will—so that they have to be taken as exogenous to any social scientific analysis? Or are the ends of action socioculturally formed in some systematic way or ways and therefore capable, at least in principle, of being endogenised?

The connection that exists between these two problems can perhaps best be brought out by reference to a protracted if intermittent debate in British philosophy and sociology which might be called the 'Algy debate', after the children's rhyme that the contending parties invoke:

Algy met a bear.
The bear met Algy.
The bear was bulgy,
The bulge was Algy.

It was Ernest Gellner (1956/1973: 13–14 esp.) who started the Algy debate in the course of a complex series of exchanges on issues of methodological individualism. Gellner was ready to concede that all social entities or events can 'in a sense' be traced back to individual action, but, he argued, only at a cost. In order to realise their programme, methodological individualists are forced to endow actors with a range of attributes—their goals, values, beliefs, attitudes, and all of what might in general be called their 'dispositions'—that determine their actions but that can in fact derive *only from* society. Thus, Gellner claimed, under methodological individualism, 'society' is, covertly and rather desperately, stuffed inside the individual, just as Algy was stuffed inside the bear. And, to the alert observer, the bulge is just as apparent. The individual actors who alone are allowed causal efficacy in regard to social phenomena can be seen to be themselves far from individualistic. They are, inevitably, socialised individuals, and it would be better if this were openly recognised.

Gellner's argument has often been invoked by later critics of methodological individualism and sometimes in regard specifically to RAT. Thus, to take a recent example, Archer (2000: 45–46) contends that neither individuals' ends nor the degree of rationality with which they pursue them can be understood without reference to the formative influence of social factors that should, analytically, be kept 'outside the bear'. At the same time, though, various responses to Gellner have been made, starting from Watkins (1957). Typically, these responses have stressed the point that while the socialisation of individuals does of course occur, this should not be seen as a process that operates in some more or less automatic fashion. Individuals do not just encounter society, as Algy encountered the bear, and then become assimilated to it. It is not in fact society that socialises individuals: society per se does not *do* anything. Individuals become socialised only as the result, intended or unintended, of the actions of other individuals, and individuals may therefore be socialised in widely differing ways. As Heckathorn has put it (1997: 13), one must recognise 'a circular relation between social action and socialisation'. Thus, to claim that socialisation is a precondition for action is arbitrary, because it is equally true that action is a precondition for socialisation.

In the face of this apparent impasse, methodological individualists would then wish to argue, as does Heckathorn, that analytical advantage in fact lies in giving priority to action. For if socialisation is made the independent variable, then the content and the force of internalised dispositions are given little more than a 'black box' explanation, whereas at least the possibility exists of showing how, under certain conditions, particular values and related social norms can derive, and gain their constraining force, from processes of action, and indeed of rational action that is its own explanation (see further Coleman, 1990: chs. 10–11).

I would certainly underwrite this argument. But I would at the same time think it important to acknowledge that, so far as RAT is concerned, a difficulty still remains in regard to socialisation, and even if this is viewed as the outcome of action. Insofar as it is the case that *both* rationality and the ends towards which rational action is oriented are conditioned by socialisation, so that they may vary strongly and systematically across different cultures or subcultures, societies or communities, then, to this extent, the explanatory potential of RAT will obviously be restricted.

On this crucial matter, the position that I would myself wish to take can be expressed in the two following arguments. First, the issues that arise in the Algy debate are in essence long-standing ones: in effect, those of 'nature and culture' and of 'individual and society' that can be traced back to the earliest origins of the social sciences or indeed of social thought more generally. Moreover, these issues are still far from any clear resolution, and it is a mistake to pretend otherwise.

Second, these issues are ultimately *empirical* ones, and thus real progress in resolving them will be made not through armchair conceptualising and reconceptualising—of the kind that, for example, has characterised the protracted 'structure-agency' debate (e.g., Giddens, 1984; Archer, 1995)—but rather through research. And relevant here will be research in various fields apart from that of sociology itself, which, however, sociologists can ill afford to ignore.

Such research has still far to go before any very firm conclusions are likely to be available to theorists. Nonetheless, what, I believe, can usefully be done at the present time is to say something about the areas of research that would seem most relevant and, further, about the progress—or lack of progress—that can so far be observed in these areas. From this standpoint, I now comment on research and related discussion that bear in turn on the problem of rationality and on the problem of ends as these were earlier outlined.

The Problem of Rationality

Critics of RAT have often maintained that its range of application is necessarily limited because the pervasiveness of rationality in action that it presupposes has itself to be seen as a sociocultural product. In its most common version, the argument is that a growing propensity for action to be guided by instrumental rationality is a distinctive, if not a defining, characteristic of western modernity. And it can thus be claimed as, for example by Wagner (2000: 25, 32; cf. Berger and Offe, 1982), that RAT is in effect reliant on a Weberian theory of modernity or, in other words, on a 'narrative of individualization and rationalization'.

Moreover, those who argue in this way can in fact invoke the authority of Max Weber himself—the great pioneer of RAT within the sociological tradition—in support of their case. In a discussion of the foundations of marginal utility theory, Weber (1908/1975: 32–33) strongly rejects the idea that these can be found in an empirical, 'universalistic' psychology—specifically, the 'psycho-physics' of his day (see ch. 7, n. 12)—and insists that they lie only in 'cultural-historical' circumstances: that is, in the historical specificity of the capitalist epoch, in which, as he puts it, the 'approximation of reality' to the theory has been 'a *constantly increasing* one' [emphasis in original]. That is to say, it is the institutional forms of capitalism that progressively facilitate, induce, or indeed compel the rationality that is assumed by the theory, and in a way that would not occur in societies characterised by what Weber, perhaps somewhat ironically, calls 'non-economic' conditions.[12]

However, what needs to be asked is how far the general position here taken up by Weber can still be regarded *as* authoritative, a century after its formulation. In the light of various lines of recent enquiry, I would believe that it does now require very serious qualification, if indeed it can stand at all. The main underlying issues are two: those of the validity, first, of the binary contrast that runs throughout Weber's work (and of course much other classical sociology) between 'traditional' and 'modern' cultures and societies; and, second, of the notion of a unilinear transition from the former to latter, in which the West plays the dominant role and essentially on account of its greater capacity to deploy, in Weber's own dramatic phrase, 'the rationality of world mastery'.

Of particular relevance here is the rich evidence, from historical, anthropological, and geographical research, that provides the basis for wide-ranging studies such as those of Blaut (1993) and Goody (1996) in which a quite explicit challenge to the Weberian view is raised.[13] These authors directly dispute the claim that modernisation has been the distinctive project of the West. Rather, they would argue, the various processes subsumed under this term are ones subject to much historical uncertainty and contingency, so that, in a long-term historical perspective, different geographical regions in both the East and the West have to be seen as taking the lead in different respects at different times. Thus, the West cannot be radically set apart from the rest of the world as regards the development of science and technology or the growth of institutional forms, as, say, in economic life, that favour or embody 'the rationality of world mastery'.[14] Western preeminence in these areas has to be recognised as in fact only a relatively recent phenomenon.

In turn, then, doubt is cast on Weber's central thesis that 'the rise of West' was associated with 'the possession of a rationality not available to others' (Goody, 1996: 11)—because in other parts of the world the growth and application of rationality were prevented, in some way never explained other than by the invocation of 'rockbound, timeless, changeless tradition' (Blaut, 1993: 5). The evidence now available, it is held, indicates that instrumental rationality has to be understood as an attribute of *all* cultures, both at an informal, 'practical' level and also, at least once literacy has been achieved, at the level of formal logical reasoning. It is an error if, as Goody puts it (1996: 46), 'rationality is seen to qualify men and cultures' in some holistic way rather than patterns of action in specific contexts.

Likewise, conformity with tradition should be seen as marking all societies in some degree—but also the ability of individuals to *break with* tradition. In this regard, Goody (1996: 40) upbraids Weber for recurrently equating action that follows tradition or custom with 'sheer habituation'. Goody's key point here is that it is *only if* traditional action can be so viewed that it can be properly treated as invariably nonrational. Actors can follow tradition or custom in a quite rational way, as in effect an evolved guide to what is best practice, *provided* that they remain ready to act differently—that is, to go against tradition—if experience indicates that, because of some situational change, traditional practice is no longer the best way to achieve their goals and can be improved on (cf. my earlier discussion of rational habits and of instrumental compliance with norms, ch. 7, pp. 154–5).[15]

If, then, it is now far less clear than it might have appeared in Weber's day that the propensity for rationality in action, and thus the range of applicability of RAT, *is* subject to close sociocultural conditioning and in effect limited to the modern West, a further question is prompted. How is the pervasiveness of instrumental rationality—its apparent resistance to sociocultural conditioning—to be itself understood? On this point, it is of interest to note that both Blaut (1993: 12) and Goody (1996: 12–15, 36) make appeal to the Kantian principle of 'the psychic unity of mankind', and reject notions of radically differing 'mentalities' corresponding to different levels of social development—such as the 'logical' and 'pre-logical' mentalities proposed by Lévy-Bruhl (1910). That is to say, they are concerned, along with a number of other recent authors, to challenge the assumption that demonstrated cross-cultural differences in patterns and contents of thought imply, to quote Lloyd (1990: 136), 'differences in the minds that do the thinking'; or in turn the assumption that cultures possess, as Boudon puts it, 'une capacité illimitée de conditionner les individus et, par suite, de les rendre hétérogènes d'une culture à l'autre' (2003c: 76; cf. also 2003a: 175–76).

Thus far, attempts to give arguments in favour of 'the psychic unity of mankind' an empirical as opposed to a purely philosophical grounding have been relatively restricted. They have had to rely largely on interpretations of data derived from anthropological fieldwork that are inevitably partial and not infrequently contested.[16] However, of late the possibility has arisen that additional, and ultimately far more systematic support might be provided by research of a quite different kind: that is, research in cognitive and evolutionary psychology. For Kant, the basis of mankind's oneness was a common and unchanging 'categorical apparatus' that provided the framework of all human cognitive capacity. In recent years, cognitive and evolutionary psychologists have developed an adventurous new version of this idea. What has been proposed is that something equivalent to Kant's categorical apparatus should now be envisaged in terms of physical—that is, neural—brain structure; and, further, that this structure, this 'cognitive architecture', should be seen as the outcome of evolutionary processes: that is, of long histories, or 'pre-histories', of environmental pressure and selection in the making of *homo sapiens*.

Such 'evolutionary Kantianism', to use Plotkin's (1997: 66) apt phrase, does then suggest a basis on which a rather radical claim might be made regarding the apparently abiding propensity for rationality in action across widely varying sociocultural contexts. It could be that through features of the evolved cognitive architecture of *homo sapiens* a capacity for such rationality has been created, analogous, say, to the capacity for language acquisition, that finds universal expression; or more specifically, as Runciman has put it (1998: 15), that 'the human mind has been programmed by natural selection to calculate the trade-off between the costs and benefits of one course of action rather than another'. In this way, then, RAT could be provided with a psychological grounding of a far more general kind than that which Weber rejected for marginal utility theory, and with one that is adequate to warrant rationality as the central tendency in individual action (even if with much individual deviation), which as I earlier argued, is the key requirement for RAT's explanatory power at the level of social phenomena.

However, what needs then to be stressed is that the rationality that is envisaged—and that has so far been empirically indicated—within the research programme of evolutionary Kantianism is *not* an infinite rationality of the kind most typically assumed in the RAT of economics. It is, rather, a form of bounded rationality. And it is of particular interest that the cognitive and evolutionary psychologists who are involved in exploring this rationality have already formed a close alliance with economists who seek to build on Simon's pioneering work (see, e.g., Gigerenzer and Selten, eds., 2001; Augier and March, eds., 2004).

What has in fact so far been added to Simon's idea of a bounded rationality based on satisficing rather than maximising or optimising is chiefly the idea of 'ecological rationality'. That is, the idea of a rationality in which decision making is guided by simple, 'fast and frugal', heuristics that are closely adapted to particular environmental conditions or domains. Experimental studies have shown that through such heuristics remarkably good inferences, and hence decisions, can often be made with only very limited time, knowledge, and calculation (Gigerenzer and Todd, 1999; Gigerenzer, 2000, 2004a, 2004b, 2005).[17] To date, only limited work has been undertaken on the operation of ecological rationality specifically in the domain of social life. But one promising focus of interest is on the way in which action that may at first sight appear nonrational, such as imitation of the action of others or indeed the following of social norms, can in fact reflect the use of heuristics that are conducive to choices of a—boundedly—rational kind (see esp. Gigerenzer, 2000, 2005; Boyd and Richerson, 2001).

To revert, then, to the Algy debate, what is implied by the kinds of research that I have considered in the foregoing is that, so far at least as rationality is concerned, the charge that this is a sociocultural variable surreptitiously, but still rather obviously, stuffed inside the individual actor may turn out to have significantly less force than would at first appear. From several different quarters there are now clear indications that, in this regard, the individualistic bear's own constitution may be such that it does not need to eat quite as much of the sociocultural Algy as Gellner and those who have followed him would suppose.

One might hope that sociologists would themselves come to play an increasingly active part in research of the kind in question, and that those who remain sceptical of RAT would at all events be ready to engage more seriously with the findings that are emerging than has hitherto been the case. However, a rather sad coda must here be added. Such positive developments would appear jeopardised by the opening up of what could be regarded as a new and highly divisive phase in the Algy debate, in which more radical evolutionary psychologists have taken the lead. That is, through the attack, initiated by Tooby and Cosmides (1992) and followed up among others by Pinker (2002) on what is taken to be 'the standard social science model' of the human individual.

According to this model, the critics charge, the individual comes into the world as virtually a 'blank slate', with innate capacities and drives of only the most generalised and plastic kind, and is then socioculturally formed— indeed created—in ways that are as various as societies and cultures themselves. Thus, since human nature is understood as essentially indeterminate, it attracts little interest either as a matter for investigation in itself or in regard to the explanation of social phenomena; it is always, as it were, the dependent rather than an independent variable. And consequently, it is held, social scientists cut themselves off, in a seriously self-damaging way, from what is now increasingly the main concern of the 'hard' human sciences—that is, 'the evolved architecture of the human mind'.

However, what the critics seek to present as the standard model of the social sciences is in fact one adhered to only by those who take up positions on the issue of 'individual and society' that would, on an overall view, have to be regarded as quite extreme. For example, Tooby and Cosmides have to sustain their characterisation of the supposed standard model (1992: 24–31) very largely by references to Durkheim and to such sociologists and anthropologists who would be ready to believe with Geertz (1973: 36–37) that 'humanity is as various in its essence as it is in its expression'. As against such positions, a number of telling points can indeed be made.[18] But, viewed from positions taken up by other social scientists, and especially, in the case of sociology, from that of adherents of the individualistic paradigm, the evolutionary psychologists' attack can only appear as unfortunately indiscriminate.[19] Furthermore, zeal in combating one form of extremism all too readily engenders another: for example, when, in as clear an expression of *ontological* individualism as one could wish, Tooby and Cosmides claim (1992: 47) that 'what mostly remains, once you have removed from the human world everything internal to individuals, is the air between them'; or again when they insist (Cosmides and Tooby, 1994), largely, it seems, as a matter of dogma, on the 'hard-wiring' of psychological mechanisms not just for rational decision making but also for the generation of the preferences by which action is in general guided—an issue to which I return in the following section.

Not surprisingly, then, in some sociological quarters a truly Durkheimian 'aggressive-defensiveness' has in turn been provoked, which has led to evolutionary psychology being denounced as a form of biological imperialism, no less dangerous than economics imperialism and carrying the same array of disciplinary, ideological, and existential threats. Thus, in a paper entitled—almost inevitably—'Colonising the Social Sciences?', Rose (2001) rejects evolutionary psychology out of hand as little more than the latest version of a long-discredited Social Darwinism that is devoid of intellectual value and that has to be resisted on all counts.[20]

In the face of such a polarisation of views, it is then difficult to be optimistic, at least for the immediate future, about sociologists joining with economists and psychologists in attempts to achieve a better understanding of the foundations of rationality, even though from the work previously referred to there are already clear indications that this is an area for co-operation across the social and the natural sciences of quite outstanding potential.

The Problem of Ends

It is a charge frequently levelled against RAT that it takes the ends towards which action is oriented simply as givens; or, in other words, that in analyses based on RAT ends (or goals, values, desires, preferences, etc.) are treated as exogenous. In response to this line of criticism, however, various attempts have of late been made to suggest how actors' ends might be accounted for either in ways that are external yet readily complementary to RAT or through being endogenised to RAT.

For example, several authors have sought to specify some limited number of goals that *all* individuals could be regarded as pursuing, whether directly or indirectly. Most systematically, perhaps, Lindenberg (1992, 1996) has proposed a 'social production function' with the universal and ultimate goals of physical and social well-being, to each of which is then linked an underlying hierarchy of instrumental goals, such as the achievement of wealth, power, or prestige (see also Harsanyi, 1969; Hechter, 1994). However, while exercises of this kind may be of classificatory value, it is not clear what they contribute to the actual explanation of goals and, in particular, of those that are taken to be universal and ultimate. In attempts to go further two, quite divergent, approaches can be identified.

The first of these starts from the belief of the more radical evolutionary psychologists, referred to above, that natural selection has produced in *homo sapiens* not only a universal capacity for rationality but, in addition, universal preferences of just the kind that Lindenberg and others would wish to postulate. Cosmides and Tooby (1994: 331) have in fact proposed that psychologists and economists should together aim to go beyond the exploration of evolved rationality to nothing less than the creation of 'a science of preferences'. So far, this proposal does not appear to have aroused any great interest on the part of economists—in significant contrast to the work of Gigerenzer and others on rationality.[21] However, some proponents of RAT in sociology, and most notably, perhaps, Kanazawa (2001), have been ready to argue that evolutionary psychology can indeed serve as a valuable adjunct to RAT by providing explanations for many preferences, and indeed underlying values, as arising either from 'universal human nature' or from its interaction with a variable environment—and including, Kanazawa would stress, preferences and values that motivate cooperation, commitment, altruism, and other forms of social action of a kind that have often created problems for RAT.

The second approach does in fact come from economics, but has little connection with evolutionary psychology. In mainstream economic analysis the 'exogeneity of preferences' has been accepted as more or less axiomatic. But a heterodox tendency has always existed whose members, whether claiming descent from Adam Smith or Karl Marx, have maintained that a society's institutions of production and distribution must in some degree influence the way in which individuals in that society form their preferences, and thus the ends that they pursue. Of late, efforts have been made to move beyond this essentially programmatic position and to specify actual causal mechanisms or processes through which such institutional influence might be exerted and thus produce variation in preferences of a systematic kind. In this regard, a leading paper is that of Bowles (1998) in which a number of possible mechanisms—such as the institutional framing of choices or shaping of norms and the effects of work tasks on personal values—are hypothesised and illustrated. In other words, a thoroughgoing endogenisation of preferences is here envisaged.[22]

The degree of divergence between the two approaches is then evident enough: the one appeals to nature, the other to culture. In terms of the Algy debate, one might say that while in the first approach it is of little consequence that Algy gets eaten—the big question being that of how the bear could manage this—in the second, the ways in which the consumption of Algy forms the very character of the bear are all important. However, in the present context, it is in fact one shared feature of the two approaches that is chiefly relevant: namely, that so far as providing a solution to the problem of ends is concerned, *both* are still almost entirely conjectural. Whether the aim is to explain preferences as an outcome of human evolution or to trace out how differences in institutional forms create systematic variation in preferences, ideas have been advanced—of greater or less plausibility—but, so far at least, with only very sparse empirical support. This is indeed acknowledged by some at least of the authors who have been cited, despite their wide-ranging efforts to search out relevant material.

Thus, Kanazawa (2001: 1144) admits that his arguments are often 'highly speculative'. In contrast, for example, to those of Gigerenzer and his associates on evolved rationality, they lack a sound basis in experimental work; and the temptation then is to lapse into the telling of 'just-so' stories of the kind that show evolutionary psychology at its worst.[23] Similarly, Bowles recognises that he can for the most part point only to possible instances, rather than to compelling evidence, of his proposed mechanisms of preference formation actually at work, and he stresses (1998: 103) how little is in fact known about cultural transmission in general—about 'who acquires what trait from whom, under what conditions and why'.

In the light of the foregoing, it might then be concluded that criticism levelled against RAT over its inability to account for the ends towards which action is directed is fully vindicated. Attempts to overcome the problem have gone in two different, and indeed contrary, directions, yet in neither case have any very compelling results been produced. But, while this is so, and the problem is clearly still far from any satisfactory resolution, a further point has at the same time to be recognised: that is, that the problem of ends remains outstanding not just for RAT *but for sociological theory in general.* And it could at all events be counted to the credit of proponents of RAT, whether in economics or sociology, that, having started from the assumption of exogeneity, they have then sought to move beyond this to address quite explicitly the question of how the ends or action might be accounted for, even if with rather little success thus far. In contrast, sociologists of other theoretical persuasions have tended to start from the—obviously far stronger—assumption that the goals of action *are* to be treated as endogenous, yet appear to have done so more or less as a matter of faith, and with very little concern for specifying and empirically demonstrating the actual social processes by reference to which this assumption might be warranted.

In this respect, the theoretical work of Parsons serves as a prime illustration. For Parsons (1937, 1952, esp.), the readiness found in the utilitarian tradition and in classical economics to accept the 'randomness of ends', and thus their exogeneity, is mistaken in principle. For if ends really were random, then human society would be impossible or at all events would be in a permanent state of chaos. If a society is to cohere, Parsons maintains, the ends of individual action have to be integrated through a shared culture. That is to say, while, on the one hand, the dominant values of this culture are institutionalised in the structure of society, on the other hand, these values, and derived social norms, are internalised by individuals in the course of their socialisation.

Parsons' position might in fact be regarded as a generalised or, alternatively, as a far less specific and vaguer version of that later taken up by Bowles. And it is not then surprising that it encounters similar empirical difficulties. It has proved very hard to establish, for any particular society, just what are the shared values that provide the basis of its integration, and through exactly what processes—and with what degree of efficacy—these values are institutionalised and internalised. And in turn it has of course become a standard criticism of Parsons (see, e.g., Lockwood, 1956; Mann, 1970) that societies can, and generally do, exist, and persist, with a far lower degree of 'integration' than he would believe to be functionally necessary or, in other words, with far higher levels of value dissensus, deviance from norms, and social conflict.

Also highly relevant here are the further criticisms of Wrong (1961) and Homans (1964) that alike focus on Parsons' 'oversocialised conception of man' and his exaggerated view of the plasticity of human nature. One point of obvious interest is the extent to which these authors anticipate *from within sociology* the later attacks of the evolutionary psychologists on the idea of the 'blank slate', even though Wrong takes his psychology chiefly from Freud and Homans, somewhat strangely, from the behaviourists.[24]

However, there is another feature of their critique, the importance of which seems often to have been overlooked. In rejecting the 'blank slate'—or what they actually called the 'social mold'—theory of human nature, Wrong and Homans do not only wish to retain some notion of human universals. In addition, they emphasise that socialisation itself should not be seen as necessarily leading to uniformity among individuals within the same culture or subculture, society or community. Even if one can appeal to socialisation to explain *grosso modo* the variation observed among collectivities in the things their members value, want, and pursue, a shared socialisation still does not prevent individuals who are members of the same collectivity from wanting, valuing, and pursuing very different things.[25] And here Wrong and Homans could surely claim support from the results of quantitative sociology (cf. ch. 6, pp. 125–6). For in most areas of research—political partisanship, religious participation, or family formation and dissolution would be obvious examples to take—the typical finding is that, whatever differences may be revealed in patterns of choice and action at the level of collectivities, still only a very modest part of the variance at the *individual* level can be accounted for; far less in fact than Parsons' theory would lead one to expect, even when a wide range of indicators of individuals' sociocultural attributes and affiliations is brought into the analysis.

Moreover, in a later comment Wrong (1999: 65) has pointed to one rather obvious reason why this should be so. The involvement of individuals in the 'recurrent webs' of relationships that define their everyday social situations is only one source of influence on their actions. Another, which sociologists have tended to neglect, is their biography. And even among individuals who at any one time are found within the same sociocultural context their life courses will often display a great diversity. To return again to the Algy debate, one might think of each individualistic bear, over his or her lifetime or at least formative years, as having eaten not just one sociocultural Algy but a number of such Algys, with the result that each bear, even if inwardly socialised, has not a largely shared, but rather a fairly distinctive social character, reflecting a unique personal history.[26]

When sociologists unsympathetic to RAT object that it treats the ends of action simply as givens, it should then be recognised that the position from which they do so is not a strong one. They argue *as if*, from some *other* theoretical standpoint, a way in which ends can be endogenised to sociological analysis is readily apparent. But if this is so at all, it is still—just as from the side of RAT—at the level only of programme, not performance. And the relevant empirical evidence would suggest that such processes as are usually appealed to—in particular, those involved in socialisation—do not in fact operate in a very effective fashion. Thus, those sociologists who insist on reiterating general statements to the effect that the ends of action are to be seen as the product of sociocultural circumstances (e.g., Archer: 2000: 46) can by now be reasonably asked when they expect to deliver on these statements. So far, they have failed to do so. As Lichbach (2003: 44) queries: 'where is the empirically verified theory . . . that they claim the rationalists lack?' And indeed, as Elster has remarked (1997: 753), why people have the goals, values, desires, and preferences that they do could well be regarded as 'the most important unsolved problem in the social sciences'.

The foregoing reviews of recent research and discussion bearing on the two key problems that I identified, those of rationality and of ends, have, then, clearly differing outcomes. In the case of rationality, significant advances can be claimed. It is, to say the least, now far more problematic than it was in Weber's day to suppose that a capacity or propensity for rationality in action is in some sense specific to individuals formed within the sociocultural matrix of western modernity; and there is indeed a growing body of evidence to underline the error—to repeat Goody's apt formulation—of taking rationality 'to qualify men and cultures' rather than particular patterns of action. Furthermore, developments in psychology are in this regard reinforcing, and giving greater content to, the idea of the psychic unity of mankind: that is, in tracing out the features of a bounded but still, in context, highly effective rationality in action that may come to be seen as the cross-culturally pervasive product of an evolved cognitive architecture. And a positive response to these developments is evident within economics, even if not, for the time being, within sociology.

In contrast, in regard to the problem of ends, progress would seem to have been made only in that—and chiefly from the side of RAT—it has been recognised that the problem cannot be overcome by programmatic *fiat* but only by demonstrating the processes that are actually involved in the determination of ends. However, whether the aim is to locate such processes in nature, that is, in evolved preference-generating mechanisms, or to show them as endogenous to differing sociocultural circumstances, little has so far been achieved beyond the formulation of hypotheses for which empirical support is still largely lacking. It is of course possible that in the course of time such support will in fact be forthcoming. But the possibility has, I think, equally to be acknowledged that the problem may not yield easily to either of the approaches in question. It may, for example, prove to be the case that even if the idea of indeterminacy—of some degree of randomness—in ends is rejected in principle, the degree of complexity that is involved in the shaping of individuals' ends, whether, say, through nature-culture or situation-biography interactions, is in practice still so great that to insist on determinacy affords rather little advantage.

Finally, then, it may be asked what conclusions may be drawn from the foregoing by proponents of RAT or by those who would at all events be prepared to regard RAT, in some version or other, as currently offering the best prospects for a sociology with the aims both of explaining and understanding the processes through which social phenomena are generated. If the several pseudo-problems that I discussed in the first part of this essay can be disposed of and attention focused on the two very real problems that I have considered in the second part, how should supporters of RAT respond to the 'present state' of these problems? There are, I would suggest, good grounds for proceeding in the two following ways.

First, the presumption should now be that a capacity for—boundedly—rational action is a human universal (the specifics of which call for much further exploration) rather than a sociocultural variable; and, in turn, that there are no societies or cultures in regard to which RAT is off limits from the start. It should then be treated as an empirical issue how well RAT performs, relative to other theories, in any particular area of social life, even though RAT should always be privileged—that is, taken as far as it will go—in view of the self-explanatory character that rational action possesses.

Second, the ends of action should continue to be treated as exogenous, and thus as needing to be established empirically case by case, until such time as the viability of doing otherwise is indicated by some genuine research breakthrough. While the explanations of social phenomena that follow will not therefore be 'rock-bottom', it is still the case, as Elster has argued (1983c, 1998), that such 'non-rock-bottom' explanations of courses and patterns of action, *given* actors' ends, can be valid and valuable.[27]

Such proposals do not, I realise, appear at all heroic. They cannot in this respect compete with the calls to the barricades made by critics of RAT in order that the true sociological faith should be defended against historic enemies. But, from the point of view of advancing sociology as a social science, they represent, I believe, the most rational course of action that can presently be taken.

CHAPTER NINE

Causation, Statistics, and Sociology*

In a paper of great insight, though sadly posthumous, Bernert (1983) noted a long-standing uncertainty among sociologists in regard to the concept of causation and its use in their work. 'Uncritical adulation' in the later nineteenth century gave way to 'complete rejection' in the early twentieth, followed in turn, in the years after World War II, by 'pragmatic utilization'—a position that, one might add, has itself been subject to rising criticism in the period since Bernert's review. These vicissitudes in the career of a concept have to be understood, as Bernert shows, in the context not only of the development of sociology itself but of larger scientific and philosophical debates.[1] In this essay I seek, much in the spirit of Bernert's contribution, to draw attention to some results of statisticians being increasingly involved in such debates, and further to consider the reception in, and potential for, sociology of the new understandings of causation that have thus emerged.

The founders of modern statistics might be regarded as representatives of the era in which the concept of causation was viewed with scepticism. At least for Pearson (1892), it was a mere 'fetish', carried over from metaphysical, prescientific thinking, which was to be abandoned and replaced by that of correlation, at once both more general and more precise. However, an opportunity for statisticians to make a more constructive contribution came at a later point with the introduction by philosophers, in the 1940s and

*This essay is a revised and extended version of the twenty-ninth Geary Lecture given at the Economic and Social Research Institute, Dublin. For helpful comments on earlier drafts I am indebted to Hans-Peter Blossfeld, Richard Breen, Pat Clancy, Tom Cook, David Collier, David Cox, Robert Erikson, David Freedman, Michael Gähler, Paul Holland, Janne Jonsson, Máire Ní Bhrolcháin, Donald Rubin, and Wout Ultee.

1950s, of the idea of probabilistic, as opposed to deterministic, causation: that is, the idea, roughly, that rather than causes being seen as necessitating their effects, they might be regarded simply as raising the probability of their occurrence (for reviews and more recent developments, see Salmon, 1980; Eells, 1991). A probabilistic view of causation might be associated with the argument that the world itself is nondeterministic; but such a view could also be favoured simply on the grounds that, whether the world is deterministic or not, it is too complicated, and our knowledge of it too error-prone, to permit anything other than probabilistic accounts to be provided. The latter position, at least, is one that would seem likely to commend itself to most sociologists—despite some recent attempts to uphold both the desirability and possibility of causal explanations in sociology that are of an entirely deterministic kind (see, e.g., Ragin, 1987; Becker, 1992; Mahoney, 2003; and for critical comment, Lieberson, 1992, 1994; Sobel, 1995; and chs. 1, 3, and 6).

In what follows, I take up three different understandings of causation that have been importantly shaped by contributions from statisticians. These I label as

1. causation as robust dependence,
2. causation as consequential manipulation, and
3. causation as generative process.

I sketch out these positions in a deliberately broad and nontechnical way. My concern is not with different individual formulations of each position and their internal coherence from a philosophical or a statistical point of view. I am interested, rather, in differences among these positions considered generically and with the question of what each might have to offer to working sociologists who wish to engage in causal analysis of some kind.[2] I treat the three ideas of causation in the above order, and then, drawing especially on the last, outline a further position which, it seems to me, could be—and indeed to some extent already is—both viable and valuable in sociology.

CAUSATION AS ROBUST DEPENDENCE

The starting point here is with the proposition, widely recognised in both philosophy and statistics, that while correlation—or, more generally, association—does not imply causation, causation must in some way or other imply association. The key problem that has then to be addressed is that of how to establish whether, or how far, the observed degree of association of variable X with variable Y, where X is temporally prior to Y, can be equated with the degree to which X is *causally significant* for Y.[3] It may indeed be that the probability of Y, given X, is greater than the probability of Y given not-X; but this is not in itself sufficient to demonstrate that X is a cause of Y. For example, it could be that a third variable (or set of variables), Z, is the cause of both X and Y, so that, if one conditions on Z, the association between X and Y disappears: that is, Y becomes statistically independent of X and any supposed causal link between X and Y is revealed as spurious. It could, though, also be that conditioning on Z does not entirely remove the association between X and Y but merely weakens it. In this case, the implication is not that X is a spurious cause of Y, but only that there is *some part* of the observed association between them that does not reflect the causal significance that X has for Y. A solution to the problem of moving from association to causation has then generally been pursued through an argument to the effect that X is a 'genuine' cause of Y insofar as the dependence of Y on X can be shown to be robust: that is to say, cannot be eliminated through one or more other variables being introduced into the analysis and then in some way 'controlled' (see esp. Simon, 1954; Suppes, 1970).

One particularly influential version of the attempt to understand causation in this way is that proposed by Granger (1969) in the context of the analysis of econometric time series, which has the further, more distinctive, feature of treating causation explicitly in terms of predictive power. A variable, X, 'Granger causes' Y if, after taking into account all information apart from values of X, these values still add to one's ability to predict future values of Y. In principle, 'all information' here refers to all information that has been accumulated in the universe up to the point at which the prediction of Y is made. In practice, however, Z has to refer to some particular information set, and what counts as a Granger cause would seem to be any non-zero partial correlation that improves the analyst's forecasting ability. Thus, as Holland (1986a) has argued, Granger causation is established essentially through the detection and elimination of spurious causal significance, or of what Granger himself calls 'non-causality': X is *not* a Granger cause of Y, relative to the information in Z, to the extent that the correlation between X and Y disappears, given Z. That is to say, the idea of robust dependence is crucial.

This same idea is also to be found, though again with a particular slant, in methodological programmes developed within sociology—most obviously, perhaps, in Lazarsfeld's proposals for 'elaboration' in the analysis of survey data (see, e.g., Kendall and Lazarsfeld, 1950; Lazarsfeld and Rosenberg, eds., 1955; Lazarsfeld, Pasanella, and Rosenberg, eds., 1972). Lazarsfeld is, like Granger, concerned with detecting spurious causation, but in the interests less of prediction than of explanation. Thus, a further and seemingly more positive strategy that Lazarsfeld advocates is to begin with a correlation between X and Y that is of substantive interest—say, a correlation between area of residence and vote; but then, rather than supposing any direct causal link, to seek *an explanation of the correlation itself* by finding one or more prior variables, Z—say, social class or ethnicity—which, when brought into the analysis, will reduce the partial correlation of X and Y to as close to zero as possible. To the extent that this is achieved, Z can be viewed as the cause of both X and Y—or, at all events, until such time as further 'elaboration' might bring the robustness of their dependence on Z itself into question.

The regression techniques taken over from econometrics and biometrics, including causal path analysis, that became familiar in quantitative sociology from the 1970s onwards marked important advances on Lazarsfeldian 'elaboration' in both their refinement and scope. But, as Davis (1985) has shown (cf. also Clogg and Haritou, 1997), so far as the basic understanding of causation is concerned—causation as robust dependence—a clear continuity can be traced. It is in fact the methodological tradition thus represented that has served as the main vehicle for the 'pragmatic utilization' of the concept of causation by sociologists, which Bernert sees as characteristic of the postwar years. However, as I suggested at the start, growing dissatisfaction with this position has of late been apparent, and among sociologists whose primary interest is in empirical research as well as among theorists and methodologists.

At the source of this dissatisfaction is a problem with the idea of causation as robust dependence to which attention has been drawn from various quarters. If causation is viewed in this way, then, it would appear, establishing causation becomes *entirely* a matter of statistical inference, into which no wider considerations need enter. Causation can be derived directly from the analysis of empirical regularities, following principles that are equally applicable across all different fields of enquiry, and without the requirement for any 'subject-matter' input in the form of background knowledge or, more crucially, theory. This implication might not appear too disturbing if, as with Granger, the essential criterion of causation is taken to be increased predictive power. But most philosophers of science would find this a too limited view, and would wish to regard causation as entailing something more than (if not other than) predictability—on the lines, say, of 'predictability *in accordance with theory*' (cf. Feigl, 1953; Bunge, 1979). Moreover, among economists, and even among econometricians (e.g., Geweke, 1984; Basmann, 1988; Zellner, 1988), there are many who would maintain that while Granger causation may be an idea of great practical utility for the purposes of forecasting, it can lead to *causal explanation* only when the demonstrated statistical relationships are provided with some rationale in theory and, moreover, in theory ultimately at the microeconomic level. In a discussion of prediction in economics, Sen (1986: 14) observes that the magnitudes of concern to the forecaster are all social magnitudes, and that variables such as prices, investment, consumption, and money supply 'do not, naturally, move on their own, untouched by human volition'. Thus, while 'mindless macroeconomics' may serve as a basis for predictions—or, at all events, for 'simple and immediate' ones—any 'deep explanation' of the movement of the magnitudes involved can, in the end, only be gained through theory, and of a kind that makes reference to the 'objectives, knowledge, reasoning and decisions' of individuals acting in society.

In sociology itself forecasting is a far less prominent activity than in economics, and it is then scarcely surprising to find that the treatment of causation in terms of predictability has been still more sharply rejected, and that arguments analogous to that of Sen on the need to go beyond the analysis of variables have been very widely expressed. Especially from the standpoint of methodological individualism, sociologists have strongly criticised the supposition that statistical techniques can in themselves provide adequate causal explanations of social phenomena. Such techniques can show only relations among variables and not how these relations are actually produced—as they can indeed only be produced—through the action and interaction of individuals (see esp. Boudon, 1976, 1987, 2003a: 169–72; Coleman, 1986a; Abbott, 1992a; also Lindenberg and Frey, 1993; Esser, 1996; Hedström and Swedberg, 1998a, 1998b).

For example, if, in a causal path analysis, a path is shown as leading from educational attainment to level of occupation or of income, it does not make much sense to talk, on this basis, of education *causing* occupation or income. Individuals get jobs because other individuals or employing organisations offer them jobs or because they make a place for themselves, as self-employed workers, in some market for goods or services. And likewise they get income because employers pay them or because they secure fees or make profits. Thus, even if it is clear from statistical analysis that how well individuals fare as regards jobs and income depends in some part on their educational attainment—and that this dependence is indeed robust—the question remains of just how this dependence comes about. It could be that education provides saleable knowledge and skills; but it could also be that education is used by employers chiefly as an indicator of job-seekers' psychological or social characteristics; or, again, that education allows individuals to pass credentialist filters chiefly set up to suit employers' convenience or to restrict the supply of labour to particular kinds of employment. To establish a causal link between education and occupation or income would then require, in the first instance, situating the variable of 'educational attainment' within some generalised narrative of action that would represent one or other such process that is of a 'causally adequate' kind (see, e.g., Jackson, Goldthorpe, and Mills, 2005). And in the interests of clarity, consistency, and subsequent empirical testing, it would then be further desirable that any narrative thus advanced should be not merely ad hoc but rather one informed by a reasonably well-developed theory of social action.

Moreover, as already remarked in Chapter 6 (pp. 121–4), such questioning of the capacity of 'variable sociology' to produce causal explanations has received strong reinforcement from objections raised by statisticians to the way in which techniques such as causal path analysis have actually been applied in sociology. Most notably, Freedman (1992a, 1992b, 1997, 1999, 2004; cf. Holland, 1988; Clogg and Haritou, 1997) has built up a cogent critique around three main points: first, that such modelling itself requires a theoretical input to determine the variables to be included, their causal ordering, the functional form of relationships between them, and so on; second, that insofar as the theory is mistaken—that is, is inconsistent with the social processes that actually generate the data used—the results of the analysis will be vitiated; and, third, that available sociological theory may just not be strong enough to help produce models that can be treated as genuinely 'structural'—that is, so parameterised that their coefficients are sufficiently invariant and autonomous to sustain claims about the consequences of changes in the variables deemed to be exogenous. For instance, a model might purport to show, on the basis of past observations, the degree to which inequalities in income among classes or ethnic groups depend on differences in their educational attainment; but if, as a result, say, of policy intervention, educational differentials were to be reduced, it could be seriously doubted whether reductions in income inequalities would then follow in the manner expected under the model.

In sum, an understanding of causation simply as robust dependence would seem best regarded more as a feature of sociology's past than of its future—of the period in which it was widely, although for the most part unreflectingly, believed that the making of causal inferences would be facilitated *pari passu* with the advance of statistical methodology. To conclude thus is not, I would stress, to imply that no such advance was achieved, nor that techniques such as causal path analysis have proved of no value in sociology. Rather, it is to suggest, and the point will in due course be developed further, that the potential of such techniques for sociology has been misjudged—though less, it should be said, by the real pioneers than by their epigoni[4]—and now stands in need of serious reevaluation.

CAUSATION AS CONSEQUENTIAL MANIPULATION

Among statisticians, the idea of causation as consequential manipulation would appear to have emerged in reaction to that of causation as robust dependence from a relatively early stage. Cook and Campbell (1979: 26) claim to be expressing a long-standing view when they contend that this latter idea, or what they themselves call the 'partialling approach', does not adequately accord with the understanding of causation in 'practical science'—which they would, apparently, see as best exemplified by medical or agricultural science. Here, attention centres specifically on 'the consequences of performing particular acts' or, in other words, on establishing causation through experimental methods; and this, they urge, is the paradigm for causal analysis that should in general be followed. Subsequently, a number of statisticians (see esp. Rubin, 1974, 1977, 1990; Holland, 1986a, 1986b) have developed and refined this position in a technically impressive way.

In outline, the argument is as follows. Causes can only be those factors that could, conceptually at least, serve as 'treatments' in experiments: that is, causes must in some sense be manipulable. In turn, the indication of genuine causation is that if a causal factor, X, is manipulated, then, given appropriate controls, a systematic effect is produced on the response variable, Y. Understood in this way, causation is always relative. It is, in principle, determined by *comparing* what would have happened to a 'unit' in regard to Y if this unit had been exposed to X (treatment) with what would have happened if it had not been exposed to X (control). This formulation gives rise to what Holland (1986a) has called the 'Fundamental Problem of Causal Inference': that is, it is not possible in the same experiment for a unit to be both exposed and not exposed to the treatment. But the problem has a statistical solution. One can take the whole population of units involved and compare the *average* response for exposed units with the average response for control units, with the difference between the two being then regarded as the average causal effect.[5] For this solution to be viable, however, it is essential that various conditions are met. Units must be assigned to the treatment or control subsets entirely at random; and the response of a unit must be unaffected either by the process of assignment itself or by the treatment (or absence of treatment) of other units. In sum, the conditions required are, ideally, those of randomised experimental design, as elaborated in statistical work from Fisher's (1935) classic study onwards.

There would seem to be wide agreement that the idea of causation as consequential manipulation is stronger or 'deeper' than that of causation as robust dependence (cf. Holland 1986a, Cox, 1992; Sobel, 1995, 1996). With the latter, it is observed, a variable X can never be regarded as having causal significance for Y in anything more than a provisional sense; for it is impossible to be sure that all other relevant variables have in fact been controlled. At any point, further information might be produced that would show that the dependence of Y on X is not robust after all or, in other words, that the apparent causal force of X is, at least to some extent, spurious. In contrast, insofar as causation is inferred from the results of appropriately designed experimental studies, the issue of spuriousness is avoided: the random assignment of units to exposure or nonexposure to the treatment variable replaces the attempt—the success of which must always be uncertain—to identify and statistically control all other variables that might be of causal significance.

Such an argument carries force. Nonetheless, it is at the same time important to recognise that, in moving from the one understanding of causation to the other, a far from negligible redefinition appears to occur of the actual problem being addressed. To put the matter briefly, while exponents of causation as robust dependence are concerned with establishing *the causes of effects*, exponents of causation as consequential manipulation are concerned—and more narrowly, it might be thought—with establishing *the effects of causes*. Holland (1986a: 959) indeed acknowledges this. Although 'looking for the causes of effects is a worthwhile scientific endeavour', he argues, 'it is not the proper perspective in a theoretical analysis of causation'. It is more to the point to take causes simply as 'given' or 'known', and to concentrate on the question of how their effects can most securely be measured. The main justification offered for this stance would seem to be (see esp. Holland, 1986b: 970; cf. also 1988) that while statements in the form 'X is a cause of Y' are always likely to be proved wrong as knowledge advances, statements in the form 'Y is an effect of X', *once they have been experimentally verified*, do not subsequently become false: 'Old, replicable experiments never die, they just get reinterpreted'.

In assessing how appropriate to sociology the idea of causation as consequential manipulation might be, this shift in focus must not be lost sight of, and I shall indeed return to it. But a more immediate issue is the extent to which the idea can be applied at all, given that most sociological research is not—and, for both practical and ethical reasons, cannot be—experimental in character.

What would in this regard be recommended by those subscribing to the principle of 'no causation without manipulation' is that in their empirical work sociologists should seek as far as possible to mimic experimental designs and, in particular, through what have been called, in a rather special sense, 'observational studies'. Such studies are those in which a treatment or, in a social context, a political or administrative intervention of some kind actually takes place; or, at very least, in which it is possible to understand the situation studied *as if* some treatment or intervention had occurred (cf. Rosenbaum, 1995: 1). The problem of approximating the requirements of randomised experimental design, it is argued, can then be addressed by making the process of unit assignment, whether actual or supposed, itself a prime concern of the enquiry. Specifically, researchers should attempt to identify, and then to represent through covariates in their data analyses, all influences on the response variable that could conceivably be involved in, or follow from, this process. Thus, in a study of, say, the effects of a vocational education and training scheme on workers' future earnings, it would be necessary to investigate any possible selection biases in recruitment to the scheme (i.e., in the assignment of individuals to the treatment rather than the control subset), any unintended effects of recruitment or nonrecruitment (e.g., on workers' motivation), any links fortuitously established with labour markets during the scheme, and so on, so that all such factors might be appropriately taken into account in the ultimate attempt to determine the effect on earnings of the treatment per se: that is, the education and training actually provided.

A difficulty at once apparent here is that of how it can be known if the set of covariates that is eventually established does indeed warrant the assumption that, given this set, treatment assignment and unit response *are* independent of each other. Have *all* relevant influences been represented and adequately measured and controlled? A whole battery of statistical techniques has in fact been developed to help answer such questions (see, e.g., Rosenbaum, 1995; Winship and Morgan, 1999). However, valuable though these techniques are, it is still difficult to avoid the conclusion that, in nonexperimental social research, attempts to determine the effects of causes will lead not to results that 'never die' but only to ones that have differing degrees of plausibility. And because this plausibility will in part depend on the existing subject-matter knowledge and theory that, presumably, guide the selection of covariates, such results will have to be provisional in just the same way and for just the same reasons as those of attempts to determine the causes of effects via the partialling approach.

Furthermore, it remains difficult to see how observational studies in the sense in question could have anything other than a rather minor role in sociology. While they could well be taken to represent the preferred design in policy evaluation research, it would appear no more than a statement of fact to say that in most other forms of enquiry in which sociologists presently engage, they could have only quite limited application—and even if this statement might then invite the conclusion that sociological research is not in general of a kind adequate to sustain causal analysis.

In this regard, the crux of the matter is of course the insistence of Rubin, Holland, and others that causes must be manipulable, and their consequent unwillingness to allow causal significance to be accorded to variables that are not manipulable, at least in principle. In this latter category are those variables that are 'intrinsic' to units—that is, part of their very constitution. Proponents of a manipulative view of causation would argue that an intrinsic variable may be considered as an *attribute* of a unit and shown to be associated with other variables, but that it cannot meaningfully be said to have 'effects' on them, since in the case of such a variable it does not make any sense to envisage a unit as taking a different value to that it actually has. The only way for an intrinsic variable to change its value would be for the unit itself to change in some way—so that it would no longer be the same unit. Thus, to give a sociological example, one could discuss the association that exists between sex (or again, say, race), on the one hand, and educational attainment, on the other. But it would be no more meaningful to speak of sex as being a cause of such attainment than it would be to make statements about what level of education Ms. M would have achieved had she been a man or Mr. N had he been a woman.

It is in fact this restriction imposed on variables that can be treated as causes that has led to most objections from sociologists and other social scientists, and also from philosophers, to the principle of 'no causation without manipulation' (see, e.g., Geweke, 1984; Glymour, 1986; Granger, 1986; Berk, 1988). However, what I wish further to suggest here is that, from a sociological standpoint at least, this restriction is worrying not just because of the difficulties that arise over the causal significance of attributes, on which discussion has in fact so far centred, but also, and indeed more so, because of those that arise in another, quite different respect: that is, over the causal significance of *action*. This argument can be developed on the basis of a simple but illuminating example from Holland (1986a).

Holland considers the three following statements, each of which could be taken to suggest causation in some sense:

(A) She did well on the exam because she is a woman.
(B) She did well on the exam because she studied for it.
(C) She did well on the exam because she was coached by her teacher.

To begin with (C), this refers to an intervention—that is, coaching by the teacher—and thus the idea of causation as consequential manipulation, which Holland supports, is clearly applicable. In apparent contrast, the reference in (A) is to an attribute—sex—and in this case the suggestion of causation would, from Holland's position, be mistaken. However, as Berk (1988: 167) has observed, in a sociological context, what may seem prima facie to be a reference to an attribute, such as sex or race, often turns out to be a reference, rather, to a social construct built up around an attribute (cf.

also Rubin, 1986). Thus, (A) could be quite plausibly taken as claiming that women do well not because of their (biologically fixed) sex but because of their (in principle, alterable) gender; and a 'manipulative' causal interpretation would then be possible, with the implication that if the social construction or perception of gender were to be changed in some way, women would do less well.

It is, though, statement (B) that, from Holland's point of view, creates the really serious problems. Here there is reference neither to an intervention in regard to a manipulable factor nor to an attribute. The obvious elaboration of (B) would be as follows: she had the goal of doing well in the exam; she believed that studying for the exam was the best way of achieving this goal; therefore she chose to study; therefore, her belief being correct, she did well. It may be noted that the form of this narrative is of the general kind that, as earlier seen, has been proposed by both economists and sociologists in order that adequate recognition may be made of the human action that must underlie all statistically demonstrated social regularities: that is, a narrative given, to use again Sen's words, in terms of individuals' 'objectives, knowledge, reasoning and decisions'. And most sociologists would, I believe, wish to regard this kind of explanatory narrative as being causal in character: the woman's doing well was caused by her taking appropriate means to this end. But, as Holland (1986a: 955) indeed appreciates, such accounts cannot in any very convincing way be reconciled with the idea of causation as consequential manipulation, and primarily because of 'the voluntary aspect of the supposed cause'.[6] Thus, either a limit to the applicability of this idea has here to be accepted or else sociologists must be required to reform, in at least one rather crucial respect, the language of causation that they are accustomed to using. This problem of agency, as it might be called, is one reason, Holland concedes, why the argument over what constitutes proper causal inference has to be left, and is likely to remain, 'without any definitive resolution'.

It has, moreover, to be noted that a version of the problem may well arise in 'observational' studies in sociology, in the special sense noted above: that is, studies that seek to determine the effects of some kind of intervention and that would thus appear to offer the best possibility for implementing a manipulative approach to causation. In such studies, it cannot be supposed that the response of the units involved—that is, ultimately of the individuals affected or potentially affected by the intervention—will be of the same nature as that of the units in an experiment in some applied natural science. These individuals are likely to know that the intervention is taking place, to have beliefs about what its aims are and what might follow from it, and then to relate their understanding of the situation to their own interests and goals and to act accordingly—which could in fact mean acting so as actually to counter or subvert the intervention. In the case, say, of the introduction of some kind of positive discrimination in education, with the aim of reducing class or ethnic differentials in attainment, it could be that members of those classes or ethnic groups whose children would not benefit and who might lose their competitive advantage in schools and labour markets could respond—that is, act—so as to preserve this advantage: as, for example, by devoting yet more of their own resources to their children's education or by trying to modify processes of educational or occupational selection so that their children would still be favoured. And such a response could indeed occur, in a preemptive way, even where the intervention was not made: that is, within educational administrations or geographical areas assigned to the 'control' rather than the 'treatment' subset.

In such circumstances, at least one of the crucial requirements of randomised experimental design would then clearly be breached: namely, that the response of a unit should not be influenced by whether other units are treated or not. And still more basic issues do in any event arise. For example, is an intervention to be regarded as causally consequential if it would have had an effect had it not at the same time caused an offsetting response? And would it make any sociological sense to try to control for such a response, even supposing that this were in some way possible?

The very fact that such questions can be asked serves then to reemphasise the difficulties of translating an approach to causation developed within applied natural science into a social science context.[7] So far at least as sociology is concerned, the ultimate source of these difficulties might be specified as follows. The approach allows conceptual space for human action, and in particular for action of a rational, outcome-oriented kind, *only in* the roles of experimenter or intervener. Once the experiment or intervention is made, all else has to follow in the manner simply of bacteria responding to a drug or plants to a fertiliser: that is, in ways to which considerations of individuals' 'objectives, knowledge, reasoning and decisions' have no further relevance. In turn, a rather paradoxical if not contradictory position is arrived at. It is maintained that only through purposive action taken in the role of experimenter or intervener can genuinely causal processes be set in motion—'no causation without manipulation'. Yet action taken by individuals in *other* roles, in the everyday pursuit of their goals by what they believe to be the best means (their response to interventions included) cannot be accorded causal significance and, in this case, precisely because of its 'voluntary aspect'.

The idea of causation as consequential manipulation does therefore face sociologists with something of a dilemma. There is wide agreement that one has here a more rigorously formulated, even if narrower, understanding of causation than that founded on the idea of robust dependence; yet it appears far less appropriate to, and applicable in, sociological analysis. Two main reactions on the part of sociologists have so far been apparent. One, which is perhaps best expressed by Sobel (1995, 1996), entails acceptance of the manipulative approach as that which, as it were, sets the standard for the making of causal inferences. Sociologists should therefore seek wherever possible to conduct research on an experimental or at least quasi-experimental basis and, if this is not possible, still to take this approach as providing the conceptual framework within which the validity of causal inferences should be judged—discomfiting though this may often be (cf. also Winship and Morgan, 1999). The other, contrasting reaction is that to be found most fully argued in the work of Lieberson (1987; cf. Lieberson and Lynn, 2002). This entails a straight rejection of the attempt to impose the experimental model (or, at any rate, that adopted in medical or agricultural research) onto sociology, on the grounds that this represents an undue 'scientism'—that is, an undue regard for the form rather than the substance of scientific method—and with the implication, then, that sociologists have to find their own ways of thinking about causation, proper to the kinds of research that they can realistically carry out and the problems that they can realistically address.

The position that I would myself wish to take up in this regard, while representing an appreciative response to those of both Sobel and Lieberson, is one that is more strongly influenced by the third understanding of causation that I initially identified, that of causation as generative process.

CAUSATION AS GENERATIVE PROCESS

This idea of causation has been advanced by statisticians in several versions. It does not, though, to the same extent as the two understandings of causation already considered reflect specifically statistical thinking. It would appear to derive, rather, from an attempt to spell out what must be *added to* any statistical criteria before an argument for causation can convincingly be made. Thus, Cox (1992: 297) introduces the idea in noting a 'major limitation' of the manipulative approach to causation—and likewise, it would seem, of the approach via robust dependence (cf. Cox and Wermuth, 1996: 220–21): namely, that 'no explicit notion of an underlying process' is introduced—no notion of a process 'at an observational level that is deeper than that involved in the data under immediate analysis'. Similarly, Simon and Iwasaki have maintained that, in moving from association to causation, more must be entailed than just time precedence or manipulation in establishing the necessary asymmetry: that is, that X has causal significance for Y rather than vice versa. The assumption must also be present that the association is created by some 'mechanism' operating 'at a more microscopic level' than that at which the association is established (1988: 157). In other words, these authors would alike insist (and cf. also Freedman, 1991, 1992a, 1992b) on tying the concept of causation to some process existing in time and space, even if not perhaps directly observable, that actually generates the causal effect of X on Y and, in so doing, produces the statistical relationship that is empirically in evidence. At the same time, it should be said, they would also recognise that the accounts that are advanced of such causal processes, in order to illuminate the 'black boxes' left by purely statistical analysis, can never be taken as definitive. They must in all cases be ones that are open to empirical test; and even where they appear to be supported, it has still to be accepted that finer-grained accounts, at some yet deeper level, will in principle always be possible.[8]

Such an approach to causation is clearly seen by its proponents as being essentially that which prevails, even if only implicitly, in general scientific practice (cf. Cox, 1992: 297; Simon and Iwasaki,1988: 149–51; Freedman, 1991) and, presumably, in nonexperimental as well as experimental fields. In fact, the subject-matter area in which this approach has perhaps been developed most explicitly is that of epidemiology (see, e.g., Bradford Hill (1965, 1991); and it is at all events this that provides the obvious paradigm case—that of smoking and lung cancer. Statistical analysis of observational data was able to show a strong association between smoking and lung cancer and, further, that this was robust to the introduction of a whole range of possible 'common' causal factors. But what was crucial to the claim for a causal link was the elaboration of an underlying, generative process on the basis of the isolation of known carcinogens in cigarette smoke, histo-pathological evidence from the bronchial epithelium of smokers and so on. Freedman (1997: 129) emphasises the diversity of sources from which the evidence that supports the proposed generative process derives, and notes that its force 'depends on the complex interplay among these various studies and the [statistical] data-sets'.

As I have said, those statisticians who have upheld the idea of causation as generative process have tended to represent it as a necessary augmentation of the two understandings of causation earlier examined. But whether the same relationship is involved in both cases alike might be questioned. In regard to causation as robust dependence, causation as generative process would indeed seem an obvious complement. It at once allows for the objection that causation cannot be established simply through general procedures of statistical inference, without need for subject-matter input. If some account is required of the processes that are believed to be creating the statistically demonstrated dependence, then this account will have to be given largely on the basis of subject-matter knowledge; and the more thoroughly the account is informed by prevailing theory, rather than being merely ad hoc, the more coherent—and testable—it will be (cf. Bradford Hill, 1965; Cox and Wermuth, 1996: 225–26).

However, in regard to causation as consequential manipulation, the idea of causation as generative process would appear not just as complement but also in certain respects as corrective. To begin with, a focus on how causal effects are brought about serves to reduce the significance accorded to different kinds of independent variables. Thus, even if it is thought improper to speak of an attribute as being a true cause of, rather than merely associated with, a dependent variable, the key issue can still be seen as that of how the relationship, however labelled, is actually produced. For example, even if 'She did well on the exam because she is a woman' is taken to refer to the fixed attribute of sex (rather than to potentially changeable gender), what is important is the nature and validity of the account given of the process that underlies the association appealed to—as, say, an account on the lines that the hardwiring of females' brains has evolved in ways that give them an advantage over men in the kind of examination in question. And at the same time, in a social science context, the attaching of causal significance to action, far from being a source of difficulty, could rather be taken as the *standard* way of constructing an account of a causal process: 'She did well on the exam because she studied for it' is no longer in any way problematic.[9]

Furthermore, it is also important to recognise that an emphasis on causal processes serves to direct attention back to the question of the causes of effects as opposed to that of the effects of (assumed or, supposedly, known) causes (cf. Smith, 1990). In turn, a shift is implied away from the strong verificationist position that would see the purpose of causal analysis as being to determine the effects of causes, via experimental methods, in a once-and-for-all way, and which, as well as being open to some philosophical doubts, is in any event scarcely supportable in sociological practice. An understanding of causation in terms of generative processes consorts far better in fact with a falsificationist position. Hypothetical but adequate accounts of such processes are advanced—that is, the processes envisaged would in principle be capable of generating the statistical relationships addressed—and further empirical enquiry is then undertaken to try to test whether it is these processes that are actually at work. This might well lead to a negative result, but even a positive one would remain no more than provisional since, as earlier remarked, it is accepted that truly 'final' accounts of causal processes will never be reached.

If, then, the idea of causation as generative process can be seen not only as augmenting the ideas of causation as robust dependence and of causation as consequential manipulation but also, in the latter case, as entailing some degree of modification and reorientation, a basis does, I believe, become discernible on which an alternative approach to causal analysis, appropriate to sociological enquiry, might be developed. That is, one that would enable sociologists to go beyond the merely 'pragmatic utilisation' of the concept of causation as, say, through unreflective causal modelling, without, however, requiring them to take up an understanding of causation too restrictive to allow them to pursue their own legitimate purposes.

AN ALTERNATIVE FOR SOCIOLOGY

The approach to causal analysis that is here proposed, in part drawing on and in part elaborating a position that I have already to some extent developed in preceding chapters, is presented in the form of a three-phase sequence:

1. establishing the phenomena that form the *explananda,*
2. hypothesising generative processes at the level of social action, and
3. testing the hypotheses.

It should, however, be stressed that such a presentation is intended primarily to ease exposition. In practice, the three phases are unlikely to be so readily separable in any particular piece of sociological work as this schematic treatment might suggest.

1. Establishing the Phenomena

This phrase is taken from Merton (1987), who seeks to make the seemingly obvious but, as he shows, often neglected point that before advancing explanations of social phenomena, sociologists would do well to have good evidence that these phenomena really exist and *that they express sufficient regularity to require and allow explanation.* Merton's emphasis on regularity has here particular importance. To begin with, it would seem necessary for sociologists to recognise (cf. the discussion in chs. 3 and 6) that their explanatory concerns are in fact with regularities rather than singularities, such as, say, individual lives or unique historical events. And further, the nature of the basic linkage between sociology and statistics is in this way clearly brought out. If sociologists' *explananda* consist of social regularities of one kind or another, then statistics is, if not the only, at all events the most reliable and versatile means of demonstrating that such regularities exist and of clarifying their nature; and especially so, it might be added, in the case of regularities that are not readily apparent to the 'lay members' of a society in the course of their everyday lives but are revealed only through the— perhaps rather sophisticated—analysis of data that have been collected extensively in time or space (see further Goldthorpe, 2005).

However, establishing the phenomena is an essentially descriptive exercise and insofar as it is achieved statistically it is statistics in descriptive mode that will be relevant. In this connection, it is of interest to note that various critics of current causal modelling methods in sociology (e.g., Lieberson, 1987: 213–19 esp.; Freedman, 1992a, 1992b; Abbott, 1998) have regretted the way in which enthusiasm for such methods has led to the disparagement of overtly descriptive statistical work, and would in effect join with Merton in urging on sociologists the importance of using quantitative data to show, in Lieberson's words, 'what is happening' before they attempt to explain 'why it is happening'.

What then may be suggested—as indeed the critics in question all in one way or another do—is that the whole statistical technology that has underpinned the sociological reception of the idea of causation as robust dependence, from Lazarsfeldian elaboration through to causal path analysis, should be radically reevaluated. That is to say, instead of being regarded as a means of inferring causation directly from data, its primary use should rather be seen *as* descriptive, involving the analysis of joint and conditional distributions in order to determine no more than patterns of association (or correlation). Or, at very most, representations of the data might serve to *suggest* causal accounts, which, however, will need always to be further developed theoretically and then tested as quite separate undertakings.[10] Moreover, once the independent role of description is in this way accepted, a range of other statistical techniques than those that have been aimed at causal analysis would seem capable of making a major contribution: for example, loglinear methods of analysing categorical data (including latent class analysis), where no distinction between independent and dependent variables need be entailed and attention centres specifically on structures of association and interaction; or again, as Abbott (1998) argues, various nonprobabilistic techniques of scaling, clustering, and sequencing that are even more clearly dedicated to descriptive tasks.

What gives arguments for the importance of description their real force is not just that instances can readily be found in the sociological literature of the recent past of what might be regarded as 'premature' causal analysis—that is, instances in which causal models were applied that later descriptive work showed to be based on mistaken suppositions (see, e.g., ch. 6, pp. 123–4). In addition, and more positively, various cases can also be cited in which the chief statistical accomplishment has been to identify and characterise important social regularities that were hitherto unappreciated, or incorrectly understood, by in effect separating out these regularities from their particular contexts. For example, loglinear modelling has been applied to demonstrate how a large degree of temporal constancy and significant cross-national commonality in relative rates of social mobility—or patterns of social fluidity—can underlie historically and geographically specific and often widely fluctuating absolute rates (see further vol. II, ch. 7). Likewise, sequential logit modelling, as pioneered by Mare (1981), has been used in order to show up persistence in class differentials in educational attainment during eras in which educational provision has steadily expanded and in which the 'effects' of class origins on educational attainment overall may indeed have declined simply on account of increased rates of participation (see further vol. II, ch. 2). Or again, event history analysis has enabled uniformities in the pattern of life-course events in relation to family formation or dissolution to be distinguished across periods and places characterised by widely differing political, economic, and social conditions (Blossfeld and Huinink, 1991; Blossfeld and Rohwer, 1995b). It is important that the use of rather advanced statistical techniques for these purposes of what might be called sophisticated description should be clearly distinguished from their use in attempts at deriving causal relations directly from data analysis.

2. Hypothesising Generative Processes

Social regularities, once relatively securely established by descriptive methods, are then to be regarded as the basic *explananda* of sociological analysis: sociological problems are ones that can all in one way or another be expressed in terms of social regularities—their formation, continuity, interrelation, change, disruption, and so on.[11] When, therefore, analysis becomes causal, social regularities represent the effects for which causes have to be discovered. And this task, contrary to what proponents of the idea of causation as robust dependence would seem to have supposed, cannot be a purely statistical one but requires a crucial subject-matter input.

From the position of methodological individualism that I would here adopt—and from which most of the critiques earlier noted of a purely 'variable sociology' explicitly or implicitly derive—this input has then to take the form of some account of the action and interaction of individuals. In effect, a narrative of action must be provided that purports to capture the central tendencies that arise within the diverse courses of action that are followed by particular actors in situations of a certain type: that is, situations that can be regarded as sharing essential similarities insofar as actors' goals and the nature of the opportunities and constraints that condition their action in pursuit of these goals are concerned. And, in turn, a case must be made to show how these central tendencies in action would, if operative, actually give rise, through their intended and unintended consequences, to the regularities that constitute the *explananda*. The theory that underlies such hypothesised processes will then obviously be a theory of social action of some kind; and, in this respect, the two main alternatives that would appear available might be labelled as rational action theory (RAT) and norm-oriented action theory. On grounds that I have set out in preceding chapters, and to which I return in Volume II, I would regard the former as having conceptual, explanatory, and interpretative privilege over the latter, though quite possibly needing to be complemented by it. RAT allows for the fuller expression of the idea of reasons as causes for action; and an appeal to the rationality of action, in the sense of its grounding in what for actors are good reasons for their actions in terms of perceived costs and benefits, represents a uniquely attractive end-point for any sociological explanation to reach. However, for present purposes, the important point is that *whatever* theory of action is favoured, it should be used to enable as explicit and coherent a formulation as possible of the generative processes that are proposed and in this way facilitate their evaluation as regards both their causal adequacy and their empirical presence.[12]

In particular, it is at this stage that questions of what might be called causal form and causal hierarchy should be clarified. Thus, authors such as Lieberson (1987: ch. 4 esp.) and Blossfeld and Rohwer (1995a: ch. 1) have stressed the need to specify whether causal processes are seen as symmetrical or, rather, one-way and irreversible, and whether they entail lags, thresholds, or other distinctive temporal features in their effects. And Lieberson (1987: ch. 7 esp.) has further emphasised the need to distinguish between 'basic' causal processes and ones of a more 'superficial' kind (the former often being less open to direct observation than the latter). Thus, to revert to an earlier example, if differentials in educational attainment are in fact treated as a basic cause of income inequalities among classes or ethnic groups, then action, such as some kind of political intervention, that brought about a reduction in these differentials would be expected to close income gaps also. But if educational differentials are seen as only a superficial cause of income inequalities, with the basic cause lying elsewhere—say, in processes grounded in more generalised social inequalities or in discrimination—then what would be expected to follow from their reduction would not be a corresponding decrease in income inequalities but simply changes *consequent on the latter remaining unaltered*: for instance, a weakening of the association between education and income while, perhaps, that between other factors—say, family contacts—and entry into well-paid employment became stronger.

3. Testing the Hypotheses

As earlier indicated, the first test of any causal explanation of a social regularity that is put forward must be that of its adequacy: would the generative process hypothesised, assuming it to be operative, in fact be capable of producing the regularity in question? It is here worth pointing out that the fuller and more refined the description of the regularity, the stronger the explanatory demands that will be made and the more likely it is that certain candidate accounts can be eliminated at this stage.[13] However, it may be supposed that more than one adequate account will be possible, and further testing is then required to try to determine which—if any—of the processes hypothesised is actually at work. In other words, the issue shifts from that of the adequacy in principle of an account of a causal process to that of its empirical validity.

In this connection, what crucially matters are the implications that follow from any account that is advanced. If the generative process suggested does in fact operate to produce, or help to produce, an established regularity, then what *else* should be empirically found? The process, or at least some features of it, could perhaps be directly observable (cf. ch. 4, pp. 84–5); but if the action and interaction of relatively large numbers of individuals is involved or interaction that is not of a localised, face-to-face kind, then this may scarcely be feasible. The alternative is to devise more indirect tests by specifying other effects to which the process should give rise apart from those constituting the regularities it purports to explain, although likewise of an empirically ascertainable kind. Such direct or indirect tests may be made through whatever methods appear most appropriate; and it is indeed important that separate tests of particular implications should be undertaken, and repeated, on the basis of different data-sets and analytical techniques (cf. Berk, 1988).[14] Thus, while it might seem that, at this stage, attention does after all come to focus on the effects of—given—causes rather than on the causes of effects, this is within the context not of randomised experimental design but of (what should be) a theoretically informed account of a generative process that is subject to ongoing evaluation; and with the outcome being falsification or, if testing is withstood, simply corroboration, rather than the verification of effects of a once-and-for-all kind.

To illustrate, one could take the case of the consequences for children of parents' marital breakup.[15] An association would appear to be established between breakup, on the one hand, and, on the other, children leaving school at the minimum age and experiencing various other seemingly adverse effects. But disagreement arises over whether, or how far, breakup can be given causal significance in these respects. For instance, it is not difficult to think of possible 'common' causes—say, personality factors or parental conflict—that could lie behind both marital instability *and* poor parenting and its consequences for children. The key issue may then be regarded as that of whether the children of those couples who *do* break up would have fared better if their parents had in fact stayed together, and in this way Holland's 'Fundamental Problem of Causal Inference' is directly encountered: the same couple cannot both break up and not break up. Moreover, a statistical solution via experimental design is here scarcely possible; and from the point of view of causation as consequential manipulation, the strategy to be pursued would then have to be that of viewing breakup as if it were an intervention, and attempting to overcome the assignment problem by introducing a set of relevant covariates into the analysis: that is, so that a comparison could be made between the children of parents who did and who did not break up on the basis of, as it were, 'all else equal to the time of breakup'. However, as earlier remarked, it remains far from clear how the completeness of such a set could ever be determined and definitive results thus claimed, any more than they could be from the standpoint of causation as robust dependence. It would indeed appear that the more attention analysts have given to the problems of defining and including appropriate covariates, the more sceptical their conclusions have become (see esp. Ní Bhrolcháin, Chappell, and Diamond, 1994).

The alternative strategy that is here proposed is that those who wish to investigate what, causally, underlies the association between marital breakup and adverse features of children's future lives should begin by spelling out as fully as they are able the way or ways in which they believe that the effects in question are produced—that is, by giving accounts of adequate generative processes; and these accounts should then be empirically tested, by reference to their further implications, as extensively as possible. The more detailed the accounts are, the more likely it is that they will differ in their implications so as to allow critical comparisons to be made: as, say, between children who have lost a parent through marital dissolution and those who have lost a parent through death; between siblings who experience their parents' breakup at different ages; between children who remain with a single parent after breakup and those who acquire a step-parent; between children experiencing breakup in differing contexts in terms of prevailing rates of breakup, the extent of social support for single parents, and so on.

In fact, one recent contribution can be taken as marking at least a first step in seeking to implement such a strategy. Jonsson and Gähler (1997), considering the possible effects of marital breakup on children's educational attainment in Sweden, first identify a number of 'plausible causal mechanisms' and then carry out analyses on a large-scale longitudinal data-set in order to test for the presence of such mechanisms. Interestingly, the mechanism, or generative process, for which strongest corroboration was found was one that had received little previous attention in the debate: that is, a 'downward mobility' process through which, when children are separated from the parent with the higher educational or occupational achievement, their own educational and occupational aspirations tend to fall (see also Gähler, 1998). There are in fact quite close analogies here, via the 'structural' theory of aspirations (Keller and Zavalloni, 1964), with processes that have been suggested, and have received some support, in explaining persistence and change in class and gender differentials in educational attainment more generally (cf. Boudon, 1974; Gambetta, 1987; and vol. II, chs. 2–4). Nonetheless, it is important to note that what the authors claim is still only evidence for, and not definitive proof of, the operation of such a process, and they are careful to point out what might prove to be special features of the Swedish case.[16]

For the present, the—diversified and repeated—testing of suggested generative processes on the basis of particular implications derivable from them is, perhaps, the most that can be asked for. It should, though, finally be said that the logical conclusion to which the entire approach outlined would lead is that of testing on the basis of statistical models *of these processes themselves*. The important distinction in this regard is that made by Cox (1990) between 'empirical' and 'substantive' statistical models, or by Rogosa (1992) between statistical models per se and scientific models expressed in statistical form (cf. also Sørensen, 1998; Hedström, 2005). Models of the former kind are those that sociologists normally use and are concerned with relations among variables that may be determined through techniques of rather general applicability. Models of the latter kind, however, are intended to represent real processes that have causal force (whether or not directly observable). They are therefore crucially informed by subject-matter theory and can in turn serve as the vehicles through which such theory is exposed to test in a fairly comprehensive way. In particular, as Cox has observed, it should be possible for such models to be applied in simulation exercises: 'The essential idea is that if the investigator cannot use the model directly to simulate artificial data, how can "Nature" [or, one could add, "Society"—JHG] have used anything like that method to generate real data?' (1990: 172). In sociology, accounts of processes capable of producing observed regularities are not yet for the most part expressed in sufficiently specific and theoretically informed ways to permit substantive models to be developed—greater efforts at formalisation might help in this respect—and, correspondingly, the simulation approach to hypothesis testing is not at a very advanced stage. Nonetheless, there are by now at least indications that its potential in helping to integrate theoretical and quantitative empirical work is becoming more fully appreciated (see, e.g., Halpin, 1999).

The general point that, I believe, emerges most clearly from the foregoing might be put as follows. If contributions made by statisticians to the understanding of causation are to be taken over with advantage in any specific field of enquiry, then what is crucial is that the right relationship should exist between statistical and subject-matter concerns.

Thus, it could be said that the idea of causation as robust dependence does have a certain appropriateness insofar as the main aim of research is prediction and, in particular, prediction in the real world rather than in the laboratory or, in other words, forecasting. The importance that this idea has had in economic forecasting is not therefore at all surprising. However, where the ultimate aim of research is not prediction per se but rather causal explanation, an idea of causation that is expressed in terms of predictive power—as, for example, Granger causation—is likely to be found wanting. Causal explanations cannot be arrived at through statistical methodology alone: a subject-matter input is also required in the form of background knowledge and, crucially, theory. This is the upshot of the critiques made by sociological theorists and statisticians alike of the pragmatic or, one could say, atheoretical use of the concept of causation by quantitative sociologists on the basis of essentially partialling procedures from Lazarsfeldian elaboration through to causal path analysis.

Likewise, the idea of causation as consequential manipulation is apt to research that can be undertaken primarily through experimental methods and, especially, to revert to Cook and Campbell, to 'practical science' where the central concern is indeed with 'the consequences of performing particular acts'. The development of this idea in the context of medical and agricultural research is as understandable as the development of that of causation as robust dependence within applied econometrics. However, the extension of the manipulative approach into sociology would not appear promising, other than in rather special circumstances. It is not just that in sociological research practical and ethical barriers to experiments, or interventions, often arise: it can be accepted that statisticians have made major advances in the methodology of quasi-experimental studies, even if the latter can scarcely claim to provide once-and-for-all results in the way that might be thought possible with true experiments. The more fundamental difficulty is that, under the—highly anthropocentric—principle of 'no causation without manipulation', the recognition that can be given to the action of individuals as having causal force is in fact peculiarly limited. That is, it extends only to those actually in the role of experimenter or intervener: otherwise, what Holland calls the 'voluntary aspect' of action, and including in the case of action taken in response to an intervention, creates major problems.

The idea of causation as generative process is not, in the same way as the two other ideas of causation that have been considered, linked to a particular body of statistical work. It does, nonetheless, appear to offer the best basis, as I have sought finally to show, on which statistical and substantive concerns can be related in causal analysis in sociology. First, it places the emphasis on the causes of effects: in other words, it implies that such analysis begins with the effects—the phenomena—for which a causal explanation is then sought. And in sociology it is in establishing the phenomena that statistics has a basic contribution to make, in an essentially descriptive mode. Second, the idea of a generative process specified at a deeper, or more microscopic, level than that of the data that constitute the *explananda* fits closely with the analytical approach of at least those sociologists adhering to the principle of methodological individualism, who would thus insist on the need for causal explanations of social phenomena to be grounded ultimately in accounts of the action and interaction of individuals, and who have criticised a purely 'variable sociology' from this point of view. Third, the recognition that final, definitive accounts of generative processes will never be reached means that empirical evaluations of such accounts, in regard to whether the processes they suggest do in fact operate to produce the effects attributed to them, are not expected to achieve once-and-for-all verification but either falsification or, at best, what might be described as corroboration pending improvement. Statistics has then again an evident role to play in testing such accounts via their particular, empirically ascertainable implications on, for now, a 'catch-as-catch-can' basis. But this role will be enlarged insofar as sociologists are able to develop their accounts of generative processes to the point at which statistical methods can also be applied in creating substantive models of these processes themselves.

NOTES

Notes to Chapter 1

1. Readers who might wish to have the grounds for the analysis more fully spelled out are referred to the Introduction to the first edition.

2. It is, for example, instructive, if disturbing, to compare the *American Journal of Sociology*, the *American Sociological Review* or the *European Sociological Review*, on the one hand, with, on the other—and taking examples from my own country—*Sociology* or the *Sociological Review*. However one may wish to assess the relative merits of these journals, it is difficult to see how they could be said to relate, in other than a purely nominal sense, to the same academic *discipline*.

3. In this connection, one should not underestimate the impact of Alan Sokal's splendid hoax on the journal *Social Text* (Sokal, 1996a, 1996b)—nor the highly counterproductive nature of the desperate efforts at damage limitation that followed.

4. Also of major significance on the philosophical front was Kuhn's forthright rejection in his Rothschild lecture of 1991 (see 2000: ch. 5) of the 'absurdity' of the 'strong programme' of the post-Mertonian sociology of science—of which he was widely, but undeservedly, regarded as a progenitor. This programme could be regarded as the major expression of cognitive relativism originating within sociology itself. Although it attracted relatively little attention from either philosophers or scientists until the 'science wars' of the 1990s, it then became increasingly a target for their criticism, and especially as regards its implication that scientific knowledge, rather then being effectively constrained by the way the world is, has an essentially contingent character. That is to say, if physics, chemistry, or biology had been historically formed within some different sociocultural matrix to that which actually obtained, then it would be possible for their present-day cognitive content to be not just more or less advanced than, but *significantly different from*, what it in fact is (cf. Hacking, 1999: ch. 3). As critics have observed, not even the vaguest accounts have ever been given of what these supposedly alternative versions might have looked like.

5. It is perhaps this outcome that is most disturbing to Steinmetz (2005: 144–

55) in his hostile response to Mahoney and Rueschemeyer—including charges of bad faith and 'identification with the aggressor'—which focuses on their 'uneasy mingling of positivism and non-positivism'. This criticism is, however, sustainable, if at all, only in relation to Steinmetz's own philosophically convoluted, yet still quite arbitrary, definition of positivism. Fortunately, as I go on to suggest in the text, the style of argumentation in which Steinmetz engages does now appear increasingly passé.

6. Steuer writes as an economist. Much of his critical commentary on what he calls 'pretend social science' is clearly directed against sociologists and, in particular, against the authors of what he calls books of 'social revelation' or 'social poetry' that trade on the buzzwords of the day such as 'globalisation', 'risk', the 'network-society', and so on. See further Goldthorpe (2004b).

7. In addition to counterposing expressive and critical sociology to sociology as social science, Boudon (2001) also distinguishes a fourth type, 'cameral' sociology: that is, sociology aimed at providing information needed for the guidance of public policy (cf. Schumpeter, 1954: part II, ch. 3). This chiefly differs from sociology as social science in having specific descriptive rather than general explanatory concerns. In previous commentary on Boudon (Goldthorpe, 2004a), I have sought to show that, despite this difference, there is little to prevent the relationship between these two types of sociology from being one of cooperation and complementarity, while they are together clearly set apart, as regards their objectives and methodological commitments, from both expressive and critical sociology.

8. I have myself sought to develop this same line of argument in detail in the case of a particular area of social research, that of social mobility (Goldthorpe, 2005). In this area, it is, I believe, readily demonstrable that progress has been made in regard not simply to data collection and analysis and the accumulation of empirical findings but, further—and despite problems posed by the greater mutability of social than of natural phenomena—in regard to the theoretical explanation of these findings.

9. Hacking prefers to speak of 'ideas' and 'objects' rather than of concepts and facts but I do not think that my translation of his argument into the terminology that I have earlier used leads to any serious misrepresentation. For a forceful application of Hacking's argument in critique of Jenkins (2002), see Voas (2003).

10. In other words, the 'double hermeneutic' proposed by Giddens (1984, 1987) and frequently appealed to by impossibilists does not appear very consequential. Contrary to what Giddens suggests, social scientists' concepts need not be, and in fact often are not, 'parasitic' on actors' concepts and can be, and often are, applied without any likelihood of feedback. This is most obviously, though not only, the case when such concepts are applied to past societies. It is, for example, difficult to see how the double hermeneutic operates when a Cobb-Douglas production function is applied in analyses of medieval agriculture or the distinction between absolute and relative rates of social mobility in a study of nineteenth-century social stratification. Moreover, insofar as interaction does occur, it can be taken

into account in social scientists' analyses—as, say, when allowance is made in testing Durkheimian explanations of suicide rates for the possibility that Durkheimian ideas may influence the official classification of dubious deaths.

11. In the foregoing, I have written as if theorists and researchers are, as it were, two separate sociological tribes, and indeed this could not be thought a wildly misleading representation of the present situation. But of course there is nothing to prevent, and much to commend, sociologists shifting between the roles of theorist and researcher or pursuing both simultaneously.

12. Peter Hedström has drawn to my attention a remark by Francis Crick (1989) to the effect that present-day biologists do in fact quite routinely think in terms of mechanisms, specified at the level of chemical processes, rather than of general laws.

13. As Elster has observed (1998: 48–49), mechanism-based explanations may be regarded as inferior to lawlike explanations in falling short of generality— that is, in being limited in their domain of application. But they still offer an increase in understanding insofar as the mechanism invoked is *more general* than the phenomena that it accounts for. Moreover, others might wish to go further than Elster in seeking to integrate different mechanisms on a common theoretical basis. As regards prediction *stricto sensu*, this would seem possible even in the natural sciences only insofar as a closed system exists or may be set up as, say, in a laboratory. In open systems, such as those with which social scientists typically deal, it would be better to think of forecasting rather than prediction. And in this regard, it is not clear that social scientists are always at a disadvantage. I would be ready to back my long-range forecast of traffic conditions in central Oxford next Christmas Day against any meteorologist's forecast of the weather conditions.

14. A little earlier Mahoney and Rueschemeyer (2003: 15, n. 14) observe that 'historians remain largely indifferent to historical comparative analyses' and that this 'represents a major unresolved problem of our research tradition'. I would suggest that lack of methodological sophistication in the use of secondary sources is at least one source of the problem, and that historians will remain unimpressed until some significant improvement in this regard is achieved.

15. I should make it clear that I do not wish to deny induction any part in the research process. I would regard 'learning from the data', as through various methods of exploratory data analysis, as being especially appropriate in the first phase of describing, with as great refinement as possible, the phenomena that are to be explained. In this connection, data-mining methods or (more politely) specification searches are often of value with complex quantitative data-sets. However, I find it odd that Collier, Brady, and Seawright (2004: 239) appear to regard such inductive procedures as being of distinctive value in theory construction and testing—specifically as 'an unavoidable step in making causal inferences from observational data'—since elsewhere, as I have noted, they underline my own argument to the effect that causation cannot in any event be simply cranked out of statistical analyses.

16. I also find Ragin's position here somewhat difficult to square with his commitment to the idea of determining often highly complex but at the same time quite deterministic patterns of causation via logical methods, such as his 'qualitative comparative analysis'. This method is, incidentally, favourably referred to throughout the collection edited by Brady and Collier (2004; though note the strong critique subsequently provided by their collaborator, Seawright, 2005) without any reference to my own or others' demonstrations of its extreme fragility (as, for example, in Wickham-Crowley, 1992 or Kangas, 1994) in the face of error or uncertainty in data and its coding—which would seem inevitable in social research, regardless of whether or not the social world is itself regarded as deterministic. Such demonstrations have the same critical force in regard to new 'fuzzy-set' versions of QCA (Ragin, 2000) as to the original version but, so far as I am aware, no response has been made by its proponents.

17. For example, from Goldstone's review (2003) of the study of revolutions, it clearly emerges that the actual phenomena to be explained have been defined in constantly shifting ways, and at the same time a basic flaw of any form of inductively generated or 'grounded' theory is shown up: namely, that making successive modifications to some initial theory as new evidence comes in carries no guarantee of theoretical advance. Rather, researchers may become caught up in a quite misleading path dependency. The possibility should always be kept open of flatly rejecting a theory as empirically untenable and of making an entirely new start (cf. ch. 4, p. 74). Goldstone remarks (2003: 78) that, in the light of several decades of research, he has now come to the view that a revolution in the theory of revolutions may be necessary: most importantly, the *explanandum* should be taken as the conditions not of state disruption but rather of state stability. One may then ask: absent the commitment to grounded theory, might not this idea have been tried out a good deal sooner?

18. It is also notable that Burawoy's typology of public, critical, policy, and professional sociology has obvious parallels with Boudon's expressive, critical, cameral, and scientific typology. My main difficulty with Burawoy's position lies with the category of 'reflexive knowledge' that, for him, appears to legitimate sociologists assuming the role of public intellectuals. I do not understand how reflexive knowledge might differ from knowledge of a common-or-garden kind.

19. One might mention the rapid development of longitudinal survey work, whether based on the repeated sampling of populations, the collection of retrospective life history data or panel designs, and also of surveys designed to produce hierarchically structured data-sets comprising both individual-level data and data relating to a series of supra-individual entities in which respondents are or have been involved. As regards techniques of analysis, the treatment of categorical data has been transformed through loglinear and logmultiplicative modelling and logistic regression; and techniques such as event history analysis and multilevel modelling have enabled new survey designs of the kind indicated to be effectively exploited (cf. Clogg, 1992).

20. The alternative behavioural version itself comes in two different forms: that grounded in psychological behaviourism and represented most directly by Homans (1961) and the more implicit and diffuse social behaviourism that is forcefully criticised by Coleman (1986a).

21. It might be objected to the idea of such a sequence that theory must be involved already at the first stage, since all empirical observations are necessarily 'theory-laden'. I would accept that all observations must take place within some *conceptual scheme*, and it might in turn be argued that all such schemes have at least an implicit theoretical basis. However, insofar as theory is in *this* way involved in the establishment of social regularities, it does not follow that circularity must then arise when the processes that are theoretically proposed as generating the observed regularities are subjected to empirical test. Even where empirical observations are underpinned by the same conceptual scheme, different and indeed contradictory explanatory arguments may be developed. Furthermore, it should not be supposed that adopting one conceptual scheme rather than another will necessarily lead to a radical change in what is observed. For example, the regularities in class differentials in educational attainment or in relative rates of intergenerational class mobility that are considered in various chapters in Volume II are revealed with varying degrees of sharpness and detail when differing conceptualisations of class are used but in no case do they disappear from view or indeed are substantially altered in their form.

Notes to Chapter 2

1. This distinction, together with that between *Geisteswissenschaften* and *Naturwissenschaften*, originates in nineteenth-century German debates on methodology in history and the social sciences. For a brief discussion, see Collingwood (1993: 165–83). An interesting example of the use of the distinction in the period referred to in the text, with the aim of differentiating, yet at the same time showing the complementarity of history and sociology, is Bierstedt (1959).

2. Clearly, my position has in important respects changed since the time of my earlier paper, as a result, I would like to think, of my having had much more experience, whether first- or secondhand, of research into societies both past and present. However, both history and sociology, and the typical orientations of their practitioners, have also changed. Today, interdisciplinary, or rather adisciplinary, enthusiasm would seem to me to have gone too far, at least on the sociological side. And I find it of interest that a similar view has also been taken from the side of history by a distinguished practitioner who is by no means unsympathetic to sociology: see Stone (1987).

3. This use of history is that with which I have in fact been most concerned in my own work on comparative social mobility (Erikson and Goldthorpe, 1992a; and see further ch. 3 and vol. II, ch. 7). The classic programme for a comparative macrosociology is that set by Przeworski and Teune (1970), which has as its ideal

objective 'the replacement of the names of nations with the names of variables'. Insofar as, in explaining cross-national variation in social structure or process (e.g., in mobility rates and patterns), the sociologist is forced into invoking institutional or cultural features, or indeed events, as specific features of national histories, then *pro tanto* the Przeworski-Teune programme must fall short of realisation.

4. For pertinent but brief comments by previous authors, see Marshall (1963: 38) and Bell and Newby (1981).

5. I was myself put through the catechism by the Dutch historian, G. J. Renier, a remarkable teacher, whose work on historiography (1950) was our main text and is now unduly neglected. Also influential was the work of Collingwood, now extensively reedited (1993).

6. The one instance of which I am aware in which historians likewise generate their evidence is when they engage in 'oral' history. Here too, though, it may be noted that problems of survival, and in turn of representativeness, are of large importance.

7. Another way of putting much of this is to say, as does Clubb (1980: 20), that 'The source materials upon which historians must rely are virtually by definition "process produced" . . . ' and that they are, moreover, 'the residual process-produced data that have survived the ravages of time'. Clubb notes that historians occasionally have at their disposal data that were collected for social scientific purposes, and that this is likely to be a more common situation for future historians. However, he then rightly comments that 'we can also imagine that historians in the future will regard these data as no less process-produced, in this case by the process of social research as archaically practised in the mid-twentieth century—and will bemoan the fact that the wrong data were collected, the wrong questions asked, and that the underlying assumptions and methods were not better documented'.

8. Skocpol (1984: 364) treats Erikson's intentions as being 'characteristic of historical sociologists who apply general models to history'. There can of course be little value in such a procedure unless there are *independent* grounds for believing that the models have some validity. But it should be noted that Erikson himself is clear that his concern is (see text) 'to examine several ideas about deviant behaviour' for which he does not appear to claim any prior validity.

9. It may also be argued that sociologists have a legitimate recourse to history when their concern is with phenomena such as revolutions, major economic crises, mass panics or crazes, and so on, which not only happen rather infrequently but are in any event more amenable to investigation in retrospect than as they occur. I am not fully convinced by this argument (on the difficulty of a sociology of rarely occurring phenomena, see further ch. 3) but for present purposes it is not necessary to contest it. Nor do I take up here a concern displayed with history by some sociologists that I would most certainly regard as illegitimate: that is, a concern with 'theorising' history so as, it is hoped, to secure a cognitive grasp on its movement or logic. I have written critically elsewhere (Goldthorpe, 1971, 1979) on the persistence of historicism in this sense.

10. An early but cogent and, I suspect, highly influential, attack on Spencer by a preeminent historian was Maitland (1911). Note also Collingwood's critique (1993: 263–66) of the last phase of 'scissors-and-paste' historiography, that of the 'pigeon-holers', whose approach was: 'Very well: let us put together all the facts that are known to historians, look for patterns in them, and then extrapolate these patterns into a theory of universal history'. On the sociological side, the late nineteenth century saw of course the beginnings in Britain of sample survey methods of data collection (see ch. 4) and a growing interest in related techniques of data analysis (see vol. II, ch. 8).

11. It might be argued that this 'new wave' of grand historical sociology was in fact led by Eisenstadt's *The Political Systems of Empires* (1963). But Eisenstadt's influence would seem to have been clearly less than that of Moore—chiefly, I suspect, because his highly academic structural-functionalism accorded far less well with the prevailing mood of the later 1960s than did the *marxisant* tone and explicitly radical commitment of Moore's work.

12. Thus, for example, in a collection of essays edited by Skocpol (1984), consideration is given to the work of historians such as Marc Bloch and E. P. Thompson alongside that of authors such as Eisenstadt, Moore, Wallerstein, and Anderson.

13. Then, as apparently later (cf. Carr, 1961: ch. 1), the classic expositors of such positivism in historiography were taken to be von Ranke and, in Britain, Lord Acton.

14. An essay important for its catalytic effect was Hexter (1961). For a more recent critique of 'social change explanations' of the English Civil War, but certainly not one that could be dismissed as sociologically unsophisticated, see Clark (1986); and for a major study sythesising much of the research of the last three or four decades, see Woolrych (2002).

15. In the Appendix, 'A Note on Statistics and Conservative Historiography', Moore takes up the difficulties posed for his interpretation of the Civil War by Brunton and Pennington's study (1954) of the members of the Long Parliament, which, as Moore notes, led Tawney himself to acknowledge that the division between Royalists and Parliamentarians 'had little connection with diversities of economic interest and social class'. Moore then tries to rework Brunton and Pennington's statistics to save what he takes to be Tawney's thesis against Tawney's own abandonment of it—but succeeds only in providing a nice example of the ecological fallacy.

It might be added here that the treatment of the English Civil War by both Wallerstein and Anderson is no more satisfactory. Wallerstein, who claims (1974–89, vol. 1: 8) that 'contrapuntal controversial work' is a positive advantage for his enterprise, reviews a wider range of literature than Moore but by an eirenical *tour de force* still ends up where he wants to be: that is, able to claim that the English Civil War, though not a direct struggle between classes, nonetheless resulted from the formation of an agricultural capitalist class, which the old aristocracy was

forced to accommodate and in part to merge with, thus leading to the early creation in England of a 'national bourgeoisie' (see 1974–89, vol. 1: 256, 269, 282,
297 esp.). It must, however, be pointed out that of the authorities whom Wallerstein cites, at least as many would reject this conclusion as would accept it. Anderson, in contrast, refers to only a very limited number of secondary (or tertiary)
sources and then, effectively disregarding all controversy, blandly asserts (1974b:
142): 'English absolutism was brought to a crisis by aristocratic particularism and
clannic desperation on its periphery: forces that lay historically behind it. But it
was felled at the centre by a commercialized gentry, a capitalist city, a commoner
artisanate and yeomanry: forces pushing beyond it. Before it could reach the age of
maturity, English Absolutism was cut off by a bourgeois revolution'. Once more it
must be emphasised that it is essentially the interpretation of the English Civil War
as a 'bourgeois revolution' that has been challenged by revisionist historians over
the last two decades or more.

My own judgment would be that the revisionists have indeed succeeded in undermining the supposed evidence for such an interpretation. But, further, I would
doubt that even if there *were* a valid 'social change explanation' of the English Civil
War, adequate relics could be found to allow its validity to be demonstrated. What
Hexter remarked (1961: 149) apropos the initial Tawney *versus* Trevor Roper debate is likely to remain the last word: 'And what such masters of the materials of
seventeenth-century history and of historical forensics cannot prove when they set
their minds to it, is not likely ever to be proved'.

16. Furthermore, the central theses that are argued for by authors such as
Moore, Wallerstein, and Anderson are ones which they themselves clearly see as
being politically highly consequential, so that questions of how far their use of secondary sources is politically influenced and of what checks on political bias *they*
would believe appropriate, inevitably arise.

17. Unlike Skocpol, the other authors earlier cited do not even appear to
recognise the need for a methodology. Their main justification for grand historical sociology would seem to be simply that it gives 'the broad view' and is thus a
necessary complement to 'specialists' history'. Thus, Moore writes (1966: xi): 'That
comparative analysis is no substitute for detailed investigation of specific cases is
obvious'. But, he goes on: 'Generalizations that are sound resemble a large-scale
[*sic*] map of an extended terrain, such as an airplane pilot might use in crossing
a continent. Such maps are essential for certain purposes just as more detailed
maps are necessary for others'. Moore's cartography inspires no more confidence
than his historiography. Assuming that in the above he means 'small-scale' not
'large-scale', a small-scale map, useful for an 'extended terrain', is dependent for
its accuracy on the detailed surveying from which it is built up. And likewise, as a
'cliometric' and a 'conventional' historian have written together (Fogel and Elton,
1983: 125), 'the quality of an historical interpretation is critically dependent on
the quality of the details out of which it is spun. Time and again the interpretation

of major historical events, sometimes of whole areas, has been transformed by the correction of apparently trivial details'. It should also be said that the methodology of grand historical sociology has attracted little attention from writers concerned with the methodology of the social sciences in general. One essay by Galtung (1979) may be noted, though its contribution to practice does not seem large.

Notes to Chapter 3

1. This discussion, it should be said, has often ended on an eirenic note, the complementary nature of quantitative and qualitative work, and the need to 'build bridges' between them being emphasised. Thus, the present essay may appear disobliging and contrary to the prevailing spirit of methodological pluralism. But it seems to me, for reasons that will become clear, that often, behind the rhetoric of pluralism, a collaborative alliance is being proposed on terms that are in fact unduly skewed in favour of the case-oriented approach.

2. 'Historicist' is thus being used here in what one might describe as the sense of Meinecke rather than the sense of Popper.

3. Whether or not Skocpol does in practice apply Mill's canons appropriately is a matter of some dispute. See, for example, Nichols (1986), Skocpol (1986), Ragin (1987: 38–42), Burawoy (1989), and Lieberson (1992). However, as will later emerge, I would see this as an issue that is overshadowed by far more serious ones.

4. Without seeking to deny the force of the general point being made here, one could question whether the illustration suggested is in fact the most apt. A good deal of the apparent conflict in results from welfare state research would appear to be resolved once differing understandings of the dependent variable are recognised: that is, whether this is taken as the amount of social welfare *expenditure* or as the extent and quality of *social rights* to welfare (cf. Korpi, 1989; Korpi and Palme, 2003).

5. It may be noted that while Skocpol invokes Mill directly, Rueschemeyer refers to Mill at one remove: that is, via Znaniecki's notion (1934) of 'analytic induction', which, however, Rueschemeyer would wish to see developed beyond its reliance on the Method of Agreement alone (1991: 36, n. 12). In the present context it is of particular interest that Znaniecki contrasts analytic induction with 'enumerative induction', based on probability theory, and asserts that, since the former is capable of providing *exhaustive* knowledge of the situation under study, the latter is rendered superfluous. Rueschemeyer, it maybe added, gives no recognition to the powerful critiques that have been made of Znaniecki's analytic induction— classically, by Robinson (1951).

6. Mill presented his canons in Book III of *A System of Logic*, which is entitled 'Of Induction'. They are first formulated in ch. viii, 'Of the Four Methods of Experimental Inquiry'. His treatment of the moral—that is, social—sciences is quite separate, coming in Book VI, 'On the Logic of the Moral Sciences'. His views

on the unsuitability in this context of methods of experimental induction are found chiefly in ch. vii. For illuminating commentary, see Ryan (1970). Skocpol's discussion of the problems of applying Mill's methods is very brief (1979: 36–40) and her dismissive response (1994: 338) to Lieberson (1992) indicates only that she has failed to grasp the force of his argument.

7. It may be found surprising that such strong 'positivistic' commitments are taken up within the qualitative camp. However, I have in the preceding essay made the point that Skocpol and other 'grand historical sociologists' are in effect compelled by their dependence on secondary works as their main empirical resource to adopt a distinctively positivistic attitude towards historiography and, specifically, the nature of historical facts. Further, Burawoy has acutely observed that Skocpol's reliance on inductive logic likewise puts limits on the doubts that she can allow herself about just what the historical facts are. For Skocpol, he remarks (1989: 773), 'the facts have a certain obviousness that they don't for historians', and she pays little attention to the controversies that rage over them: 'She is forced into this blindness in order to get her induction machine off the ground.' It may be observed that a similar penchant for inductive and deterministic accounts is to be found among exponents of case studies at a microsociological level—or at all events among those following in the Chicago or symbolic interactionist tradition. See, for example, the very explicit statements made in this regard by Becker (1992: 212) and also the discussion in Chapter 4.

8. As an illustration of the critical point here made, one may take the application of QCA reported by Kangas (1994) in the context of a comparative study of the quality of health insurance provision. Through reanalysis of the data given in Table 14.2 of his paper, it is possible to show that the result Kangas achieves—that high quality provision (as of 1950) is associated with strong Christian Democracy in combination with a unified bloc of bourgeois political parties, but not with the level of working-class mobilisation—depends crucially on two things: first, the coding on the dependent variable in a single, borderline case, that of Switzerland; and second, on the particular solutions that are adopted to problems of contradictory cases and of missing combinations of explanatory variables—which regularly arise with QCA. If these problems are treated in a somewhat different but equally defensible way and Switzerland is taken as having high rather than low quality provision, which would certainly seem arguable (cf. also Kangas, 1991), then the result of the entire analysis changes very significantly. Now, in fact, all that matters is the strength of Christian Democracy, and the unity or fragmentation of bourgeois parties joins the level of working-class mobilisation as a quite irrelevant factor. Kangas, I should make clear, is not unaware of the problem of QCA here demonstrated; the main purpose of his paper is to compare the results he obtains from QCA with those deriving from different analytical approaches to the same problem and data.

9. Skocpol chiefly bases her claim on the work of Wickham-Crowley (1992). However, this author's applications of QCA reveal exactly the same difficulties as

those found in the instance discussed in the previous note. Thus, his analysis of causal factors in peasant support for guerrilla movements in Latin America turns crucially on certain codings that, as he himself recognises, are highly doubtful on account of data problems. Readers who enjoy Boolean algebra can work out for themselves what would happen to Wickham-Crowley's conclusions if (accepting his way of handling problems of contradictory cases and missing combinations of explanatory variables) just a few of these problematic codings were changed: if, say (see his Table 12-1, 1992: 306), positive rather than negative codes were given to Cuba (Las Villas) on factor B (agrarian disruption) and to Guatamala (Zacapa) on factor D (peasant linkage); or—yet more dramatically—if, in addition, positive codings on factor D were also given to Nicaragua (N. Central rural and Northwest towns).

Ragin's more recent efforts (2000) at developing QCA do not seem to me to help in any major way in overcoming the basic problems of the method. For further criticism, see Achen (2005) and Seawright (2005).

10. Another quantitative technique that can be used to help overcome the small N problem, and that could also have its qualitative analogues, is that of event history analysis. For example, Korpi and Palme (2003) test hypotheses on factors influencing welfare state retrenchment in the late twentieth century by taking as their dependent variable all instances of *changes made* in replacement rates in un-employment, sickness, and accident benefits across 18 nations.

11. Lack of data quality, and especially in regard to cross-national compa-rability, does of course still often impose serious limitations on macrosociological studies, whatever the technical resources they may command. However, it can be said that this problem does now attract growing critical attention among those engaging in quantitative research. See, for example, in the case of research in social stratification and mobility, the issues taken up in Treiman (1975), Gold-thorpe (1985), Ganzeboom, Luijkx, and Treiman (1989), Erikson and Goldthorpe (1992a: ch. 2; 1992b). In some contrast, advocates of historical case studies espe-cially would appear to resort to double standards. Thus, one finds Rueschemeyer, Stephens, and Stephens (1992: 26) commenting, with good reason, on the problem of 'not always reliable information' in quantitative studies of capitalist development and democracy—but just one page after an encomium on the 'towering achieve-ment' of Moore (1966). Why, one wonders, do they not consider in an equally crit-ical way the question of the reliability, or even of the very existence, of the evidence to which Moore appeals in support of his central thesis—for instance (see ch. 2) as regards the social sources of the English Civil War?

12. Even in public policy research the importance of diffusion and also of international economic or political pressure can be exaggerated. As regards the development of welfare state institutions, see, for example, Flora and Alber (1981), Garrett and Lange (1991), Huber, Ragin, and Stephens (1993), and Scharpf and Schmidt, eds. (2000). For an insightful review of the recurrent problems of dif-fusionist theory itself, and in an area of prime application—fertility studies—see

Kreager (1993). Sociological fashion as well as real world developments would seem to play a large part in current writing on globalisation (see further ch. 5). It is not long since the emphasis was rather on the non-exportability of institutions— for example, of those of the 'Westminster model' to the new nations of the former British empire or of Soviet institutions to the satellite nations of the USSR. Recall discussion of Stalin's comments about 'saddling cows'.

13. Several contributors to the collection edited by Castles do in fact make at least implicit moves in the direction suggested. See in particular Busch (1993) on differences in anti-inflation policies and Schmidt (1993) on differences in male and female workforce participation rates and their determinants.

14. I have in mind here the various arguments that have been advanced on the possibility of historical explanation being achieved without reference to general theories through the use of narratives that show how specific events form part of 'continuous series' (Oakeshott, 1933), have 'followability' (Gallie, 1964), are 'colligated' within a 'continuing process' (Walsh, 1974), or are otherwise 'internally' rather than 'externally' connected. For a valuable brief review, see Dray (1993).

15. Again a close parallel can be noted with case studies oriented towards microsociological issues. Even a sympathetic commentator (Hammersley, 1989: chs. 7 and 8) is forced to acknowledge that problems of theory testing are acute with both 'analytic induction' and with the no less inductive 'grounded theory' (Glaser and Strauss, 1967) to which it seems more common for case analysts working at a micro-level to appeal (see further ch. 4). It is of interest that Ragin (1994a: 94; cf. also 1997) should acknowledge that 'analytic induction'—of which his own QCA is in effect a systematisation—is to be seen as primarily concerned with 'the degree to which the image of the research subject has been refined, sharpened, and elaborated in response to both confirming and disconfirming evidence', or, that is, with no more than *conceptualisation.*

16. I would, as it happens, entirely agree with the *substantive* criticisms that Rueschemeyer and his colleagues make of earlier efforts at explaining the association between capitalism and democracy—that is, via modernisation theory. But I would totally disagree that it should be seen as a fault of this, or of any other theory, that it is insufficiently grounded in prior research or is indeed 'pure conjecture' (1992: 29). Theories must be judged not by their empirical origins but by their empirical implications. And what better epitaph could a theory possibly hope for than that it was bold enough to provoke research and clear enough to be proved wrong by it?

17. The responses to Kiser and Hechter of which I am aware are those of Quadagno and Knapp (1992), Skocpol (1994), and Somers (1998). The two former seem to me to concede far more than they effectively contest. That is, their authors show themselves ready to accept a much less demanding idea of theory than that of Kiser and Hechter and, in turn, the implication that comparative historical sociologists are not interested in testing theories in the way Kiser and Hech-

ter would require. Somers, however, resorts to a position of cognitive relativism, appealing to a 'historical epistemology' supposedly—but, I would suggest, very questionably—derived from Kuhn. What this proposes is 'that all our knowledge, our logics, our presuppositions, indeed our very reasoning practices, are indelibly (even if obscurely) marked with the signature of time' (Somers, 1998: 731). Such a position would appear to remove the possibility of any rational debate about the specifics of methodology.

18. While it is surely disappointing, it should not be thought a disgrace for sociologists to admit that they have not been able to develop a theory that will adequately account for their empirical findings. This is so because one cannot expect effective theory, in the sense I intend, to be produced at will, nor by following specified procedures or guidelines—as would appear the case with grounded theory. I do not find it accidental that it is in case-oriented, qualitative sociology that the rather absurd use of 'theorise' as a *transitive* verb has become most common: that is, it can, apparently, be demanded that a topic be theorised in the same way as it can be demanded that the kitchen be cleaned or the shopping brought home. This confirms me in my belief that, typically, no more than (re)conceptualisation is in fact involved.

19. In other words (cf. ch. 2), I would here again see force in the nomothetic-idiographic distinction as applied to sociology and history, if, that is, it is understood as referring essentially to the direction of intellectual effort (and without any implication either that sociological theory must be entirely universal or that historiography must avoid all general concepts). Claims that comparative historical studies applying some form of analytic induction are capable of overcoming this distinction (e.g., Zaret, 1978: 118; Skocpol, 1979: 33–37) seem to me, for reasons given above, not to be borne out on the evidence of these studies themselves. And I would take leave to doubt that the further attempt apparently being made via 'sociological narrativism' (see, e.g., Griffin, 1992; Quadagno and Knapp, 1992) is any more likely to succeed. While I would certainly sympathise with efforts such as those of Abbott (1992a, 1992b) to establish analogues between narrative accounts and causal explanations, there are still basic differences to be recognised among the kinds of narrative that may be deployed. For example, one may understand rational choice theory in terms of narratives but ones which, in contrast to historical narratives, are generalised rather than specific, set in analytic rather than real time, and implicative rather than conjunctive in their structure (see further ch. 6, pp. 126–27 and chs. 7 and 8 more generally).

Notes to Chapter 4

1. Ethnographic research is essentially qualitative and almost all ethnographies could be counted as case studies, while survey research can scarcely avoid being quantitative and variable oriented in some degree. However, there are of course various other qualitative methods than ethnography, and case studies may be based

on a variety of qualitative *and* quantitative methods. At the same time, quantitative methods can also be applied in research that is neither case oriented nor survey based, as, say, in that which utilises official statistical data that are collected via censuses or other legally enforced recording or registration procedures. I should further make it clear that in this essay, as its title indicates, the main focus of my attention is on ethnographic research *in the context of sociology* rather than social anthropology, following the lines of demarcation that have been conventionally, if somewhat arbitrarily, drawn between these disciplines: that is, I concentrate on ethnographic research as conducted within relatively large-scale and technologically and economically advanced societies.

2. Elite groups may also be studied, but in this case ethnography is then often directed to the purposes, as Katz (1997: 405) puts it, of 'debunking charisma' and 'deconstructing deference'.

3. This position, it may be added, is highly consistent with the frequently made argument that it is not the task of philosophers of science to prescribe methodology for practitioners but rather to reconstruct, and perhaps refine and elaborate, the logic that the latter in fact use. The idea of a single logic of inference informing all scientific methods and in turn the case for its application in qualitative, just as in quantitative, work in the social sciences are cogently set out in King, Keohane, and Verba (1994: ch. 1 esp.) to which I am much indebted. If underwriting the position that these authors adopt is to be regarded as the *differentia specifica* of a positivist, then I would be happy to be classified as one, and also pleased that this much-abused term could in this way be given some clear meaning in sociological debate. It should, though, be noted that accepting the idea of a single logic of inference does *not* imply accepting the natural science 'experimental model' of scientific enquiry, *nor* the covering law model of scientific explanation, *nor* the possibility of a neutral observational language—each of which tenets has been taken as the infallible mark of Cain.

4. At the present time, 'reflexive' seems to be the favourite word to conjure with. It has, however, to be said that what would be the distinctive features of a reflexive sociology, at the level of research and analytical procedures, remains desperately obscure. Thus, while Burawoy (1998) acknowledges the 'vagueness' of the idea in previous work (e.g., Bourdieu and Wacquant, 1992), his attempts at greater clarity and specificity are scarcely impressive. Do we gain much in understanding just what a reflexive sociology would entail by being told that it 'enunciates the idea of *structuration*, which implies a reciprocal but asymmetrical constitution of local processes and extralocal forces—forces that can be economic, political or cultural, and more or less systematic' (1998: 14)? Nor is a later essay (Burawoy, 2003) any more helpful in this regard. Similarly, Hammersley and Atkinson introduce a new edition of their text on ethnography (1995) by saying that 'The central theme of the book remains the importance of a reflexive approach'. But the few pages they devote to the idea of reflexivity (1995: 16–21) does little to show how the key tenets of proponents of this approach would differentiate them from many

'non-reflexive' sociologists (the present writer included) who would, for example, have no difficulty whatever in accepting that 'the orientations of researchers will be shaped by their socio-historical locations', or that 'behaviour and attitudes are often not stable across contexts and . . . the researcher may influence the context', or that 'data should not be taken at face value but treated as a field of inferences'. Moreover, when Hammersley and Atkinson come to treat actual issues of data collection and analysis, the idea of reflexivity, rather than being 'the central theme', seems more or less to disappear.

5. One such consequence would obviously be that of relinquishing all claims on public resources devoted to social science. Furthermore, if the secession also involves a rejection of the very idea of science, and of associated ideas of rationality and truth, there would seem no grounds for, or point in, trying to argue the matter with the seceders. One cannot argue rationally with principled irrationalists; and those who hold that truth is merely 'political' (see, e.g., Denzin, 1997: 12) can have no complaints if they meet with a political response. See further the courageous remarks by Huber (1995) and also, from within sociological ethnography, by Hammersley (1999: 6).

6. Emile Cheysson, one of the most talented of the Le Playistes, writing in 1890 and quoted in Desrosières (1993: 263).

7. It might be added here that the poverty surveys carried out by Booth and Rowntree in Britain in the late-nineteenth and early twentieth centuries, and often highlighted in English-language accounts of the history of empirical social research, in fact contributed rather little so far as the methodology of surveys was concerned. In contrast, the major contribution of Kiaer (who wrote mainly in Norwegian or French) has been grossly neglected.

8. Within the broad agreement thus characterised, there are, of course, some evident divisions. Most notable, perhaps, is that identified by Campbell (1996). On the one hand, there are those ethnographers who believe that the meaning of action is constituted entirely intersubjectively in the course of the face-to-face interaction of individuals in particular situations, and who therefore concentrate on questions of how actors manage to interpret and understand what each other is doing rather than on the courses and patterns of action that they in fact follow. On the other hand, there are those who would believe that it is on actual courses and patterns of action that interpretative effort should focus and that the meaning of these to individuals, and likewise individuals' definitions of the situations in which they act, do not have to be, and indeed often are not, themselves situationally specific. The presence of this, and other, divisions does not, I think, have any great bearing on at least the critical part of my argument.

9. In Cambridge in the 1960s I often attended Meyer Fortes' seminars, at which papers by graduate students and others based on fieldwork in West Africa were the staple. I several times asked questions about how the choice of informants was made, how important to the findings reported this choice might be, and so on. After one such intervention Fortes was driven to expostulate: 'Dammit, if I want to

learn French, I don't need a random sample of Frenchmen to teach me. One competent native speaker is enough!' But the issue then arises of just how far in this regard the analogy between a language and a culture or set of social institutions holds up. While some linguists at least would maintain that a native speaker cannot in fact make a mistake in his or her own language, there are few sociologists who would suppose that 'lay members' cannot hold mistaken, or at any rate radically divergent, beliefs about their own society. It should, however, be added that some social anthropologists have seriously engaged with problems of fieldwork sampling (see, e.g., Honigman, 1973).

10. Certainly, in the—now rather many—instances in which attempted replications or reexaminations of older anthropological ethnographies have led to their being challenged, the possibility is almost always raised (cf. Bryman, 1994) either of their authors having being misled by informants, whether deliberately or not, or of informants having in fact represented only particular subcultures or social groupings.

11. For example, problems arising in this way are suggested in the case of two classic 'street' ethnographies: that is, via the undue influence of 'Doc' in Whyte's *Street Corner Society* (1943) and of 'Tally' in Liebow's *Tally's Corner* (1967).

12. One of the first ethnographies I ever read, and by which I was totally persuaded, was Redfield's study (1930) of Tepoztlán. But I then discovered the restudy by Lewis (1951). Should I have been so convinced by Redfield—or were, perhaps, my first impressions right? In regard to this and other similarly disputed cases, Bryman (1988: 76) has aptly observed that 'Brief conversations, snippets from unstructured interviews, or examples of a particular activity are used to provide evidence for a particular contention. There are grounds for disquiet in that the representativeness or generality of these fragments is rarely addressed. Further, field notes or extended transcripts are rarely available'. In his long essay on ethnographic 'revisits', Burawoy (2003) manages largely to avoid such questions of inadequacy of data and the problems thus created for any attempt at rational evaluation of conflicting accounts or any assessment of how far discrepancies might be due to real changes between visits.

13. For example, the laboratory ethnographies of Latour (1987; Latour and Woolgar, 1979) have many admirers within the sociology science but, for me, Latour's choice and presentation of material has always seemed highly slanted and tendentious (cf. Gross and Levitt, 1994: 57–62; Cole, 1996).

14. 'Theoretical sampling' is a key component in Glaser and Strauss's more general programme for grounded theory that is characterised by an extreme inductivism (as well as, I would argue, by a failure to make a sufficiently clear distinction between theory and concepts). Thus, there seems to be little to prevent a situation in which a theory that, as initially formulated, is quite unsound is not rejected outright but is rather 'developed' through a series of ad hoc adaptations made in the face of uncongenial empirical findings. This risk can, moreover, only be increased by Glaser and Strauss's preference for conceptual fission and elabora-

tion—to the point of 'saturation'—rather than for conceptual parsimony. Another form of nonprobabilistic sampling that could easily lead to systematically biased results is 'snowball' sampling: that is, in cases where the snowballing is limited by the social networks existing within one particular grouping in the locale (cf. Burgess, 1984: 57).

15. My own awareness of this problem dates from my reading of the study of a Yorkshire mining village by Dennis, Henriques, and Slaughter (1956), which was fairly close to the village in which I grew up. In relation to my own village, the authors' ethnography appeared to me to apply well to just *one* subculture among several that were generally recognised and that had their own rather distinctive social bases. But what grounds had I for judging whether the authors had given only a very partial account of 'their' village or whether this was in fact much more homogeneous than mine, despite being a good deal larger?

16. Where this particular objection to probabilistic sampling is made, it is notable that the emphasis tends to be placed—in a rather positivistic way?—on the 'hard', factual information that only certain individuals can provide.

17. Thus, Hammersley (1992: 189; though cp. 1991: 28) argues that at least with some ethnographies 'the issue of generalisability does not arise' since the case studied represents 'a population of one', and he cites as an instance of this Fielding's study (1981) of the National Front in Britain. However, it is evident enough from a reading of this study that Fielding is in fact concerned with far more than idiographic description. He is interested in the National Front as an example of a right-wing extremist movement, as an expression of political deviance, and as a context in which to study the role of individual will in participation in such deviance. And in all these respects, generalisation from the case of the National Front is clearly involved (Fielding, 1981: chs. 1, 10 esp.).

18. This is, though, less surprising than it might at first seem. Mitchell's position is in direct line of descent from that of Znaniecki, and the latter's proposals for analytic induction amount in fact to little more than a highly simplified version of the canons of induction proposed by John Stuart Mill for theory construction in the experimental—though *not*, it should be stressed, in the moral (i.e., social)—sciences (cf. ch. 3, pp. 42–3, 44–5). It would seem that most of the authors who have approvingly cited Mitchell's arguments on generalisation from ethnographies have simply not appreciated the nature of the theory that these arguments entail. I might add here that in clarifying my own position on these matters, I owe much to energetic but always good-natured and illuminating argument with Clyde Mitchell over many years up to his death.

19. Yin (1994: 30–32, 48–50) and Stewart (1998: 47–49) present what are in effect weaker versions of Mitchell's argument, in claiming that in ethnographic (or other case study) work, generalisation should not be seen as being from sample to population but rather from case to theory, hypothesis or 'insight', with, in Yin's view, instances where a theory is supported from one case to another (little is said about *dis*confirmation) being the equivalent of the replication of results in experi-

mental research. This is, however, to neglect the obvious but crucial fact that in experiments contextual conditions are controlled either physically or by randomisation in a way that they cannot be in research undertaken in natural settings. Burawoy (1998: 14) likewise argues in favour of generalisation from case to theory with the aim, however, of theory reconstruction rather than confirmation, and maintains that 'Because we begin with theory, a single case is quite sufficient for a progressive reconstruction'. This may be so but it is certainly not enough for theory testing unless, again, theory of a quite deterministic character is supposed. Analytic induction itself would by now appear to have been effectively abandoned in ethnographic work, at all events as a method of causal analysis in the way intended by Znaniecki. Insofar as it is still defended, it is simply as an aid in theory development (cf. Manning, 1982).

20. What would seem an unacceptable away of evading this challenge is to seek to compartmentalise Jankowski's work by taking it, as does Burawoy (1998: 17), as simply representing the 'positive tradition' within ethnography.

21. Two points might be added here. First, in regard to problems of the reliability and validity of data in ethnography, even the best discussions (e.g., Kirk and Miller, 1986) would seem, just like discussions of problems of within- and across-locale variation, to be much stronger on diagnosis than on prescription. Second, in regard to contextual effects, results from the multilevel modelling of survey data would indicate that these effects are often far *less* important than ethnographers' claims or indeed much textbook sociology would lead one to expect.

22. As is recognised in the text, ethnographic research may indeed suggest theory; but, contrary to what is claimed by proponents of grounded theory, there is no reason for supposing that having inductive, rather than deductive, or indeed purely speculative, origins in itself contributes to the validity of a theory. Theories, like all ideas, are to be judged by their consequences—specifically, by whether they stand up to test—and not by their antecedents.

23. A consequence of the failure, earlier noted, of Willis (1977) to deal adequately with problems of within-locale variation in his study of working-class boys is that the processes of alienation from school on which he concentrates are not in fact adequate to account for the rates and patterns of educational participation or of subsequent social mobility on the part of such children that are demonstrated at a macro-level by survey research. Willis, like many other qualitative researchers in the field of educational sociology, appears to be remarkably ill informed about such rates and patterns (see further vol. II, chs. 2, 4, and 7).

24. In this regard, hypothesis testing via ethnography is still likely to be troubled by the small N problem (cf. ch. 3). One potentially valuable way in which this problem could be addressed is through the use of meta-analyses. But here again developments in the context of ethnography would seem so far to lag well behind those in other, more quantitatively oriented fields. Compare, for example, Glass, McGaw, and Smith (1981) with Wolf (1986).

25. And to this the point may be added that in modern societies important social processes within which actors' orientations may be formed will tend, rather than being confined to a particular locale, to extend over several different locales and associated social networks—for example, those of family, work, friendship, and so on—so that the difficulty of achieving adequate ethnographic coverage becomes immense. (See further vol. II, ch. 4, in regard to the study of social class differences in educational choice.)

26. See, for example, within economics, the interesting reflections of a heterodox institutionalist such as Piore (1983) and of an orthodox econometrician such as Manski (1993).

27. It might be added that in this respect major benefits are to be expected from the increasing use of computers in ethnographic work: not so much from what is thus to be gained analytically, at least with existing ethnographic software (cf. Hammersley and Atkinson, 1995: 193–204), but simply from the requirement thereby imposed on ethnographers to constitute the results of their research as a data-set with accompanying documentation that is fully open to examination and criticism in the public domain (see further vol. II, ch. 1). The improvement in standards of survey research consequent on the establishment of survey data archives and the requirement for publicly accessible documentation was immense.

28. As support for this view, I would cite the recent *Handbook of Qualitative Research*, edited by Denzin and Lincoln (1994), which, for a volume which was presumably supposed to give a balanced review of the field, reveals a strong postmodernist bias in both the choice of contributors and the slant of their contributions.

Notes to Chapter 5

1. I recognise that there is not a complete consensus among the globalisation theorists whose work I consider (although they do cite each others' work approvingly to a rather remarkable extent). I focus on views that can be shown to be fairly widely held and also note occasional disagreements.

2. Further anomalous facts are that significant differences in unemployment rates exist among EZ countries and that there are several instances of these rates being relatively low in countries with very open economies *and* a good deal of labour protection—for example, Austria, the Netherlands, and Norway.

3. Although both Giddens (2000: 93–95) and Castells (2000b: 134–36) indicate some awareness of the complexity of the issue of trade effects, neither attempts to engage with it in any depth. Of the theorists in question, Giddens gives least weight to the role of freer international trade in creating increased earnings inequality, but without then making clear in what other way, if any, globalisation is involved.

4. Schulze and Ursprung do moreover raise the question of just how far an

antithesis between economic efficiency and welfare-state development should be accepted. This issue is also of concern to Atkinson (1999a, 1999b; cf. also Korpi, 1985) who, like Schulze and Ursprung, rejects 'necessitarian' arguments about the future of the welfare state and stresses the continuing importance of policy choices and political mobilisation. Of further relevance is the 12-nation comparative study by Scharpf and his associates of advanced welfare states within the international economy (Scharpf and Schmidt, eds., 2000). In a summary report on this study Scharpf (2000) concludes that such welfare states differ in the degree of their vulnerability to international economic pressures and in the policy options that are open to them in seeking to maintain their viability but that there is no reason why they need abandon their 'employment, social security and egalitarian aspirations'. In the UK, it may be added, New Labour administrations between 1997 and 2004—though only very modestly egalitarian—have nonetheless introduced tax and social security changes that are estimated to have kept the increase in income inequality over the period down to around a half of what it would otherwise have been (Brewer et al., 2004).

5. This position could be seen as an intermediate one among political economists as between, on the one hand, that adopted by Rodrik (1997), who believes that the effects of globalisation in limiting the capacity of nation states to provide adequate social insurance for their citizens against external risk are underestimated by some more 'Panglossian' authors, and who fears a populist and protectionist backlash; and, on the other hand, that taken by Iversen (2000; cf. also Iversen and Cusack, 2000), who would regard the main source of economic and social risk in modern societies—and thus the greatest challenge to welfare states—as being not globalisation at all but rather *deindustrialisation*, driven almost exclusively by domestic factors. For a comparable position on the specific issue of the role of multinationals, see Hirst and Thompson (1999: ch. 3).

6. In his most recent work, Beck (2000c) himself does indeed seem more concerned to stress the transformation rather than the disappearance of work, although, as is characteristic (cf. Steuer, 1998), the claims he makes are often quite contradictory.

7. In earlier work (1994: 144–48), Giddens also takes up the idea of an underclass but with his adoption of the language of social exclusion he would appear to abandon it—perhaps because it is difficult to think of members of an underclass *not* 'having fewer resources' than others.

8. See, for example, for Ireland—a key case for theories of globalisation— the work of Nolan and Whelan (1999) referred to in the text below, and for an illuminating Anglo-German comparison, McGinnity and Hillmert (2004). The latter study also considers the degree of cross-national variation in class patterns of unemployment that may result from differences in labour market institutions and forms of social protection.

9. An instructive debate on these issues is that between Jacoby (1999a, 1999b) and Cappelli (1999). It should, however, be noted that Cappelli does not dissent

from Jacoby's main argument concerning the persistence of 'good jobs' in the U.S. economy, and that the main point of difference arises over whether jobs offering career prospects *within one firm* are in decline.

10. Jacoby's work underlines the force of a theoretical argument that I and others have emphasised from the side of class analysis (see, e.g., Breen, 1997; also vol. II, chs. 5 and 6) but which is largely ignored by exponents of the 'transformation of work' thesis. With increasing competitiveness and economic turbulence, employers may well wish to reduce the burden of risk that they assume on behalf of their employees, but how far they can go in this direction is constrained by limits to the range of work that can in fact be commodified without loss of organisational effectiveness. In particular, where employees are required to deploy expertise or exercise delegated authority on behalf of their employing organisation, employment contracts approximating a spot form are unlikely to be efficient contracts.

11. Even where the argument is made that the origins-destinations association shows a long-term tendency to weaken, the extremely slow nature of this change is emphasised rather than any 'epochal change' (see, e.g., Ganzeboom, Luijkx, and Treiman, 1989).

12. The idea that with modernisation increasing intergenerational mobility is largely offset by decreasing intragenerational or worklife mobility (i.e., the 'counterbalance' thesis) did not in fact hold for British society (nor for many others) over the middle decades of the twentieth century, since the very rapid expansion of the salariat allowed upward mobility to increase both inter- *and* intragenerationally (Goldthorpe, 1987: ch. 2). But with a larger salariat expanding more slowly than before, the counterbalance thesis does now start to apply.

13. Kleinman (1998) makes perceptive observations on the political uses and ideological implications of the social exclusion concept. The extent of its acceptance within the social scientific community has undoubtedly had much to do with its political currency and the consequent pressure to introduce it into applications for research funding—as might indeed also be said of the concept of globalisation itself. It would be to the advantage of social science if what is often admitted in private in these respects could be publicly stated.

14. The continuing research of Nolan, Whelan, and their associates has two further important implications. First, it brings out the point that one of the chief supposed mechanisms of social exclusion—social isolation arising from area of residence—has to be demonstrated as a contextual effect, not just asserted (cf. ch. 3, p. 83), and that this may well prove difficult to do (Nolan and Whelan, 2001; see also Friedrichs, 1998). And, second, it shows up a major limitation of the work of Leisering and Leibfried (1999), the empirical study perhaps most often cited by proponents of the thesis of the individualisation (or 'democratisation') of poverty. If poverty is measured not by income level alone (as in Leisering and Leibfried's study) but also through various indicators of deprivation, its relation to social class emerges far more strongly; and, consequently, both the idea of the individualisation of poverty and that of the socially excluded as a distinct grouping

in some way outside the class structure are called into question (Layte and Whelan, 2002; Whelan, Layte, and Maître, 2002, 2004).

15. The clearest examples of class dealignment in voting come from the Scandinavian nations. Here, in effect, very high levels of class voting around the middle of the twentieth century have 'regressed towards the mean' of the western democracies in general. The evidence of low levels of class voting in Britain in the 1930s is just one of many indications presently emerging from the work of both social scientists and historians of the very dubious usage, in the work of Giddens and Beck in particular, of the concept of the 'traditional'. This, it seems, serves as a vast residual category, to be invoked as convenient across time and space and without need for serious documentation, in order to create a required contrast with the 'modern' (cf. ch. 8, pp. 177–79).

16. There would seem to be good reason for this concern. In current research my colleague, Tak Wing Chan, and I find evidence from British General Election Surveys that while from 1997 the association between class and vote does weaken, from 2001 an association, not previously evident, develops between class and nonvoting: that is, members of the working class, and especially nonskilled wage workers, are now significantly less likely to vote than are members of other classes. The most striking and best documented case of such class-linked nonvoting is of course the United States. See, e.g., Verba, Nie, and Kim (1978) and Vanneman and Cannon (1987).

17. It may be thought that I have here concentrated too much on electoral rather than social movement politics. But the claims of globalisation theorists do specifically relate to the former as well as to the latter; and moreover, the social movements that they cite as examples of the new politics (see, e.g., Castells, 1997: chs. 2–4) could scarcely be regarded as ones that, in advanced societies at least, have so far played a transformatory, or indeed any central, role. As Iversen (2000) observes, the distributional—including class conflicts that are likely to continue around the welfare state are in themselves sufficient to ensure that post-materialist politics of the kind envisaged by Inglehart will not dominate, nor, one could add, will identity or life politics. For an empirically well-founded critique of the thesis that late twentieth-century welfare state retrenchment is better explained in terms of 'new politics' than of 'class politics', see Korpi and Palme (2003).

18. Social stratification is one area in which persistence seems in many respects to be more striking than change—in contrast, say, with that of family and sexual relations where over recent decades change has been quite dramatic. This 'revolution' has indeed attracted the attention of most grand globalisation theorists. However, their attempts to show the connection with globalisation amount to little more than placing two trends of change alongside each other, with no clear specification of the causal processes supposedly linking one to the other (see, e.g., Giddens, 1998).

19. The chief exception here, among the theorists with whom I have been

chiefly concerned, might appear to be Castells, whose books have extensive bibliographies and also contain swathes of statistics. However, Castells refers little more than the others to material in mainstream economics, political science, and sociology journals, and the statistical material remains largely in form of univariate or bivariate tables rather than forming a basis for analyses in support of his theoretical arguments, for sharp criticism of which see Abell and Reyniers (2000).

20. For an illustration of how comparativists would seek to address this problem, and specifically in regard to the possible effects of globalisation on cross-national variation in class structure and mobility, see Breen and Rottman (1998).

Notes to Chapter 6

1. I recognise, indeed insist (see further chs. 7 and 8), that there is an entire family of rational action theories, and that, as well as family resemblances, significant differences have also to be observed. I opt for the designation of rational action theory rather than the more common 'rational choice theory' since the latter tends to be used in a narrower sense than suits my purposes: that is, as referring, as I would see it, to the version of rational action theory that is characteristic of mainstream economics and of some political science (see further ch. 8).

2. See further in this connection the fascinating exchange between Hauser (1976) and Boudon (1976), in which, it might be said, Hauser wins most of the battles but Boudon wins the war.

3. While Freedman's major published contribution (1992a) is ostensibly directed against an instance of causal path modelling in Hope (1984), its real target, as Duncan (1992) has recognised, should be taken as Blau and Duncan's *The American Occupational Structure* (1967)—the *locus classicus* of causal path modelling in sociology (though see n. 5). This latter work was in fact the subject of an earlier critique by Freedman (1983) that remained unpublished.

4. Thus, Holland (1986a, 1988) argues that what statistics can contribute to causal inference (even when allied to experimental designs) lies not in the *identification of the causes* of known effects, which is the task of theory, but rather in the *measurement of the effects* of the causes that theory postulates. For further discussion of Holland's position, see Chapter 9.

5. It should in this connection be noted that 30 years ago, in an introductory text on structural equation modelling, Duncan (1975: 151–52 esp.) not only elaborated the technical problems involved but warned of the dangers of regarding such modelling as being in itself a way of conducting sociological analysis and emphasised the essential role of theory. More recent contributions that likewise serve to bring out the full extent of the theoretical demands of causal modelling in sociology include Lieberson (1987) and Blossfeld and Rohwer (1995a: ch. 1 esp.).

6. To make such a distinction is not to suppose that the phenomena to be explained can be established without recourse to *concepts*, which may then in turn reflect some theoretical stance. But even where data are constituted in terms of a

conceptual approach that is theoretically well-derived, it does not follow that the explanation of any regularities that are revealed will, for this reason, be at once apparent. As Popper has emphasised (e.g., 1976b: 18–31), the same problem or *explanandum* may well be arrived at through quite different conceptual approaches; and if an explanation is then to be provided, *further* theoretical advance will obviously be required.

7. It is of interest that, as Clogg (1992) has documented, loglinear modelling and event history analysis are alike instances of statistical techniques that have to a significant extent advanced *via* their sociological applications, in contrast to those on which sociology tended previously to rely which were mostly imports from biometrics, psychometrics, or econometrics. And further of interest is the growing readiness to reject the idea, deriving from Stevens' (1946) theory of scale types, that using categorical or discrete data entails an inferior form of measurement (see esp. Duncan, 1984: ch. 4).

8. Thus, for example, from the loglinear modelling of intergenerational social mobility tables that also incorporate an educational variable (see, e.g., Ishida, Müller, and Ridge, 1995), it has become apparent that the part played by education cannot be realistically treated as being uniform across all origin-to-destination transitions alike, as causal path models usually suppose. Or again, event history analyses (cf. Blossfeld and Rohwer, 1995a) have indicated that it is inadequate in such models simply to suppose a temporal ordering of variables (e.g., education comes before 'first job'), without also considering the 'temporal shapes' of the dependencies that are taken to be involved.

9. This, I would emphasise, should not be thought of as a shortcoming. As Stinchcombe (1993: 27) has aptly observed (and see further vol. II, ch. 9), it is scarcely desirable, from an explanatory point of view, that the mechanisms invoked to account for regularities observed at a higher—that is, more macro—level should then entail 'complex investigations' at a lower level. See also Popper (1966: ch. 14).

10. See further in this connection Lindenberg's (1985, 1990) useful distinction between the concepts of individual$_1$, appropriate to psychology, where both analytic *and* explanatory primacies lie at the individual level, and individual$_2$, appropriate to RAT as applied in sociology (or economics), where explanatory primacy remains at the individual level, via the principle of methodological individualism, but analytic primacy is shifted to the aggregate level. See also the insightful reflections on this issue of Boudon (1990: 42–43; 2003a: 169–71), inspired by passages from Simmel. From the position here taken, criticisms both of RAT and of survey data of the kind advanced by Scheff (1992) become strictly irrelevant.

11. See further Chapter 4, pp. 78–9. An analogous determinism is supposed at the macro-level in the work of sociologists such as Skocpol and Ragin, insofar as they eschew quantitative and probabilistic, in favour of qualitative and logical analyses that are inspired more or less directly by the methodology of John Stuart Mill.

12. And as Duncan has aptly commented (1975: 166–7), having argued that a complex social system could hardly operate other than to some degree stochastically, 'The sociologist who despairs of his low R^2s would do well to ask himself if he would want it otherwise—would he care to live in the society so structured that his particular collection of variables accounts for 90 percent instead of 32 percent of the variance in Y?'

13. A further standard objection raised against RAT is that it offers no systematic account of how the ends (or goals) towards which rational action is directed are themselves formed. Proponents of RAT have readily acknowledged the correctness of this observation but have replied—quite appropriately, I would believe—that neither has any other theoretical approach contributed much of significance in this regard. I take up this issue at greater length in Chapter 8.

14. Such potential failures of rationality and their implications have been exhaustively analysed at a theoretical level in the work of Elster (see esp. 1979, 1983b, 1989a, 1989c).

15. Stinchcombe's more general concern is with the way in which 'proportionality factors' of any kind within a population can remain close to constant over time, despite rapidly changing individual characteristics. The basic mathematical idea involved can be traced back to Penrose (1946) if not indeed to Quetelet. Hechter (1987: 31–33) also takes up Stinchcombe's argument in a RAT context, but for the more limited purpose of defending the assumption of actors' similar preference orderings over a given set of choices.

16. The possibility does of course remain that there may be other common—that is, nonidiosyncratic—influences bearing on the collectivity of actors apart from that of rationality. The most obvious alternatives are shared beliefs that cannot be understood as rational, even in the given conditions; or shared commitments to values and related social norms that cannot be understood in rational—that is, instrumental—terms (see further ch. 8). It is then in no way accidental that the most engrossing and consequential of current debates in modern sociological theory should centre on issues raised in this connection (see, e.g., Boudon 1994; Elster, 1989a: ch. 3 esp.; Coleman, 1990: chs. 10, 11 esp.; Hechter, 1994); and it is, moreover, encouraging that these appear also to be debates to which, as I seek to show in Volume II, empirically based interventions can significantly contribute.

17. There are several accounts of the disaster by naval historians. Watkins draws primarily on Hough (1959).

18. Moreover, insofar as mechanism-based theory draws on RAT, these arguments also sit ill with claims for its paradigmatic privilege.

19. It is of interest that even a philosopher of science such as Hausman (1992), who upholds the importance of models (as distinct from theories) in economics as a means of conceptual elaboration and who emphasises the problems of a falsificationist methodology, should still believe that economists need to give more serious attention to theory appraisal via data collection and analysis, and that this might in turn lead to a sharper recognition of the point at which the qualification

of a theory is less appropriate than its radical modification or indeed abandonment. I should add that although Elster does not address the problem of the relation of theory and research that I here raise, he is entirely clear about the crucial distinction from which it stems: that is, between theory in a restricted sense—or what he would prefer to call the specification, or model, of a causal mechanism—and what he would regard as theory proper. Theory in this latter sense must *include* a statement of its domain of application: 'it is supposed to tell you which mechanisms operate in which situations' (1990: 247).

20. A cautionary tale in this regard is provided by the ingenious attempt made by Boudon (1974; cf. also 1982: ch. 2) to explain, from a RAT standpoint, what he took as a puzzling conjunction in modern societies of increasing educational provision, declining class differentials in educational attainment but more or less constant rates of intergenerational social mobility. While, in its spirit, this attempt is entirely in accord with what is here being advocated, it is now apparent, in the light of better data and more appropriate analyses than were available to Boudon, that his problem scarcely exists. A decline in class differentials in educational attainment is *not* a marked and general feature of modern societies or, at all events, not in the sense of a declining influence of class origins on children's 'transition probabilities' at successive branching points in their educational careers—with which Boudon was crucially concerned (see Shavit and Blossfeld, eds., 1993). Thus, the lack of a consistently increasing trend in (relative) mobility rates need not, on this account at least, occasion any great surprise (see further vol. II, chs. 2–4).

21. The most detailed analyses have concerned the effects of mobility on voting (see, e.g., De Graaf and Ultee, 1990; Clifford and Heath, 1993; De Graaf, Nieuwbeerta, and Heath, 1995; Cautrès, 1995). With reference to the argument of the preceding section, it is of interest to note that Cox (1990: 169–70), in a general review of the differing roles that models may play in statistics, takes diagonal reference models as a social science example of the bridging of 'empirical' and more 'substantive' concerns; or, that is, of a movement towards models that 'aim to explain what is observed in terms of processes (mechanisms), usually via quantities that are not directly observed, and some theoretical notions as to how the system under study "works"'.

22. Two further features of the work of Gambetta and of Weakliem and Heath alike should in this connection be noted. First, the models they fit are mostly ones inspired by RAT-based hypotheses, and the extent to which these fail to account for their data is then assessed in effect by reference to the residuals (in the statistical sense) under these models. This could, however, be unfair to RAT insofar as the models are misspecified (which is a particular worry with the relatively crude ones applied by Gambetta). Second, these authors themselves acknowledge difficulties even in suggesting, let alone demonstrating, plausible explanations of how the residual effects, assuming them to be real, are actually generated. Gambetta (1987: 93–99 esp.) considers, among other possibilities, that of distorted cognitive or

judgmental processes, while Weakliem and Heath speculate about 'subconscious conformity' with class opinion.

Notes to Chapter 7

1. On the—crucial—distinction between methodological and ontological individualism, see Chapter 8, p. 169.

2. Reference is often here made to 'social systems'. However, I see no point in committing oneself to this concept unless it is going to be put to explanatory use— as, typically, in conjunction with that of 'equilibrium'. While RAT can of course operate as an element within such an explanatory strategy—as, most obviously, in mainstream economics—it is not dependent on it; and whether a sociological generalisation of the equilibrium theory of economics (see, e.g., Coleman, 1990) will prove of much value remains, in my view, highly debatable.

3. Among distinctions that I do not consider, perhaps the most notable is that between RAT as based on 'parametric' rationality, where a passive environment is supposed, and on 'strategic' rationality, where the rational action of one actor depends on that of all others involved—that is, game theory (cf. Elster, 1983b: ch. 1). Because both approaches have been shown to have important sociological applications, the distinction is not of great consequence for my present purposes.

4. Some further comments on terminology may be helpful here. I follow Elster (1983a: ch.3) and various other authors in distinguishing action from behaviour (or, alternatively, treating action as a special kind of behaviour) in that action is *intentional*, in contrast with behaviour that can be understood as 'externally' caused. However, as will later be seen, I differ from Elster in wishing to subdivide intentional action so that nonrational, as well as rational and irrational action is specifically recognised.

5. Some proponents of RAT (e.g., Harsanyi, 1969; Hechter, 1994) have sought to identify the goals towards which rational action is *in general* directed: for example, economic gain, social acceptance, or power. But it is not clear whether this entails more than providing a series of heads under which any more specific goals can, in some way or other, be catalogued. The fact that RAT does not seek to endogenise actors' ends or goals is frequently referred to as a major limitation; but given the lack of success of theories of action that have attempted this move, the strategy of proceeding empirically might appear well judged. This issue is taken up at greater length in Chapter 8.

6. An addendum made to this argument by some economists is that the prevalence of such subconscious rationality is guaranteed by natural selection exerted through market forces. Thus, for example, firms led by entrepreneurs or managers who are not profit maximisers will simply be eliminated. For pertinent critical comment, see Langlois (1986: 243–47), Sen (1987), and Blaug (1992: 99–105).

7. The essential similarity between the positions reached by Popper and von Wright—independently, it would seem—has attracted remarkably little com-

ment, even where it might have been expected (see, e.g., Koertge, 1975, 1979). It is, however, of interest that Watkins (1970: 209), in a discussion of the rationality principle, remarks that this principle 'effects a two-way connection . . . It says that a man who has a decision-scheme issuing in a practical conclusion will try to act in accordance with that conclusion. . . . It also says that, given that a man was not drugged, hypnotized, sleep-walking, etc. but *acting*, then his action was the acting out of the practical conclusion of a decision-scheme'.

8. Becker (1976: 7) argues that the important question is whether or not the theory is closed in a 'useful' way—that is, one that allows testable propositions to be formulated. But even supposing that this is the case, what then matters is how theorists respond to empirical evidence indicating that such propositions are false (Schoemaker, 1982: 539–41, 554 esp.). Are they ready to consider that the theory might be misconceived, and perhaps radically so, or do they draw on the possibilities for immunising stratagems that its closure offers? Becker rarely, if ever, indicates what kind of evidence he himself would regard as being inconsistent with the theories he advances; but for a review—by sociologists—of empirical findings that stand in apparent contradiction to a range of his theoretically grounded claims, see Baron and Hannan (1994). Of late, it should be recognised, more economists have shown themselves ready to criticise Becker's position (see, e.g., Blaug, 1992: ch. 14) and at the same time to work with conceptions of bounded rationality. Of particular sociological interest in this regard are the transaction cost economics of Williamson (1985, 1996) and others (see further vol. II, ch. 5).

9. That is to say, if traditional action is rendered rational by dint of supposing the maintenance of tradition to be itself the goal. A similar approach to that outlined in the text could be taken in regard to the distinction between rational and habitual action. It has been advanced as a critique of RAT that a man does not decide anew each morning how to shave his face but just acts 'out of habit'. This could, however, be entirely rational. If one believes that one has worked out the best way to shave, why constantly return to the problem? What would be irrational would be not to adapt to change: that is, not to reconsider the matter if information became available to suggest that by using other equipment or a different technique one could achieve a worthwhile improvement.

10. The view here taken of the scope of RAT thus implies significantly more restriction than that of Boudon (1996, 1998, 2003b, 2003c) who, in advancing his 'cognitivist model', argues that the 'good reasons' that actors may have for their actions need *not* be limited to 'the cost-benefit comparison type': for example, rational action can be 'axiological', rather than outcome oriented, in following consistently from a value. Although Boudon here appeals to Weber's notion of *Wertrationalität*, it should be noted that Weber himself recognised (1922/1968:26), that, from the standpoint of *Zweckrationalität*, action of a *wertrational* kind must always be judged *ir*rational.

11. As Sen puts it (1977: 327) 'One way of defining commitment is in terms

of a person choosing an act that he believes will yield a lower level of personal welfare to him than an alternative that is also available to him'.

12. A further distinction that would obviously call for attention is that between rational and expressive action. Action pursued 'for its own sake' could be regarded as rational where, for example, actors set its intrinsic rewards against the costs involved. This, incidentally, I would see as the most promising approach to the 'paradox of voting' that has often been invoked in critiques of RAT (e.g., Green and Shapiro, 1994). However, instances of enthusiasm, rapture, or fervour have also to be recognised where action clearly does not derive from any kind of cost-benefit considerations.

13. Weber's most extended discussion of the issue is to be found in a neglected paper (1908/1975) in which he forcefully criticises an attempt by Lujo Brentano to provide marginal utility theory with a foundation in experimental psychology—specifically, in the Weber-Fechner law that the strength of a stimulus must increase in geometric ratio if the perceived strength of sensation is to increase in arithmetic ratio. (The coproposer of the law was Ernst Heinrich Weber—no relation of Max.) Though I know of no direct evidence that Popper was influenced by this paper, there are frequent references in his work to Weber's *Gesammelte Aufsätze zur Wissenschaftslehre* in which it was reprinted.

14. Consider a trickster attempting to exploit the tendency discussed by Boudon (1994: 235–36) for individuals to miscalculate how best to bet on the toss of a coin known to be heavily biased. The trickster might make some money initially, but knowledge of how to win (even if not of the underlying mathematics) would soon spread among the public. In contrast, the tendency which Boudon further considers (1994: 247–48) of many teachers to believe, in a context of educational expansion, that standards of educational achievement are falling, even if this is not in fact so, is likely to have much greater social persistence. For the source of the error here is not the inability of the individuals concerned to calculate correctly but the situationally restricted, and thus partial and misleading, nature of the relevant knowledge that is most immediately available to them.

15. This does not of course imply or warrant any neglect of material resources and of related patterns of opportunity and constraint in the situation of action. RAT, at least in the version I would favour, is very readily allied with class analysis, as I seek to show at some length in the second volume of this work. In the following chapter I discuss the misconception that RAT is unduly voluntaristic.

16. If sociologists have available respondents' own accounts of their action, as, say, through interviews, the rationality that is reconstructed in situational analyses can be subjected to a further check, which is likely to be especially relevant where unorthodox utilities are postulated. As Cohen (1976: 149) has remarked, it is easier for historians and ethnographers to make the conduct studied by them appear rational in that 'dead men can never answer back and ethnographers' informants used not to be able to do so'. At the same time, though, actors' accounts

need not be regarded as entirely privileged, but rather as being open to criticism, on grounds of fact and logic, in just the same way as sociologists'. This latter point is an important one in considering the issue of the place of attitudinal and other subjective data in the development and evaluation of RAT-based explanations (cf. Opp, 1998).

17. It is also by proceeding on these lines, I would believe, that sociologists can best address the central macro-to-micro issue that arises with RAT: that of whether RAT differs in its potential across different kinds of society and culture. I take up this issue in the chapter that follows but it is evident that underlying the claims that I have made for the privilege of RAT must be the assumption of what Popper (see esp. 1966: chs. 23, 24), echoing Kant, has called 'the intellectual [or psychic] unity of mankind'—to which the idea of rationality provides the *passe partout*.

Notes to Chapter 8

1. Terminological issues have, I am afraid, to be taken seriously. Other sociologists use RAT in much the same way as I do or in some cases make much the same kind of distinction between rational choice theory and the larger body of theory of which it forms part but by means of other terminology. For example, Boudon (2003c: ch. 1) distinguishes between rational choice theory and 'the general rational model' (*modèle rationnel général*). However, it should be noted that Macy (1998) uses 'rational action theory' in an entirely different way: that is, to refer to theory that is concerned with action (or behaviour) that can be regarded as rational simply by reference to its *outcome*, and not, necessarily, to the decision-making processes (if any) from which it results.

2. An exception might be made in the case of the concluding essay by Beckford (2000), which has, moreover, a significantly less oppositional tone than the others.

3. If this suspicion is thought unworthy, further grounds for it are provided by the rather remarkable fact that in the collection there is little if any reference to, let alone any consideration of, the work of leading figures in the development of versions of RAT specifically in the context of sociology: for example, Boudon, Esser, Hechter, Heckathorn, Hedström, Lindenberg, or Opp.

4. Schütz and Popper are of particular interest in that both were influenced by, but also in part reacted against, developments in economics, in particular, the subjectivism of the Austrian school (Prendergast, 1986). Esser (1993) well brings out the partiality of the purely 'interpretivist' view of Schütz that most recent commentators have favoured.

5. Schumpeter, who actually coined the term 'methodological individualism', did so expressly to try to avoid any confusion between individualism as a principle of analysis in the social sciences and individualism in other senses (Udéhn, 2001: 104–105).

6. Archer and Tritter (2000), along with other contributors to the Warwick collection, make no mention of rational choice Marxism.

7. In his wide-ranging treatise on methodological individualism, Udéhn (2001: 186–89 esp.) sees the key issue as being that of whether or not cultural or social entities are allowed to 'enter into' sociological explanations. But I would think it more helpful—as Udéhn does at certain points appear to acknowledge—to ask about exactly *how* they may do so. For proponents of methodological individualism, they quite properly enter as *conditions* of action, while individuals remain as the sole causal agents. A crucial contrast thus arises with the position of those who would argue that social phenomena are generated directly by causal mechanisms that are in some way inherent in social systems or cultures themselves, and in relation to which individual action can then be no more than epiphenomenal.

8. The fact that critics of RAT want to argue *both* that it sees actors as being purely self-interested *and* that it is unconcerned with the nature of their ends leads often to inconsistency or to rather strange arguments to the effect that if RAT can allow for the pursuit of altruistic goals, this can only be by defining altruism out of existence since the pursuit of altruism is made as selfish as the pursuit of any other preference. See, for example, in the Warwick collection (Archer and Tritter, eds., 2000) the differing positions that are represented on pp. 2, 5, 13, 36, 53, 75, and 80.

9. Edling (2000) objects that what he—quite aptly—calls my 'Gaussian' argument need not hold if only subjective rather than objective rationality is involved and rationality is thus limited by actors' beliefs—which may differ from actor to actor. I would certainly accept that what I see as the crucial assumption underlying RAT is more likely to be wrong if subjective rather than objective rationality is supposed. However, whether it is in fact wrong, in any particular case, is an empirical matter. My concern is to make clear just what the assumption is, not to claim that it is irrefragable. As should be evident from what immediately follows in the text, I would wish RAT-based explanations always to be formulated so that they are open to empirical rejection—one source of which could of course be that the crucial assumption fails.

10. Implicit in Sen's argument, and likewise in my own, is the idea that in the social sciences *any* theory of action that has explanatory ambition and potential will need to be based on a model of the actor that is a simplification in one way or another. Those theoretical approaches that are reluctant to simplify may provide a whole range of categories for (re)description but at the same time their explanatory power is likely to be undermined. Symbolic interactionism provides, I believe, a prime example of this point.

11. In what follows, I refer to the ends of action as a way of covering not only the specific goals towards which action may be directed but also the more general values, desires, or preferences that may shape such goals.

12. It should be noted that Weber does here still preserve his commitment to

methodological individualism by arguing that these institutions had themselves to be created by action of a quite new, indeed revolutionary kind—that is, action that was an unintended consequence of the secular ethic of ascetic Protestantism (cf. Marshall, 1982; Hernes, 1989).

13. I place the emphasis here on the evidence from primary research on which these works are based (both are impressively well documented), and specifically on that relevant to their authors' critiques of Weber, rather than on the works themselves since I would not necessarily wish, and, for my present purposes, do not need, to underwrite all of the authors' more positive arguments. I should also note that both authors recognise that Weber's own writings are often more subtle and nuanced than many of those who have invoked his authority would seem to be aware.

14. Thus, Blaut (1993) gives particular attention to Chinese scientific and technological achievement—and to the rather desperate attempts of some authors to minimise its significance. Goody (1996: ch. 2) takes up one of Weber's own favourite examples of western rationality in economic affairs, that of double-entry accounting, and reviews evidence to show that this practice did not represent a 'quantum jump' from traditional into modern or 'scientific' accounting but simply one step in a long process of the rationalisation of monetary transactions, with origins in both the near East and China.

15. A body of empirical research that is especially illuminating in this connection is that which of late has transformed the economics and sociology of so-called traditional—that is, largely peasant agriculture. In the view that previously prevailed, such agriculture was seen as dominated by custom, so that innovation and long-term investment were discouraged and low levels of productivity persisted. However, while peasants and other traditional agriculturalists may well show a deep respect for customary practices—which often turn out to provide quite rational solutions to problems of resource allocation, risk management, and dispute settlement—recent research reveals that this does not prevent them from departing from such practices when they can gain advantage from so doing. In both historical and present-day cases, peasant agriculture has been regularly found to be capable of sustained increases in productivity driven by technological innovation and investment. For a major study and literature reviews, see Allen (1992, 2001). For an interesting critique of Weber's own treatment of traditional agriculture and its disruption, in his study (Weber, 1892) of the East Elbian region in the late nineteenth century, see Grant (2002).

16. These defences were made largely in the context of debates over the role of a shared rationality in providing for the very possibility of cross-cultural understanding (see, e.g., Hollis and Lukes, eds., 1982). Hollis (1982: 75) sums up his position at one point by arguing that if such understanding is to occur, then there must, in Strawson's striking phrase, be 'a massive central core of human thinking which has no history'.

17. Also of interest in the present context is the critique made by Gigerenzer and his associates, from the standpoint of ecological rationality, of aspects of the celebrated 'heuristics and biases' research programme of Kahnemann and Tversky—in particular of the latter's claim to have shown that there are systematic fallacies built in to human reasoning involving some violation of a rule of logic or probability. Against this, strong experimental evidence is presented (see, e.g., Gigerenzer, 2000: ch. 6 esp.) to show how cognitive illusions disappear and human reasoning is greatly improved simply as a result of information being presented in a form—for example, natural frequencies—to which the human mind is adapted rather than in a form too recent for this to be the case—for example, conditional probabilities.

18. For example—and the point is of particular relevance in the present context—Tooby and Cosmides are surely right to underline the difficulties that arise in seeing human psychology as being essentially dependent on sociocultural context without any consideration being given to the psychological requirements for the existence of human society and culture in the first place.

19. It is rather ironic that the critics of the standard social science model of the individual would appear no less ignorant or disregarding of the individualistic paradigm as are the more vehement critics of RAT. Tooby and Cosmides do at one point (1992: 31) acknowledge that they leave out of account 'important dissident sub-communities' in the social sciences that 'have sloughed off or never adopted' the standard model. However, this does little to mitigate the partiality of their characterisation of sociology—to say nothing of economics.

20. An especially unfortunate development in encouraging such alarmist reactions is Pinker's attempt (2002: part I) to establish a close association between evolutionary psychology and behavioural genetics. In contrast, it should be noted, Tooby and Cosmides (1992: 25) emphasise the extent to which human genetic variation 'is overwhelmingly sequestered into functionally superficial biochemical differences', thus leaving human functional design 'universal and species-typical', and further the fact that such genetic variation as does occur is found largely among individuals rather than among collectivities.

21. My interpretation of this situation would be that in general the arguments of evolutionary psychologists are far more convincing, in both theoretical and empirical terms, when concerned with human *capacities* rather than with human *motivations*. It is certainly possible in the present state of knowledge—and this would indeed represent my own position—to be entirely receptive to the idea of 'hard-wired', and thus universal, capacities, while still believing that insofar as universal motivations can be identified, these will indeed be quite plastic: that is, subject to very significant sociocultural modification, and thus variation, in their actual expression.

22. Bowles's approach to endogenisation has, however, still to be distinguished from that of Becker (1996), which is of a yet more radical kind. Becker's

aim is to explain preference formation on the part of actor A not just as the result of the rational choices of other actors who wish to shape A's preferences or as the unintended result of A's own rational choices in some other respect but, further, if need be, as the result of A himself or herself deciding in a quite direct and instrumental way to have or to develop certain preferences, consistently with some immanently conceived metapreference function. I would agree with the cogent criticisms directed against this approach by Elster (1997) in respect of both its conceptual coherence and empirical plausibility. Bowles, in contrast (1998: 80), would give only a minor role to intentional preference formation and, as indicated in the text, is primarily concerned with the indirect and often unintended effects on preferences of institutions of production and distribution that have their own economic rationale.

23. For example, this seems to me to occur with Kanazawa's (2001) attempt to explain young people's participation in protest movements as resulting from the fact that this allows young men to display their leadership and innovatory potential and young women to assess possible partners from this point of view. The freerider problem in collective action is thus overcome, Kanazawa argues, since such action provides ideal opportunities for courtship, and these opportunities are taken up because of unconscious motivations to seek reproductive success.

24. The behaviourists were, of course, themselves rather extreme 'blank slaters'.

25. In this connection, Wrong (1961: 192) makes a helpful distinction between two ways in which 'socialisation' can be understood. On the one hand, it may refer to the transmission to the individual of the content of a specific culture; on the other hand, it may refer simply to 'the process of becoming human', of acquiring uniquely human attributes from interaction with others. As Wrong points out, all individuals are socialised in the latter sense 'but this does not mean that they have been completely molded by the particular norms and values of their culture'.

26. It is considerations of the kind outlined in the preceding two paragraphs that lead me to be relatively optimistic that what I earlier referred to as the crucial underlying assumption of RAT—that rational action is the decisive 'central tendency' in the generation of macrosocial regularities—will prove far more robust than critics suppose simply on the basis of pointing to ways in which it *could* be undermined. There is, I suspect, a kind of *déformation professionelle* that leads to many sociologists exaggerating the homogenising effects on the components of action of socialisation and networks of interpersonal relations.

27. More effort should, however, be made to improve on methods that are currently available for determining actors' ends empirically. Here again sociologists could usefully join forces with economists who are becoming increasingly aware of problems that arise with the idea of revealed preferences or, that is, with the practice of simply inferring ends from action (cf. Manski, 2000, 2004; and also vol. II, ch. 4).

Notes to Chapter 9

1. Bernert's paper concentrates on the concept of causation in American sociology but is in fact of quite general relevance.

2. Other reviews of issues of causality from a statistical point of view, from which I have greatly benefited, are Holland (1986a), Berk (1988), Cox (1992), Sobel (1995), and Winship and Morgan (1999).

3. I am aware of some special cases in which it might be argued that causation is present in the absence of association: for example, where X does have an effect on Y which, however, happens to be *exactly* cancelled out by a further and opposing effect that X exerts on Y via a third variable, Z. For present purposes, I believe that such cases can be safely disregarded. I might also add that here, as throughout, I assume that effects cannot precede causes and further that plural or 'multifactorial' causation may operate.

4. Lazarsfeld, for example, always urged that elaboration should go together with 'interpretation' that involved specifying intervening variables in the supposed causal connection and the provision of some appropriate narrative or 'story-line' (see further vol. II, ch. 9). Again, Duncan's standard work (1975) could scarcely be more explicit on the problems that sociologists must face, and overcome, if they are to produce valid causal path models. It is of particular interest to read one of his main cautionary passages in conjunction with Freedman's (1975: 152) critique, outlined in the text above:

> A strong possibility in any area of research at a given time is that there are *no* structural relations among the variables currently recognized and measured in that area. Hence, whatever its mathematical properties, no model describing covariation of those variables will be a structural model. What is needed under the circumstances is a theory that invents the proper variables . . . There were no structural equation models for the epidemiology of malaria until the true agent and vector of the disease were identified, although there were plenty of correlations between prevalence of the disease and environmental conditions.

5. Holland (1986a: 947) distinguishes this 'statistical' solution from the 'scientific' solution typically pursued in laboratory experiments which rests on various assumptions concerning the homogeneity of units and the invariance of measurements made of their properties.

6. The difficulty for Holland here is that of reconciling purposive or 'outcome-oriented' and rational action on the part of an individual with the idea of 'caused' action in the sense he would favour, which must take on the character of a response to an intervention. It might be noted that a somewhat related objection to treating the reasons for actions as their causes was advanced by chiefly neo-Wittgensteinian philosophers on the lines that causation must entail causes and effects that are logically independent, whereas the reasons for an action and the actual course it follows will, at least in the case of rational action, be logically con-

nected (see e.g., MacIntyre, 1962). However, the force of this objection has been increasingly questioned and the idea of reasons for action as representing at all events one kind of causation among others would appear by now to have gained rather wide philosophical acceptance (see, e.g., Toulmin, 1970; Mackie, 1974: ch. 11; Davidson, 1980: chs. 1 and 14 esp.). On the application of this same idea in economics, see Helm (1984).

7. It might be thought that similar problems with experiments to those envisaged in the text could also arise in applied natural science. For example, the (perhaps apocryphal?) case is sometimes cited of an agricultural experiment in which the treatment of certain plots resulted in very heavy crops, which then, however, attracted large numbers of foraging birds, so that the eventual yield on these plots was less than on those not treated. But the birds just wanted to eat: they were not trying to stop the treatment working by countering its effects. Again, there are well-known problems of how to take into account patient noncompliance in clinical trials, which clearly involves action (or inaction) on the part of patients. But it would still not be generally supposed that patients have the objective of actually subverting trials.

8. As Suppes (1970: 91) has aptly observed, the accounts of causal processes or mechanisms given by one generation become themselves the black boxes for the next. It may be added that it is essentially Holland's recognition of this point that leads him to wish to concentrate, as a statistician, on determining the effects of causes rather than the causes of effects—'on what can be done well rather than on what we might like to do, however poorly' (1988: 451). But it could be replied, first, that this is to be unduly discouraged by what is a quite general feature of the pursuit of scientific knowledge; and second that, at least in the case of sociology, what can be done well and less well by statistics appears less clear-cut than Holland might suppose (cf. Smith, 1990).

9. Nor would be: 'They took measures to counter the policy intervention because they believed it was detrimental to their interests'.

10. In this regard, the use of graph theoretical representations of structures of conditional independence and association among variables would seem to have potential value (Cox and Wermuth, 1996), although this method has not so far been widely applied in sociology. More ambitiously, computerised algorithms have been developed to search for possible representations of this kind on the basis of correlation matrices from particular data-sets and thus, it is hoped, to lead to the discovery of causal relations with little need for subject-matter input (Spirtes, Glymour, and Scheines, 1993; Pearl, 2000). However, the assumptions involved seem often questionable and, again, no very convincing applications have been presented, at least in sociology. For lively debate, see McKim and Turner, eds., (1997) and also the exchanges culminating in Freedman and Humphreys (1999) and Freedman (2004).

11. It is important to note that such problems do in fact arise not only, as it

were, endogenously to the development of sociology but also exogenously to this development—most obviously, perhaps, from various kinds of applied, even purely 'administrative', social research (see further Goldthorpe, 2004a). While I would then entirely agree with authors such as Hedström and Swedberg (1998a, 1998b) in their insistence that the main requirement of theory is that it should explain, I believe that they place a too exclusive emphasis on the role of theory in the discovery of problems and, correspondingly, underestimate that of empirical research— and especially of large-scale survey research—which may itself have primarily descriptive goals (cf. Erikson, 1998).

12. A concern for the theoretical basis of hypothesised generative processes is also important to prevent purely ad hoc switching. As an example of this, one could cite the case of sociologists drawing on versions of RAT in seeking to explain regularities in the class-vote relationship but then reverting to norm-oriented action theory to explain why individuals vote at all. Such switching *may* be appropriate but the grounds for it have always to be spelled out: that is, the attempt must be made to specify which kinds of process will operate under which conditions. As argued in Chapter 6, there are dangers in the idea that sociologists can simply accumulate a collection of models of causal processes or mechanisms of many different kinds, items from which can then be used (or discarded) just as seems convenient.

13. For example (and as is argued at greater length in vol. II, chs. 2 and 4 especially), once it is recognised just what it is that needs to be explained about class differentials in education—that is, why in most modern societies they have remained surprisingly little changed at successive transitions, despite substantial educational expansion—it at once becomes apparent that culturalist accounts (e.g., Bourdieu, 1973; Willis, 1977) do not meet the initial requirement of causal adequacy. For if the main source of these differentials were indeed to lie in radically divergent class subcultures, with working-class families attaching a lower value to education than families in more advantaged class positions and their children being thus systematically alienated from the educational system, then what one would have to expect in course of educational expansion would be *widening* differentials. But there is no evidence of this. Working-class children have in fact taken up expanding educational opportunities at least at the same rate as children of other class origins.

14. It is of course quite likely that the data-sets that are used to establish particular social regularities will not be those most suitable, from the point of view of the information they contain, for purposes of testing supposed generative processes. This points up the importance of recognising the distinction between these phases of enquiry.

15. What follows is much influenced by, and draws on, Ní Bhrolcháin (2001).

16. Another relevant study, though more psychological in orientation, is that reported by Rutter (1981; and cf. also 1994) who advances the hypothesis that, in explaining the association between marital breakup and children's disorderly be-

haviour, the 'mediating mechanism' is tension resulting from marital conflict rather than the breakup itself. Rutter is then able to show how this hypothesis can be tested, again on the basis of longitudinal data, through the comparison of cases of temporary separations arising from marital conflict and those arising for other reasons and also of cases where, following such a separation associated with conflict, a reduction or increase in conflict was subsequently recorded.

BIBLIOGRAPHY

Abbott, A. (1992a), 'What Do Cases Do? Some Notes on Activity in Sociological Analysis' in C. C. Ragin and H. S. Becker (eds.) *What Is a Case?* (Cambridge: Cambridge University Press).
Abbott, A. (1992b), 'From Causes to Events: Notes on Narrative Positivism', *Sociological Methods and Research*, 20: 428–55.
Abbott, A. (1997), 'On the Concept of Turning Point', *Comparative Social Research*, 16: 85–105.
Abbott, A. (1998), 'The Causal Devolution', *Sociological Methods and Research*, 27: 148–81.
Abbott, A. (2001), *Chaos of Disciplines* (Chicago: University of Chicago Press).
Abell, P. (1992), 'Is Rational Choice Theory a Rational Choice of Theory?' in J. S. Coleman and T. J. Fararo (eds.) *Rational Choice Theory: Advocacy and Critique* (Newbury Park: Sage).
Abell, P. and Reyniers, D. (2000), 'On the Failure of Social Theory', *British Journal of Sociology*, 51: 739–50.
Abrams, P. (1980), *Historical Sociology* (Bath: Open Books).
Achen, C. A. (2005), 'Two Cheers for Charles Ragin', *Studies in Comparative International Development*, 40: 27–32.
Adams, J., Clemens, E. S., and Orloff, A. S. (2005), 'Introduction: Social Theory, Modernity, and the Three Waves of Historical Sociology' in *idem* (eds.) *Remaking Modernity: Politics, History, and Sociology* (Durham: Duke University Press).
Agassi, J. (1975), 'Institutional Individualism', *British Journal of Sociology*, 26: 144–55.
Albrow, M. (1996), *The Global Age* (Cambridge: Polity Press).
Allardt, E. (1990), 'Challenges for Comparative Social Research', *Acta Sociologica*, 33: 183–93.
Allen, R. C. (1992), *Enclosure and the Yeoman* (Oxford: Clarendon).
Allen, R. C. (2001), 'Community and Market in England: Open Fields and Enclosures Revisited' in M. Aoki and Y. Hayami (eds.) *Communities and Markets in Economic Development* (Oxford: Oxford University Press).

255

Amenta, E. and Poulsen, J. D. (1994), 'Where to Begin: A Survey of Five Approaches to Selecting Independent Variables for Qualitative Comparative Analysis', *Sociological Methods and Research*, 23: 22–53.

Anderson, M. (1971), *Family Structure in Nineteenth Century Lancashire* (Cambridge: Cambridge University Press).

Anderson, P. (1974a), *Passages from Feudalism to Antiquity* (London: New Left Books).

Anderson, P. (1974b), *Lineages of the Absolutist State* (London: New Left Books).

Andersen, R., Yang, M., and Heath, A. F. (2006), 'Class Politics and Political Context in Britain: 1964–1997: Have Voters Become More Individualized?', *European Sociological Review*, 22: 215–28.

Appleby, L. and Starmer, S. (1987), 'Individual Choice Under Uncertainty: A Review of Experimental Evidence Past and Present' in J. D. Hey and P. J. Lambert (eds.) *Surveys in the Economics of Uncertainty* (Oxford: Blackwell).

Archer, M. S. (1995), *Realist Social Theory: The Morphogenetic Approach* (Cambridge; Cambridge University Press).

Archer, M. S. (2000), 'Homo Sociologicus, Homo Economicus and Home Sentiens' in M. S. Archer and J. Q. Tritter (eds.) *Rational Choice Theory: Resisting Colonisation* (Routledge: London).

Archer, M. S. and Tritter, J. Q. (eds.) (2000), *Rational Choice Theory: Resisting Colonization* (Routledge: London).

Archer, M. S. and Tritter, J. Q. (2000), 'Introduction' in *idem* (eds.) *Rational Choice Theory: Resisting Colonization* (Routledge: London).

Atkinson, A. B. (1997), 'Bringing Income Distribution in from the Cold', *Economic Journal*, 107: 297–321.

Atkinson, A. B. (1998), 'Social Exclusion, Poverty and Unemployment' in A. B. Atkinson and J. Hills (eds.) *Exclusion, Employment and Opportunity* (London: Centre for Analysis of Social Exclusion, London School of Economics).

Atkinson, A. B. (1999a), *The Economic Consequences of Rolling Back the Welfare State* (Cambridge, Mass.: MIT Press).

Atkinson, A. B. (1999b), 'Is Rising Inequality Inevitable? A Critique of the Transatlantic Consensus'. WIDER Annual Lecture, 1999, Helsinki.

Augier, M. and March, J. G. (eds.) (2004), *Models of Man: Essays in Memory of Herbert A. Simon* (Cambridge, Mass.: MIT Press).

Baert, P. (1998), *Social Theory in the Twentieth Century* (Cambridge: Polity Press).

Bairoch, P. (1996), 'Globalization Myths and Realities' in R. Boyer and D. Drache (eds.), *States against Markets: The Limits of Globalization* (London: Routledge).

Barbera, F. (2004), *Meccanismi sociali* (Bologna: Il Mulino).

Baron, J. N. and Hannan, M. T. (1994), 'The Impact of Economics on Contemporary Sociology', *Journal of Economic Literature*, 32: 1111–146.

Basmann, R. L. (1988), 'Causality Tests and Observationally Equivalent Representations of Econometric Models', *Journal of Econometrics*, 39: 7–21.

Beck, U. (1992), *Risk Society* (London: Sage).

Beck, U. (2000a), *What Is Globalization?* (Cambridge: Polity Press).

Beck, U. (2000b), *The Brave New World of Work* (Cambridge: Polity Press).

Beck, U. (2000c), 'The Cosmopolitan Perspective: Sociology in the Second Age of Modernity', *British Journal of Sociology*, 51: 79–105.

Becker, C. (1955), 'What Are Historical Facts?' in H. Meyerhoff (ed.) *The Philosophy of History in Our Time* (New York: Doubleday).

Becker, G. (1976), *The Economic Approach to Human Behavior* (Chicago: Chicago University Press).

Becker, G. (1996), *Accounting for Tastes* (Cambridge, Mass.: Harvard University Press).

Becker, H. S. (1992), 'Cases, Causes, Conjunctures, Stories and Imagery' in C. C. Ragin and H. S. Becker (eds.) *What Is a Case?* (Cambridge: Cambridge University Press).

Beckford, J. A. (2000), 'When the Battle's Lost and Won' in M. S. Archer and J. Q. Tritter (eds.) *Rational Choice Theory: Resisting Colonization* (Routledge: London).

Bell, C. and Newby, H. (1981), 'Narcissism or Reflexivity in Modern Sociology?', *Polish Sociological Bulletin*, 1: 5–19.

Berk, R. A. (1988), 'Causal Inference for Sociological Data' in N. J. Smelser (ed.) *Handbook of Sociology* (Newbury Park: Sage).

Berger, J. and Offe, C. (1982), 'Functionalism vs. Rational Choice?', *Theory and Society*, 11: 521–26.

Bernert, C. (1983), 'The Career of Causal Analysis in American Sociology', *British Journal of Sociology*, 24: 230–54.

Berry, B. J. L. (1970), 'Some Methodological Consequences of Using the Nation as a Unit of Analysis in Comparative Politics'. Social Science Research Council, New York, Committee on Comparative Politics.

Bierstedt, R. (1959), 'Toynbee and Sociology', *British Journal of Sociology*, 10: 95–104.

Blalock, H. M. (1984), 'Contextual-Effects Models: Theoretical and Methodological Issues', *Annual Review of Sociology*, 10: 353–72.

Blau, P. M. and Duncan, O. D. (1967), *The American Occupational Structure* (New York: Wiley).

Blaug, M. (1991), 'Afterword' in N. de Marchi and M. Blaug (eds.) *Appraising Economic Theories* (Aldershot: Elgar).

Blaug, M. (1992), *The Methodology of Economics*, 2nd ed. (Cambridge: Cambridge University Press).

Blaut, J. M. (1993), *The Colonizer's Model of the World* (New York: Guilford).

Blossfeld, H.-P., and Huinink, J. (1991), 'Human Capital Investments or Norms of Role Transition? How Women's Schooling and Career Affect the Process of Family Formation', *American Journal of Sociology*, 97: 143–68.

Blossfeld, H.-P. and Prein, G. (eds.) (1998), *Rational Choice Theory and Large-Scale Data Analysis* (Boulder: Westview).

Blossfeld, H.-P. and Rohwer, G. (1995a), *Techniques of Event History Modeling: New Approaches to Causal Analysis* (Hillsdale, N.J.: Erlbaum).

Blossfeld, H.-P. and Rohwer, G. (1995b), 'West Germany' in H.-P. Blossfeld (ed.) *The New Role of Women: Family Formation in Modern Society* (Boulder: Westview).

Boudon, R. (1974), *Education, Opportunity and Social Inequality* (New York: Wiley).

Boudon, R. (1976), 'Comment on Hauser's Review of *Education, Opportunity and Social Inequality*', *American Journal of Sociology*, 81: 1175–187.

Boudon, R. (1982), *The Unintended Consequences of Social Action* (London: Macmillan).

Boudon, R. (1987), 'The Individualistic Tradition in Sociology' in J. C. Alexander et al. (eds.) *The Micro-Macro Link* (Berkeley: University of California Press).

Boudon R. (1989), *The Analysis of Ideology* (Cambridge: Polity Press).

Boudon, R. (1990), 'Individualism or Holism in the Social Sciences' in P. Birnbaum and J. Leca (eds.) *Individualism* (Oxford: Clarendon).

Boudon, R. (1994), *The Art of Self-Persuasion* (Cambridge: Polity Press).

Boudon, R. (1996), 'The "Cognitivist Model": A Generalized "Rational-Choice" Model', *Rationality and Society*, 8: 123–50.

Boudon, R. (1998), 'Social Mechanisms Without Black Boxes' in P. Hedström and R. Swedberg (eds.) *Social Mechanisms* (Cambridge: Cambridge University Press).

Boudon, R. (1998–2000), *Études sur les sociologues classiques*, 2 vols. (Paris: Presses Universitaires de France).

Boudon, R. (2001), 'Sociology that Really Matters', *European Sociological Review*, 18: 371–78.

Boudon, R. (2003a), *Y-a-t-il encore une sociologie?* (Paris: Odile Jacob).

Boudon, R. (2003b), 'Beyond Rational Choice Theory', *Annual Review of Sociology*, 29: 1–21.

Boudon, R. (2003c), *Raison, bonnes raisons* (Paris: Presses Universitaires de France).

Boudon, R. and Cherkaoui, M. (eds.) (1999), *Central Currents in Social Theory* (London: Sage).

Bourdieu, P. (1973), 'Cultural Reproduction and Social Reproduction' in R. K. Brown (ed.) *Knowledge, Education and Cultural Change* (London: Tavistock).

Bourdieu, P. and Wacquant, L. (1992), *An Invitation to Sociology* (Chicago: University of Chicago Press).

Bowles, S. (1998), 'Endogenous Preferences: The Cultural Consequences of Markets and Economic Institutions', *Journal of Economic Literature*, 36: 75–111.

Bowley, A. L. (1906), 'Address to the Economic Science and Statistics Section of the British Association for the Advancement of Science', *Journal of the Royal Statistical Society*, 47: 607–25.

Bowley, A. L. (1926), 'Measurement of the Precision Obtained in Sampling', *Bulletin of the International Statistical Institute*, 22, Supplement: 6–62.

Bowley, A. L. and Burnett-Hurst, A. R. (1915), *Livelihood and Poverty* (London: Bell).

Boyd, R. and Richerson, P. J. (2001), 'Norms and Bounded Rationality' in G. Gigerenzer and R. Selten (eds.) *Bounded Rationality: The Adaptive Toolbox* (Cambridge, Mass.: MIT Press).

Bradford Hill, A. (1991), *Principles of Medical Statistics*, 12th ed. (London: Arnold).

Bradford Hill, A. (1965), 'The Environment and Disease: Association or Causation?', *Proceedings of the Royal Society for Medicine*, 58: 295–300.

Bradshaw, Y. and Wallace, M. (1991), 'Informing Generality and Explaining Uniqueness: the Place of Case Studies in Comparative Research' in C. C. Ragin (ed.) *Issues and Alternatives in Comparative Social Research* (Leiden: E. J. Brill).

Brady, H. E., Collier, D., and Seawright, J. (2004), 'Refocusing the Discussion of Methodology' in H. E. Brady and D. Collier (eds.) *Rethinking Social Inquiry: Diverse Tools, Shared Standards* (Lanham: Rowman and Littlefield).

Brady, H. E. and Collier, D. (eds.) (2004), *Rethinking Social Inquiry: Diverse Tools, Shared Standards* (Lanham: Rowman and Littlefield).

Breen, R. (1997), 'Risk, Recommodification and Stratification', *Sociology*, 31: 473–89.

Breen, R. (ed.) (2004), *Social Mobility in Europe* (Oxford: Oxford University Press).

Breen, R. and Rottman, D. (1998), 'Is the National State the Appropriate Geographical Unit for Class Analysis?', *Sociology*, 32: 1–21.

Brewer, J. D. (2000), *Ethnography* (Buckingham: Open University Press).

Brewer, M., Goodman, A., Myck, M., Shaw, J., and Shephard, A. (2004), *Poverty and Inequality in Britain: 2004* (London: Institute for Fiscal Studies).

Brooks, C. (1994a), 'Class Consciousness and Politics in Comparative Perspective', *Social Science Research*, 23: 167–95.

Brooks, C. (1994b), 'The Selectively Political Citizen?', *Sociological Methods and Research*, 22: 419–59.

Brooks, C., Nieuwbeerta, P., and Manza, J. (2006), 'Cleavage-Based Voting Behavior in Cross-National Perspective: Evidence from Six Postwar Democracies', *Social Science Research*, 35: 88–128.

Brunton, D. and Pennington, D. H. (1954), *Members of the Long Parliament* (London: Allen and Unwin).

Bryant, C. G. A. (1995), *Practical Sociology* (Cambridge: Polity Press).

Bryant, J. M. (1994), 'Evidence and Explanation in History and Sociology', *British Journal of Sociology*, 45: 3–19.

Bryman, A. (1988), *Quantity and Quality in Social Research* (London: Routledge).

Bryman, A. (1994), 'The Mead/Freeman Controversy: Some Implications for Qualitative Researchers', *Studies in Qualitative Methodology*, 4: 1–27.

Bunge, M. (1979), *Causality and Modern Science* (New York: Dover).

Burawoy, M. (1989), 'Two Methods in Search of Science: Skocpol versus Trotsky', *Theory and Society*, 18: 759–805.

Burawoy, M. (1998), 'Critical Sociology: A Dialogue between Two Sciences', *Contemporary Sociology*, 27: 12–20.

Burawoy, M. (2003), 'Revisits: An Outline of a Theory of Reflexive Ethnography', *American Sociological Review*, 68: 645–79.

Burawoy, M. (2004a), 'Public Sociologies: Contradictions, Dilemmas and Possibilities', *Social Forces*, 82: 1603–618.

Burawoy, M. (2004b), 'For Public Sociology', *American Sociological Review*, 70: 4–28.

Burgess, R. G. (1984), *In the Field* (London: Allen and Unwin).

Busch, A. (1993), 'The Politics of Price Stability: Why the German-Speaking Nations Are Different' in F. G. Castles (ed.) *Families of Nations: Patterns of Public Policy in Western Democracies* (Aldershot: Dartmouth).

Caldwell, B. J. (1991), 'Clarifying Popper', *Journal of Economic Literature*, 29: 1–33.

Calhoun, C. (1996) 'The Rise and Domestication of Historical Sociology' in T. J. McDonald (ed.) *The Historic Turn in the Human Sciences* (Ann Arbor: University of Michigan Press).

Campbell, C. (1996), *The Myth of Social Action* (Cambridge: Cambridge University Press).

Campbell, M. (1942), *The English Yeoman* (New Haven: Yale University Press).

Cappelli, P. (1999), 'Career Jobs *Are* Dead', *California Management Review*, 42: 146–67.

Carr, E. H. (1961), *What Is History?* (London: Macmillan).

Castells, M. (1997) *The Power of Identity* (Oxford: Blackwell).

Castells, M. (2000a), *The Rise of the Network Society*, 2nd ed. (Oxford: Blackwell).

Castells, M. (2000b), *End of Millenium*, 2nd ed. (Oxford: Blackwell).

Castles, F. G. (1993), 'Introduction' in *idem* (ed.) *Families of Nations: Patterns of Public Policy in Western Democracies* (Aldershot: Dartmouth).

Castles, F. G. (ed.) (1993), *Families of Nations: Patterns of Public Policy in Western Democracies* (Aldershot: Dartmouth).

Cautrès, B. (1995), 'Mobilité sociale et comportement électoral: modèles sociologiques et modélisations statistiques', *Revue française de sociologie*, 36: 185–224.

Cherkaoui, M. (2005), *Invisible Codes: Essays on Generative Mechanisms* (Oxford: Bardwell).

Clark, J. C. D. (1986), *Revolution and Rebellion* (Cambridge: Cambridge University Press).

Clifford, J. (1988), *The Predicament of Culture: Twentieth Century Ethnography, Literature and Art* (Cambridge, Mass.: Harvard University Press).

Clifford, J. and Marcus, G. E. (eds.) (1986), *Writing Culture: the Poetics and Politics of Ethnography* (Berkeley: University of California Press).

Clifford, P. and Heath, A. F. (1993), 'The Political Consequences of Social Mobility', *Journal of the Royal Statistical Society*, Series A, 156: 51–61.

Clogg, C. C. (1992), 'The Impact of Sociological Methodology on Statistical Methodology', *Statistical Science*, 7: 183–207.

Clogg, C. C. and Haritou, A. (1997), 'The Regression Method of Causal Inference and a Dilemma Confronting this Method' in V. R. McKim and S. P. Turner (eds.) *Causality in Crisis?* (Notre Dame, Ind.: University of Notre Dame Press).

Clubb, J. M. (1980), 'The "New" Quantitative History: Social Science or Old Wine in New Bottles?' in J. M. Clubb and K. Scheuch (eds.) *Historical Social Research* (Stuttgart: Klett-Cotta).

Cohen, A. P. (1984), 'Informants' in R. F. Ellen (ed.) *Ethnographic Research* (London: Academic Press).

Cohen, P. C. (1976), 'Rational Conduct and Social Life' in S. I. Benn and G. W. Mortimore (eds.), *Rationality and the Social Sciences* (London: Routledge).

Cole, S. (1996), 'Voodoo Sociology: Recent Developments in the Sociology of Science' in P. R. Gross, N. Levitt, and M. W. Lewis (eds.) *The Flight from Science and Reason* (New York: New York Academy of Sciences).

Cole, S. (ed.) (2001), *What's Wrong with Sociology?* (New Brunswick, N.J.: Transaction Books).

Coleman, J. S. (1964), *Introduction to Mathematical Sociology* (New York: Free Press).

Coleman, J. S. (1986a), 'Social Theory, Social Research and a Theory of Action', *American Journal of Sociology*, 91: 1309–335.

Coleman, J. S. (1986b), *Individual Interests and Collective Action* (Cambridge: Cambridge University Press).

Coleman, J. S. (1990), *Foundations of Social Theory* (Cambridge, Mass.: Belknap).

Coleman, J. S. and Fararo, T. J. (1992), 'Introduction' in *idem* (eds.) *Rational Choice Theory: Advocacy and Critique* (Newbury Park: Sage).

Collier, D., Brady, H. E., and Seawright, J. (2004) 'Sources of Leverage in Causal Inference: Toward an Alternative View of Methodology' in H. E. Brady and D. Collier (eds.) *Rethinking Social Inquiry: Diverse Tools, Shared Standards* (Lanham: Rowman and Littlefield).

Collingwood, R. G. (1993), *The Idea of History*, 2nd ed. (Oxford: Oxford University Press). Originally published 1946.

Conlisk, J. (1996), 'Why Bounded Rationality?', *Journal of Economic Literature*, 34: 669–700.

Converse, P. A. (1964), 'The Nature of Belief Systems in Mass Publics' in D. Apter (ed.) *Ideology and Discontent* (New York: Free Press).

Converse, P. A. (1970), 'Attitudes and Non-Attitudes: Continuation of a Dialogue' in E. R. Tufte (ed.) *The Quantitative Analysis of Social Problems* (Reading, Mass.: Addison-Wesley).

Cook, T. D. and Campbell, D. (1979), *Quasiexperimentation* (Chicago: Rand McNally).

Corti, L. and Thompson, P. (2003), 'Secondary Analysis of Archive Data' in C. Seale et al. (eds.) *Qualitative Research Practice* (London: Sage).

Cosmides, L. and Tooby, J. (1994), 'Better than Rational: Evolutionary Psychology and the Invisible Hand', *American Economic Review*, 84: 327–32.

Cox, D. R. (1990), 'Role of Models in Statistical Analysis', *Statistical Science*, 5: 169–74.

Cox, D. R. (1992), 'Causality: Some Statistical Aspects', *Journal of the Royal Statistical Society*, Series A, 155: 291–301.

Cox, D. R. and Wermuth, N. (1993), 'Linear Dependencies Represented by Chain Graphs', *Statistical Science*, 8: 204–18.

Cox, D. R. and Wermuth, N. (1996), *Multivariate Dependencies* (London: Chapman Hall).

Cressey, D. R. (1953), *Other People's Money* (New York: Free Press).

Crick, F. (1989), *What Mad Pursuit? A Personal View of Scientific Discovery* (London: Penguin).

Davidson, D. (1976), 'Psychology as Philosophy' in J. Glover (ed.) *The Philosophy of Mind* (Oxford: Oxford University Press).

Davidson, D. (1980), *Essays on Actions and Events* (Oxford: Clarendon).

Davis, J. A. (1985), *The Logic of Causal Order* (Beverly Hills: Sage).

De Graaf, N. D. and Ultee, W. (1990), 'Individual Preferences, Social Mobility and Electoral Outcomes', *Electoral Studies*, 9: 109–32.

De Graaf, N. D. and Heath, A. F. (1992), 'Husbands' and Wives' Voting Behaviour in Britain: Class-Dependent Mutual Influence of Spouses', *Acta Sociologica*, 35: 311–22.

De Graaf, N. D., Nieuwbeerta, P., and Heath, A. F. (1995), 'Class Mobility and Political Preferences: Individual and Contextual Effects', *American Journal of Sociology*, 100: 997–1027.

Dennis, N., Henriques, F., and Slaughter, C. (1956), *Coal Is Our Life* (London: Eyre and Spottiswoode).

Denzin, N. K. (1989), *Interpretive Interactionism* (Newbury Park: Sage).

Denzin, N. K. (1990), 'Reading Rational Choice Theory', *Rationality and Society*, 2: 172–89.

Denzin, N. K. (1997), *Interpretive Ethnography* (Thousand Oaks, Calif.: Sage).

Denzin, N. K. and Lincoln, Y. S. (eds.) (1994), *Handbook of Qualitative Research* (Thousand Oaks, Calif.: Sage).

Desrosières, A. (1991), 'The Part in Relation to the Whole: How to Generalise? The Prehistory of Representative Sampling' in M. Bulmer, K. Bales, and

K. K. Sklar (eds.) *The Social Survey in Historical Perspective, 1880–1940* (Cambridge: Cambridge University Press).

Desrosières, A. (1993), *La politique des grands nombres* (Paris: La Découverte).

Diebold, F. X., Neumark, D., and Polsky, D. (1997), 'Job Stability in the United States', *Journal of Labour Economics*, 15: 206–33.

DiPrete, T. and Forristal, J. D. (1994), 'Multilevel Models: Methods and Substance', *Annual Review of Sociology*, 20: 331–57.

Dogan, M. (1994), 'Use and Misuse of Statistics in Comparative Research' in M. Dogan and A. Kazancigil (eds.) *Comparing Nations* (Oxford: Blackwell).

Douglas, M. and Ney, S. (1998), *Missing Persons: A Critique of the Social Sciences* (Berkeley: University of California Press)

Dray, W. (1993), *Philosophy of History*, 2nd ed. (Englewood Cliffs: Prentice Hall).

Duncan, O. D. (1975), *Introduction to Structural Equation Models* (New York: Academic Press).

Duncan, O. D. (1982), 'Rasch Measurement and Sociological Theory'. Hollingshead Lecture, Yale University.

Duncan, O. D. (1984), *Notes on Social Measurement* (New York: Russell Sage).

Duncan, O. D. (1992), 'What If?', *Contemporary Sociology*, 21: 667–68.

Dupré, J. (2001), *Human Nature and the Limits of Science* (Oxford: Oxford University Press).

Edling, C. (2000), 'Rational Choice Theory and Quantitative Analysis: A Comment on Goldthorpe's Sociological Alliance', *European Sociological Review*, 16: 1–8.

Eells, E. (1991), *Probabilistic Causality* (Cambridge: University of Cambridge Press).

Eisenstadt, S. N. (1963), *The Political Systems of Empires* (New York: Free Press).

Elias, P. and McKnight, A. (2003), 'Earnings, Unemployment and the NS-SEC' in D. Rose and D. Pevalin (eds.) *A Researcher's Guide to the National Statistics Socio-Economic Classification* (London: Sage).

Elster, J. (1979), *Ulysses and the Sirens* (Cambridge: Cambridge University Press).

Elster, J. (1983a), *Explaining Technical Change* (Cambridge: Cambridge University Press).

Elster, J. (1983b), *Sour Grapes* (Cambridge: Cambridge University Press).

Elster, J. (1983c), 'Reply to Comments', *Theory and Society*, 12: 111–20.

Elster, J. (1985), *Making Sense of Marx* (Cambridge: Cambridge University Press).

Elster, J. (1989a), *The Cement of Society* (Cambridge: Cambridge University Press).

Elster, J. (1989b), *Nuts and Bolts for the Social Sciences* (Cambridge: Cambridge University Press).

Elster, J. (1989c), *Solomonic Judgments* (Cambridge: Cambridge University Press).

Elster, J. (1990), Interview in R. Swedberg (ed.) *Economics and Sociology* (Princeton: Princeton University Press).

Elster, J. (1991), 'Rationality and Social Norms', *Archives européennes de sociologie*, 32: 109–29.

Elster, J. (1993), 'Some Unresolved Problems in the Theory of Rational Behavior', *Acta Sociologica*, 36: 179–90.

Elster, J. (1997), 'More Than Enough', *University of Chicago Law Review*, 64:748–64.

Elster, J. (1998), 'A Plea for Mechanisms' in P. Hedström and R. Swedberg (eds.) *Social Mechanisms* (Cambridge: Cambridge University Press).

Erikson, K. (1966), *Wayward Puritans* (New York: Wiley).

Erikson, R. (1998), 'Thresholds and Mechanisms' in H.-P. Blossfeld and G. Prein (eds.) *Rational Choice Theory and Large-Scale Data Analysis* (Boulder: Westview).

Erikson, R. and Goldthorpe, J. H. (1992a), *The Constant Flux: A Study of Class Mobility in Industrial Societies* (Oxford: Clarendon).

Erikson, R. and Goldthorpe, J. H. (1992b), 'The CASMIN Project and the American Dream', *European Sociological Review*, 8: 283–305.

Esser, H. (1993), 'The Rationality of Everyday Behaviour: A Rational Choice Reconstruction of the Theory of Action by Alfred Schutz', *Rationality and Society*, 5: 47–57.

Esser, H. (1993–2001), *Soziologie: Spezielle Grundlagen*, 7 vols. (Frankfurt: Campus).

Esser, H. (1996), 'What Is Wrong with "Variable Sociology"?', *European Sociological Review*, 12: 159–66.

Etzioni, A. (1988), *The Moral Dimension: Toward a New Economics* (New York: Free Press).

Evans, G. (1999), 'Class Voting: from Premature Obituary to Reasoned Appraisal' in *idem* (ed.) *The End of Class Politics? Class Voting in Comparative Context* (Oxford: Clarendon).

Evans, G. (2000), 'The Continued Significance of Class Voting', *Annual Review of Political Science*, 3: 401–17.

Evans, G. (ed.) (1999), *The End of Class Politics? Class Voting in Comparative Context* (Oxford: Clarendon).

Evans, G., Heath, A. F., and Payne, C. (1999), 'Class: Labour as a Catch-All Party?' in G. Evans and P. Norris (eds.), *Critical Elections* (London: Sage).

Fararo, T. J. (1996), 'Foundational Problems in Theoretical Sociology' in J. Clark (ed.) *James S. Coleman* (London: Falmer).

Farber, H. S. (1997), 'The Changing Face of Job Loss in the United States, 1981–1995', *Brookings Papers on Economic Activity: Microeconomic Supplement*, 55–128.

Farmer, M. K. (1982), 'Rational Action in Economic and Social Theory: Some Misunderstandings', *Archives européennes de sociologie*, 23: 179–97.

Farmer, M. K. (1992), 'On the Need to Make a Better Job of Justifying Rational Choice Theory', *Rationality and Society*, 4: 411–20.

Farr, J. (1983), 'Popper's Hermeneutics', *Philosophy of the Social Sciences*, 13: 157–76.

Farr, J. (1985), 'Situational Analysis: Explanation in Political Science', *Journal of Politics*, 47: 1085–107.

Feigl, H. (1953), 'Notes on Causality' in H. Feigl and M. Brodbeck (eds.) *Readings in the Philosophy of Science* (New York: Appleton-Century Crofts).

Fetterman, D. (1998), *Ethnography* (Thousand Oaks, Calif.: Sage).

Fielding, N. (1981), *The National Front* (London: Routledge).

Fischer, C. (1982), *To Dwell Among Friends* (Chicago: Chicago University Press).

Fisher, R. A. (1935), *The Design of Experiments* (Edinburgh: Oliver and Boyd).

Flora, P. and Alber, J. (1981), 'Modernization, Democratization, and the Development of Welfare States in Western Europe' in P. Flora and A. J. Heidenheimer (eds.) *The Development of Welfare States in Europe and America* (New Brunswick, N.J.: Transaction Books).

Flyvbjerg, B. (2001), *Making Social Science Matter* (Cambridge: Cambridge University Press).

Fogel, R. W. and Elton, G. R. (1983), *Which Road to the Past?* (New Haven: Yale University Press).

Frank, R. H. (1990), 'Rethinking Rational Choice' in R. Friedland and A. F. Robertson, (eds.) *Beyond the Marketplace* (New York: Aldine de Gruyter).

Freedman, D. A. (1983), *Structural-Equation Models: A Case Study*. Technical Report No. 22, Department of Statistics, University of California, Berkeley.

Freedman, D. A. (1985), 'Statistics and the Scientific Method' in W. Mason and S. Fienberg (eds.) *Cohort Analysis in Social Research* (New York: Springer).

Freedman, D. A. (1991), 'Statistical Analysis and Shoe Leather', *Sociological Methodology*, 21: 291–313.

Freedman, D. A. (1992a), 'As Others See Us: A Case Study in Path Analysis' in J. P. Shaffer (ed.) *The Role of Models in Nonexperimental Social Science: Two Debates* (Washington, DC: American Educational Research Association and American Statistical Association).

Freedman, D. A. (1992b), 'A Rejoinder on Models, Metaphors and Fables' in J. P. Shaffer (ed.) *The Role of Models in Nonexperimental Social Science: Two Debates* (Washington, DC: American Educational Research Association and American Statistical Association).

Freedman, D. A. (1997), 'From Association to Causation via Regression' in V. R. McKim and S. P. Turner (eds.) *Causality in Crisis?* (Notre Dame, Ind.: University of Notre Dame Press).

Freedman, D. A. (1999), 'From Association to Causation: Some Remarks on the History of Statistics', *Statistical Science*, 14: 243–58.

Freedman, D. A. (2004), 'On Specifying Graphical Models for Causation and the Identification Problem'. Technical Report 601, Department of Statistics, University of California, Berkeley.

Freedman, D. A. and Humphreys, P. (1999), 'Are There Algorithms that Discover Causal Structures?', *Synthèse*, 121: 29–54.

Frey, B. (1992), *Economics as a Science of Human Behavior* (Boston: Kluwer).

Friedman, D. and Hechter, M. (1988), 'The Contribution of Rational Choice Theory to Macrosociological Research', *Sociological Theory*, 6: 201–18.

Friedman, M. (1953), *Essays in Positive Economics* (Chicago: University of Chicago Press).

Friedrichs, J. (1998), 'Do Poor Neighbourhoods Make their Residents Poorer?' in H-J. Andress (ed.) *Empirical Poverty Research in a Comparative Perspective* (Aldershot: Ashgrave).

Froude, J. A. (1884), *Short Studies on Great Subjects*, vol. 1 (London: Longmans).

Gähler, M. (1998), *Life After Divorce* (Stockholm: Swedish Institute for Social Research).

Gallie, D., White, M., Cheng, Y., and Tomlinson, M. (1998), *Restructuring the Employment Relationship* (Oxford: Clarendon).

Gallie, W. B. (1964), *Philosophy and the Historical Understanding* (London: Chatto and Windus).

Galton, F. (1889), 'Comments' on E. B. Tylor 'On a Method of Investigating the Development of Institutions; Applied to Laws of Marriage and Descent', *Journal of the Royal Anthropological Institute*, 18: 245–56, 261–69.

Galtung, J. (1979), 'Om Makrohistoriens Epistemologi og Metodologi: en Skisse' in Nordisk Fagkonferanse for Historik Metodelaere, *Makrohistorie* (Oslo: Universitetsforlaget).

Gambetta, D. (1987), *Were They Pushed or Did They Jump? Individual Decision Mechanisms in Education* (Cambridge: Cambridge University Press).

Ganzeboom, H. G. B., Luijkx, R., and Treiman, D. J. (1989), 'Intergenerational Class Mobility in Comparative Perspective', *Research in Social Stratification and Mobility*, 8: 3–55.

Garrett, G. and Lange, P. (1991), 'Political Responses to Interdependence: What's Left for the Left?', *International Organization*, 45: 539–64.

Garrett, G. (1998), *Partisan Politics in the Global Economy* (Cambridge: Cambridge University Press).

Garrett, G. (2000), 'Globalization and Government Spending Around the World', Istituto Juan March Working Paper 155, Madrid.

Geertz, C. (1973), *The Interpretation of Cultures* (New York: Basic Books).

Gellner, E. (1956/1973), 'Explanation in History' reprinted with additions from the *Proceedings of the Aristotelian Society* in *Cause and Meaning in the Social Sciences* (London: Routledge).

Gellner, E. (1990), 'The Gaffe-Avoiding Animal or a Bundle of Hypotheses' in P. Birnbaum and J. Leca (eds.), *Individualism* (Oxford: Clarendon).

Gellner, E. (1992), *Postmodernism, Reason and Religion* (London: Routledge).

Gershuny, J. (1993), 'Post-Industrial Career Structures in Britain' in G. Esping-Andersen (ed.) *Stratification and Mobility in Post-Industrial Societies* (London: Sage).

Geweke, J. (1984), 'Inference and Causality in Economic Time Series' in Z. Griliches and M. D. Intriligator (eds.) *Handbook of Econometrics*, vol. 2. (Amsterdam: North Holland).

Gibson, Q. (1976), 'Arguing from Rationality' in S. I. Benn and G. W. Mortimore (eds.) *Rationality and the Social Sciences* (London: Routledge).

Giddens, A. (1979), *Central Problems in Social Theory* (London: Macmillan).

Giddens, A. (1984), *The Constitution of Society* (Cambridge: Polity Press).

Giddens, A. (1987), *Social Theory and Modern Sociology* (Cambridge: Polity Press).

Giddens, A. (1990), *The Consequences of Modernity* (Cambridge: Polity Press).

Giddens, A. (1994), *Beyond Left and Right* (Cambridge: Polity Press).

Giddens, A. (1998), *The Third Way* (Cambridge: Polity Press).

Giddens, A. (2000), *Runaway World* (London: Profile Books).

Gigerenzer, G. (2000), *Adaptive Thinking: Rationality in the Real World* (Oxford: Oxford University Press).

Gigerenzer, G. (2004a), 'Fast and Frugal Heuristics: the Tools of Bounded Rationality' in D. Koehler and N. Harvey (eds.), *Blackwell Handbook of Judgment and Decision-Making* (Oxford: Blackwell).

Gigerenzer, G. (2004b), 'Striking a Blow for Sanity in Theories of Rationality' in M. Augier and J. G. March (eds.), *Models of Man: Essays in Memory of Herbert A. Simon* (Cambridge, Mass.: MIT Press).

Gigerenzer, G. (2005), 'What Makes *Homo Sapiens* Smart? The Rationality Controversy' in R. Stainton (ed.), *Contemporary Debates in Cognitive Science* (Oxford: Blackwell).

Gigerenzer, G. and Todd, P. M. (1999), *Simple Heuristics that Make Us Smart* (New York: Oxford University Press).

Gigerenzer, G. and Selten, R. (eds.) (2001), *Bounded Rationality: The Adaptive Toolbox* (Cambridge, Mass.: MIT Press).

Glaser, B. G. and Strauss, A. L. (1967), *The Discovery of Grounded Theory* (Chicago: Aldine).

Glass, G. V., McGaw, B., and Smith, M. L. (1981), *Meta-Analysis in Social Research* (Beverly Hills: Sage).

Glymour, C. (1986), 'Comment: Statistics and Metaphysics', *Journal of the American Statistical Association*, 81: 964–66.

Goldfrank, W. (1972), 'Reappraising Le Play' in A. Oberschall (ed.) *The Establishment of Empirical Sociology* (New York: Harper Row).

Goldstone, J. A. (1997), 'Methodological Issues in Comparative Macrosociology', *Comparative Social Research*, 16: 107–120.

Goldstone, J. A. (2003), 'Comparative Historical Analysis and Knowledge Accumulation in the Study of Revolutions' in J. Mahoney and D. Ruesechmeyer (eds.) *Comparative Historical Analysis in the Social Sciences* (Cambridge: Cambridge University Press).

Goldthorpe, J. H. (1962), 'The Relevance of History to Sociology', *Cambridge Opinion*, no. 28: 26–29.

Goldthorpe, J. H. (1971), 'Theories of Industrial Society', *Archives européennes de sociologie*, 12: 263–88.

Goldthorpe, J. H. (1979), 'Intellectuals and the Working Class in Modern Britain', Fuller Memorial Bequest Lecture, University of Essex.

Goldthorpe, J. H. (1985), 'On Economic Development and Social Mobility', *British Journal of Sociology*, 36: 549–73.

Goldthorpe, J. H. (with Llewellyn, C. and Payne, C.) (1987), *Social Mobility and Class Structure in Modern Britain*, 2nd ed. (Oxford: Clarendon).

Goldthorpe, J. H. (1994), 'The Uses of History in Sociology: A Reply', *British Journal of Sociology*, 45: 55–77.

Goldthorpe, J. H. (1997), 'A Response to the Commentaries', *Comparative Social Research*, 16: 121–32.

Goldthorpe, J. H. (2001), 'Class and Politics in Advanced Industrial Societies' in T. Clark and S. M. Lipset (eds.), *The Breakdown of Class Politics* (Washington: Woodrow Wilson Centre).

Goldthorpe, J. H. (2004a), 'Sociology as Social Science and Cameral Sociology: Some Further Thoughts', *European Sociological Review*, 20: 97–105.

Goldthorpe, J. H. (2004b), 'The Scientific Study of Society', *British Journal of Sociology*, 55: 123–26.

Goldthorpe, J. H. and Mills, C. (2004), 'Trends in Intergenerational Class Mobility in Britain in the Late Twentieth Century' in R. Breen (ed.) *Social Mobility in Europe* (Oxford: Oxford University Press).

Goldthorpe, J. H. (2005), 'Progress in Sociology: The Case of Social Mobility Research' in S. Svallfors (ed.) *Analyzing Inequality: Life Chances and Social Mobility in Comparative Perspective* (Stanford: Stanford University Press)

Goldthorpe, J. H. and McKnight, A. (2006), 'The Economic Basis of Social Class' in S. Morgan, D. B. Grusky and G. S. Fields (eds.) *Mobility and Inequality: Frontiers of Research from Sociology and Economics* (Stanford: Stanford University Press).

Goodman, A. and Oldfield, Z. (2004), *Permanent Differences? Income and Expenditure Inequality in the 1990s and 2000s* (London: Institute for Fiscal Studies).

Goody, J. (1996), *The East in the West* (Cambridge: Cambridge University Press).

Granger, C. W. J. (1969), 'Investigating Causal Relations by Econometric Models and Cross-Spectral Methods', *Econometrica*, 37: 424–38.

Granger, C. W. J. (1986), 'Comment', *Journal of the American Statistical Association*, 81: 967–68.

Grant, O. (2002), 'Max Weber and "Die Lage der Landarbeiter im ostelbischen Deutschland": A Statistical Examination', *Jahrbuch für Wirtschaftsgeschichte*, 2: 61–84.

Gray, J. (1998), *False Dawn: The Delusions of Global Capitalism* (London: Granta).

Green, D. P. and Shapiro, I. (1994), *Pathologies of Rational Choice Theory: a Critique of Applications in Political Science* (New Haven: Yale University Press).

Griffin, L. J. (1992), 'Temporality, Events, and Explanation in Historical Sociology', *Sociological Methods and Research*, 20: 403–27.

Gross, P. R. and Levitt, N. (1994), *Higher Superstition* (Baltimore: The Johns Hopkins University Press).

Gross, P. R., Levitt, N., and Lewis, M. W. (eds.) (1996), *The Flight from Science and Reason* (New York: New York Academy of Sciences).

Haack, S. (1998), *Confessions of a Passionate Moderate* (Chicago: Chicago University Press).

Hacking, I. (1999), *The Social Construction of What?* (Cambridge, Mass.: Harvard University Press).

Halaby, C. N. and Weakliem, D. L. (1989), 'Worker Control and Attachment to the Firm', *American Journal of Sociology*, 95: 549–91.

Halbwachs, M. (1933), *L'Evolution des besoins dans les classes ouvrières* (Paris: Alcan).

Hall, J. (1985), *Powers and Liberties* (Harmondsworth: Penguin).

Halle, D. (1993), *Inside Culture: Art and Class in the American Home* (Chicago: Chicago University Press).

Halpin, B (1999), 'Simulation in Sociology: A Review of the Literature', *American Behavioural Scientist*, 42: 1488–1508.

Hammel, E. A. (1980), 'The Comparative Method in Anthropological Perspective', *Comparative Studies in Society and History*, 22: 145–55.

Hammersley, M. (1989), *The Dilemma of Qualitative Method: Herbert Blumer and the Chicago Tradition* (London: Routledge).

Hammersley, M. (1991), *Reading Ethnographic Research* (London: Longman).

Hammersley, M. (1992), *What's Wrong with Ethnography?* (London: Routledge).

Hammersley, M. (1999), 'Not Bricolage but Boatbuilding: Exploring Two Metaphors for Thinking About Ethnography', *Journal of Contemporary Ethnography*, 28: 574–85.

Hammersley, M. and Atkinson, P. (1995), *Ethnography* (London: Routledge).

Handl, J. (n.d.), 'Heiratsmobilität und berufliche Mobilität von Frauen', VASMA Project Working Paper, 8, Institüt für Sozialwissenschaften, University of Mannheim.

Hands, D. W. (1985), 'Karl Popper and Economic Methodology: A New Look', *Economics and Philosophy*, 1: 83–100.

Hansen, M. H. (1987), 'Some History and Reminiscences of Survey Sampling', *Statistical Science*, 2: 180–90.

Harsanyi, J. C. (1969), 'Rational-Choice Models of Political Behavior vs. Functionalist and Conformist Theories', *World Politics*, 22: 513–38.

Hart, N. (1994), 'John Goldthorpe and the Relics of Sociology', *British Journal of Sociology*, 45: 21–30.

Hauser, R. M. (1976), 'On Boudon's Model of Social Mobility', *American Journal of Sociology*, 81: 911–28.

Hausman, D. M. (1992), *The Inexact and Separate Science of Economics* (Cambridge: Cambridge University Press).

Heath, A. F., Jowell, R., and Curtice, J. (1985), *How Britain Votes* (Oxford: Pergamon).

Heath, A. F., Curtice, J., Jowell, R., Evans, G., and Field, J. (1991), *Understanding Political Change* (Oxford: Pergamon).

Hechter, M. (1987), *Principles of Group Solidarity* (Berkeley: University of California Press).

Hechter, M. (1994), 'The Role of Values in Rational Choice Theory', *Rationality and Society*, 6: 318–33.

Heckathorn, D. D. (1997), 'Overview: The Paradoxical Relationship between Sociology and Rational Choice', *The American Sociologist*, 28: 6–15.

Hedström, P. (1996), 'Rational Choice and Social Structure: On Rational Choice Theorizing in Sociology' in B. Wittrock (ed.) *Social Theory and Human Agency* (London: Sage).

Hedström, P. (2005), *Dissecting the Social: On the Principles of Analytical Sociology* (Cambridge: Cambridge University Press).

Hedström, P. and Swedberg, R. (1998a), 'Social Mechanisms: An Introductory Essay' in *idem* (eds.) *Social Mechanisms* (Cambridge: Cambridge University Press).

Hedström, P. and Swedberg, R. (1998b), 'Rational Choice, Situational Analysis, and Empirical Research' in H.-P. Blossfeld and G. Prein, (eds.) *Rational Choice Theory and Large-Scale Data Analysis* (Boulder: Westview).

Hedström, P., Swedberg, R., and Udéhn, L. (1998), 'Popper's Situational Analysis and Contemporary Sociology', *Philosophy of Social Sciences*, 28: 339–64.

Hedström, P. and Swedberg, R. (eds.) (1998), *Social Mechanisms* (Cambridge: Cambridge University Press).

Held, D., McGrew, A., Goldblatt, D., and Perraton, J. (1999), *Global Transformations* (Cambridge: Polity Press).

Helm, D. (1984), 'Predictions and Causes: A Comparison of Friedman and Hicks on Method', *Oxford Economic Papers*, 36: 118–34.

Hernes, G. (1989), 'The Logic of *The Protestant Ethic*', *Rationality and Society*, 1: 123–62.

Hernes, G. (1992), 'We are Smarter than We Think', *Rationality and Society*, 4: 421–36.

Hexter, J. H. (1961), 'Storm over the Gentry' in *Reappraisals in History* (London: Longmans).

Hicks, A. M. (1994), 'Introduction to Pooling' in T. Janoski and A. M. Hicks (eds.)

The Comparative Political Economy of the Welfare State (Cambridge: Cambridge University Press).

Hirsch, P., Michaels, S., and Friedman, R. (1987), '"Dirty Hands" versus "Clean Models": Is Sociology in Danger of being Seduced by Economics?', *Theory and Society*, 16: 317–36.

Hirshleifer, J. (1985), 'The Expanding Domain of Economics', *American Economic Review*, 75: 53–68.

Hirst, P. and Thompson, D. (1999), *Globalization in Question*, 2nd ed. (Cambridge: Polity Press).

Hogarth, R. M. and Reder, M. W. (eds.) (1986), *Rational Choice* (Chicago: University of Chicago Press).

Holland, P. (1986a), 'Statistics and Causal Inference', *Journal of the American Statistical Association*, 81: 945–60.

Holland, P. (1986b), 'Rejoinder', *Journal of the American Statistical Association*, 81: 968–70.

Holland, P. (1988), 'Causal Inference, Path Analysis, and Recursive Structural Equation Models', *Sociological Methodology*, 18: 449–84.

Hollis, M. (1982), 'The Social Destruction of Reality' in M. Hollis and S. M. Lukes (eds.) *Rationality and Relativism* (Cambridge, Mass.: MIT Press).

Hollis, M. (1987), *The Cunning of Reason* (Cambridge: Cambridge University Press).

Hollis, M. (1994), *The Philosophy of Social Science* (Cambridge: Cambridge University Press).

Hollis, M. and Lukes, S. M. (eds.) (1982), *Rationality and Relativism* (Cambridge, Mass.: MIT Press).

Homans, G. C. (1961), *Social Behavior* (New York: Harcourt, Brace and World).

Homans, G. C. (1964), 'Bringing Men Back In', *American Sociological Review*, 29: 809–18.

Honigman, J. J. (1973), 'Sampling in Ethnographic Fieldwork' in R. Naroll and C. Cohen (eds.) *Handbook of Method in Cultural Anthropology* (New York: Columbia University Press).

Hope, K. (1984), *As Others See Us: Schooling and Social Mobility in Scotland and the United States* (Cambridge: Cambridge University Press).

Hope, K. (1992), 'Barren Theory or Petty Craft? A Response to Professor Freedman' in J. P. Shaffer (ed.) *The Role of Models in Nonexperimental Social Science: Two Debates* (Washington, D.C.: American Educational Research Association and American Statistical Association).

Hopkins, T. K. and Wallerstein I. (1981), 'Structural Transformations of the World Economy' in R. Rubinson (ed.) *Dynamics of World Development* (Beverly Hills: Sage).

Hough, R. (1959), *Admirals in Collision* (London: Hamish Hamilton).

Hout, M., Manza, J., and Brooks, C. (1999), 'Classes, Unions and the Realignment of US Presidential Voting, 1952–1992' in G. Evans (ed.) *The End of Class Politics?* (Oxford: Oxford University Press).

Huber, E., Ragin, C. C., and Stephens, J. D. (1993), 'Social Democracy, Christian Democracy, Constitutional Structure and the Welfare State', *American Journal of Sociology*, 99: 711–49.

Huber, J. (1995), 'Institutional Perspectives on Sociology', *American Journal of Sociology*, 101: 194–216.

Hutchison, T. W. (1988), 'The Case for Falsification' in N. de Marchi (ed.) *The Popperian Legacy in Economics* (Cambridge: Cambridge University Press).

Inglehart, R. (1977), *The Silent Revolution* (Princeton: Princeton University Press).

Inglehart, R. (1990), *Culture Shift in Advanced Industrial Societies* (Princeton: Princeton University Press).

Inglehart, R. (1997), *Modernization and Postmodernization* (Princeton: Princeton University Press).

Ishida, H., Müller, W., and Ridge J. M. (1995), 'Class Origin, Class Destination, and Education: A Cross-National Study of Ten Industrial Nations', *American Journal of Sociology*, 60: 145–93.

Iversen, T. (2000), 'The Dynamics of Welfare State Expansion: Trade Openness, Deindustrialization and Partisan Politics' in P. Pierson (ed.) *The New Politics of the Welfare State* (Oxford: Oxford University Press).

Iversen, T. and Cusack, T. R. (2000), 'The Causes of Welfare State Expansion: Deindustrialization or Globalization?', *World Politics*, 52: 313–49.

Jackson, M., Goldthorpe, J. H., and Mills, C. (2005), 'Education, Employers and Class Mobility', *Research in Social Stratification and Mobility*, 23: 3–34.

Jacoby, S. (1999a), 'Are Career Jobs Headed for Extinction?', *California Management Review*, 42: 123–45.

Jacoby, S. (1999b), 'Reply: Premature Reports of Demise', *California Management Review*, 42: 168–79.

Jacoby, S. (2000), 'Melting into Air? Downsizing, Job Stability and the Future of Work', *Chicago-Kent Law Review*, 76: 1195–234.

Jankowski, M. S. (1991), *Islands in the Street* (Berkeley: University of California Press).

Jankowski, M. S. (2002), 'Representation, Responsibility and Reliability in Participant Observation' in T. May (ed.) *Qualitative Research in Action* (London: Sage).

Janoski, T. and Hicks, A. M. (eds.) (1994), *The Comparative Political Economy of the Welfare State* (Cambridge: Cambridge University Press).

Jarvie, I. C. (1964), *The Revolution in Anthropology* (London: Routledge).

Jarvie, I. C. (1972), *Concepts and Society* (London: Routledge).

Jenkins, R. (2002), *Foundations of Sociology* (Basingstoke: Palgrave MacMillan).

Johnson, J. C. (1990), *Selecting Ethnographic Informants* (Newbury Park: Sage).

Jonsson, J. O. and Gähler, M. (1997), 'Family Dissolution, Family Reconstitution, and Children's Educational Careers: Recent Evidence for Sweden', *Demography*, 34: 277–93.

Kahnemann, D. and Tversky, A. (1979), 'Prospect Theory: An Analysis of Decision under Risk', *Econometrica*, 47: 263–91.

Kanazawa, S. (2001), 'De Gustibus *Est* Disputandum', *Social Forces*, 79:1131–163.

Kangas, O. (1991), *The Politics of Social Rights: Studies on the Dimensions of Sickness Insurance in 18 OECD Countries* (Stockholm: Swedish Institute for Social Research).

Kangas, O. (1994), 'The Politics of Social Security: on Regressions, Qualitative Comparisons, and Cluster Analysis' in T. Janoski and A. M. Hicks (eds.) *The Comparative Political Economy of the Welfare State* (Cambridge: Cambridge University Press).

Katz, J. (1997), 'Ethnography's Warrants', *Sociological Methods and Research*, 25: 391–423.

Keller, S. and Zavalloni, M. (1964), 'Ambition and Social Class: a Respecification', *Social Forces*, 43: 58–70.

Kendall, P. L. and Lazarsfeld, P. F. (1950), 'Problems of Survey Analysis' in R. K. Merton and P. F. Lazarsfeld (eds.) *Continuities in Social Research: Studies in the Scope and Method of 'The American Soldier'* (Glencoe, Ill.: Free Press).

Kiaer, A. N. (1895), 'Observations et expériences concernant des dénombrements représentatifs', *Bulletin of the International Statistical Institute*, 9: 176–83.

Kiaer, A. N. (1901), 'Sur les méthodes représentatives ou typologiques', *Bulletin of the International Statistical Institute*, 13: 66–70.

King, G., Keohane, R. O., and Verba, S. (1994), *Designing Social Inquiry* (Princeton: Princeton University Press).

Kirk, J. and Miller, M. L. (1986), *Reliability and Validity in Qualitative Research* (Beverly Hills: Sage).

Kiser, E. and Hechter, M. (1991), 'The Role of General Theory in Comparative-Historical Sociology', *American Journal of Sociology*, 97: 1–30.

Kiser, E. and Hechter, M. (1998), 'The Debate on Historical Sociology: Rational Choice Theory and Its Critics', *American Journal of Sociology*, 104: 785–816.

Kleinman, M (1998), 'Include me Out? The New Politics of Place and Poverty'. Centre for the Analysis of Social Exclusion, London School of Economics.

Koertge, N. (1975), 'Popper's Metaphysical Research Program for the Human Sciences', *Inquiry*, 18: 437–62.

Koertge, N. (1979), 'The Methodological Status of Popper's Rationality Principle', *Theory and Decision*, 10: 83–95.

Koertge, N. (ed.) (1998), *A House Built on Sand* (New York: Oxford University Press).

Korpi, W. (1983), *The Democratic Class Struggle* (London: Routledge).

Korpi, W. (1985), 'Economic Growth and the Welfare State: Leaky Bucket or Irrigation System?', *European Sociological Review*, 1: 97–118.

Korpi, W. (1989), 'Power, Politics, and State Autonomy in the Development of Social Citizenship: Social Rights during Sickness in Eighteen OECD Countries since 1930', *American Sociological Review*, 54: 309–28.

Korpi, W. and Palme, J. (2003), 'New Politics and Class Politics in the Context of Austerity and Globalization: Welfare State Regress in 18 Countries, 1975–95', *American Political Science Review*, 97: 425–46.

Kreager, P. (1993), 'Anthropological Demography and the Limits of Diffusionism', *Proceedings of the International Population Conference, Montreal*, 4: 313–26.

Kronauer, M. (1998), ' "Social Exclusion" and "Underclass"—New Concepts for the Analysis of Poverty' in H.-J. Andress (ed.) *Empirical Poverty Research in a Comparative Perspective* (Aldershot: Ashgate).

Krüger, L., Daston, L. J., and Heidelberger, M. (eds.) (1987), *The Probabilistic Revolution*, vol. 1, *Ideas in History* (Cambridge, Mass.: MIT Press).

Krüger, L., Gigerenzer, G., and Morgan, M. S. (eds.) (1987), *The Probabilistic Revolution*, vol. 2, *Ideas in the Sciences* (Cambridge, Mass.: MIT Press).

Krugman, P. (1999), *The Accidental Theorist* (London: Penguin).

Kruskal, W. and Mosteller, F. (1980), 'Representative Sampling, IV: the History of the Concept in Statistics', *International Statistical Review*, 48: 169–95.

Kuhn, T. (2000), *The Road Since Structure* (Chicago: University of Chicago Press).

Lakatos, I. (1970), 'Falsification and the Methodology of Scientific Research Programmes' in I. Lakatos and A. Musgrave (eds.) *Criticism and the Growth of Knowledge* (Cambridge: Cambridge University Press).

Langlois, R. N. (1986), 'Rationality, Institutions and Explanation' in *idem* (ed.) *Economics as Process* (Cambridge: Cambridge University Press).

Latour, B. (1987), *Science in Action* (Milton Keynes: Open University Press).

Latour, B. and Woolgar, S. (1979), *Laboratory Life* (Beverly Hills: Sage).

Latsis, S. J. (1976), 'A Research Programme in Economics' in *idem* (ed.) *Method and Appraisal in Economics* (Cambridge: Cambridge University Press).

Layte, R. and Whelan, C. (2002), 'Cumulative Disadvantage or Individualisation?', *European Societies*, 4: 209–33.

Lazarsfeld, P. F. (1959), 'Problems of Methodology' in R. K. Merton, L. Broom, and L. S. Cottrell (eds.) *Sociology Today: Problems and Prospects* (New York: Basic Books).

Lazarsfeld, P. F. (1961), 'Notes on the History of Quantification in Sociology—Trends, Sources and Problems', *Isis*, 52: 277–333.

Lazarsfeld, P. F. and Rosenberg, M. (eds.) (1955), *The Language of Social Research* (New York: Free Press).

Lazarsfeld, P. F., Pasanella, A. K., and Rosenberg, M. (eds.) (1972), *Continuities in the Language of Social Research* (New York: Free Press).

Leisering, L. and Leibfried, S. (1999), *Time and Poverty in Western Welfare States* (Cambridge: Cambridge University Press).

Le Play, F. (1855), *Les Ouvriers européens* (Paris: Imprimerie Impériale).

Levi, M. (1997), 'A Model, a Method, and a Map: Rational Choice in Comparative

Historical Analysis' in M. I. Lichbach and A. S. Zuckerman (eds.) *Comparative Politics* (Cambridge: Cambridge University Press).

Lévy-Bruhl, L. (1910), *Les fonctions mentales dans les sociétés inferieures* (Paris: Presses Universitaires de France).

Lewis, O. (1951), *Life in a Mexican Village: Tepoztlan Revisited* (Urbana: University of Illinois Press).

Lichbach, M. I. (2003), *Is Rational Choice Theory All of Social Science?* (Ann Arbor: University of Michigan Press).

Lieberson, S. (1987), *Making It Count* (Berkeley: University of California Press).

Lieberson, S. (1992), 'Small Ns and Big Conclusions: An Examination of the Reasoning in Comparative Studies Based on a Small Number of Cases' in C. C. Ragin and H. S. Becker (eds.) *What Is a Case?* (Cambridge: Cambridge University Press).

Lieberson, S. (1994), 'More on the Uneasy Case for Using Mill-Type Methods in Small-N Comparative Studies', *Social Forces*, 72: 1225–237.

Lieberson, S. and Lynn, F. B. (2002), 'Barking Up the Wrong Branch: Scientific Alternatives to the Current Model of Sociological Science', *Annual Review of Sociology*, 28: 1–19.

Liebow, E. (1967), *Tally's Corner* (London: Routledge).

Lindenberg, S. (1982), 'Sharing Groups: Theory and Suggested Applications', *Journal of Mathematical Sociology*, 9: 33–62.

Lindenberg, S. (1983), 'Utility and Morality', *Kyklos*, 36: 450–68.

Lindenberg, S. (1985), 'An Assessment of the New Political Economy: Its Potential for the Social Sciences and Sociology in Particular', *Sociological Theory*, 3: 99–114.

Lindenberg, S. (1989), 'Choice and Culture: The Behavioral Basis of Cultural Impact on Transactions' in H. Haferkamp (ed.) *Social Structure and Culture* (Berlin: de Gruyter).

Lindenberg, S. (1990), 'Homo Socio-Economicus: The Emergence of a General Model of Man in the Social Sciences', *Journal of Institutional and Theoretical Economics*, 146: 727–48.

Lindenberg, S. (1992), 'The Method of Decreasing Abstraction' in J. S Coleman and T. J. Fararo (eds.) *Rational Choice Theory: Advocacy and Critique* (Newbury Park: Sage).

Lindenberg, S. (1996), 'Continuities in the Theory of Social Production Functions' in H. G. B. Ganzeboom and S. Lindenberg (eds.) *Verklarende Sociologie: Opstellen voor Reinhard Wippler* (Amsterdam: Thesis).

Lindenberg, S. and Frey, B. (1993), 'Alternatives, Frames and Relative Prices: A Broader View of Rational Choice Theory', *Acta Sociologica*, 36: 191–205.

Lindenberg, S. and Wippler, R. (1978), 'Theorienvergleich: Elemente der Rekonstruktion' in K. O. Hondrich and J. Matthes, (eds.) *Theorienvergleich in den Sozialwissenschaften* (Darmstadt: Luchterhand).

Lindesmith, A. (1948), *Opiate Addiction* (Bloomington: Principia).

Lloyd, G. E. R. (1990), *Demystifying Mentalities* (Cambridge: Cambridge University Press).

Lockwood, D. (1956), 'Some Remarks on "The Social System"', *British Journal of Sociology*, 7: 134–46.

Lustick, I. S. (1996), 'History, Historiography, and Political Science: Multiple Historical Records and the Problem of Selection Bias', *American Political Science Review*, 90: 605–17.

MacIntyre, A. (1962), 'A Mistake about Causality in Social Science' in P. Laslett and W. G. Runciman, (eds.) *Philosophy, Politics and Society* (Oxford: Blackwell).

Mackie, J. L. (1974), *The Cement of the Universe: A Study of Causation* (Oxford: Clarendon).

Macy, M. W. (1998), 'Social Order and Emergent Rationality' in A. Sica (ed.) *What Is Social Theory?* (Oxford: Blackwell).

Mahoney, J. (2003), 'Strategies of Causal Assessment in Comparative Historical Analysis' in J. Mahoney and D. Rueschemeyer (eds.) (2003), *Comparative Historical Analysis in the Social Sciences* (Cambridge: Cambridge University Press).

Mahoney, J. and Rueschemeyer, D. (2003), 'Comparative Historical Analysis: Achievements and Agendas' in *idem* (eds.) *Comparative Historical Analysis in the Social Sciences* (Cambridge: Cambridge University Press).

Mahoney, J. and Rueschemeyer, D. (eds.) (2003), *Comparative Historical Analysis in the Social Sciences* (Cambridge: Cambridge University Press).

Maitland, F. M. (1911), 'The Body Politic' in H. A. L. Fisher (ed.) F. M. Maitland, *Collected Papers* (Cambridge: Cambridge University Press).

Mann, J. M. (1970), 'The Social Cohesion of Liberal Democracy', *American Journal of Sociology*, 35: 423–31.

Mann J. M. (1986), *The Sources of Social Power* (Cambridge: Cambridge University Press).

Mann, J. M. (1994), 'In Praise of Macro-Sociology', *British Journal of Sociology*, 45: 37–54.

Manning, P. K. (1982), 'Analytic Induction' in R. B. Smith and P. K. Manning (eds.) *Qualitative Methods* (Cambridge, Mass.: Ballinger).

Manski, C. F. (1993), 'Adolescent Econometricians: How Do Youth Infer the Returns to Schooling?' in C. T. Clotfelter and M. Rothschild (eds.) *Studies of Supply and Demand in Higher Education* (Chicago: Chicago University Press).

Manski, C. F. (2000), 'Economic Analysis of Social Interactions', *Journal of Economic Perspectives*, 14: 115–36.

Manski, C. F. (2004), 'Measuring Expectations'. Department of Economics and Institute for Policy Research, Northwestern University.

Manza, J. and Brooks, C. (1999), *Social Cleavages and Political Change: Voter Alignments and US Party Coalitions* (Oxford: Oxford University Press).

March, J. G. (1978), 'Bounded Rationality, Ambiguity, and the Engineering of Choice', *Bell Journal of Economics*, 9: 587–608.

Mare, R. D. (1981), 'Change and Stability in Educational Stratification', *American Sociological Review*, 46: 72–87.

Marsh, C. (1982), *The Survey Method: the Contribution of Surveys to Sociological Explanation* (London: Allen and Unwin).

Marshall, G. (1980), *Presbyteries and Profits: Calvinism and the Development of Capitalism in Scotland* (Oxford: Clarendon).

Marshall, G. (1982), *In Search of the Spirit of Capitalism* (London: Hutchinson).

Marshall, T. H. (1963), *Sociology at the Crossroads* (London: Heinemann).

McClintock, C. C., Brannon, B., and Maynard-Moody, S. (1983), 'Applying the Logic of Sample Surveys to Qualitative Case Studies: the Case Cluster Method' in J. Van Maanen (ed.) *Qualitative Methodology* (Beverly Hills: Sage).

McGinnity, F. and Hillmert, S. (2004), 'Persisting Class Inequality', *European Societies*, 6: 383–408.

McKim, V. R. and Turner, S. P. (eds.) (1997), *Causality in Crisis?* (Notre Dame: Notre Dame University Press).

McMichael, P. (1990), 'Incorporating Comparisons Within a World-Historical Perspective: an Alternative Comparative Method', *American Sociological Review*, 55: 385–97.

Merton, R. K. (1987), 'Three Fragments from a Sociologist's Notebook: Establishing the Phenomenon, Specified Ignorance and Strategic Research Materials', *Annual Review of Sociology*, 13: 1–28.

Meyer, J. W. (1987), 'The World Polity and the Authority of the Nation-State' in G. M. Thomas et al., *Institutional Structure* (Newbury Park: Sage).

Miles, M. B. (1983), 'Qualitative Data as an Attractive Nuisance' in J. Van Maanen (ed.) *Qualitative Methodology* (Beverly Hills: Sage).

Miles, M. B. and Huberman, A. M. (1984), *Qualitative Data Analysis* (Beverly Hills: Sage).

Mill, J. S. (1843/1973–74), *A System of Logic Ratiocinative and Inductive* in J. M. Robson (ed.) *Collected Works of John Stuart Mill* (Toronto: University of Toronto Press).

Mitchell, J. C. (1983), 'Case and Situation Analysis', *Sociological Review*, 31: 187–211.

Moore, B. (1966), *The Social Origins of Dictatorship and Democracy* (Boston: Beacon).

Mouzelis, N. (1994), 'In Defence of "Grand" Historical Sociology', *British Journal of Sociology*, 1994: 31–36.

Müller, W. (1999), 'Class Cleavages in Party Preferences in Germany—Old and New' in G. Evans (ed.), *The End of Class Politics?* (Oxford: Oxford University Press).

Müller, W. and Karle, W. (1993), 'Social Selection and Educational Systems in Europe', *European Sociological Review*, 9: 1–23.

Murphey, M. G. (1973), *Our Knowledge of the Historical Past* (Indianapolis: Bobbs Merrill).

Nagel, T. (1997), *The Last Word* (Oxford: Oxford University Press).

Naroll, R. (1970), 'Galton's Problem' in R. Naroll and R. Cohen (eds.) *A Handbook of Method in Cultural Anthropology* (New York: The Natural History Press).

Neyman, J. (1934), 'On the Two Different Aspects of the Representative Method: The Method of Stratified Sampling and the Method of Purposive Selection', *Journal of the Royal Statistical Society*, 97: 558–606.

Ní Bhrolcháin, M., Chappell, R., and Diamond I. (1994), 'Scolarité et autres caractéristiques socio-démographiques des enfants de mariages rompus', *Population*, 6: 1585–612.

Ní Bhrolcháin, M. (2001), '"Divorce Effects" and Causality in the Social Sciences', *European Sociological Review*, 17: 33–57.

Nichols, E. (1986), 'Skocpol on Revolution: Comparative Analysis vs. Historical Conjuncture', *Comparative Social Research*, 9: 163–86.

Nolan, B. and Whelan, C. (1999), *Loading the Dice? A Study of Cumulative Disadvantage* (Dublin: Oak Tree).

Nolan , B. and Whelan, C. (2001), 'Urban Housing and the Role of Underclass Processes: The Case of Ireland', *Journal of European Social Policy*, 10: 5–21.

Norkus, Z. (2000), 'Max Weber's Interpretive Sociology and Rational Choice Approach', *Rationality and Society*, 12: 259–82.

Oakeshott, M. (1933), *Experience and Its Modes* (Cambridge: Cambridge University Press).

O'Connell, P. J. (1994), 'National Variation in the Fortunes of Labor: A Pooled and Cross-Sectional Analysis of the Impact of Economic Crisis in the Advanced Capitalist Nations' in T. Janoski and A. M. Hicks (eds.) *The Comparative Political Economy of the Welfare State* (Cambridge: Cambridge University Press).

O'Connor, J. S. and Brym, R. J. (1988), 'Public Welfare Expenditure in OECD Countries', *British Journal of Sociology*, 39: 47–68.

Ogburn, W. F. (1922), *Social Change with Respect to Culture and Original Nature* (New York: Huebsch).

Ohmae, K. (1995), *The End of the Nation State: The Rise of Regional Economies* (New York: Free Press).

Olewiler, N. (1999), 'National Tax Policy for an International Economy: Divergence in a Converging World?' in T. J. Courchene (ed.) *Room to Manoeuvre? Globalization and Policy Convergence* (Montreal: McGill-Queens University Press).

Oman, C. (1999), 'Globalization, Regionalization and Inequality' in A. Hurrell and N. Woods (eds.), *Inequality, Globalization and World Politics* (Oxford: Oxford University Press).

Opp, K.-D. (1998), 'Can and Should Rational Choice Theory be Tested by Survey Research? The Example of Explaining Collective Political Action' in H.-P.

Blossfeld and G. Prein (eds.) *Rational Choice Theory and Large-Scale Data Analysis* (Boulder: Westview).

Orloff, A. S. and Skocpol, T. (1984), 'Why Not Equal Protection? Explaining the Politics of Public Spending in Britain, 1900–1911, and the United States, 1890s–1920', *American Sociological Review*, 49: 726–50.

O'Rourke K. H. and Williamson, J. G. (1999), *Gobalization and History* (Cambridge: Cambridge University Press).

Orum, A. M., Feagin, J. R., and Sjoberg, G. (1991), 'Introduction' in *idem* (eds.) *A Case for the Case Study* (Chapel Hill: University of North Carolina Press).

Pampel, F. C. and Williamson, J. B. (1989), *Age, Class, Politics, and the Welfare State* (Cambridge: Cambridge University Press).

Parry, O. and Mauthner, N. S. (2004) 'Whose Data Are They Anyway? Practical, Ethical and Legal Issues in Archiving Qualitative Research Data', *Sociology*, 38: 139–52.

Paugam, S. (1996), 'La Constitution d'un paradigme' in *idem* (ed.) *L'Exclusion: l'état des savoirs* (Paris: La Découverte).

Parsons, T. (1937), *The Structure of Social Action* (Glencoe: Free Press).

Parsons, T. (1952), *The Social System* (Glencoe, Ill.: Free Press).

Pearl, J. (2000), *Causality: Models, Reasoning and Inference* (Cambridge: Cambridge University Press).

Pearson, K. (1892), *The Grammar of Science* (London: Black).

Penrose, L. S. (1946), 'The Elementary Statistics of Majority Voting', *Journal of the Royal Statistical Society*, 109: 53–57.

Pinker, R. (2002), *The Blank Slate: The Modern Denial of Human Nature* (Cambridge, Mass.: MIT Press).

Piore, M. (1983), 'Qualitative Research Techniques in Economics' in J. Van Maanen (ed.) *Qualitative Methodology* (Beverly Hills: Sage).

Platt, J. (1988), 'What Can Case Studies Do?', *Studies in Qualitative Methodology*, 1: 1–23.

Plotkin, H. (1997), *Evolution in Mind* (London: Allen Lane).

Popper, K. R. (1957), *The Poverty of Historicism* (London: Routledge).

Popper, K. R. (1966), *The Open Society and its Enemies*, 2nd ed. (London: Routledge).

Popper, K. R. (1972), *Objective Knowledge* (Oxford: Clarendon).

Popper, K. R. (1976a), 'The Logic of the Social Sciences' in *The Positivist Dispute in German Sociology* (London: Heinemann).

Popper, K. R. (1976b), *Unended Quest* (London: Fontana).

Popper, K. R. (1994), *The Myth of the Framework* (London: Routledge).

Portocarero, L. (1987), *Social Mobility in Industrial Societies: Women in France and Sweden* (Stockholm: Almqvist and Wicksell).

Prendergast, C. (1986), 'Alfred Schutz and the Austrian School of Economics', *American Journal of Sociology*, 92: 1–26.

Przeworski, A. (1987), 'Methods of Cross-National Research, 1970–83: An Overview' in M. Dierkes, H. N. Weiler, and A. B. Antal (eds.) *Comparative Policy Research* (Berlin: WZB-Publications).

Przeworski, A. and Teune, H. (1970), *The Logic of Comparative Social Inquiry* (New York: Wiley).

Quadagno, J. S. (1987), 'Theories of the Welfare State', *Annual Review of Sociology*, 13: 109–28.

Quadagno, J. S. and Knapp, S. J. (1992), 'Have Historical Sociologists Forsaken Theory?', *Sociological Methods and Research*, 20: 481–507.

Quetelet, A. (1835/1842), *A Treatise on Man and the Development of his Faculties* (Edinburgh: Chambers).

Quinn, D. (1997), 'The Correlates of Changes in International Financial Regulation', *American Political Science Review*, 91: 531–52.

Ragin, C. C. (1987), *The Comparative Method* (Berkeley: University of California Press).

Ragin, C. C. (1991), 'Introduction: Cases of "What Is a Case?"' in C. C. Ragin and H. S. Becker (eds.) *What Is a Case?* (Cambridge: Cambridge University Press).

Ragin, C. C. (1994a), *Constructing Social Research* (Thousand Oaks, Calif.: Pine Forge).

Ragin, C. C. (1994b), 'Introduction to Qualitative Comparative Analysis' in T. Janoski and A. M. Hicks (eds.) *The Comparative Political Economy of the Welfare State* (Cambridge: Cambridge University Press).

Ragin, C. C. (1997), 'Turning the Tables: How Case-Oriented Research Challenges Variable-Oriented Research', *Comparative Social Research*, 16: 27–42.

Ragin, C. C. (2000), *Fuzzy-Set Social Science* (Chicago: Chicago University Press).

Ramirez, F. O. and Boli, J. (1987), 'Global Patterns of Educational Institutionalization' in G. M. Thomas (ed.) *Institutional Structure* (Newbury Park: Sage).

Redfield, R. (1930), *Tepoztlan: A Mexican Village* (Chicago: University of Chicago Press).

Reich, R. (1991), *The Work of Nations* (New York: Knopf).

Renier, G. J. (1950), *History: Its Purpose and Method* (London: Allen and Unwin).

Robbins, L. (1949), *The Nature and Significance of Economic Science*, 2nd ed. (London: Macmillan).

Robinson, W. S. (1951), 'The Logical Structure of Analytic Induction', *American Sociological Review*, 16: 812–18.

Rodrik, D. (1997), *Has Globalisation Gone Too Far?* (Washington, D.C.: Institute for International Economics).

Rodrik, D. (1998), 'Why Do More Open Economies have Bigger Governments?', *Journal of Political Economy*, 106: 997–1032.

Roemer, J. (1982), *A General Theory of Exploitation and Class* (Cambridge: Cambridge University Press).

Rogosa, D. (1992), 'Causal Models Do not Support Scientific Conclusions: A Comment in Favour of Freedman' in J. P. Shaffer (ed.) *The Role of Models in*